BUSINESS COACHING INTERNATIONAL

BUSINESS COACHING
INTERNATIONAL
Transforming Individuals
and Organizations

Sunny Stout Rostron

with contributing authors

Marti Janse van Rensburg
Daniel Marques Sampaio

KARNAC

First published in 2009 by
Karnac Books Ltd
118 Finchley Road
London NW3 5HT

British Library Cataloguing in Publication Data

A C.I.P. for this book is available from the British Library

ISBN: 978-1-85575-713-4

Typeset by Vikatan Publishing Solutions (P) Ltd, Chennai, India

www.karnacbooks.com

"Coaching is unique, helping individuals to systematize their conscious thoughts about the immediate actions needed to address specific practical issues, and to understand the unconscious processes that may be sabotaging their success"

—Sunny Stout Rostron

ENDORSEMENTS

"This book is, in my opinion, an important milestone in the coaching literature and it comes at the right time, one when coaching is maturing into an influential profession in the mainstream. Coaching has long needed a comprehensive guide and reference book of this nature, and now it has one. Coaching must be continuously self-reflective, and this book will stimulate that too. It explores and explains in a readable, credible and academically sound form the variety of different principles, methods, models and responsibilities of coaches and coaching. It lays out the field for the reader to choose from, in unusual depth. It is a real quality Handbook, in the best meaning of the word."

—Sir John Whitmore PhD, author of Coaching for Performance: GROWing People, Performance and Purpose; Executive Chair of Performance Consultants.

"The world of business coaching can rejoice—the book we have been wanting and needing is here. This book harnesses the vast and complex world of excellence in coaching and offers it to us digestibly, delectably and with impressively accessible scholarship. I want every coach and soon-to-be coach to read this book. The inner world of coaching, cogently, warmly, thoroughly presented is a *tour de force* and a gift to us all. There are many kinds of bible in the world—this will be one of them."

> —Nancy Kline, President of Time To Think, Inc., and author of *Time To Think: Listening To Ignite The Human Mind* and *More Time To Think: A Way Of Being In The World*.

"Finally a coaching *Whole Earth Catalogue* in the form of a user-friendly book has emerged that addresses the needs of practicing coaches versus someone's theory about coaching. What comes through loud and clear is that Stout Rostron is the voice of the coach—she is in the marketplace and has tested what works and what does not. This is a masterful work that enables anyone who wishes to coach, whether they are a peer coach or an executive, to find guidelines as well as skills, tools, attitudes and behaviours that become developmental building blocks in any good coaching process. This is a must-read, essential for anyone wishing to help others in any corporate, educational or group setting. Very inspiring to read."

> —Mark R. Rittenberg EdD, Guest Professor, Executive Education Division, Kellogg School of Management, Northwestern University in Illinois, and President of Corporate Scenes Inc in California.

"You simply must read this book if you are serious about being a top-notch business coach. It is an excellent guide to best practices based on clear theory, experience and business wisdom."

> —Carol Kauffman PhD ABPP PCC, co-founder and Director of the Coaching and Positive Psychology Initiative at Harvard Medical School, and Co-Editor-in-Chief of *Coaching: An International Journal of Theory Research and Practice*.

"This is an extraordinarily thorough book. It covers a great range of practical guidance on matters that will concern the new coach, and it also addresses the current issues for those concerned with coaching worldwide, including the deliberations of the Global Convention on Coaching. It is clearly written and very widely referenced. It addresses a wide range of approaches to coaching while remaining firmly embedded in an experiential learning tradition."

—David Megginson, Professor of Human Resource Development, Sheffield Hallam University, UK.

"I am struck by the incredible generosity of this book. Readers are presented with a rich and thorough blend of theoretical understanding and practical wisdom, delivered in a way that is highly accessible and will be of considerable value to experienced and inexperienced business coaches alike. The book reflects a deep passion and caring for the emerging discipline of coaching; one that has been rarely seen to date, and should be widely applauded. It is a very welcome addition to my library!"

—Gordon Spence PhD MAPS, leading Australian coaching psychologist and Co-Director of The Nardoo Partnership, lecturer in the Coaching Psychology Unit at the University of Sydney, and member of the Research Advisory Board of the Institute of Coaching.

"Business coaching is so many different things to the diversity of practitioners around the world. Each of us gets tricked into believing that it is only how we define coaching within our own minds, from our own training, and our own geographical bias. This book takes the diversity of multiple world perspectives on coaching. Read it if you are ready for an adventure in coaching; where you see new things in new contexts that can change how you live and work. Your adventure can be short or long, reading parts of chapters or the whole book at a time. The trip comes with its own translator—everything is put in language we can all make sense of and use on the spot. The author brings to this adventure one of the best minds and practical guides to challenge us to think and act differently in our coaching. Enjoy it as I have."

—Lew Stern PhD, co-founder and Chairman of the Executive Coaching Forum, founder and past director of the Graduate Certificate Program in Executive Coaching at the Massachusetts School of Professional Psychology, President of Stern Consulting, Co-author of *The Executive Coaching Handbook*, and author of *Executive Coaching: Building and Managing Your Professional Practice*.

"A book that will further advance your appreciation for and understanding of the powerful intervention known as business coaching."

—Wendy Johnson, President and CEO, Worldwide Association of Business Coaches (WABC).

CONTENTS

PREFACE

This book aims to provide a wide spectrum of coaching theory and standards, with a clear and accessible overview of business coaching practice. It is structured as a practical, easy-to-access guide to the most important aspects of business coaching, with a link to the foundation-stones of business coaching internationally.

This book is not the publication of my own researched executive coaching model—which will be my next project—but aspires to offer practitioners a general handbook or encyclopaedia of the very best theoretical models, current practice and thinking in business coaching.

Coaching is a new, dynamic and emerging profession, and this book was written to explore the dynamics of this discipline as it matures and grows worldwide. I have tried to accommodate a variety of learning styles in the book, and hope you will dip in and find the chapters most relevant to you. My aim is to offer a wide perspective of differing approaches and models that coaching professionals and practitioners will find immediately useable and applicable to their business coaching interventions.

This book is dedicated to all coach practitioners and coaching professionals in the hope that this helps take our emerging discipline forward into a new and exciting chapter.

—Sunny Stout Rostron

FOREWORD

We are delighted to offer *Business Coaching International* as our latest edition in the Professional Coaching Series. We wanted to produce a book which would provide a scholarly yet accessible overview of key frameworks influencing business coaching alongside a perspective on global developments in the field.

The author, Sunny Stout-Rostron, is ideally placed as she combines extensive practice with a researcher's insights and unrivalled contacts worldwide. She takes a varied set of concepts and links them through frameworks which enable the reader to explore difference in a coherent way. She does so with a lightness of touch which nevertheless builds on an extensive underpinning of scholarship. Her own experience and those of her contributing authors is clear throughout the text.

Coaching has emerged globally as a key intervention, drawing on a very diverse range of theories to inform practice. It has also attracted practitioners from an equally wide range of backgrounds who draw upon their various experiences in business, psychology, therapy, management and organizational development, sports, consultancy, and more. This means that different professional traditions have influenced practice. Such a diverse base has been a considerable source of strength. It has, however, made it difficult for those new to the field to find an accessible source book that reflects the full range of ideas. For experienced practitioners, the tendency to draw upon their profession of origin has meant that an awareness of the breadth as well as the depth of coaching knowledge has been lacking. This book answers both needs.

It takes an in-depth look at the coaching process, its question frameworks, coaching competences, and how to use current coaching models. Through an exploration of ethics, contracting, supervision, the "relationship"—and a detailed look at the coaching conversation—we believe that the authors have outlined the crucial elements for individual, team and organizational transformation. This understanding is deepened by a detailed examination of issues such as diversity within the international coaching marketplace, management of the existential issues that affect meaning and purpose for the executive, and emotional intelligence.

However, this variety is not tackled as a recipe for one approach but rather takes a deeper look at being an effective business coach.

So what can our readers expect from their investment in reading this book?

First, they will gain an accessible overview of the keys ideas influencing coaching today and a source to explore further through detailed referencing and suggestions in the "Coach's Library". The balance in this overview will provide the reader with a base point to develop their own thinking about useful models.

Second, through an investigation of "the significance, meaning and structure of the coaching intervention within the coach-client conversation", it will help you to look at what you need to be to become a coach and to coach more effectively. It will take you on a philosophical journey and into a series of approaches you can use to inform your work. The book, therefore, does not just provide an overview but is a practical resource for coaching.

Third, it will explore specific areas relevant to the business coach, such as leading a team; thinking strategically; managing people, processes and tasks; maintaining relationships; promoting; networking; succession planning; and continuing professional development.

Fourth, it will explore issues relevant for the coach working with the individual around issues such as developing self-awareness;

managing oneself in the workplace; becoming aware of relationships, values and culture at work; managing relationships in a complex and diverse environment; and developing a healthy lifestyle.

Finally, it will offer insights into ways of ensuring that coaching happens effectively in organizations—covering strategy, implementation, measurement, competencies and supervision.

We have asked a number of leading exponents of coaching to review the book and their comments (included) echo our own view that the authors have exceeded our aim of providing a comprehensive, practical, informed yet accessible introduction to business coaching.

We are delighted to offer this book to you—to guide your journey to becoming the coach you want to be (and that your clients deserve).

Professor David Lane
Series Editor
Professional Development Foundation

ABOUT THE AUTHORS

Sunny Stout Rostron, DProf MA

Sunny Stout Rostron is a director of the Manthano Institute of Learning (Pty) Ltd, and a founding faculty member of The Coaching Centre (TCC) in Cape Town. She has a wide range of experience in leadership and management development, business strategy and executive coaching. With 18 years' experience as an executive coach, Sunny believes there is a strong link between emotional intelligence and business results—she works with executives and their teams to help them achieve individual, team and organizational goals.

Sunny is founding chair of the Working Group on a Research Agenda for Development of the Field within the Global Convention on Coaching (now the Global Coaching Community), whose role is to research the emerging profession of coaching worldwide. She is a research advisor to the Institute of Coaching based at Harvard, and is Founding President of the professional association Coaches and Mentors of South Africa (COMENSA). She has developed a range of international programmes in the corporate, legal and education fields, and is the author of seven books including *Business Coaching Wisdom and Practice* (Knowledge Resources, 2009), *Accelerating*

Performance: Powerful New Techniques to Develop People (Kogan Page, 2002) and *Managing Training* (Kogan Page, 1993). She is a contributing author to *Sharing the Passion: Conversations with Coaches* (Advanced Human Technologies, 2006), and *The Sage Handbook of Coaching* (Sage, 2009).

Sunny has developed a succession of leadership and management development programmes within the corporate sector in the UK, USA and South Africa. Her clients include Sasol, Standard Bank, Pick n Pay, Cummins Filtration International, Foschini Group, Eskom, Chaswill Process Technologies, and VWSA. Sunny completed her professional doctorate in Executive Coaching at Middlesex University, London, in 2006. She frequently speaks at conferences in the USA, UK and South Africa. A member of the Worldwide Association of Business Coaches (WABC), and a founding faculty member in South Africa of the Thinking Environment® programme (developed by Nancy Kline), Sunny has recently collaboratively set up the Manthano Institute of Learning (Pty) Ltd, whose aims include the promotion and development of academic and practitioner coaching research in South Africa.

Sunny manages an executive coaching practice, while continuing to develop new education and supervision programmes for coach practitioners. She plays a leading role in building the emerging profession of coaching in South Africa and abroad. Currently an active member of the International Coaching Research Forum (ICRF) and the Transitional Steering Group (TSG) for the Global Coaching Community (GCC), Sunny's passion is to develop the knowledge base for coaching through research and the critical reflective practice of dedicated coach practitioners.

Marti Janse van Rensburg, MBA (contributing author)

Marti Janse van Rensburg brings an extensive and varied business background to her successful coaching practice. This broad experience, ranging from scientific research to corporate management, gives her invaluable, hands-on knowledge and insight, both of which provide a critical key to understanding clients and coaching in the corporate world.

Marti's clients range from Woolworths, Johnnic Publishing, Standard Bank, Eskom, Sasol, Discovery, Liberty, IS, McKinsey & Company, and AngloGold Ashanti, to the Southern Africa-United

States Centre for Leadership and Public Values (a joint venture of the University of Cape Town and Duke University). Marti coached and facilitated the Accelerated Leadership Development Programme (ALDP) at Sasol through the Gordon Institute of Business Science (GIBS) in Johannesburg.

In addition to one-on-one coaching, Marti facilitates team coaching and leadership development for clients such as the Eskom CEO Programme. She designed a countrywide training programme for Standard Bank managers on how to give and receive feedback. She also designed a performance coaching programme for Standard Bank in conjunction with their Leadership Development Team, and started their Leader-as-Coach Programme at the Global Leadership Centre (GLC).

In 2003, Marti was involved in the ground-breaking Action Reflection Learning (ARL) programme at the MIL Institute in Sweden. Marti was a founding director of the professional association Coaches and Mentors of South Africa (COMENSA), and is a member of the Worldwide Association of Business Coaches (WABC). She took part in the Global Convention on Coaching (GCC) Working Group on a Research Agenda for Development of the Field during 2007–2008.

In her previous career, Marti was a researcher at the CSIR before moving into the high fashion industry where she worked as a designer and the owner of a training facility for designers. She taught and consulted for ten years in fashion retail, which gave her business experience in Asia. Marti has a degree in Chemical Engineering from the University of Pretoria, and an MBA from the Gordon Institute of Business Science (GIBS) of the University of Pretoria with a focus on executive coaching. Her coaching and leadership development career over the past eight years has introduced her to a range of international coaches, consultants and clients in Africa, the UK, Europe and the USA.

Daniel Marques Sampaio PhD
(contributing author)

Daniel Marques Sampaio was born in Rio de Janeiro and has lived in London for two decades. He gained degrees in the Arts from Goldsmiths College, University of London, before being awarded a

PhD in Urban Studies (Brunel University, 2003), for a thesis on recent regeneration initiatives in South and Southeast London. He has worked in the UK, France, Holland, and Hong Kong. His recent projects include the interdisciplinary research presented in *Capital Corporations Consumers Communications* at the Alsager Arts Centre of Manchester Metropolitan University (2007), and *Private/Public*, a photographic project with Michael Jones Architects in London (2009). He has also lectured widely in cultural and urban studies in the UK, and spoken at several conferences. Daniel is currently Programme Leader in Critical and Theoretical Studies at the Faculty of Arts and Media at Croydon Higher Education College, and Lecturer in Cultural Studies at the University of Hertfordshire in the UK.

ACKNOWLEDGEMENTS

The purpose of this book is to share our research, teaching and practice in order to contribute to the growing expertise and developing knowledge about our emerging profession of coaching. In the preparation of this book, we owe a large debt of gratitude to Nick Wilkins, Business Manager of the newly-formed Manthano Institute of Learning (Pty) Ltd, for his astute advice on editing issues.

Appreciation is extended to all of our readers: Carol Kauffman, David Lane, David Megginson, Helena Dolny, Lew Stern, David Peterson, Marc Kahn, Shani Naidoo, and Mark Rittenberg. In addition, I would particularly like to thank Marti Janse van Rensburg and Daniel Marques Sampaio for their contributions to: "Chapter 6: Diversity, Culture and Gender" and the Appendix.

The core concept underpinning this book is experiential learning. We constantly returned to how we work with clients: reflecting, observing and sharing—knowing that, as a result, our coaching practice and teaching will be the stronger for it. We hope yours will be enriched too.

CHAPTER ONE

About this book

CHAPTER OUTLINE
- What's different about this book?
- Where does coaching fit into the business?
- Who should read this book?
- Chapter contents
- Coach's library

What's different about this book?

Everything! This book is about the essential "practice" and "practices" of a business coach. The authors speak from their experience, with practical examples, analyzing the complexities of the coaching conversation—the basic tool of the business and executive coach. They believe that business coaching can make a huge contribution to leadership competence inside organizations and, in this book, comprehensively integrate their practical experience as business coaches with their own research and teaching.

Business Coaching International takes an in-depth, dynamic and integrative look at the coaching process, question frameworks, coaching competences, and how to use current coaching models. It examines key coach/client concerns such as ethics, contracting, supervision and the "relationship" between coach and client. The book also focuses on the hub of the coaching conversation—learning from experience. The authors believe this is crucial for individual, team and organizational transformation.

This book also explores:

- the diversity of the international coaching marketplace and how the business coach needs to adapt accordingly;
- how to handle existential issues that affect meaning and purpose for the over-stretched executive;
- where emotional intelligence fits into the matrix of core competences for the business coach; and
- the core theoretical underpinnings of business coaching that will transform your business coaching practice.

Although there are many excellent studies available about coaching, this book is specifically targeted to the diverse and multifaceted marketplace of coaching, coaching psychology and coaching research. Whereas the majority of publications look at coaching as a recipe, this book takes a deeper look at what it takes to become an effective business or executive coach.

Business Coaching International investigates the significance, meaning and structure of the coaching intervention within the coach-client conversation, and takes a look at what, how and who you need to be to coach. At the heart of the business coaching process, irrespective of the model or approach, is "the relationship". This means that business coaching is not necessarily about "doing" for the client, but more about "being"—creating a safe thinking environment: a space where thinking, feeling, insight and creative decision making can take place. Applying the knowledge and techniques within this book will deepen your practice.

Some of the tools and processes explored in this book will help you to coach your executive clients in:

1. Business issues such as leading a team; thinking strategically; managing people, processes and tasks; maintaining relationships; promoting; networking; succession planning; and continuing professional development.

2. Emotional intelligence (EQ) issues such as developing self-awareness; managing oneself in the workplace; becoming aware of relationships, values and culture at work; and managing relationships in a complex and diverse environment.
3. Relationship issues, which dominate if executives do not lead a healthy lifestyle, thus diminishing their effectiveness at work. The anxiety of not coping, either at home or in the office, impacts on the other half of an executive's life.
4. Body, mind and stress issues such as maintaining health and fitness, a balanced diet, and getting enough sleep.

Each chapter is designed to be a world unto itself. What we suggest to make it fun, useful and intriguing for yourself is to read the first chapter, then read those chapters most relevant to you right now. Immediately you can begin to apply new thinking that will help build the rigour of your own business coaching practice—whether you oversee a stable of business coaches or run your own individual practice.

As authors who coach, consult and lecture internationally, we have written this book specifically for practising coaches and coaching consultants with tools, techniques, case studies and applications relevant to any business coach anywhere. We share with you from our personal experience as executive coaches—two of us having worked in organizations for nearly 30 years, much of that time engaged in coaching senior managers and executives at the highest level. We also share our various learning and research findings from coaching inside organizations in the UK, Europe, USA and South Africa. Marti and I have been involved in the Working Group on a Research Agenda for Development of the Field within the Global Convention on Coaching (GCC), looking at the development of the coaching profession worldwide. This book also explores several international developments that may have an impact on the supervision and regulation of coaching worldwide.

Where does coaching fit into the business?

Whether you are an external coaching consultant, head of Human Resources (HR) or Organizational Development (OD) within your organization, it is important that coaching is aligned with both the business and the talent strategies. Within most organizations there tends to be a unique combination of **internal coach** programmes combined with training and mentoring to develop the "manager as coach", or the "leader as coach", as well as team coaching—in addition to some kind of schema to recruit and bring in **external coaches** for senior executives. There is some confusion between "team coaching" and "group facilitation". It is important for anyone coaching teams or groups to be skilled not just in facilitating group learning processes, but also in teaching coaching skills and competences for individual team members who need to develop their own direct reports in a coaching manner.

What we recommend is that both internal and external coaching programmes are in alignment with each other, and with the business and talent development strategies. It is crucial to be able to measure the efficacy of internal and external coaching programmes, and we would encourage some qualitative or quantitative measurement of all coaching that takes place in the organization. One of the ways to measure success is to have feedback sessions with the coaches two or three times a year, with the coaches giving feedback on what is working and not working within the system, and on that which impedes or supports the coaching and/or mentoring processes. Secondly, ensure that there is a process in place to adequately supervise internal and external coaches, and build a systemic coaching programme that is fully integrated with the company's talent management systems and processes to create a feedback loop to senior management and line managers as well as internal and external coaches.

Also crucial is some kind of qualitative and quantitative measurement of the coaching process, identifying the return on investment (ROI) for the organization. We recommend clearly specifying the aims and objectives of the coaching process, both internal and external. This requires the development of criteria for external coaches that you recruit, as well as building a bespoke training programme for internal coaches to cover the basics: the coaching process; an understanding of coaching models and question frameworks; and the theoretical and psychological underpinnings of coaching, including the competences required for the coach.

These competences range from attention, active and deep listening, intervention skills such as questions, reframing and giving feedback, and experiential learning techniques, to an understanding of ethics and confidentiality, psychological processes and organizational systems. Equally important are the ability to interpret and understand management and/or psychological profiles, an understanding of and ability to work with diversity and cultural competence, and the requirements of continuing professional development.

Who should read this book?

If you are a business coach working within a business, entrepreneurial, organizational or corporate environment, then this book is for you. If you are a practising business coach hired externally into organizations, an internal organizational coach working with junior, senior and executive managers, a managerial leader who uses coaching to develop your team, an HR manager/director setting up an internal coaching programme, or if you are facilitating coach-training programmes within an organization—then this book is definitely for you.

No manager or executive leaves their personal life behind when they walk into work. It is simply another role or function that frames who they are. So it follows that business coaching cannot be effective without looking at clients holistically. Even if business coaches primarily help clients to identify their core purpose, strategies, developmental objectives, strengths, weaknesses and obstacles to be overcome, business coaching also takes in all aspects of an executive's life, from the meaning and purpose of the work that they are doing, to managing people, processes and systems, as well as creating a balance between work and personal life.

This book is for you if you are:

- a master business or executive coach with an existing, successful practice wishing to deepen your competence, knowledge and skills because you believe in your own continuous improvement;
- a practising business or executive coach with varying levels of expertise;
- a business coach new to the field keen to develop your expertise;
- a business coach who wishes to expand and improve your skills and competence in the coaching process with a deeper understanding of the coaching conversation and its impact in the workplace;

- a coach who wants to understand the coaching process within the coaching conversation more fully, as well as the entire coaching intervention over a period of time;
- an HR professional responsible for setting up the coaching interventions within the organization, and often find yourself in a coaching role;
- a senior managerial leader who wants to understand the principles of business coaching because you are experiencing coaching or considering it as a profession;
- a senior leader who needs to understand the role of the business coach because you are responsible for leading, managing and coaching your team or organization;
- an experienced external and/or internal business coach actively engaged in business coaching;
- a coach or coach researcher actively engaged in business coaching-related matters, for example, one-on-one coach training or leadership/management development programmes;
- a coach who has one or more years of business coaching and who needs an in-depth understanding of the coaching process and coaching models;
- someone at the beginning stages of coaching in business, with over five years' business and organizational experience; or
- a coach practitioner who has delivered coaching services to small, medium and large organizations, including public and private institutions.

We hope the following chapters will give you a broader perspective on your practice and the challenges that you face when coaching individuals and teams. This is a growing field built on the cumulative experience of business coaches, and we firmly believe that our most powerful learning comes from experience. As a business coach, you are helping your clients to learn from and interpret their own experiences, and to understand the complexity of the environment in which they work. We hope that our learning will make a substantial contribution to your competence and practice.

It is critical in any organization that the coaching strategy is in alignment with both the business and the talent strategies. Often the HR department is not in alignment with the Coaching and Mentoring unit, and often neither is in alignment with Organizational or

Leadership Development. Only when these are all working together in an integrated way will you be able to develop a successful internal and external coaching programme and process with sustainable and measurable outcomes.

Chapter contents

Chapter 2: The business coaching process

Chapter 2 takes a brief look at the origins and foundation-stones of business coaching worldwide. Examined here are the core theoretical and psychological underpinnings of coaching, with an overview of the current reality for business coaching in the USA, UK, and Australia, as well as in Argentina, India, China and other East Asian countries, and South Africa. We outline modern management theory from the 1970s to the twenty-first century, from transformational leadership to the learning organization, managing complexity and talent development—and the way it influenced the beginnings of corporate coaching.

Business coaches encourage their clients to think for themselves and to develop an awareness of their own conscious and unconscious behaviours, which may influence performance in the workplace. Business coaching is essentially about the results experienced through the dynamic relationship between coach and client, and how those results impact on individual, team and organizational performance.

This chapter addresses the influence of adult learning and experiential learning on the business coaching process, where coach and client probe the essence of an experience to understand its significance and the learning that can be gained from it. Ultimately, however, business coaching needs to be aligned with all the leadership and management development initiatives within the organization.

Chapter 3: The coaching conversation

This chapter explores the purpose and focus of the "coaching conversation" and the competences useful to the business coach. The "coaching conversation" is the face-to-face or telephonic interaction between coach and client. It is a "thinking partnership" (Kline, 1999/2004) where coach and client reflect on the client's experience, transforming it into potential for learning and action. How the client takes responsibility for change can emerge from the coaching conversation.

The focus of a coaching conversation is to help the client work towards achieving their desired outcomes. The coach primarily explores with each client what it is that is holding back or stopping the client from achieving their goals. One example would be to identify and replace disempowering assumptions and paradigms with empowering ones.

The final section of this chapter outlines the general approach to competence frameworks developed by four international coaching bodies in an effort to promote professionalism within the industry, and recommends specific core competences to build your capacity as a business coach.

Chapter 4: Working with question frameworks

This chapter explores the range of coaching question frameworks available in the marketplace, e.g. those of John Whitmore, Nancy Kline and Jinny Ditzler. It includes descriptions of how to use two-, three-, four-, five-, six-, eight- and ten-stage frameworks, including neuro-linguistic programming (NLP) and Nancy Kline's Thinking Environment® processes, with examples for understanding. This chapter is designed to have you look specifically at how you can develop your own questioning process.

One of the most difficult paradigms for a coach to understand, as opposed to being a teacher or a therapist, is to not provide answers or solve the client's problems for them. The greatest gift you can offer is to help the client "consider ideas, approaches, strategies, behaviours, and other approaches and actions" not previously considered (Ting and Scisco, 2006:51). Although technically coaches do not offer advice, clients sometimes ask for an opinion, information or advice; it is important that the coach give the required support or guidance without telling the client what to do.

Chapter 5: Understanding and exploring coaching models

Today, coaches are trained in an eclectic range of coaching models. This chapter explores a cross-section of coaching models which influence the work of business and executive coaches worldwide.

Models help us to develop flexibility as coach practitioners. They offer structure and an outline for both the coaching conversation and the overall coaching journey. However, although models create a system within which coach and client work, it is essential that they are not experienced as prescriptive or rigid.

Coaching models help us to understand the coaching intervention from a systems perspective, and the "structure" of the interaction between coach and client. This chapter takes a practical look at how coaching models are constructed, and how they can help you to flexibly structure the overall coaching journey as well as the individual coaching conversation with your business client.

Chapter 6: Diversity, culture and gender

The importance of acknowledging diversity is increasingly recognized in our globalized world. In this chapter, Sunny Stout Rostron introduces the subject of diversity and power relations, looking at how assumptions limit individuals and groups. Marti Janse van Rensburg examines and analyzes race, gender and linguistic issues in practical terms, and Daniel Marques explores the challenge to worldviews and cultural understanding based on power relations, privilege and binary opposites.

Power relations not only have deep roots in our cultural matrix—our shared ways of doing things, of making sense of the world—but can often also inform our personal views, choices, and actions. Any form of power exacerbates difference and influences how we perceive and react to behaviour. This is true in any area of life, and nowhere more so than in the business context, specifically due to the hierarchical nature of organizational systems.

In the business environment, the coach needs to become aware of, and to manage, their own responses to questions of diversity, before they can begin to coach a client on similar issues. This chapter focuses on raising the business coach's awareness of crucial diversity issues both within themselves and their clients.

Chapter 7: Existential and experiential learning issues

Existential philosophy regards human existence as unexplainable, and stresses freedom of choice and taking responsibility for one's acts. Within the business coaching context, the coach helps the client to articulate existential concerns such as freedom, purpose, choice and anxiety, and to identify and replace limiting paradigms with empowering paradigms, thus leading to positive change.

These existential issues are relevant to the coach too. For example, if you look at purpose—the coach might be tempted to confuse their own individual purpose with that of the client, and in the process be seduced to use their position or power to influence the client. In existential terms, the meaning of individual experience is not a given; it is subject to interpretation. This chapter explores existential and experiential learning issues which confront the coach and client at every stage during their coaching conversation.

Chapter 8: Supervision, contracting and ethical concerns

Coaching supervision is in its infancy, worldwide—and is influenced by the role supervision plays for psychotherapists and psychologists, who are required to be in supervision throughout their training and years of clinical practice. This chapter examines how supervision is defined and practised worldwide. COMENSA (2006b:1), for example, defines the importance of supervision as follows: "Accountability, effectiveness and professionalism are core values for coaches and mentors. Supervision helps the coach/mentor manage high levels of complexity, maintain continued professional development, and have a mechanism for ensuring accountability and ethical practice."

This chapter discusses how you should go about being supervised and/or play the role of supervisor. We look at the role ethics plays in business coaching, and detail ethical codes that have been developed in recent years through professional bodies such as the Worldwide Association of Business Coaches (WABC), the European Mentoring and Coaching Council (EMCC), the International Coach Federation (ICF), and Coaches and Mentors of South Africa (COMENSA). Ethical dilemmas are as important as the professional codes themselves, and the author explores some of the potential dilemmas that can arise during a coaching intervention. A third corporate governance issue for business coaches is the standard contract they draw up for the client. Accordingly, the chapter makes recommendations on key aspects to incorporate into a coaching contract.

Chapter 9: Building a body of knowledge—coaching research

One of the emerging disciplines in coaching is research. Another way to describe it is to see it as an ongoing "critical appraisal" of your own coaching practice. This chapter examines current global thinking in terms of coaching research, stressing the importance of writing up your findings as you work within the business environment. This requires more than just being coached yourself and taking part in supervision.

This chapter seeks to broaden the definition of research, having identified possible contributing roles for coach practitioners, academic researchers and coaching psychologists. Collaboration provides a dynamic and realistic way forward, meeting the needs of all coaching stakeholders in order to cultivate the sustainability of practice through a growing body of knowledge.

Chapter 10: Integration and synthesis

How can you move to the next level in your practice? If we talk about "adult stages of development", coaching as an emerging profession is currently journeying from adolescence into its adult phase. A danger is that it becomes a fashion to call oneself a "coach", or to be a coach in training. In other words, rather than a respected profession, coaching becomes a passing bandwagon.

Chapter 10 looks at coaching today in terms of its global life curve. Some markets are more mature, while others are working through adolescence, with "hormones racing up and down". Today, worldwide, coaching needs direction and the continual building of a knowledge base in order to define its move towards professional practice. This may be where you, the reader, have a part to play.

Appendix: Competences in business coaching

The Appendix clearly lays out the required skills and competences defined for general coach practitioners and business coaches by four professional bodies, *viz.* the International Coach Federation (ICF), the Worldwide Association of Business Coaches (WABC), the European Mentoring and Coaching Council (EMCC), and Coaches and Mentors of South Africa (COMENSA).

These national and international bodies represent a valuable spectrum of international standards and requirements for business coaches today. There is considerable consistency among the professional bodies with respect to the skills and competences required for a coach. However, until there is some kind of worldwide consensus on core coaching competences, this chapter outlines the competence frameworks offered by four of the professional bodies for coaching practice.

Coach's library

The Coach's Library at the end of each chapter is an abbreviated list of useful resources to include in your library for that topic. A full bibliography is listed at the end of the book.

Coaches and Mentors of South Africa (COMENSA). (2006b). *Interim Policy on Supervision*. Cape Town: COMENSA. Webpage: www.comensa.org.za/dotnetnuke/ ProfessionalPractice/Supervision/tabid/79/language/en-ZA/Default.aspx.

Lane, D.A. and Corrie, S. (2006). *The Modern Scientist-Practitioner: A Guide to Practice in Psychology*. Hove: Routledge.

Stout Rostron, S. (2006c). *Interventions in the Coaching Conversation: Thinking, Feeling and Behaviour*. Published DProf dissertation. London: Middlesex University.

Ting, S. and Scisco, P. (2006). *The CCL Handbook of Coaching: A Guide for the Leader Coach*. San Francisco, CA: Jossey-Bass.

Worldwide Association of Business Coaches (WABC). (2008a). *Code of Business Coaching Ethics and Integrity*. Webpage: www.wabc coaches.com/includes/popups/code_of_ethics_2nd_edition_december_17_2007.html.

CHAPTER TWO

The business coaching process

CHAPTER OUTLINE
- What is business coaching?
- Coaching and mentoring
- Foundation-stones of business coaching
  - The Socratic method
  - Modern management theory
  - Managing complexity
- Guidelines therapy offers business coaching
  - The impact of psychological theory on business coaching
  - Behaviour, goals and performance
  - Motivation and goal setting
  - Adult learning
  - Experiential learning
- Business coaching worldwide
  - USA
  - UK and Europe
  - Australia
  - South Africa
  - India

– China and other East Asian countries
– Argentina and Chile
• International standards
• The future of business coaching worldwide
• Coach's library

This chapter takes a brief look at the origins and foundation-stones of business coaching worldwide. Examined here are the core theoretical and psychological underpinnings of coaching, with an overview of the current reality for business coaching worldwide as it is emerging in the USA, UK and Europe, Australia, South Africa, India, China and East Asia, and Argentina. Modern management theory from the 1970s to the twenty-first century is outlined, from transformational leadership to the learning organization, managing complexity and talent development—and the way it influenced the beginnings of corporate coaching.

Business coaches encourage their clients to think for themselves and to develop an awareness of their own conscious and unconscious behaviours, which may influence performance in the workplace. Business coaching is essentially about the results experienced through the dynamic relationship between coach and client, and how those results impact on individual, team and organizational performance.

The chapter addresses the influence of adult learning and experiential learning on the business coaching process, where coach and client probe the essence of an experience to understand its significance and the learning that can be gained from it. Ultimately, however, business coaching needs to be aligned with all the leadership and management development initiatives within the organization.

What is business coaching?

Research shows that one of the fastest-emerging disciplines in the field of coaching is business coaching (WABC, 2008b). Business coaches work with managers, leaders and senior executives to improve their performance. One aim is to achieve long-term results: to manage people, communication, conflict, projects and systems more effectively. Business coaches also help their clients to manage the stresses which arise from balancing work and personal life in the midst of a highly competitive and challenging work environment.

The Worldwide Association of Business Coaches (WABC, 2008b:1) defines business coaching as:

> The process of engaging in meaningful communication with individuals in businesses, organizations, institutions or governments, with the goal of promoting success at all levels of the organization by affecting the actions of those individuals. ... There is a clear focus on achieving business objectives. It is this focus that distinguishes business coaching from other types of coaching. Business coaching addresses the client's development for the purpose of achieving business outcomes rather than achieving personal or career goals.

It is here that I differ somewhat from the WABC definition, as I see the inherent importance of aligning the executive's intrinsic drivers with their personal and professional goals. If an individual client is unable to do so, the organizational environment within which they work will be a source of stress to them, making it difficult—sometimes impossible—for them to achieve specific, set targets.

Business coaching is essentially about the results experienced through the dynamic relationship between coach and client, and how such results impact on individual, team and organizational performance. Business coaching focuses on an effective, sustainable and measurable way of developing managerial leaders and their teams. I view "managerial leadership" similarly to the way Jaques and Clement (1991:4–6) describe it in their book *Effective Leadership*; I see leadership as a process and an accountable function of management, rather than as a role in itself.

One of the reasons why business coaching has become increasingly popular is because organizations understand the importance of getting the best out of talented people. It is now widely accepted that the best way to do this is by investing in people's professional development and encouraging them to participate in decision-making processes. It follows, therefore, that a key component of business coaching is a focus on **executive** coaching—on the development of senior managers and executives to improve their individual performance, and by doing so to optimize organizational results.

A recent study by the American Management Association (AMA) underlines that most coaching is provided to high-performing middle managers and junior managers on the fast track, while executive coaching targets high potentials, problem employees, executives and expatriates (American Management Association, 2008:20).

The origin of the word "coach" is from the French *coche*. It derives from the Hungarian town, Kòcs, where the first coach/wagon was built in the sixteenth century. As a verb, "to coach" was to convey a valued person from where they were to where they wanted to be. At the end of the nineteenth century, American college students had coaches to support them in achieving their best; this is true for executive coaching today (Stout Rostron, 2006a).

Although our modern-day use of the term "coaching" originated from the world of professional sport, business coaching is a distinct, unique, emerging profession—differentiated from teaching, training, counselling or mentoring. Particularly in countries where sport is such a passion, many executives perceive themselves to be more akin to high-performing athletes, developing competence and achieving results through professional coaching, rather than dealing with "personal problems" as in therapy or counselling.

Coaching and mentoring

Coaching may share some ancient roots with the discipline of "mentoring". The word "mentor" is often attributed to Homer's *Odyssey*, wherein Mentor is referred to as an advisor to Odysseus' son, Telemachus. In 1699 *Les Aventures de Telemaque* (*The Adventures of Telemachus*) was published by François de Salignac de la Mothe-Fenelon (1651–1715), a French writer and educator. It has been argued that in Homer's original work, Mentor acted as more of a caretaker than a "mentor", and Fenelon reinterpreted this to idealize his own role as tutor to the Dauphin (Stout Rostron, 2006a). In so doing, Fenelon created the modern-day mentor who embodies the attributes of teacher, guide and counsellor—a definition which has entered contemporary organizational jargon.

Whatever its origins, mentoring takes place in conversations with clients, as does coaching—but while the coach uses question frameworks and coaching models to help the client work out solutions to specific issues, the mentor simply acts as an adviser, directly sharing their experience, expertise, advice and wisdom with the mentee.

Not surprisingly, there is currently a great debate among experienced business coaches as to whether being "directive" and "giving advice" is a mentoring rather than a coaching activity, possibly encouraging the client to be too reliant on the coach.

Foundation-stones of business coaching

This section, an adapted excerpt from Stout Rostron (2006a), summarizes the origins and evolution of business coaching.

The Socratic method

The first great coach is often considered to be Socrates (469–399 BCE), who massively influenced modern thought. His greatest contribution to modern-day coaching is the Socratic method, characterized by persistent questioning and self-analysis. The philosophical statement "the unexamined life is not worth living" is attributed to Socrates, and although he encouraged individuals to think for themselves, he never called himself a teacher nor published any of his thoughts. Perceived to be a threat by the established Greek governing powers of the time, Socrates was tried and found guilty of subverting the good order of Athens. In other words, he encouraged his followers to think, ask questions and to challenge the traditional "common wisdom" and assumptions of his epoch.

Today, best-practice business coaching uses a structured yet flexible question framework to help clients think for themselves without interference. Business coaches encourage their clients to think for themselves and to develop an awareness of their own conscious and unconscious behaviours which may impact on performance in the workplace. The coach thus acts more as a "thinking partner" than as a mentor, enabling the executive to operate at the top of their game and to maintain the cutting edge of business innovation.

A great thinker of our own day, Nancy Kline, in her book *Time to Think*, says that "one of the most valuable things we can offer each other is the framework in which to think for ourselves", and that "as the thinker, knowing you will not be interrupted frees you to truly think for yourself" (Kline, 1999/2004). In Chapter 4, we examine a range of question frameworks used by business coaches today in order to tease out the issues and concerns in which their clients are struggling to take decisions.

Modern management theory

1970s—A mental approach to performance excellence

In the early 1970s, a seminal work by Timothy Gallwey (1974), *The Inner Game of Tennis*, advocated that "learning how to learn" led to a mental approach which would result in greater success than any mere perfection of technique ever could. His approach initiated a trend within organizations worldwide, developing a deeper awareness for executives: that in order to improve individual and organizational performance they first needed to access their own internal resources. This "mental" approach to performance excellence was later perfected by the neuro-linguistic, cognitive-behavioural approach to coaching which advocated "using the brain for a change" (Bandler, 1985).

1980s—Corporate coaching for transformational leadership

Building on this mental approach to managerial performance, the development of corporate leadership became big business in its own right—and the advent of corporate coaching was a logical extension of this movement. There are a variety of opinions as to when the discipline of executive coaching began its ascent. Morris and Tarpley (2000:144) suggest that it was in the late 1980s when a huge gap became increasingly evident between what managers were competently trained to do and what they were actually being asked to achieve.

At the same time, the popularity of organizational gurus such as Peter Senge and Stephen Covey encouraged the growth of the self-help and pop psychology sections of bookshops. Today many executives won't be seen dead without their copy of the latest, most fashionable manual on organizational thinking.

Covey advocated that individuals need to be the first to change if any organizational transformation was to be sustainable. His work signalled the beginning of the shift in the late 1980s towards corporate coaching. He advocated that the critical element of trust be built up within the organization, and he insisted that leadership began with the individual executive.

1990s—The learning organization and executive leadership

The 1990s gave birth to the management concept of the "learning organization". This stressed that, in the face of complexity and uncertainty, individuals and organizations needed to adapt capably and continuously to changing work and social environments. The learning organization provided a fresh perspective on how "learning" provided a key to more democratic organizational structures and flexible processes.

In other words, the capacity to learn reinforced the ability to make choices. Peter Senge's *The Fifth Discipline* (1990) emphasized systems thinking and the importance of organizational learning. According to Senge (1990:14), a learning organization is "an organization that is continually expanding its capacity to create its future". Senge (1990:376) also identified five critical practices within the learning organization: personal mastery, mental models, shared vision, team learning and systems thinking.

Traditionally, the development of organizations and corporations supported business and performance development models, but ignored the importance of values to individuals and teams. This crucial lack therefore laid the foundation for the development of coaching—not just for leaders and senior executives, but for individuals at all levels in the workforce looking to enhance their personal and professional lives.

At the same time, facilitating successful corporate leadership succession became a critically important need. As a result, corporate consultants began to work in organizations with senior managers and executives, and by the late 1990s the emergence of corporate coaches contributed to the perception that "visionary leadership training" (Hudson, 1998:3) was the way forward, in alignment with executive coaching programmes.

Managing complexity

Today, in the twenty-first century, Shaw and Linnecar suggest dispensing with the "compelling" myth of the "super-executive" that has been built up since the early 1990s. They maintain that "leadership cannot be mythical because we see it in action around us every day" (Shaw and Linnecar, 2007:xiii). Perhaps one of the reasons that the myth of the super-executive continues, apart from media hype, is due to the complexity that executives have to manage daily. This complexity comprises the number and ambiguity of variables operating within the organization, including the rate and scale of change, and the environment in which people and systems attempt to work together effectively.

Jaques and Clement (1991:xiv–xv) define the qualities that they believe managerial leaders need to acquire as being

> ... the necessary level of cognitive complexity to carry the level of task complexity; a strong sense of value for the particular managerial work, and for the leadership of others; the appropriate knowledge, and skills, plus experienced practice in both; the necessary wisdom about people and things; and the absence of abnormal temperamental or emotional characteristics that disrupt the ability to work with others.

The growing complexity of the twenty-first-century organization puts great pressure on postgraduate business schools to develop competent, experienced coaches who are able to walk alongside managerial leaders learning to juggle enormous levels of cognitive, emotional and organizational complexity. Every business leader needs to balance the corporate mission, vision, culture, values, organizational targets, as well as guide transformational development of resources and systems, as part of the complexity of the organizational context. In addition, the business coach has a responsibility to be a thinking partner to the managerial leader, and to keep a clear vision of yet another complex system—that of client, coach and organization, sometimes referred to as client, coach and sponsor.

LEADERSHIP AND TALENT DEVELOPMENT
Standard Bank, a leading banking and financial services group in South Africa, has built a Global Leadership Centre (GLC) to develop cognitive, behavioural and emotional competence for their managerial leaders. Executives are able to make their own choice of external coach from a suite of candidates selected

through a rigorous screening process. Helena Dolny, Founding Director of the GLC's Coaching and Mentoring Unit, explains that "Conducted behind closed doors, the executive coaching relationship is private. Coaching is an unregulated industry; the benefit of the screening process is greater confidence in terms of the fit between the coach and what the company is trying to achieve."

Dolny says that the focus has been on providing a range of coaching programmes for different purposes: performance coaching skills for all line managers, peer coaching and team coaching, as well as the flagship executive coaching programme. She points out that, "The issues we constantly address are about clarifying the difference between coaching approaches and varying purpose, and secondly peoples' concerns about the sustained value of coaching and return on investment. Getting data to support measurability is a major challenge." Dolny believes that a systemic implementation of coaching and mentoring programmes is the key to developing talent and supporting transformation in the changing financial marketplace of a fledgling democracy (Dolny, 2008).

Guidelines therapy offers business coaching

In this chapter, I refer to various psychologists and psychotherapists whose practice and research have made a substantial impact on the development of coaching: Irvin Yalom, an existential psychotherapist at Stanford University, California; Dr Ernesto Spinelli, an existential professor of psychology at Regent's College London; Carl Rogers, psychologist and developer of the client-focused approach; and Bruce Peltier, psychologist and executive coach based in San Francisco, and author of *The Psychology of Executive Coaching*. The core skills of the Rogerian client-centred approach—i.e. active listening, respecting clients, and adopting their internal frame of reference—is in alignment with the central aim of achieving results within the coaching conversation.

Because coaching is currently a service industry and an "emerging profession", it does not yet meet the requirements for a "true profession". It is here that psychology and psychotherapy research offer much insight into the complexity of human behaviour and organizational systems for the business coach. For example, it is crucial for the business coach always to refer pathology appropriately and to keep coaching and therapy separate.

As defined by Grant and Cavanagh (2006:3), the key criteria to becoming a profession are:

- creating significant barriers to entry;
- a shared common body of knowledge;
- formal qualifications at university level;
- regulatory bodies with the power to admit, discipline and meaningfully sanction members;
- an enforceable code of ethics; and
- some form of state-sanctioned licensing or regulation.

Once a more rigorous and empirical body of academic and practitioner research is available for the business coach, we will see the emergence of professional coaches, both internal and external to the organization. As a result of the International Coaching Research Forum (ICRF), which was sponsored by the Foundation of Coaching in September 2008 at Harvard University, a community of coaching researchers has developed a range of research proposal outlines to advance the emerging profession. The Foundation of Coaching is backing the initiative with grants for academic and organizational coaching research worldwide. In all countries worldwide, it is essential that practising business coaches are encouraged to reflect the rigour of their work in reflective practice, evidence-based research or peer-reviewed journals. It is for this reason that I encourage an awareness of the scientist-practitioner model of coaching aligned with the development of a common body of "empirically tested knowledge" (Grant and Cavanagh, 2006:2).

Historically, the models of therapy have shifted over the years. The first model of the therapist-patient relationship was the "blank screen", where the therapist stayed neutral hoping the patient would project onto this "blank screen major transference distortions". The second model was the therapist as archaeologist, digging through the past to understand "the original trauma" (Yalom, 2001:75). Although Freud often enquired into the personal lives of his patients, Carl Rogers in his early years advocated non-directive therapy with minimal direction to the client. He later abandoned this for a more participative, interactive style.

Harry Stack Sullivan defined psychotherapy as "a discussion of personal issues between two people, one of them more anxious than the other" (Yalom, 2001:108). Although the coach is not dealing with the neuroses of their clients, a great deal of anxiety arises in the professional working life of clients that needs to be addressed. In therapy, the therapist gives feedback on the client/patient relationship as it occurs; in coaching, on the other hand, the feedback is more focused on relationships the client experiences out in the workplace.

This is where the coach needs to have a great deal of awareness in order not to become part of the "client's system". Sometimes it is useful to observe what is happening between coach and client, and how this mirrors blind spots or areas of difficulty for the client. This requires the coach to be able to ask questions, make candid observations—or challenge the client's perspective or view of a situation—when this would be helpful to remove limiting assumptions or lead to a more positive result. A key difference is that therapists interpret behaviour; coaches challenge and make observations about client behaviour.

OBSERVING CLIENT BEHAVIOUR

One of the senior executives with whom I work would periodically "explode" about an emotional event that had occurred between him and another at work. It took me a few months to help my client understand the impact of his "explosive" behaviour on others, and the need for greater self-awareness on his part. The client's own behaviour, in fact, was triggering a strong emotional reaction in others. Once we began to discuss the types of reactions that were occurring and to help the client see what role he played in the interactions, he became aware of his own defensiveness.

As his self-awareness grew, regarding the impact his behaviour had on others, we started to discuss how to build alliances and heal a few broken relationships in a proactive and positive way. His insight into his own behaviour produced gradual change that, over a period of a year, began to result in a more positive response towards him by subordinates and colleagues. Eventually trust and respect developed into strong support for the work he was initiating in the organization. To this day, however, he still has to work on his own self-defensive tendencies. Nevertheless, he has developed greater self-awareness, and his gradual change in behaviour has given more authenticity to his transformational projects—which, in turn, are beginning to impact positively on the organization. He continues to grow the trust that is now being placed in his abilities.

According to Peltier (2001:xxx), the positive themes to be gained from therapy, and which impact the coaching intervention, are insight, awareness of the goal, self-examination, intra-personal understanding, talking about things (i.e. making things explicit), rapport building, and special relationship feedback from an impartial party within a confidential relationship.

Therapists can offer insight into the dynamics and motivations of others, adult development, effective listening skills (restatement, summarizing, physically listening, deep listening), resistance, and co-operation. According to Peltier (2001), the basic ingredients of the executive coaching relationship are based on a few common themes from the psychology literature. I have paraphrased and reordered these themes:

- active listening;
- adopting the client's internal frame of reference;
- being a confidante, listener, personal advisor;
- being engaging and responsive;
- building trust and understanding;
- coaching for skill, performance, development, and the executive's agenda;
- directing the client toward a desired outcome;
- empathy;
- equal working partnership;
- forging the partnership;
- listening skills;
- providing challenge and support;

- understanding the dynamics of human behaviour;
- offering an active partnership;
- offering two-way feedback;
- patience;
- respecting clients;
- being an objective, trustworthy source of feedback; and
- wanting to empower others by helping them to take responsibility for change.

In terms of the coaching intervention, Rogerian principles also lead to success for the business coach (Rogers, 1961:61–63):

- creating a genuine, authentic, one-on-one relationship with the client;
- achieving accurate empathy through unconscious positive regard and acceptance;
- by really hearing the client and fully accepting them as they currently are; and
- reflecting what you hear back to the client so that they can fully appreciate their situation as it is.

The impact of psychological theory on business coaching

Many countries around the world are in a period of rapid transformation—economically, politically and socially. Individuals must learn to adapt to and manage constant change, multi-cultural diversity, and educational and linguistic differences. They also have to confront major economic and life transitions within the workplace. To be successful, business coaches require an understanding of organizational systems and complexity, as well as an informed "hands-on" familiarity with psychological theory.

In grappling with the development of managerial leaders, it is critical that business coaches understand the intrapersonal and interpersonal realms. Psychology and psychotherapy have well-established traditions of specialized fields of study, ethics, supervision and published research that are highly relevant to our fast-changing, complex organizational and societal systems. I am **not** saying that business coaches need to be psychologists; simply that they need a practical grounding or "literacy" in psychological theory.

Business coaches work with executive behaviour and performance—and behaviour is determined by the individual's perception of their social situation. Peltier, in *The Psychology of Executive Coaching*, says that contemporary psychotherapy literature is relevant and invaluable for executive coaches because it is systems-oriented, drawing from models of humanistic, existential, behavioural and psychodynamic psychology. This helps executives to develop themselves and become more effective (Peltier, 2001:ix–xx).

Cognitive psychology focuses on current perceptions and on subjective reality, and is the study of the mind, its ways and patterns. Cognitive therapy helps people to begin to notice, and change, their own thought patterns with powerful emotional and behavioural benefits (Peltier, 2001:82). Neuro-Linguistic Programming (NLP) is based on cognitive behavioural psychology, and involves an understanding of the mental and cognitive processes behind behaviour—hence providing vital coaching tools for the development of communication and for the process of change:

> NLP ... provides psychological skills for understanding the mental processes and patterns we use to achieve results. NLP addresses how we use our senses to think, how language relates to thought, and how our thinking strategies control our experience and achievements. NLP provides a practical understanding of how the brain works: how people think, learn and motivate themselves to change. It is essentially about how we process information, and how this manifests itself in behaviour. It is how we use the language of the mind to achieve specific desired goals. Like many learning tools, NLP refers to how you organize your mental life: the basis of all learning (Stout Rostron, 2002:117).

Behaviour, goals and performance

To help clients improve their behaviour and performance, it is useful for business coaches to understand the psychology behind adult behaviour, goals and motivation. Sigmund Freud's five stages

THIRD-POSITION THINKING

Third-position thinking is an NLP coaching technique to help the client work with a situation involving another party (with whom the client is having difficulty); the other party is not actually physically present in the coaching conversation. The coach helps the client to think through a situation from three positions (first position/the client's own; second position/the other's position; third position/the client as their own "coach"). This is a technique the coach uses to help the client physically stand in first position (their own position); second position (the other's position); and third position (client adopts a meta-position or that of the "coach") in order to resolve a conflict or to see the other person's point of view. I use this frequently when the client has an issue or difficulty with another party and needs to hear, see and feel perspectives from all points of view. Because coach and client enact it—and the client actually verbalizes what they, as well as the other person, are thinking and feeling—it helps the client to understand the bigger picture, and to determine what needs to change in their own behaviour in order to effect change in the other party's behaviour.

of psycho-development (oral, anal, phallic, latency, genital) have remained a benchmark for the interpretation and study of psychotherapy. According to Freud, the early years of infancy and childhood establish the strengths, weaknesses and dynamics that continue into adult life (Freud, 1960/1980).

Alfred Adler, who worked with Freud for ten years, reasoned that adult behaviour is purposeful and goal-directed, and that life goals provide individual motivation. He focused on personal values, beliefs, attitudes, goals and interests. Adler recommended that adults engage in the therapeutic process using goal setting and reinventing their future, using techniques such as "acting as if", role-playing and goal setting—all tools utilized and recognized by well-qualified business coaches.

Carl Jung diverged from Freudian thinking, viewing the adult years of an individual's life as the phase where true identity emerges in a process he called "individuation". The terms "individuation", "archetype", "extraversion" and "introversion" are based on the psychological model of the relations between conscious and unconscious minds. Jung suggested that individuals carry the world in microcosm, and that the personal psyche is embedded in the archetypal psyche (Stevens, 1994). In his pioneering work, *Psychological Types*, Jung (1977) suggested that people have different preferences, which give them alternative perspectives on situations. These varying perspectives and "attitudes" are now seen as highly relevant to understanding organizational and cultural requirements and the needs of people in relation to motivation and leadership (Stout Rostron, 2006a).

Erik Eriksson, who influenced the NLP movement, further investigated the adult phases of development. Eriksson viewed development as a lifelong process, in which each individual must resolve a series of polarities, which may be stimulated by crises or turning points, to become a normal, healthy person (Stout Rostron, 2006a:25). Hudson's renewal cycle helps us to understand an adult's experience of life and change.

Abraham Maslow, like many other psychologists, believed that we need to resolve certain issues before we can move on to the next ones that need resolution (from physiological needs, to safety needs, to social needs, to esteem and self-actualization needs). Maslow broke the mould of exploring pathology to understand human nature. He looked at motivation and at motivators, believing that "individuals naturally actualize themselves unless circumstances in their development are so adverse that they must strive for safety rather than for growth" (Yalom, 1980:280).

It is nevertheless important that the business coach be able to discern pathology. As Jaques and Clement so succinctly put it, it is important to discern "abnormal temperamental or emotional characteristics that disrupt the ability to work with others" (Jaques and Clement, 1991:xiv–xv). The coach must be able to distinguish when the client should be referred to a registered psychotherapist for such pathologies to be explored and resolved.

John Whitmore in *Coaching for Performance* (2002) highlights the mind as the source of self-motivation, and insists that for people to perform they must be self-motivated. Maslow said that all we have to do is to overcome "our inner blocks to our development and maturity" (Whitmore, 2002:110). The highest state in Maslow's hierarchy of human needs was the self-actualizing person who emerges when "esteem needs are satisfied and the individual is no longer driven by the need to prove themselves, either to themselves or to anyone else" (Whitmore, 2002:111). Maslow saw this as a never-ending journey.

Associated with self-actualizing is the need to develop meaning and purpose. Clients "want their work, their activities and their existence to have some value, to be a contribution to others"; this relates to motivation because "people seek to engage in those activities that help them to meet their needs" (Whitmore, 2002:112). Through my work with coaching clients, I have come to believe that coaches are responsible for helping both themselves and their clients become aware of their own unconscious thinking processes, and how these impact on their behaviour in the world. To understand their own behaviour, clients need to understand their own intrinsic drivers at a conscious level.

Motivation and goal setting

Motivational theories primarily focus on the individual's needs and motivations. I have typically worked with coaching clients to help them understand more fully their intrinsic motivators (internal drivers such as values, beliefs, and feelings), and how to use extrinsic motivators (external drivers such as relationships, bonuses, environment, and titles) to motivate their teams. An important part of my research, therefore, has been to develop an understanding of limiting assumptions which create anxiety and prevent the client from making decisions—or which may interfere with self-belief, self-esteem, and self-management; with social or interpersonal management; and even with understanding how to work effectively within a system (such as the work environment).

The exercise below frequently forms part of an initial coaching session with a client. This is often where I start a coaching intervention, to determine what are the core values, beliefs and feelings which guide or drive this particular client. It is a powerful experience for a client to come to grips with their own intrinsic drivers, providing you, as the coach, with a tool to begin to understand your client's inner world. I recommend practising this exercise with another coach before using it with a client.

Adult learning

The goal of adult learning is to achieve balance and transition between new learning, skills development, and the cycles of adult

CLIENT EXERCISE: INTRINSIC MOTIVATORS
This involves asking two questions. But write down all the answers to the first question before asking the second question.

1. What is important to you professionally? (anything else?), and
2. What is important to you personally? (anything else?).

Write down the answers in the client's own words, exactly as they say them. What I mean by "important" are the intangibles, the unmeasurables, such as making a difference, collaboration, integrity, leadership, professionalism, balance between work and personal life, family, friends, health.

These intrinsic drivers are values, beliefs and feelings, which are not to be confused with goals. Goals are measurable, often quantifiable and tangible. Values are intangible and unmeasurable.

Finally, ask:

3. What else is important? (anything else?)

This third question is to check that nothing has been missed. Once clients have answered all the questions, have them integrate their list of personal and professional drivers, eliminating any duplicates. Ask if there is any one that is most important, or which supersedes the others. Then rank the rest in decreasing order of importance.

ALIGNING INTRINSIC DRIVERS WITH GOALS
Use this list to examine any goals to be set for this individual. An individual's goals always need to be in alignment with their own internal, intrinsic drivers, otherwise there will be difficulties for them in trying to achieve those goals. Intrinsic drivers and motivators need to be in alignment with all goals set.

An example of a conflict between goals or job responsibilities and personal intrinsic drivers was a client who had given up smoking; her top driver had become "health". This executive's job was to edit an international journal for tobacco regulation worldwide. Part of her role entailed translating regulations from various countries into English; she herself was a qualified linguist speaking 15 languages. Every day she was translating "smoking can damage your health" over and over again. Eventually her health began to be affected as her key job responsibilities and targets were in direct conflict with her new core intrinsic driver—health. Her personal coach helped her begin to think about the need to look for a new job.

Personal versus business goals
Another approach to this exercise, particularly if your client has a tendency to view personal and business goals holistically, is to identify business goals as short-term, medium-term and long-term. A clear indication, when asked the question: "What are your goals?" or "Where do you want to be in a year's time?" is that the client often responds with business goals. The next question would then be: "What would you like people to say about you at your funeral?" Typically, the answers here are different. The conversation can then proceed to the difference between personal and business goals, with a further question as to the appropriate timeframe to achieve personal goals.

An example is a client who lists short- and medium-term business goals as "moving up the corporate ladder to a senior position" and a long-term goal as "owning my own business". The same client responded to the "funeral" question that he would like to be seen as adding value to his community, being loving and kind and always available for people who matter to him. Often the drive to achieve business goals is in alignment with the drive to achieve personal goals.

life. Frederick Hudson (1998:106) researched four phases in which individuals and organizations experience change. Hudson's four stages of change (**go for it; doldrums; cocooning; getting ready**) are useful in order to understand cycles of change, and the continuous process of growth throughout adult life. In Chapter 5, we look at how to use Frederick Hudson and David Kolb's learning models as processes in your coaching conversation.

Adult learning theory has influenced coaching from the start. Because the world is in constant flux, the goal of adult learning is to achieve a balance between work and personal life. Although training was the methodology used in the 1980s and 1990s to develop managers, today training is preferred as a methodology for skills transfer. Coaching is thought to be a more powerful method to develop a managerial leader's ability to learn from experience and to develop professional competence. Recent coaching research shows that leadership development is often viewed as the purpose of most coaching assignments (Underhill, McAnally and Koriath, 2007; cited in AMA, 2008:2).

The coaching conversation is an excellent adult learning and developmental space. Most business coach-client relationships involve an integration of personal and systems work. Personal work is intended to help the client develop the mental, physical, emotional and spiritual competence to achieve their desired goals; systems work may be found within a partnership, marriage, family, organizational team or matrix structure. Business coaching is holistic and encompasses the systems of which the individual client finds themselves a part.

Experiential learning

A powerful influence on coaching, experiential learning is an active process where coach and client probe the essence of an experience to understand its significance and the learning which can be gained from it. Experiential learning is directly influenced by the seminal works of John Dewey, Kurt Lewin, Jean Piaget, David Boud, and David Kolb.

The importance of experiential learning is that it emphasizes a client's individual, subjective experience. In existential terms, the meaning of experience is not a given; it is subject to interpretation. Coach and client use the business coaching conversation to actively reconstruct the client's experience, with a focus on setting goals which are aligned with the client's intrinsic drivers, i.e. values, beliefs and feelings.

How clients construct their experience is what Boud, Cohen and Walker (1996:11), in *Using Experience for Learning*, term the individual's "personal foundation of knowledge". Coaches need to be aware that, often, more is lost than gained by ignoring the uniqueness of each person's history and ways of experiencing the world. This is why many coaches will begin their first conversation with a client by asking to hear their life story.

Boud, Cohen and Walker (1996) have defined the differences between cognitive, affective and conative (i.e. expressing endeavour or effort) learning. Cognitive learning is more concerned with **thinking**, where affective learning is concerned with **values and feelings**, and conative or psychomotor learning is concerned with **action and doing**. If learning at work is cognitive, affective and psychomotor, then it involves feelings and emotions (affective), the intellectual and cerebral processes (cognitive) and action (conative) (Boud, Cohen and Walker, 1996:46–58).

We now know that not only is learning socially and culturally constructed, but it does not occur in isolation from social and cultural norms and values. Clients will reconstruct their own experience within the context of a particular social setting and range of cultural values. In other words, coach and client do not exist independently from their environment. The client's experience impacts on their own cultural competence, which we explore in Chapter 6 when looking at issues of diversity, culture and gender in coaching.

Other considerations may be language, social class, gender, ethnic background, and the individual's style of learning. In learning from experience, it is useful to understand which barriers prevent the client from learning. Often it is a matter of developing self-reflective skills as much as self-management skills. What clients learn from their experience can transform their perceptions, their limiting and liberating assumptions, their way of interpreting the world—and their ability to achieve results.

Business coaching worldwide

Internationally, coaching as a leadership discipline is fresh and vibrant—with theoretical roots that are deep and strong. Underpinning the field of coaching are the various disciplines of psychology, and the relatively new disciplines of adult and experiential learning, organizational development, and systems thinking. Coaching, as a young and developing profession, has integrated a number of mental models from existing professions: psychological, systemic, and organizational.

In the 1990s, professional coaching was in its formative years in Australia, the UK, Europe and the USA, while in emerging markets such as Argentina, India, China and East Asia, and South Africa, coaching is only just beginning to trail-blaze its way into the 2000s.

However, in all countries, there continues to be some confusion between psychology and coaching. Although coaching is not psychotherapy, it is developmental, and involves a similar format of "conversation" with the client as psychotherapy. Influenced by a diverse range of disciplines, academics and practitioners alike view business coaching as related to organizational development, management consulting, leadership development, and human resources management.

Even though the importance of academic and practitioner research into the successes and failures of business coaching has been sign-posted by both the Global Convention on Coaching (GCC) and the newly formed International Coaching Research Forum (ICRF) at Harvard, a much greater awareness and consciousness of practitioner research is needed worldwide. A growing number of Masters and Doctoral students are in the process of completing research projects with papers beginning to be circulated worldwide. And, in addition, new coach-training programmes are springing up worldwide in university graduate schools of business at practitioner, Masters and Doctoral level.

Some of the difficulties in the global marketplace stem from there being too small a pool of diverse, qualified and experienced business coaches to satisfy the growing needs of small, medium and large organizations. Companies who employ internal and external coaches are beginning to be more demanding of quantifiable and measurable results, value for money, distinguished accreditation, membership of a recognized professional body with a clear ethical code, and an assurance of continuing professional development (CPD) aligned with published or organizational standards of competence.

Although it can be quite difficult to find information on business coaching in the international marketplace, I refer to a number of publications below which you may find useful depending on the market in which you are interested. I have not mentioned every country in the world in which coaching is taking place. However, I have tried to give a flavour of some of the issues and cultural differences emerging in different parts of the world.

USA

Diane Brennan (2008) discusses the emergence of coaching as an industry in the USA during the early 1990s. Brennan explains that the early coaching pioneers included individuals such as Thomas Leonard and Laura Whitworth, who, along with the formation of the International Coach Federation (ICF) in the mid-1990s, raised the media profile of coaching. Other organizations which emerged a few years later were "Coachville and the International Association of Coaching (IAC)" (Brennan, 2008:185).

Brennan (2008:185) explains that "what started as a handful of individuals coming together in the US in the early 1990s" has emerged as coaching, "an industry with services sought by organizations and individuals across the country". An international study of coaching for the ICF by PricewaterhouseCoopers (2007) showed that US coaches were "split nearly equally among the top three specialties of Life (18 per cent), Leadership (17 per cent) and Executive Coaching (16 per cent)" (Brennan, 2008:185–186). As in most countries today, the focus of coaching in US organizations tends to be dominated by leadership and executive coaching, with an emphasis on coaching for individual executives and their teams.

The trend began in the US with coaches being recruited into a variety of organizational departments, from organizational development, to human resources, leadership and development, as well as coaching and mentoring units. What is lacking today is valid benchmarking and a measurement of the value coaching brings to organizations, and its actual return on investment (ROI). The impact today is seen in the burgeoning of commercial coach training programmes, and the development of educational coaching programmes inside graduate schools of business.

However, what is important is that the providers, educators and buyers of coaching work together at an international level to debate and fulfil the various recommendations of the ten groups who contributed to the *Dublin Declaration on Coaching* (GCC, 2008g) produced as a result of the Global Convention on Coaching in 2008. And, although coaching draws on multiple disciplines and is used by many types of people in many environments, it is not necessarily the case that everyone in the coaching community wants to see the creation of a profession. Only by working together can the diverse perspectives and diverse points of view be heard—and alliances built. The "stakes in the ground" planted by all of the GCC working groups urge a collaborative and international approach—in particular, recommending guidelines and agreement concerning ethical codes, education and development, core competences, supervision, and research by 2010 (GCC, 2008c). The importance of international collaboration in the field of coaching cannot be over-emphasized; collaboration prevents isolation, creates equality, and brings together stakeholders from all corners of the globe. And although the GCC has inspired participation by scores of stakeholders, many more voices need to be heard.

UK and Europe

Although there is no officially recognized professional body overseeing the field of coaching in the UK and Europe, there are a variety of coaching organizations promoting best practice. You will know those most relevant to you, depending on the market within which you work. A few of these organizations are:

- Association for Coaching (AC).
- Association for Management Education and Development (AMED).
- Association for Professional Executive Coaching and Supervision (APECS).
- Special Group in Coaching Psychology (SGCP) of the British Psychological Society (BPS).
- British Association for Counselling and Psychotherapy (BACP).
- Chartered Institute of Personnel and Development (CIPD).
- European Mentoring and Coaching Council (EMCC).
- ECI (European Coaching Institute).
- The Work Foundation (formerly The Industrial Society).
- Institute of Directors (IoD).
- Chartered Management Institute (CMI) (formerly the Institute of Management).
- International Coach Federation (ICF).

Robin Linnecar (2008:1) explains that in the UK there has recently been an attempt to "pull all these [organizations] together under a common banner by issuing a Statement of Shared Values", even though there are "fundamental disparities on approaches to supervision of coaches, to name but one area".

Dr Annette Fillery-Travis (2009:1) talks about the importance of developing a coaching culture within the organizational context. "In the UK, the coaching capability of organizations is a 'hot topic'. ... The question is: How do we embed coaching within organizations in a way that fits their culture, context and needs and achieves all (or most) of the benefits?". Fillery-Travis (2008a:26) suggests that "as the coaching profession develops, we are becoming increasingly aware that we need to delineate coaching from other offers in the market; identify the real value we can bring to our clients; and be able to advise the buyers of coaching on which coaching interventions are fit for their purpose. To do this we need to have evidence of what works and how. In effect, we need a thorough grounding in both the theory and practice of what we do and the research which underpins it".

In *Coaching and Buying Coaching Services: A Guide*, published by the Chartered Institute of Personnel and Development (CIPD) in the UK, Jessica Jarvis (2004:21) states that one of the CIPD's surveys found that "four-fifths of respondents now use coaching in their organizations", but there remains a major concern about the "number of 'cowboy' coaches entering the market who are inexperienced, have little training and lack the appropriate knowledge and skills". Jarvis explains that one of the key problems in the UK is that the "coaching industry is highly fragmented, with no single professional body or sets of standards and qualifications to guide buyers of coaching services" (Jarvis, 2004:3).

Although coaching is a growing and emerging area of HR practice in the UK, business coaching seems to be moving into a more mature phase, similar to the USA. There is, however, some confusion about the impact of coaching and its return on investment. According to the UK CIPD survey (Jarvis, 2004:9), the key reasons that coaching is being used in UK organizations are to:

1. Improve individual performance.
2. Deal with underperformance.
3. Improve productivity.
4. Career planning/personal development.
5. Grow future senior staff.

6. Foster a culture of learning and development.
7. Motivate staff.
8. Accelerate change in the organization.
9. Demonstrate the organization's commitment to staff.
10. Improve staff retention and reduce the cost of sending staff to external courses.

There is a vast array of coaching services in the UK, ranging from self-employed coaches, through small and large firms of coaches, to large consultancies who offer coaching services with an interest in securing the larger-volume contracts. According to the CIPD, other self-styled coaches operate "within a business psychology model of coaching where their coaches are qualified occupational, counselling or clinical psychologists, or come from the relatively new field of coaching psychology" (Jarvis, 2004:11–12).

One of the challenges in the UK is a "growing number of business advisers and consultants who have reinvented themselves as coaches and, without any further training, now operate as full-time coaches" (Jarvis, 2004:11–12). This adds to the complexity of a discipline which is moving into maturity, but still lacks legislation and regulation as an industry. For the time being, coaching continues to be self-regulated worldwide.

According to the CIPD, coaching in the UK is at a critical juncture. Coaching has "very quickly become a fairly significant part of many organizations' learning and development strategy", although "few HR professionals have in-depth expertise of managing coaching activities, and in particular selecting and supervising external coaches" (Jarvis, 2004:69).

It seems that, as in most other countries, there is not yet consensus on what are the criteria for a good coach, or the best way to evaluate the individual coaches or the results produced as a consequence of coaching. The range and experience of coaching bodies in the UK and Europe are in a position to encourage other professional coaching bodies worldwide to continue to work together to push for greater professionalism, quality standards and adherence to ethical practice.

Australia

The state of the coaching industry in Australia is on a par with that of the USA, particularly in the field of coaching research. According to Anthony Grant at the University of Sydney's Coaching and Psychology Unit, "coaching is now mainstream in Australia" (Grant, 2008:93). An increasing number of professional development programmes in coaching are being offered at Australian universities and management schools, with Australian commercial coach training organizations offering government-accredited coach training programmes (Grant, 2008:93–95).

Grant adds that "some of this research is genuinely cutting-edge and world-leading. In addition to the coaching-related research being generated by a number of different universities, the Australian Research Council (a government research funding body) has recently awarded at least three large government grants for research into coaching". As a result, coaching in Australia "shows important signs of being a significant contributor to the global coaching movement" (Grant, 2008:93–95).

The role of research is to determine the competences necessary to educate and develop coaches worldwide, as well as to create a definition of coaching that the global community will accept.

South Africa

In the UK, Europe and Australia there are a range of professional coaching organizations. However, to date, there is no officially recognized professional body overseeing the discipline for coaching, although, as is discussed above, a number of associations are actively attempting to work together to establish formal coaching accreditation. In South Africa, in response to this need for a professional body to which coaches can belong, an important development has been the founding of Coaches and Mentors of South Africa (COMENSA).

COMENSA's overriding brief has been to provide for the regulation of coaching and mentoring in South Africa, in order to develop the credibility of coaching as an emerging profession, and to align national standards of professional competence to international standards. One of the crucial and continuing roles of COMENSA is to build relationships and alliances between the organizational buyers of coaching and the individual and small-company providers of coaching services, and to build connections with other professional bodies such as the Worldwide Association of Business Coaches (WABC), the European Mentoring and Coaching Council (EMCC), and the International Coach Federation (ICF).

Since 1994 South Africa has been undergoing a process of transformation from an apartheid racial tyranny to a democracy. While leadership succession has been of paramount importance in both developed and developing nations, the move to executive and leadership coaching for individual executives in South Africa emerged as a strong trend only during the early 2000s.

The emergence of business coaching in South Africa is related to an explosion of talent development as the nation fast-tracks its managers into executive positions in every field of industry, government and education. Like much else in South Africa, coaching was isolated from mainstream professional development due to international restrictions during the years of apartheid. Only within the last five to ten years has coaching sprung to the forefront of managerial leadership development in South Africa, whereas in the global marketplace coaching is beginning to mature.

Coaching became more visible and accessible in South Africa at the turn of the twenty-first century, as new coach training schools sprang up, and graduate business schools accommodated "leader as coach" programmes. Since 2005, organizational development (OD) and human resources (HR) departments of large corporations have been training "internal" coaches, and designing assessment programmes to bring external coach consultants into the organizational "suite" of coaches needed for their top executives.

Supervision may be the new and innovative context in South Africa for coach practitioners to contribute to the development of self-reflective practice and practitioner research. This might be a contributing factor to the move towards becoming more "professional".

India

The relevance of coaching to senior executives in India began to be acknowledged in the early 2000s due to the growing complexity of business. Deepak Chandra, Associate Dean of the Centre for Executive Education (CEE) at the Indian School of Business (ISB) explains that "As a concept, Executive Coaching is still new in India. In our past, the Gurukul system was an example of the one-to-one coach for individual students. It was built on a deeper interpersonal relationship." He acknowledges that in today's globalized world, senior management has been prompted "to counsel, seek, and simply talk to a person who can be an amalgam of a sounding-board, a critic, a seer, a friend, etc." (ISB, 2007:1).

India is in the early phase of coaching development. Gopal Shrikanth, in his article "Coaching in the Land of Gurus and Sooth-sayers", says that "As in ancient Greece, Rome and China, India had its share of historical 'royal coaches' like Krishna and Chanakya, whose wisdom is enshrined in the *Gita* and *Arthashastra*. These ancient 'case studies' are still analyzed by MBAs and corporate leaders at business schools and research institutes." He explains that multinational corporations currently rely on their global coaching partners to bring executive coaches into India. In fact, he encourages English-speaking coaches from other countries to take advantage of the opportunity to work with Indian executives. He explains that it may not yet be well-known internationally that "India has made such rapid strides over the last two decades in adopting and propagating Western management practices" (Shrikanth, 2009:1).

In "Five Keys to Successful Business Coaching in India", Kim Benz and Sasmita Maurya (2007:22) note that Indian businesses are largely a mix of two groupings:

1. The first group includes multi-national organizations, entrepreneurs who have taken their business offshore, and local business organizations with public holdings and stock market listings. This group acknowledges that there is a need for coaching, but only in a limited sense; in-company mentorship is the wider practice. As long as there continues to be investment in developing high-potential employees by these organizations, the need of this group for business coaches will increase.
2. The second group are "closely-held businesses with no stock market listing, partnership business/trading companies, and independent business owners". This group has less concern in investing in the development of their staff, and tend to view coaching "as an expense".

What seems to set India apart in its adaptation to business coaching practice, is that the coach/client association is spiritual as well as professional. According to Commander Girish Konkar, CEO of Beyond Horizons, "coaching is looked upon as a spiritual association, as opposed to a 'business/commercial' association. Indian history describes the strong association with a guru throughout any learning process" (Benz and Maurya, 2007:24).

China and other East Asian countries

In "Hybrid World: Coaching and the Complexities of Age, Values and Asian Business", Maya Hu-Chan (2007:7) suggests that "any understanding of how to coach Asian leaders must begin with an awareness of the generational changes sweeping the globe". In support, she cites a lead article in *Fast Company* magazine contending that Generation Y in China has presented the corporate world with a new creative class which blends youthful innovation with more traditional Chinese culture (Chen, 2007; cited in Hu-Chan, 2007:7).

Hu-Chan (2007:7) notes that "The business coach entering today's global marketplace is challenged to address new dualities in business and culture. In Asia in particular, a radical shift toward business is blending with, but not eliminating, traditional values. The coach must meet clients in a new virtual space". She advocates a greater understanding of the emerging synthesis of "traditional Asian veneration of age as wisdom ... counter-balanced by a wave of upstart entrepreneurs" (Hu-Chan, 2007:7).

One of Hu-Chan's (2007:8) key recommendations to coaches working in Asia is to "develop a hybrid model for Asia meets the West" and "flip the model for the West meets Asia". She cites a survey by Korn/Ferry International in 2006, who polled 300 senior executives as to what makes a business executive successful in Asia. In response to the question "Should a Western business leadership model be replaced in Asia by an Asian business leadership model?", 35.5 per cent of the executives said no: a business leadership model is required that is neither "Western nor Asian," but includes "elements of all best practices" (Hu-Chan, 2007:7).

Hu-Chan (2007:8) makes the salient point that when coaching business leaders in Asia, coaches should be careful not to be lured by their own individual assumptions about Asian culture: "Don't assume that just because the leader is Asian he or she will have an indirect communication style. Don't assume that young Asian leaders are all petulant children". And she warns coaches to be aware that "Asians aren't always of the same ethnic background.

For example, in the Greater China region, there are 56 cultures and ethnicities in Hong Kong, the mainland, and Taiwan" (Hu-Chan, 2007:9).

The main message is to "understand emerging Asian business and adapt your approach". Hu-Chan talks about the rapidly transforming culture of business in Asia, but certainly, one of the key learnings that we can take from her study is that the coach needs to be culturally well-informed and constantly aware of their own assumptions, keeping pace with "the emergence of Asia as a dominant force in the world economy with China at the helm" (Hu-Chan, 2007:8).

Argentina and Chile

The following case study is a contribution from Professor Thomas Kottner at the Institute for Integral Studies, and Director of the Swilcan Institute for Integral Leadership in Buenos Aires. Professor Kottner shares a brief history on the evolution of coaching in Argentina with reference to the development of coaching in Chile (Kottner, 2008).

CASE STUDY: ARGENTINA AND CHILE
In Argentina, coaching had its start at the Organizational Learning Center (OLC) as part of the Technological Institute of Buenos Aires (ITBA); the OLC was initially launched in agreement with the OLC at the Massachusetts Institute of Technology. A range of corporate organizations sponsored the programme in exchange for executive coaching interventions. The original coaching programme, "Leading Learning Communities" (LLC), was delivered to middle and senior management levels. However, at the time, coaching did not achieve enough serious commitment at executive level, which would have meant a greater systemic impact on the organizations involved in the project. Because the programme was considered to be too costly for organizational budgets, the OLC was eventually disbanded.

The Argentinean OLC was managed by Fred Kofman, an Argentinean who, at the outset, worked closely with Peter Senge at MIT. Kofman trained in coaching at the Newfield Network in Chile, which today has the strongest foundation for coaching in Latin America. The Newfield Network, devoted to ontological coaching, originated with Fernando Flores. Jim Selman, who trained with Flores, later founded the Institute for Professional Coaching in Buenos Aires when the Newfield Network split up. Today this is the only state-approved institute for coaching in Argentina. The specific type of coaching practiced in Argentina is primarily onto-logical coaching, with a focus on personal change processes.

During the last few years, businesses have facilitated two types of coaching intervention:

1. *Executive coaching*—with a focus on cognitive aspects for sen-ior management, and a behavioural focus for middle manag-ers. There is a deliberate distinction made between leadership and management; leadership matters are managed with onto-logical coaching.
2. *Team building and performance coaching for operational teams*— there is a concern about the lack of measurable results for team coaching, but it provides an alternative to individual executive coaching, to which there is some resistance.

Kottner suspects that the OLC was unable to expand because it did not embody a cross-cultural focus. He explains that local businesses are not yet ready for long-term systemic learning and development processes. This is primarily because, for the last 60 years, Argentina has had a significant economic crisis every five years.

In Chile the situation is somewhat different. Coaching based on neuro-linguistic programming (NLP) is more popular in Chile; NLP coaching is perceived to offer a more scientific approach to leadership and management development. The majority of coaches in the Chilean Association for Coaching have a strong background in NLP, reinforced by the fact that Joseph O'Connor, co-author of the book *Introducing NLP* (1990), is the Honorary President.

During the last few years there has been a proliferation of short courses in Argentina, mainly because it is good business. How-ever, many coaching programmes are offered without an appro-priate level of education or an understanding of the requirements for professional delivery. One of the key issues with the expansion of executive and business coaching is that coaches with a strong or academic background in business and top management still represent a small minority.

A few years ago the Argentinean Association of Professional Coaches was formed. It currently has about 280 active members, with Jim Selman as an honorary member. The institution has facilitated an annual Congress, with the previous Congress inviting presenters from other Latin American countries to share their coaching experience. Even though there are a myriad of training offers, there are only 12 institutions or educational initiatives approved with a standards seal by the Association. There is still no certification from international coaching bodies, which presents an interesting market opportunity.

Argentina has evolved as an individualistic society, and so there is still little active involvement from members who wish to expand the frontiers of coaching for the general benefit of the profession. Language also presents a barrier to the incorporation of the diverse approaches which are sustained globally.

In Argentina, coaching is on a growth path as more and more business executives are informed about its benefits, with a growing ability to discern the differences between the variety of programmes and types of coaching. The educational programmes and the coaching on offer inside organizations will become more professional as market demand grows. There is an absence of relevant practices such as **coaching supervision**, and **coaching research** is almost non-existent; both may grow, however, due to the need for benchmarked evidence if the coaching marketplace is to develop (Kottner, 2008).

International standards

As the demand for business and executive coaching continues to expand internationally, there is another area of development inside organizations. Individual corporations are in the process of defining their own standards of assessment to regulate the employment of internal and external coaches. A key prerequisite for the future will be that business coaches conform to organizational demands with the specific ethics, supervisory framework, standards and competences of those organizations. Business coaches are beginning to collaborate and form alliances in order to offer coaching services to corporate executives and their teams; this is taking place in professional bodies and at graduate school level with, for example, the Graduate School Alliance in the USA, which is conducting research into competences and criteria for post-graduate coaching programmes.

Business coaching is the trend of the moment. If it continues to develop at its current rate, conforming to internationally acceptable standards, it will make a significant difference in developing the competence and performance of individuals, managerial leaders, their teams and their organizations. However, coaching on its own is not a guarantee of success for senior executives in any organization in any country; it is a critical component which needs to be aligned with all the other leadership and management development initiatives for managers, leaders and executives within a company.

Business coaching should be aligned strategically with the overall values and objectives of an organization. A question is then raised for executives: if goals are to be motivationally achieved, are they also aligned with the individual's values, beliefs and feelings? Often organizations merely pay lip service to organizational values, and don't necessarily create them as a synthesis of the core individual values which make up the culture of the organization. Ethical dilemmas can arise during the coaching process if the executive needs to make difficult choices which are incompatible with their own value system.

Ethical challenges among executives are fairly universal. Whatever country you are coaching in, one hears stories which are almost identical to the situations faced by clients in other countries and continents. Let me tell you the story of Jim.

EXECUTIVE DILEMMAS

"Jim" (for confidentiality purposes, this and all other executives' names in this book have been changed) is a senior dispensing pharmacist who manages a major pharmaceutical retail chain in southern California. He grappled with a personal and professional dilemma, having been asked to lay off highly qualified and experienced staff in order to increase bottom-line profits for shareholders—not an uncommon position for business executives today. His inner turmoil was highlighted by the fact that the families of his pharmacists would be economically affected by the loss of one family member's income with no guarantee of replacing it, plus the loss of quality service to loyal customers. This was balanced against the short-term profits to be made by shareholders, including himself as the owner of a recently inherited share portfolio.

Jim also faced the problem of having to employ less qualified, less experienced and therefore less expensive dispensers, who would be unable to provide the quality service for which the pharmacy was reputed. One of Jim's concerns was that, although larger profits would be made for the retail organization's shareholders, these would be at the expense of a seriously reduced quality of expertise offered to a trusting public. A second unease was that all of his experienced staff already worked extensive hours; the enforced cuts to qualified staff would mean even more gruelling working hours for those still gainfully employed, with no seeming concern for the public on the part of shareholders.

"It's a moral dilemma for me, not only because I am faced with laying off people who are providing an expert quality service, but the staff who remain will be asked to take even greater strain, working longer hours yet providing an inferior service. My heart absolutely goes out to the people who are being sacrificed for short-term profits, as well as those who will step into their shoes.

"The guy in the boardroom in LA who looks only at the figures, and never has to look people in the eye like I do, is only interested in immediate gains. By the time those top executives have departed the company in a few years, with large bonuses and share options in return for their quick-buck strategy, my dispensing pharmacists who meet the public will be facing the serious frustration of the people we serve. Our customers will be experiencing a steady decline in the service they have become accustomed to. This may produce financial results for a few years, but the real business decision would be a far-sighted chairman who leaves a business that will flourish for 50 years. This short-sightedness for easy gains is, fundamentally, not good business sense.

"On the other hand, I must admit that a couple of years ago my pharmacist father left me a very solid portfolio of shares, on which I need to make good financial returns as part of my retirement planning. In the end, my decision has been to implement what I know to be a fundamentally unfair, unbusinesslike, yet profit-driven decision. It is not business-driven in the long term, because having built up our customer base on loyalty and good service, we will now sacrifice quality of service and expertise for immediate cash returns—but in the end I fear our customers will drift away to our rivals."

This is one of the most common dilemmas faced by executives today all over the world. It is a direct result of intense "bottom-line" pressure, and is a repeated theme expressed to me by many clients worldwide. Critically important is that coaching helps the client to think through such issues and dilemmas, asking questions, making observations and challenging the client's thinking—rather than offering advice on how they should manage them.

The future of business coaching worldwide

If coaching is to emerge as a discipline with a professional future, a wide variety of difficult conversations needs to take place in forums such as the GCC, and at the events of other professional bodies, where practitioners and stakeholders can share their expertise and work collaboratively together. Currently, there is an emerging collaboration among coaching industry bodies, who are working together to develop ethical codes, supervisory recommendations, professional standards of competence, and regulations for coaching certification. of coaches worldwide.

Working at a global level to develop coaching as a profession are bodies such as the Worldwide Association of Business Coaches (WABC), the International Coach Federation (ICF), the European Mentoring and Coaching Council (EMCC), Coaches and Mentors of South Africa (COMENSA), and the Chartered Institute of Personnel and Development (CIPD) in the UK. Worldwide, these and other professional coaching associations are involved with the Global Community of Coaches (GCC), which continues to facilitate a global dialogue to understand the needs of coaching consumers, practitioners and educators, in order to develop commonly agreed understandings, guidelines and frameworks for coaching practice and coach training.

As a result of the GCC process and the work done by the International Coaching Research Forum at Harvard (ICRF), it has been recommended that we need empirical evidence proving that coaching makes a difference for individuals, organizations, and society. Because there still remains a lack of clarity and consensus as to what professional coaching actually is, and what makes for an effective and reputable coach, it has been agreed that research needs to be conducted around the globe.

Business coaching has been defined in many different ways, but is essentially a one-on-one collaborative partnership to develop the client's performance and potential, personally and professionally, in alignment with the goals and values of the organization. In its formative stages as a profession, coaching sits at an interesting juncture worldwide—and business coaching, which is viewed as the primary way to develop managerial leaders, is at the very cutting edge of the way forward for this new, dynamic discipline.

Coach's library

Baez, F. (2006). Coaching across cultures. WABC *Business Coaching Worldwide eZine*, 2(4):20–23. Webpage: www.wabccoaches.com/bcw/2006_v2_i4/edge.html.

Benz, K., and Maurya, S. (2007). Five keys to successful business coaching in India. WABC *Business Coaching Worldwide eZine*, 3(2):22–24. Webpage: www.wabccoaches.com/bcw/2007_v3_i2/hottopics.html.

Bernthal, P. R., Bondra, J., and Wang, W. (2005). *Leadership in China: Keeping Pace With a Growing Economy*. Pittsburgh, PA: Development Dimensions International.

Burger, A. P (Ed.). (1996). *Ubuntu: Cradles of Peace and Development*. Pretoria: Kagiso.

Economist Intelligence Unit (EIU) and Korn/Ferry International (2007). *The Dream Team: Delivering Leadership in Asia*. Los Angeles: Korn/Ferry.

Fillery-Travis, A. (2008a). Where's the evidence? First steps into the literature. Based on the evidence, WABC *Business Coaching Worldwide eZine*, 4(1):26–28. Webpage: www.wabccoaches.com/bcw/2008_v4_i1/based-on-the-evidence.html.

Fillery-Travis, A. (2009). Collaboration and research—all for one and one for all. WABC *Worldwide Business Coaching eZine*, 5(1). Webpage: www.wabccoaches.com/bcw/2009_v5_i1/based-on-the-evidence. html.

Grant, A. M. (2008). Coaching in Australia: A view from the ivory tower. *Coaching: An International Journal of Theory, Research and Practice*, 1(1):93–98.

Hu-Chan, M. (2007). Hybrid world: Coaching and the complexities of age, values and Asian business. WABC *Business Coaching Worldwide eZine*, 3(3):6–9. Webpage: www.wabccoaches.com/bcw/2007_v3_i3/ feature.html.

Kline, N. (1999/2004). *Time to Think: Listening with the Human Mind.* London: Ward Lock.

Kottner, T. (2008). *A Short Brief on Coaching Evolution and Situation in Argentina.* Mimeo.

Legrain, E., and Fox, (2008). *Leadership Coaching: Inspiration from Asia.* Singapore: Banksia Coaching International. Webpage: www.banksia-coaching.com.

Peltier, B. (2001). *The Psychology of Executive Coaching: Theory and Application.* New York, NY: Brunner-Routledge.

Shrikanth, Gopal (2009). Coaching in the land of gurus and soothsayers. WABC *Business Coaching Worldwide eZine*, 5(1). Webpage: www. wabccoaches.com/bcw/2009_v5_i1/hot-topics.html.

Stout Rostron, S. (2006a). The history of coaching. In: McLoughlin, M. (Ed.), *Sharing the Passion: Conversations with Coaches* (pp. 16–41). Cape Town: Advanced Human Technologies.

Stout Rostron, S. (2006b). Business coaching in South Africa. WABC *Business Coaching Worldwide eZine*, 2(2):7–10. Webpage: www.wabc-coaches.com/bcw/2006_v2_i2/feature.html.

CHAPTER THREE

The coaching conversation

CHAPTER OUTLINE
- The coaching conversation as a thinking partnership
- Deepening your understanding of the business coaching process
- Listening, equality and the genuine encounter
- Learning from experience
- Purpose of the coaching conversation
- Measuring results
  - Visible behavioural change
  - Improved performance and business results
  - Personal and professional development
- Value of positive regard, empathy and appreciation
- Goals and the coach/client relationship
- Competences in business coaching
  - Why skills and competences
  - Global Convention on Coaching
  - International Coach Federation (ICF)
  - Worldwide Association of Business Coaches (WABC)
  - European Mentoring and Coaching Council (EMCC)
  - Coaches and Mentors of South Africa (COMENSA)

- Recommended competences
  - Building the coaching relationship
  - Listening and questioning
  - Developing self-awareness through the process of self-reflection
  - Continuous learning and development
  - Expanding your knowledge and core coaching skills base
  - Business and leadership coaching abilities
  - Upholding ethical guidelines and professional standards
- The need for research into core coaching competences
- In conclusion
- Coach's library

The coaching conversation provides a thinking environment where business professionals are able to develop self-awareness and a depth of understanding of themselves and others—embedding newly-acquired skills, competences and attitudes which subsequently impact the actions they take, and visibly demonstrate new behaviours. This chapter explores critical aspects of the coaching conversation, and outlines the key competences required by the coach to ensure successful outcomes.

The coaching conversation as a thinking partnership

This chapter explores the purpose and focus of the coaching conversation and the competences useful to the business coach. The "coaching conversation" is the face-to-face or telephone interaction between coach and client. It is a "thinking partnership" (Kline, 1999/2004) where coach and client reflect on the client's experience, transforming it into potential for learning and action. How the client takes responsibility for change can emerge from the coaching conversation.

The focus of a coaching conversation is to help the client work towards achieving their desired outcomes. The coach primarily explores with each client what it is that is holding back or stopping the client from achieving their goals, for example by identifying and replacing disempowering assumptions and paradigms with empowering ones.

The final section of this chapter outlines the general approach to competence frameworks developed by four international and national coaching organizations in an effort to promote professionalism within the industry, and recommends seven specific core competences to build your capacity as a business coach.

Deepening your understanding of the business coaching process

I define coaching as "a process that creates sustained shifts in thinking, feeling and behaviour—and ultimately in performance. By asking the right questions, coaches help clients find their own solutions". Cavanagh and Grant (2002:4) define coaching as a "solution-focused, results-oriented systematic process in which the coach facilitates the enhancement of performance, self-directed learning and personal growth of other individuals". The AMA/Institute for Corporate Productivity defines coaching as: "a short- to medium-term relationship between a manager or senior leader, and a consultant (internal or external) with the purpose of improving work performance" (Douglas and McCauley, 1999; cited in AMA, 2008:8).

I see the business coaching process as one that helps business executives and leaders to develop a clear understanding of their roles and responsibilities. Business coaching, like sports coaching, is about high performance, and is ultimately about sustained behavioural change and breakthrough results.

Some practitioners have had a difficult time differentiating coaching from other areas of practice or approaches by virtue of its supposed lack of "unique characteristics" (GCC, 2008a:1). One of the reasons for this is that some coaching providers see themselves as business consultants with their coaching services structured around the coaching process. It has been challenging to find one authoritative definition of coaching in the marketplace, not just because every professional body has its own slant on the coaching process, but because there is no agreed global definition available.

So what do business coaches do? The critical value of business coaching is in helping the individual executive to think clearly about the core issues which present challenges to them in their job, career and daily working life. Coaching is unique, helping individuals to systematize their conscious thoughts about the immediate actions needed to address specific practical issues, and to understand the unconscious processes that may be sabotaging their success.

Mentors focus on the development of the learner, and convey knowledge of organizational values and routines, plus the managerial system, thus helping the learner to navigate the organization's political system. Mentoring is personalized and domain-specific, and creates an atmosphere in which to acknowledge and recognize people.

In contrast, counselling is more personal and is aimed at specific personal problems. Counsellors and psychologists bring to coaching powerful, interpersonal change skills. The skills highly relevant to the coaching world, which come to us from psychotherapy literature, are:

- active listening;
- assertive communication;
- cognitive restructuring;
- conflict resolution;
- empathy;
- giving and getting feedback;
- learned optimism;
- process observation;
- self-awareness; and
- systems theory.

Robert Hargrove (2003) suggests in *Masterful Coaching* that "Coaching is having both the toughness and the compassion to skilfully intervene in people's learning processes, and that a successful coaching relationship is always a story of transformation, not just of higher levels of performance". John Whitmore (2002:8) in *Coaching for Performance* says, "Coaching is unlocking a person's potential to maximize their own performance; it is helping them to learn rather than teaching them".

These definitions suggest that **learning** is the key. This indicates that helping your clients grow, develop and become who they want to be, requires asking for their best thinking, rather than sharing yours. Your asking of incisive questions to open up the thinking of your client is "a powerful alliance designed to forward and enhance the lifelong process of human learning, effectiveness and fulfilment" (Whitworth, Kimsey-House and Sandahl, 1998:202).

The three levels of coaching intervention with which we are working as coaches are interconnected:

1. Doing: **What** tasks and goals need to be accomplished?
2. Learning: **How** will you develop the competences needed?
3. Being and becoming: **Who** are you as you grow, develop and transform? (Weiss, 2004)

The coach needs to ask: what does the client need to learn to perform better? And which skills and competences do they need to develop to "do the doing" better? Then, as they develop new skills and competences in the workplace, how does that impact on how they "be who they are"; and who is it that they want to become? When we look at coaching models in Chapter 5, we will explore the various levels of the coaching intervention that impact on the learning, growth and development of the client.

Listening, equality and the genuine encounter

The structure of the coaching intervention needs to be framed by the coach's ability to listen, and to actively intervene only when needed. **Listening, asking questions** and **silence** are core skills for the business coach—as they help to create safety for clients within the external physical environment, as well as enhancing the client's internal thinking environment.

A competence is simply a set of skills, and I include as part of the competence **active listening**: listening for feelings, asking relevant questions, giving feedback on clients' listening skills, giving feedback on the impression the client makes on you, paraphrasing, physical listening, reflection, restatement, and summarizing.

It is also important that the coach/client relationship be based on an assumption of equality. This is different to the therapist/patient relationship, which is often not considered an equal relationship. In a coaching relationship, neither coach nor client is superior to the other; both are travellers on the client's journey. A "safe thinking environment" is built through the development of the relationship, and research shows that the relationship is what can help with the onset of change (Stout Rostron, 2006c:79).

Equality also means being willing to be influenced by the client. I see this as a very important aspect of coaching. It is important that coach and client change as the relationship grows. Yalom (2001:26–27), well-known for his work with existential individual and group coaching, urges us to let our clients matter to us, "to let them enter your mind, influence you, change you—and not to conceal this from them".

For example, I recently learned a useful, amusing lesson from one of my clients. Both client and coach are raising teenage girls, and the thought from the client was "join them rather than fighting them"—in other words, take out a page in Facebook as a way to communicate at the level so desired by teenagers! This was quite an amusing and valuable lesson to me as coach—I was willing to listen to how my client related to her teenagers on the web forum as a different way to keep the lines of communication open.

However, although coaching is an egalitarian relationship, the focus is that of the coach on the client. Both individuals bring their experience, expertise and wisdom to the relationship. In coaching, the coach will adapt their style according to their model, but if the major presupposition of the coaching interaction is one of equality, it would be difficult to imagine a coach adopting the road of "minimal direction" or interaction. More important is the development of the relationship through the client/coach interactions.

Thus, I think it is important to share certain facets of yourself as they relate to the situation at hand, or are related to the topic of conversation. This brings you into the conversation as a human being. For example, I have shared with clients if there has been a particularly stressful or emotional event in the life of our families, sad or joyful (such as high school examinations, a wedding anniversary, or even the loss of a loved one).

It is critical that the coach should not dwell on their own personal issues, positive or negative—but only to comment if relevant to the conversation in developing rapport and trust. After all, the purpose of the conversation is about "them". For example, one of my clients was undergoing a divorce and was grateful that I had experienced the turbulent emotions of divorce myself. She trusted me to help her articulate her feelings and to think about the benefit of counselling for herself and her children. Yalom (2001:92) talks about the "genuine encounter", and asks the difficult question: "How can one have a genuine encounter with another person while remaining so opaque?"

Learning from experience

Learning, and particularly learning from experience, seems to be one of the major components of the coaching conversation. Learning from experience implies an understanding of the language and content of the client's story, with the coach helping the client to reconstruct their own reality by searching for meaning through dialogue.

In the context of the coaching conversation, when the client talks about their experience, they are actually creating a narrative or story. This type of storytelling constructs meaning in a different way from merely describing an experience. There is so much power in language and content that the significance of the client's story comes from both the structure of the telling as well as the interpretation and significance given. In some cultures, for example in Latin America, Africa and India, oral history and storytelling remain very important methods of passing on ritual, tradition and customs. The coaching conversation can literally be seen as an extension of "telling one's story" and looking for meaning and significance in the telling.

As humans, we are "meaning-seeking creatures" and we have been "thrown into a world devoid of intrinsic meaning" (Yalom, 2001:133). It is not uncommon in the coaching conversation for a client to ask the coach to help them figure out the "meaning of their life". Once trust has been established, these important philosophical questions arise as business clients come to terms with the complexities, stresses and ambiguities of the corporate environment.

In therapy, the essential first step is for individuals to recognize their role in resolving their own life predicament; it is similar in the coaching context. The reason is simply that the client is the one with the power to change their situation.

One of the roles of the coach is often to help the client identify where they have control, and where they do not. An example would be when the client's stress is due to focusing on the behaviour of others, over which they have little if any control. On the other hand, the client has control over their own reaction and behaviour.

Learning, change and growth are the key principles of the coaching environment. Experiential learning in education is common to Kolb, Jung and Freire, with an emphasis on developing a self-directed, purposeful life (Freire, 1973: 65). Further, experiential learning in education is seen as an active exploration of the personal, experiential meaning of abstract concepts through dialogue among equals. With this as a precedent, we can look at the "coaching conversation" not just as experiential learning, but as experiential education: learning from one's own life experiences.

The coaching intervention ranges from questions which explore feelings, motivations, perceptions, assumptions and attitudes, to reflected statements, reframed questions, role-plays, structured question frameworks, observation, or silence. In this respect, Boud, Cohen and Walker's *Using Experience in Learning* (1996) had a profound effect on my thinking about the coaching conversation, and the space it opens up for coaches to help clients to learn from their own personal experience.

Purpose of the coaching conversation

There are some key questions to consider when setting out on the coaching journey with your client. For example, what is the objective of the coaching conversation? Will part of your coaching process be to create a "personal learning" or "professional development plan" with your client (Harri-Augstein and Thomas, 1991:24;38)? What is your overall strategy for working together, and what resources are available to support you and the client at work (e.g. regular meetings with the client's line manager, or the Human Resources or Organizational Development departmental heads)? Development plans should contain the overall aims for the entire coaching journey, the strategy of how to achieve them, developmental objectives, and the "learning tactics" and core tasks that will enable the client to achieve and implement their plan.

CASE STUDY: DRAFT MANAGEMENT DEVELOPMENT PLAN
Below is an example of a draft Leadership Development Plan for one of my clients. The purpose and developmental objectives are continually reviewed, and the actions change with each coaching conversation. The Leadership Development Plan is an organic, evolving document that is shared with the Line Manager. Rather than sharing the content of the coaching conversation, client and coach can share the development plan and results achieved with other stakeholders in the coaching process. This protects client confidentiality.

Purpose:

1. To strategically position my professional career development within the organization and consistently deliver results that exceed expectations.
2. To motivate and empower my senior management team to acquire specific competences to drive results and performance.

Developmental objectives:

1. Collaboration and team work—Building an effective team that champions best practices, and puts the interests of the organization first, as well as building strong, productive relationships across the organization.
2. Organization and talent development—Demonstrating the ability to motivate and empower the team to achieve targeted results, while putting the right people in the right jobs and giving constructive, candid feedback to develop them.
3. Self-awareness and adaptability—Asserting personal ideas and opinions through productive influence, and maintaining an awareness of how my actions and behaviours impact on others.

Strategy:

1. To develop leadership and management competence by working with my coach, and developing the strategic management skills of my team.
2. To develop self-awareness and adaptability by being willing to listen to diverse points of view, developing some patience, being flexible and adaptable as and when required.
3. Being focused on the career path development for my team, and for myself in terms of succession planning.

Monthly actions:

Obstacles to achievement:

Results achieved:

Overall learning from the coaching journey:

Measuring results

In working with an individual client, there is no point in simply developing a leadership plan in isolation from the rest of the business processes. If the coaching intervention is to be successful in organizations, it is critical to develop a systemic, fully integrated coaching strategy that is in alignment with both the business and the talent strategies for the organization. Two key factors will be to identify the efficacy of internal and external coaching interventions, and the use of group or team coaching to develop key leaders (Peterson and Little, 2008:46–47). I would add to this the complementary mentoring programmes that are often aligned with business coaching inside organizations as a way to develop talent at subordinate levels.

Moreover, although I agree that, in the business context, results are often measured in three specific areas: behavioural change, improved performance, and the individual's personal and professional development (Shaw and Linnecar, 2007; cited in Ting and Scisco, 2006:58–9), I define these categories a bit differently.

1. Visible behavioural change

It is essential that any changes in self-awareness and relationship awareness show up visibly in the workplace through the client's behaviour; otherwise, it is difficult to measure what has changed as a result of the coaching. Coaching is a complex process with both qualitative and quantitative goals set. Your job as a business coach is to develop the core competences of the managerial leader. The development of those competences needs to show up visibly in work-related and behavioural changes. The client's work often starts with growing self-awareness, increased emotional maturity and improved interpersonal skills and competence.

2. Improved performance and business results

Performance improvement should have a direct effect on business results. Although it is not always possible to quantify how coaching has directly impacted performance, it is one of the key criteria linked to business coaching. This may require a systemic and developmental approach on the part of coach and client, integrated with an understanding of the complexities of the client's working context, market environment and level of competence. In Chapter 6, we look at the issues of diversity, culture and gender, and examine the impact these may have on the individual coaching client, the context within which they work, and the developmental needs of certain leaders due to their individual perspectives, culture, gender, ethnicity and experience of isolation.

3. Personal and professional development

The personal development plan you create with your client relates directly to the areas where it is perceived that they need to work. Their plan will be linked to individual management assessment profiles, 360° feedback surveys, and shadow coaching which help you to identify emotional, behavioural, cognitive and performance-related issues. One of the essentials in creating this personal development plan is to identify the skills and competences that will impact each area, creating medium-term and long-term plans. This includes the client's learning journey, the importance of identifying their learning style, and how they will be able to develop themselves personally and professionally when they have ceased to work with an external coach or internal organizational coach.

MISSING A CUE

Sometimes the coach misses a cue. A senior coach, working on a contract with a successful international multimedia agency, was tasked to help a bright young star, James (not his real name), to improve his communication skills with his team. Considered one of the most brilliant up-and-coming directors in the industry, James' intellectual capabilities overshadowed his "perceived" ability to delegate, communicate his vision to his team, and to motivate all those who worked alongside him. His ideas often stayed in his head and, although he was adored by clients, his team were sometimes confused as to their brief.

The coach and James regularly enjoyed an intellectual, if perhaps less goal-directed or action-oriented conversation. The result, after six months of coaching, was a very frustrated senior board, which did not see behavioural or performance change as a result of the coaching. The objective had been to improve James' leadership and communication competence and, although James had matured emotionally and definitely increased his awareness of himself and others, he had not translated his learning into visible behavioural change.

Insight leads to change. The business coach's job is to facilitate insight, which leads to observable behavioural change impacting on performance. This is because organizations expect to see clear effective deliverables. The AMA's 2008 research study into the reasons why organizations use coaching revealed that 79 per cent wished to improve individual performance/productivity; 63 per cent to address leadership development succession planning; 60 per cent to increase worker skill levels; and 56 per cent to improve organizational performance (AMA, 2008:11).

Value of positive regard, empathy and appreciation

A vital aspect of the coaching intervention is to be positively supportive of the client. Carl Rogers called it "unconditional positive regard". Rogers identified three essential characteristics for an effective therapist/patient relationship that are useful to us in a business coaching environment: **unconditional positive regard**, **genuineness**, and **accurate empathy** (Rogers, 1961:47–49).

The business coach both models and communicates empathy in each present moment of the coaching conversation. Not only do empathy and positive regard build trust in the relationship, but this may be one of the few places where the client is unconditionally supported in their personal and professional life. That does not mean that the coach never challenges the client. It does mean, however, that the client and coach work in a context that is safe for the client to discuss weaknesses, failures, limiting thinking and obstacles to achievement—and yet to feel neither threatened nor judged.

Empathy and positive regard are aligned with the fourth component of Nancy Kline's coaching process, appreciation. Kline's (1999/2004:62) definition of appreciation is "practising a 5 to 1 (5:1) ratio of appreciation to criticism". The most important feature of appreciation is that it needs to be a genuine appreciation of a particular quality in the client, and it needs to be communicated authentically. Appreciation may include positive comments about a particular action or behaviour, or a quality the coach has recently noticed in the client.

The quality of your appreciation for the client will come not only through your words, but also from your body language: your tone of voice, facial expression, the look in your eyes ... and, finally, by the enthusiasm and sincerity of your appreciation. Furthermore, and most importantly, the human mind seems to work best with a full picture of reality, and that realistic picture is completed with the positive, appreciative comments of the coach as listener.

What is interesting about the concept of appreciation is that we usually expect to hear "bad news" from others. It is rare that human beings really truly appreciate each other on a regular basis. We are used to hearing where we have failed, messed up, created chaos or uncertainty. In other words, it is not our personal accomplishments for which we often gain recognition, but for our mistakes or where things have gone wrong. For some reason it is the negative side of life that seems to be considered to be reality—especially in the more aggressive corporate environment.

Appreciation highlights the importance of empathy, which is a core component of emotional competence. When the client feels they are being understood, it can contribute not just to their thinking, but also to their ability to make difficult decisions, transitioning through difficult stages of personal learning and development. Empathy is critical for the coach's competence in giving direct feedback, handling uncomfortable feelings and encouraging self-awareness on the part of the client. The emotional competences I refer to here are the underlying skills of Goleman's (2002:39) model: self-awareness, self-management, social awareness, and social management.

The coach's emotional competence has a direct impact on their ability to offer support to their client. Giving support means a willingness to "model" the giving of support. This modelling of excellence is a key role for the business coach. However, it does not take away from the importance of the coach being able to challenge, make observations and ask questions about behaviour or performance that is not appropriate or going well.

CASE STUDY: AN EXAMPLE OF APPRECIATION
I have noticed that it is extremely difficult for people in the business environment to be appreciative of each other; this is because being appreciative of another acknowledges the essence of the other's "being". It was wonderful to receive a message from the CEO of an organization that I worked with recently that she has started to include "appreciations" into her "blue hat" meetings

(meetings where facts only are discussed). These appreciations allow people's emotions or feelings to come to the fore in a safe environment and in a business-like manner.

This CEO indicated that the appreciations would take the form of acknowledgement for deadlines met, projects completed even with a lack of resources, the "up-skilling" of new staff, the reaching of a target for the first time, as well as the recognition of qualities that enabled the different individuals to meet stringent requirements on a project, or to make it through a particularly difficult training, or to handle a difficult client or customer. This client, operating as "leader coach" with her team, has begun to create an environment in meetings where achievements are recognized alongside the difficulties posed by the fast pace of the working environment, the lack of resources or the lack of staff to follow up once a project has been completed.

Research shows that appreciations help us to think better. Experience has shown that appreciation is the one component when coaching in a thinking environment that people feel most fiercely about. They either defend or support the need for appreciations, or fight against the need for them.

Appreciation offsets the thinking of individuals in the team that they are not focused enough, not thinking critically enough, not strong enough, skilled enough—just not good enough. Appreciation also demonstrates a commitment on the part of team members to their own quality of thinking and decision making—and the value they place on the other team members.

Goals and the coach/client relationship

Business coaching places great emphasis on clarifying and achieving goals. Often within the complexity of the organizational environment, the client's overarching goals may be set by a more senior power; where that senior individual may have different worldviews, different paradigms, and differing limiting and empowering assumptions. It is therefore important that, as goals are set, they be related to the intrinsic and extrinsic drivers of the client themselves. The client must have a "living sense" of what their goal may be (Spinelli, 1989). In other words, the goal must be aligned with the values of the individual as much as to those of the organization if it is to be achieved.

A secondary consideration is that goals change for the client over time as the relationship develops. For example, as he grew in competence and confidence over a two-year period, one of my clients working in an international organization based in Johannesburg changed his overarching goal from that of developing strong leadership competence, to being considered one of the most competent business leaders—not just within his own country, South Africa, but in the whole of sub-Saharan Africa!

To develop the relationship effectively, the principles and concepts of the Rogerian, person-centred approach is useful to us. This is a relationship-oriented experiential approach, requiring the practitioner to listen with acceptance and without judgement if clients are going to be able to change (Rogers, 1961:33–35). If one of the core aims of the coaching intervention is to help clients understand and manage themselves and their own interpersonal communications, and if we as the coaches are going to enable rather than teach our clients, then our coaching interventions and the coaching process constantly need to have goals in mind, and we need to be able to clearly define the types of goals.

O'Neill (2000:104) maintains that sustaining your goals as a coach gives you more focus. If you as the coach are aware of your goal, you will stay in response mode rather than revert to automatic mode when your stress is high. The next step is to ensure that your goal is related to your client's goal. This is an interesting way to look at goals, as most executive coaches would first identify the client's goals and coach the client accordingly. O'Neill says be very clear about your goal as coach throughout the session, so that you lose neither **signature presence** nor **backbone**, nor **heart**.

The coach is responsible to ensure that goal-setting conversations get the best results. However, O'Neill suggests that it is best if goal setting is slowed down at first, in order to speed up action later (O'Neill, 2000:104). She differentiates between two kinds of client goals, business and personal, and links the coaching effort to a business result, highlighting and prioritising the business areas that need attention. Business goals are about achieving external results; personal goals are what the leader has to do differently in the way they conduct themselves in order to get the business results they envision. O'Neill (2000:104) cites Robert Crosby who has defined three other types of goals:

1. Bottom-line goals—aligned with the reason the organization exists.
2. Work-process goals—how the work is accomplished.
3. Human relations goals—how people collaborate to accomplish goals.

In setting goals, O'Neill reflects on Hargrove's use of "breakthrough thinking to achieve stretch goals" (O'Neill, 2000:104). Her suggested interventions to achieve this are:

1. Which business results are needed?
2. What are the team behaviours needed to be different to accomplish the results?
3. Which personal leadership challenges is the executive facing in improving these results and team behaviours?
4. What are specific behaviours the leader needs to enhance or change in themselves?

Yalom talks about two types of goals: content (what is to be accomplished), and process goals (how the coach wants to be in a session). However, he also describes the importance of setting concrete attainable goals—goals that the client has personally defined, and which increase their sense of responsibility for their own individual change (Yalom, 1980:243).

Competences in business coaching

> ... being explicit about competences gives an identified path for progression as a coach, and so can reduce any sense amongst aspiring coaches that in the distribution of client work smoke and mirrors are the governing factor (Ahern, 2003:374).

This section outlines the general approach to competence frameworks developed by four international, regional and national coaching organizations in an effort to promote professionalism within the industry. Two questions that need to be addressed worldwide is why we need competences in business coaching, and once we have identified the relevant competences for business coaching, how should we measure them?

Four professional bodies have identified the skills and competences required for general coach practitioners and business coaches: the International Coach Federation (ICF), the Worldwide Association of Business Coaches (WABC), the European Mentoring and Coaching Council (EMCC), and Coaches and Mentors of South Africa (COMENSA).

These bodies represent a valuable spectrum of national and international standards for business coaches today. There is considerable consistency among the professional bodies with respect to the skills and competences required for a coach. From their work I recommend seven specific core competences to build your capacity as a business coach. See the Appendix for greater detail as to how the selected competences are structured and benchmarked for the coaching process.

Why skills and competences?

As coaching is at this stage very much a self-regulated industry, coaching skills are rarely measured or assessed using valid and reliable assessment tools (Lidbetter, 2003). In general, skills and competence are defined by coaching associations as part of a philosophy, or as a means to an end or a goal.

Defined and benchmarked skills and competences serve a dual purpose: they give clarity in terms of how we might be selected as a coach, and they give the emerging coaching profession guidelines on what is expected and how to develop and improve. Although there are currently no such barriers to entry for coaching, if coaching is to progress further, from an emerging discipline to a fully-fledged profession, it will require the definition of specific skills and competences as part of a theoretically sound and empirically verified body of knowledge.

This process is being investigated and promoted by the Global Convention on Coaching (GCC). It is also under scrutiny by the newly-established Institute of Coaching based at Harvard Medical School, a research institute looking to build the body of knowledge for coaching worldwide, and the International Coaching Research Forum (ICRF). In September 2008, the ICRF, consisting of internationally-recognized researchers, coaching professionals and other stakeholders, met at Harvard University to produce 100 research proposal outlines aimed at advancing coaching as an evidence-based discipline. These papers are available online at www. coachingresearchforum.org.

In the meantime, various national and international coaching organizations have drawn up competence frameworks in an attempt to self-regulate and professionalize the industry as far as possible. These frameworks are outlined in the following section.

Global Convention on Coaching (GCC)

At the July 2008 GCC in Dublin, the Working Group on Core Competences emphasized that coaching competences are not unique and are shared with other disciplines. The Working Group defined competence as "... an underlying characteristic of an individual (e.g. motive, trait, attitude, value, belief, knowledge, behaviour, skill) that is causally related to effective or superior performance in a role or job", and defined a formal competence model as "... a systematic list of core competences of an effective coach, with procedural descriptions for use in the coaching process with the relevant skills" (GCC, 2008f:1).

The *Dublin Declaration on Coaching* (GCC, 2008g:6) recommends a collaborative approach among all stakeholders to identify commonalities, stressing the importance of research. The *Declaration* proposes that an "international best practice competence framework" be developed through dialogue and a research process. A key question remaining, however, is "How to apply the framework to make it usable in terms of coach selection, membership, training of coaches, code of ethics?" (GCC, 2008g:16–17).

As a coaching practitioner or professional, the key lies in your continuing self-assessment, supervision, learning and development. As a result of critically reflecting on your own practice, I suggest that you identify the core focus for your business ensuring you have competence in areas where you need to strengthen your practice. Lew Stern in *Executive Coaching: Building and Managing Your Professional Practice* suggests four areas of core competence for executive coaches (Stern, 2008:29):

- psychological knowledge;
- business acumen;
- organizational knowledge; and
- coaching knowledge, tasks and skills.

In terms of your coaching knowledge, tasks and skills, I strongly recommend that you focus on the following core competences which have been studied or researched to some degree by the various global coaching bodies to build your capacity as a business coach:

1. Building the coaching relationship;
2. Listening and questioning;
3. Self-awareness and the process of self-reflection;
4. Continuous learning and development;
5. Developing your knowledge and core coaching skills base;
6. Business and leadership coaching abilities;
7. Upholding ethical guidelines and professional standards.

International Coach Federation (ICF)

The ICF (2008a:1) points out that its framework of core coaching competences was developed in order to:

- support greater understanding about the skills and approaches used within the coaching profession;
- support members in calibrating their level of alignment between the coach-specific training the ICF expects and the training members have experienced; and
- be used as the foundation for the ICF Credentialing process examination.

The core competences are grouped into four clusters according to those that fit together "logically". The ICF (2008a:1) emphasizes that the groupings and individual competences are not weighted, i.e. they do not represent any kind of prioritization but "are all core or critical for any competent coach to demonstrate".

The ICF has definitions and related behaviours for each competency, distinguishing between behaviours that should always be present and visible and those that are called for only in certain coaching situations. The 11 ICF competences are listed below in their four groupings (with the related behaviours omitted for the sake of clarity) with significant more detail in the Appendix (ICF, 2008a:1):

A. **Setting the foundation:**
   1. Meeting ethical guidelines and professional standards.
   2. Establishing the coaching agreement.

B. Co-creating the relationship:
   3. Establishing trust and intimacy with the client.
   4. Coaching presence.
C. Communicating effectively:
   5. Active listening.
   6. Powerful questioning.
   7. Direct communication.
D. Facilitating learning and results:
   8. Creating awareness.
   9. Designing actions.
   10. Planning and goal setting.
   11. Managing progress and accountability.

A recent study tested the validity of these 11 competences. Griffiths and Campbell (2008) interviewed five ICF-certified master coaches and nine of their clients, and found that some competences were well-supported, while others were not. They discovered some inconsistency in the competency grouping, suggesting that the competences were devised somewhat unscientifically rather than through an empirically validated process. This supports the view that these are guidelines only until further research is undertaken. Griffiths and Campbell (2008) appears to be one of only two studies which endeavour to test the validity of competences. The complete ICF competence framework can be found on the Federation's website at www.coach-federation.org, with more information in the Appendix to this book.

Worldwide Association of Business Coaches (WABC)

Since 1997, the WABC has worked to define the emerging profession of business coaching and to distinguish it from other types of coaching. In partnership with the Professional Development Foundation in the UK, the WABC conducted extensive in-depth research, literature reviews and consultations with business coaches and their clients, into what defines a competent business coach.

The business coaching competences are divided into three areas (WABC, 2008b:2):

- self-management—knowing oneself and self-mastery;
- core coaching skill-base; and
- business and leadership coaching capabilities.

Each area is defined with a list of competences, and each competency is illustrated by examples of the behaviour expected of a proficient master coach with at least five years' experience (WABC, 2008b:2). WABC also includes a section on the knowledge they believe the business coach should have, which encompasses business experience, as well as knowledge of leadership and business theories (WABC, 2008b:7–10). They are the only professional body to our knowledge which lists diversity and multicultural issues as a competency (see Competency 7 under "Business and leadership coaching capabilities" in the Appendix).

WABC (2008b:2) states that "Newer business coaches are not expected to demonstrate every competency listed here. Rather, the competences provide a framework against which individuals can map their training and experience. In this way, individual coaches can use the competences to gauge their progress toward master-level proficiency."

The WABC (2008b) business coaching competence framework is outlined in the Appendix, and the complete *WABC Business Coaching Competencies* can be found on the Association's website at www.wabccoaches.com.

European Mentoring and Coaching Council (EMCC)

The *EMCC Competence Standards* define core competences in four categories as a basis for the training of coaches and mentors, as follows (EMCC, 2008a:1–3):

1. **Who we are**—the incremental hierarchy of personal attributes for coaching and mentoring.
2. **Our skills and knowledge**—we will use during the coaching/mentoring process.
3. **How we coach and mentor**—how we will demonstrate that we are able to apply what we have learned.
4. **How we manage the process**—what we will do as part of our coaching/mentoring practice to maintain and develop an effective and professional approach.

The EMCC's European Quality Award for trainers of coaches and mentors is based on these competence standards, in terms of a quality standards project launched by the EMCC in 2006 (EMCC, 2008a:1). Eric Parsloe, chief executive officer of the Oxford School of Coaching and Mentoring, said of the initiative: "Until now the market has been awash with over-simplistic communication skills programmes or pet theories presented in pseudo-technical formats. Everyone can now distinguish the genuine article" (Scott, 2007:17).

The complete *EMCC Competence Standards* can be found on the Council's website at www.emccouncil.org.

Coaches and Mentors of South Africa (COMENSA)

During 2005–2006, Coaches and Mentors of South Africa (COMENSA) developed a simple framework of standards of professional competence for coaches, which defined competences in five functional areas at four levels of expertise. The five functional areas were (COMENSA, 2006a:1):

- questioning;
- listening;
- building rapport;
- delivering measurable results; and
- upholding ethical guidelines and professional standards.

The four levels of competence within each functional area ranged from Level 1 (i.e. unacceptable) to Level 4 (i.e. master/expert) (COMENSA, 2006a:1–3).

During 2007, COMENSA developed a revised competence framework, the draft *Membership Criteria and Standards of Competence (MCSC) Framework*, based on the EMCC's Competence Standards, defined in terms of the following "measurable outcomes" (COMENSA, 2007b:21–26):

1. **Self-awareness/Who we are**—personal attributes for coaching:
   1.1 Beliefs and attitudes.
   1.2 Self-awareness.
2. **Managing the process**—what we will do as part of our coaching practice to maintain and develop an effective and professional approach:
   2.1 Managing the relationship.
   2.2 Managing the contract.

3. **Ability to coach**—skills we will use during the coaching process:
   3.1 Communication skills.
   3.2 Technical skills.
   3.3 People development skills.
4. **Facilitate learning and development**—how we will demonstrate that we are able to apply what we have learned.

The draft *MCSC Framework* includes examples of how the competences should be demonstrated within each of the following levels of practice (COMENSA, 2007b:22–26):

- Minimum competence standards for all coach practitioners.
- Registered Practitioner (in addition to minimum competence standards).
- Certified Practitioner (in addition to minimum competence standards).
- Master Practitioner (in addition to minimum competence standards).

The complete COMENSA draft *Membership Criteria and Standards of Competence Framework* can be found on the Association's website at www.comensa.org.za.

Recommended competences

All of these bodies recommend the competences of **listening, questioning** and **managing the relationship**. The WABC and COMENSA (in its draft MCSC Framework) both identify **self-awareness** as a core competence. COMENSA and the EMCC do not explicitly recommend goals or outcomes. The WABC is the only body that requires **business competence**. The Griffiths and Campbell (2008) study suggested that a crucial process missing from the ICF competence framework (and therefore from the competence frameworks of the other bodies as well) is the establishment of a process of **self-reflection** in the client. We discuss Kolb's learning cycle in Chapter 5, and if one of the intended outcomes of coaching is learning how to learn, then the ability to reflect is critical on the part of both client and coach.

Connerley and Pedersen (2005:70) define "competences" as "the skills, abilities, personal characteristics and other person-based factors that help distinguish between outstanding performance and average performance". There are six competences singled out by the ICF, EMCC, WABC and COMENSA as essential for the coaching process (see the Appendix for more details on each one):

- building the coaching relationship;
- listening;
- questioning;
- self-awareness;
- self-reflection.
- continuous learning and development

Based on the current competency frameworks of the four professional bodies outlined above, and global studies undertaken to date, the competences which deserve the focus of any business coaching practitioner to build their capacity, and to influence the developing discipline of coaching, are:

1. Building the coaching relationship;
2. Listening and questioning;
3. Developing self-awareness through the process of self-reflection;
4. Continuous learning and development;
5. Expanding your knowledge and core coaching skills base;
6. Business and leadership coaching abilities;
7. Upholding ethical guidelines and professional standards.

1. Building the coaching relationship

Coaching is ultimately defined by the relationship between the coach and the client, as Flaherty (1999:10) states in defining his operating principles of coaching: "Relationship is the most important one and is based on mutual trust, mutual respect and freedom of expression".

Because coaching is a relationship-based process, the coach must be aware of their own potential assumptions, as well as those of the client. Ideally coaches divest themselves of their own limiting paradigms, so that they can more effectively question and probe the client's articulated reality and assumptions.

A relationship develops as a result of the "coaching conversation", with client issues and concerns teased out by the skill of the coach's interventions. These interventions need, however, to be part of a larger structure, such as a coaching model—as long as the coach operates with complete flexibility within the model to cater for the concerns of the client. A safe "thinking environment" is built through the development of the relationship, and the relationship is what helps with the onset of change. The coach must be conscious, however, of staying outside the "system"—and in particular, not be drawn into the client's narrative or "story". In this way, the coach works with the client to assume responsibility for change.

To date, most of the research on the "relationship" or "encounter" between client and practitioner has been undertaken in the field of psychotherapy. My own research highlights the importance of the coach working within a flexible coaching model, developing the relationship as the central focus of the conversation. At the heart of the coaching process, irrespective of the model or approach, is the relationship. This means that it is not necessarily about "doing", for the client, but more about "being"—creating a safe space: a container for thinking, feeling and insight to take place. (Stout Rostron, 2006c:v).

If the relationship is the ultimate determinant of success in the client/practitioner relationship, then the "encounter" between coach and client is where the real work is done, and. it is not only "the relationship" that affects the outcome—it is the "quality" of the relationship that is of importance (Stout Rostron,, 2006c:37).

2. Listening and questioning

The coach practitioner "holds the space" (i.e. creating a safe thinking environment), and needs the skill of "immediacy" and empathy in the immediate moment. Holding the here and now—holding the client "where the client is"—is to do with support. And how does the coaching intervention (in conjunction with specific components such as listening, empathy, attention and ease) help to create the safe thinking environment for the relationship to develop?

Listening, observation and the skill of **asking questions** help the coach to develop the ability to be "inside" the coaching conversation, as well as to be "observing" the conversation. It is taking up a meta-position, while never leaving the micro level of being present for the client. It's crucial through listening, observation and asking questions to observe the client's patterns of thinking, linguistic use of words, content and structure of the client narrative, and specifically to begin to understand the client's world view and patterns of think-ing (Stout Rostron, 2006c:152).

According to Spinelli, the three levels of listening are mental, emo-tional and physical. For example, as a coach when you intervene in the conversation with the client, what of **you** is in your question, in your statement, in your intervention? How can you as coach be open in the way you ask questions, intervene, or ask for clarification? As coach you are asking to understand, and I would suggest that in coaching, the coach turns toward the client with the same "listening intensity" as is developed in psychotherapy (Stout Rostron, 2006c:52).

The core skills of the client-centred approach—i.e. active listening, respecting clients and adopting their internal frame of reference—is in alignment to achieving results within the coaching conversation. However, it is crucial to refer pathology appropriately and to keep coaching and therapy separate (Stout Rostron, 2006c:86).

3. Developing self-awareness through the process of self-reflection

> I am able to control only that of which I am aware. That of which I am unaware controls me. Awareness empowers me (Whitmore, 2002:33).

Experiential learning is a theoretical underpinning of coaching throughout this book—for the client and for the coach in developing their own individual skills and competence. Coaching differs from consulting in that coaching does not solve problems or give advice. It also differs in that the aim of coaching is to establish a sustainable process of experiential learning for both coach and client. In essence, your coaching is deemed successful if you have worked yourself out of a job with your client.

If the client is to learn how to learn, they need to cultivate self-awareness through reflection on their experience, values, intrinsic drivers, the impact of these on others, the environment, and on their own future goals. This process is often implicit in the coaching relation-ship through the process of questions and actions that develop critical reflection and practice. Griffiths and Campbell (2008:8) confirm that:

> The ICF competencies, by focusing on coach competency, fail to articulate reflection as an essential coaching process ... but

what emerged as an interesting phenomenon in this study, was the tendency for clients to take on the role of questioning themselves. Through engagement with the coach in powerful questioning, gradually clients began to demonstrate the ability and tendency to self-manage this process.

The ICF study further confirms that coaches often assume clients are aware of their values, but within the confines of the study this appeared to be incorrect (ICF, 2008a). The clients interviewed indicated they were not aware of their values, and that acquiring a process of awareness and reflection led them to become more aware of their emotions, their values and of the need to clarify their goals. Whitmore (2002) supports this and states that the goal of the coach is to build awareness, responsibility and self-belief.

CASE STUDY: JOURNALING

Marti recently met with a client with whom she had worked a few years ago. The client took out a journal during the session, and paged through it, filling Marti in on what was happening in her life. She shared her reflections from the journal on her values, drivers and goals—and how she planned to achieve each one. She shared her thoughts on whether her designed plan was working effectively or needed adjustment. This is an example of how she has embraced self-reflection, self-coaching and a continuing development of self-awareness as a lifelong process. She referred to her own process of self-coaching as one of reading, listening to tapes, and journaling on a daily basis. She continually checks her own personal and professional plan to make adjustments and to reflect on whether she is on schedule.

The ICF lists creating awareness as a competency, even though developing self-reflection in the client is not explicitly stated. Creating awareness is defined as the "Ability to integrate and accurately evaluate multiple sources of information, and to make interpretations that help the client to gain awareness and thereby achieve agreed-upon results" (ICF, 2008a:1).

On the other hand, as a coaching practitioner, what can you do to develop your own self-reflective practice; and how can you encourage critical self-reflection in your smaller coaching forums, as well as in individual and group supervision? Finally, how can you advocate, influence and set up academic, practitioner or organizational research into your larger coaching interventions as a way of reflecting on the success and failure of coaching for the individual client, their team and the organization?

4. Continuous learning and development

> Coaching is not a collection of techniques to apply or dogma to adhere to, rather it's a discipline that requires freshness, innovation and relentless correction according to the outcomes being produced (Flaherty, 1999:10).

Shaw and Linnecar (2007) state that a coach training programme doesn't make a good coach; instead it shows that the coach has **started** the process of learning about themselves and what they are doing in any given situation.

The importance of being coached or "in supervision" cannot be over-emphasized. Both ensure that the coach practitioner understands what the client experiences, and both encourage the coach to work on their own issues so that they do not become entangled with those of the client. With the emerging professionalization of coaching, clients are now asking: "What are your coaching qualifications and experience, and how do you continually develop your competence?"

It's crucial to create your own professional development plan, no matter how experienced you are. Although not yet mandatory in coaching (in the way it is a fundamental underpinning of psychological therapeutic practice), supervision is recommended by coaching professional bodies worldwide. In addition, you can take part in the variety of professional organizations available to you, e.g. by joining a committee in your country's relevant professional association, as a way to develop yourself and the discipline of coaching.

The WABC Business Coaching Competencies include requirements for self-management, including "Acknowledging your strengths and development needs: Having a realistic perception of your strengths and development needs" (WABC, 2008b:3). The important point is to know your strengths and limitations, and to commit to your own continuous learning and self-development.

5. Expanding your knowledge and core coaching skills base

At the Global Convention on Coaching in July 2008 in Dublin, the GCC's Working Group on a Knowledge Base for Coaching defined "knowledge" in the broadest sense, to include: "... the knowledge that coach and client bring to the coaching session, the emergent knowledge that is borne out of the coaching process; and the dynamic of the coaching relationship" (GCC, 2008e:1). One of the Working Group's key discoveries during its year-long dialogue was that the knowledge base for coaches at present is largely driven by the needs of the client, and is continually evolving.

Working with our own individual experience is a key to learning. In actively reflecting on our experience, we can draw meaning from it, literally entering into a dialogue with experience (Kolb, 1984) and thereby turning it into useable knowledge.

For us as coach practitioners, this implies that we can never stop learning. We must learn to reflect critically on our own core skills and competences. Primarily, our responsibility is to use our own practice as a way to continue our own learning process. The secret is to balance the experiential learning that emerges in your coaching practice, with a continual building of your core competence—with capacity as a practitioner through continuing professional development. This will help you to develop elasticity and flexibility in every situation that you encounter in your coach/client sessions.

Gladwell (2008:47) mentions the 10 000 hour rule of practice to achieve self mastery. He talks about the pattern of successful sports professionals, musicians and computer geeks who had practiced up to 10 000 hours to develop competence before they turned 20 years old! Daniel Levitin, a neurologist, writes that "The emerging picture ... is that ten thousand hours of practice is required to achieve the level of mastery associated with being a world-class expert—in anything" (Gladwell, 2008:40). Gladwell's research shows that the competences required for success are a combination of **talent, opportunity, practice, wanting to learn** and **vision**.

For business coaching professionals, **learning, reflection** and **practice** seem to be the key.

6. Business and leadership coaching abilities

Coaching can help business executives to fine-tune skills that are crucial within today's economic and market constraints. These include, for example, the ability to exert influence across organizational boundaries, to manage conflicts, and to create and articulate a vision. Coaching has also been shown to help leaders develop a clearer understanding of their roles and responsibilities. But perhaps more importantly, coaching can help new leaders deal with the aspects of transition, transformation and change.

There is a strong link between business results and emotional intelligence (defined as self-awareness, self-management, social awareness and social skill). In essence, coaching ensures that leaders improve their emotional intelligence skills, leading to better organizational performance. This includes achieving an optimal balance between the needs of the individual, the team and the organization. If the client has grown in term of self-awareness, the organization will want to see this "demonstrated" at work: in relationships, management competence, leadership behaviours and EQ.

But, in order to do so—the coach needs to have an in-depth understanding of organizational systems: seeing the coaching intervention from a systems perspective, and understanding the need for "structure" in the interaction between coach, individual client and the organizational system. A danger of not understanding the "system" in which the client operates is that the coach risks becoming another part of that system.

7. Upholding ethical guidelines and professional standards

One competence that is often neglected in the coaching field is ethics. One of the reasons that it is important for coach practitioners to belong to a professional coaching body is that this commits them to the ethical code of that body. Psychologists and psychotherapists are bound to their professional ethical code, and can be disciplined or struck off their professional register if they violate the code in any way.

Because coaching is not yet a profession, and is not yet regulated, it is up to each individual practitioner to uphold their own individual, or their professional body's, ethical standards.

The importance of an ethical code is that it identifies the core values, standards and fundamental principles with which coaching practitioners align themselves, and to which they agree to adhere. Also, an ethical code provides a benchmark against which individual practitioners agree to be assessed.

The need for research into core coaching competences

The value of this section is to enhance your understanding of the quality and type of existing competence frameworks. It is also important to understand that the competence frameworks presented in this chapter have not yet been empirically researched, and that such research is a critical next step. Given that competence frameworks underpin the accreditation programmes that the marketplace is keen to purchase, both coaches and organizations alike are encouraged to better evaluate any research which claims to support these frameworks.

The question is: "Where is the research?" The future of coaching really depends in large measure on providing evidence-based research to the end-user. With this in mind, those providing competence frameworks need to ensure that they conduct empirical research to back up their claims, which will in turn enable their frameworks to be aligned with education and credentialing programmes worldwide.

The Foundation of Coaching in New York has folded their Research Division into the Institute of Coaching at Harvard. They sponsor coaching research grants worldwide up to US$100 000 per year. A research advisory board decision taken in September 2008 agreed the importance of continuing research into core coaching competences, as a key next step in identifying criteria for practitioner excellence, and to take coaching educational requirements to the next level.

In conclusion

In this chapter, we have examined the purpose and focus of the coaching conversation and the need for it to be a solution-focused, results-oriented, and systemic process which skilfully develops the client's learning processes. We have defined the coaching conversation as an alliance between coach, client and organization, designed to maximize and transform thinking, behaviour and performance.

The coaching conversation provides a thinking environment where business professionals develop self-awareness and a depth of understanding of themselves and others. Personal and experiential learning is the key to coaching's ability to embed newly-acquired skills, competence, attitudes and behaviours, thereby unlocking an individual executive's potential.

Coach's library

Goldsmith, M., Lyons, L., and Freas, A. (Eds.). (2000). *Coaching for Leadership: How the World's Greatest Coaches Help Leaders Learn*. San Francisco, CA: Jossey-Bass/Pfeiffer.

Goleman, D. (1996). *Emotional Intelligence*. London: Bloomsbury.

Hargrove, R. (2003). *Masterful Coaching: Inspire an "Impossible Future" While Producing Extraordinary Leaders and Extraordinary Results*. San Francisco, CA: Jossey-Bass/Pfeiffer.

Kets de Vries, M.F.R. (2006). *The Leader on the Couch*. London: Wiley.

Kline, N. (1999/2004). *Time to Think: Listening with the Human Mind*. London: Ward Lock.

O'Neill, M.B. (2000). *Coaching with Backbone and Heart: A Systems Approach to Engaging Leaders with Their Challenges*. San Francisco, CA: Jossey-Bass.

Peltier, B. (2001). *The Psychology of Executive Coaching: Theory and Application*. New York, NY: Brunner-Routledge.

Peterson, D. and Little, B. (2008). Growth market. *Coaching at Work*, 3(1):44–47.

Shaw, P. and Linnecar, R. (2007). *Business Coaching: Achieving Practical Results Through Effective Engagement*. London: Capstone.

Stern, L. (2008). *Executive Coaching: Building and Managing Your Professional Practice*. Hoboken, NJ: Wiley.

Ting, S. and Scisco, P. (2006). *The CCL Handbook of Coaching: A Guide for the Leader Coach*. San Francisco, CA: Jossey-Bass.

Weiss, P. (2004). *The Three Levels of Coaching*. San Francisco, CA: An Appropriate Response. Webpage: www.newventureswest.com/three_levels.pdf.

West, L. and Milan, M. (2001). *The Reflecting Glass: Professional Coaching for Leadership Development*. New York, NY: Palgrave.

Whitworth, L., Kimsey-House, H. and Sandahl, P. (1998). *Co-active Coaching: New Skills for Coaching People Toward Success in Work and Life*. Palo Alto, CA: Davies-Black.

Yalom, I. D. (1980). *Existential Psychotherapy*. New York, NY: Basic Books.

CHAPTER FOUR

Working with question frameworks

CHAPTER OUTLINE
- Structure—working with question frameworks
- Two-stage frameworks
  - Understanding intrinsic drivers or motivators
  - Functional analysis: the ABC of behaviour management
  - Functional analysis
  - Action learning approach
- Three-stage frameworks
  - Contracting
  - What needs work?
- Four-stage frameworks
  - Whitmore's GROW model
  - O'Neill's "executive coaching with backbone and heart"
- Five-stage frameworks
  - Framework for change
  - Working with the CLEAR model
- Six-stage frameworks
  - Nancy Kline's Thinking Partnership®
  - Six-stage Thinking Environment® coaching process

83

- Eight-stage frameworks
  - Well-formed outcomes (NLP)
- Ten-stage frameworks
  - Business Best Year Yet®
- Developing your own question frameworks
- Coach's library

> At its core the coaching relationship is a strong personal connection between two individuals that typically occurs out of public view and whose workings may even appear mysterious to outsiders. Coaching is fundamentally a process for facilitating learning and change which is another way to describe development (Ting and Scisco, 2006:36).

This chapter explores the range of coaching question frameworks available in the marketplace, for example those of John Whitmore, Nancy Kline and Jinny Ditzler. A framework is a structure that tends to be **linear, progressive** and **visible**. A question framework is a sequence of questions with steps or stages. **Stages** indicate the possibility of nonlinear "movement" between the parts; **steps** indicate a number of linear or progressive questions as part of its process. The GROW and CLEAR models have developed detailed, linear question frameworks as part of their process.

Descriptions on how to use two-, three-, four-, five-, six-, eight- and ten-stage frameworks, include NLP and the Thinking Environment® processes, with examples for understanding. This chapter is designed to have you look specifically at how you can develop your own questioning process.

One of the most difficult paradigms for a coach to understand, as opposed to being a teacher or a therapist, is to not provide answers or solve the client's problems for them. The greatest gift you can offer is to help the client "consider ideas, approaches, strategies, behaviours, and other approaches and actions" (Ting and Scisco, 2006:51) not previously considered. Although, as I have outlined, coaches typically don't offer advice, clients will sometimes ask for an opinion, information or guidance. It is important, in the circumstances, that the coach gives the required support or observation without telling the client what to do. The client's own insight and learning is crucial for change to happen.

Structure—working with question frameworks

Whether your practice is aligned or not to a specific coaching model, your question framework creates a structure for the coaching conversation. Each individual coaching session synchronizes with the overall journey you embark on with your client. I will refer to the "coaching intervention" as the questions, observations and challenges that the coach makes during the coaching conversation with the client.

There needs to be a clear structure to your conversation. Accordingly, this chapter examines creative uses of existing question frameworks, while Chapter 5 explores coaching models in depth, examining how question frameworks are integrated into those models. The purpose of this chapter is to consider various linear question processes which help coaches explore client issues from a neutral perspective, i.e., one that is non-directive of the client.

Specific sequences of questions are useful for the business coach, either as a way to get started with a new client, or simply as a tool to be used as part of their own coaching model. Common experiences, which shape the culture of a society, may impact on those frameworks that are more useful to you than others. Most countries are increasingly complex, multicultural societies, yet within organizations there will be commonly shared values, beliefs and assumptions about leadership, management, responsibility, experience and language.

There are also subtle influences on organizational culture and individual behaviour due to the mix of history, family background, language, religion and education within an organization. Another important factor may be whether an organization works with an individualist or collectivist attitude to leadership and management. Within some societies there is often a mixture of the two.

The culture of the coach may also differ from the culture of the client. For example, I originate from a results-driven, action-oriented, continual-learning American culture, which emphasizes an approach that is "individualistic, egalitarian, performance-driven, comfortable with change, and action-oriented" (Hoppe, 2004:135; cited in Ting and Scisco, 2006:133). This may reflect a belief about leadership and development which may need to be aligned with the client's beliefs if their cultural assumptions reflect a collective rather than an individualist focus. This collectivist preference could put more emphasis on relationship-oriented group results. We discuss the impact of diverse cultural experiences and various cultural frameworks on the coaching context in Chapter 6. What is important is for the coach to be open and flexible to the assumptions, beliefs and culture within the client organization.

The following examples of question frameworks are generic. It is up to the individual coach to determine where and when these frameworks may be useful as a structure for a coaching conversation, or simply as a tool to be used within the conversation. I indicate at the end of the chapter where you can find more information on each framework.

For the remainder of this chapter we will look at two-, three-, four-, five-, six-, eight- and ten-stage question frameworks to begin to understand the basic structure of coaching interventions. My aim is to help you to look at how—and what—you do as a business coach to develop and expand your own competence through new learning.

Two-stage frameworks

In the early 1990s, when I first started to coach team leaders and executives who headed the teams I was training, I worked with simple question frameworks (two-, three- and four-question frameworks). The first question framework I worked with was a two-stage framework, which ultimately led to an understanding of the core components of emotional intelligence, i.e., self-awareness, self-management, social/relationship awareness, and social/relationship management (Goleman, 1996).

At that time, I used this two-stage question framework to help clients determine their underlying values, beliefs and feelings as a preparation for setting goals and understanding their own intrinsic drivers and sources of stress and conflict at work. It was an insightful position to begin a coaching conversation as it went to a deeper level than just understanding what was working, what was not working and what (if anything) could be done differently. This two-stage framework looks at intrinsic drivers or motivators and helps us to understand if the client's goals are in alignment with their key drivers.

Understanding intrinsic drivers or motivators

This simple two-stage framework provides an insightful position from which to begin a coaching conversation. Part of the briefing before doing this exercise is to talk with the client about the difference between intrinsic and extrinsic motivation. Motivation is intrinsic to our underlying values, beliefs and feelings. The coach wants to find out what constitutes those internal or intrinsic drivers for their client. I explain to the client that external (or extrinsic) motivators come into action when someone else tries to tap into or engage our internal motivators, to encourage us or make us want to do something.

The questions help the client to discover their own intrinsic drivers or motivators, and help both coach and client to identify whether the client's personal and organizational goals are in alignment with their personal and professional internal drivers. As suggested in Chapter 2, the team and the organization depend on the individual achieving their goals. In order to do so, goals must be in alignment with internal drivers or motivators, otherwise there will be internal conflict or stress.

When I demonstrated this in front of a group of learner practitioner coaches, they were surprised at the depth of the answers. This is because the coach is uncovering the individual's core feelings, values and beliefs. These can touch on individual existential anxieties. It will be very difficult to achieve the individual's goals without harnessing their intrinsic drivers. This process is important, as the individual's motivators must be aligned not just to their own goals, but also to the goals of the team and the organization.

Typical responses are intangibles which cannot be measured e.g., achievement, balanced life, peace of mind, recognition and acknowledgement, a higher purpose, affiliation, financial security, honesty, integrity, balance, freedom to choose, doing something of value, and giving something back, support, and teaching.

If you use this question framework, explain to the client that external motivators come into effect when someone tries to "engage" our internal motivators, to encourage us or to make us want to do something. Examples of extrinsic motivators are the working environment, feedback, recognition and titles, salaries and bonuses, personal health plans, holiday leave, education and training, an overall salary package, and benefits such as a company car or share options.

To understand what makes the client tick and what drives them, and before setting goals, it is important, firstly, to understand values, beliefs and feelings that underpin their individual behaviour. As coach, you are looking for the intangibles, the unmeasurables. If the client replies with a measurable goal (such as a specific salary or titled position in the organization), ask "What is important about that?" (you are helping them to search for an intangible such as financial security or recognition/acknowledgement). As I indicated in Chapter 2, for each motivator, the coach can ask "What's important about that?" Another important question for the coach to ask is "Anything else?" At the end of this activity, ask the client which motivator, if achieved, would allow the rest to follow:

1. **What is important to you about your professional life?** What is important about that? Anything else?
2. **What is important to you about your personal life?** What is important about that? Anything else?

Other applications of this framework are to ask questions relevant to a particular project or issue, such as:

1. What is important to you about your job/this project?
2. What is important about that?
3. Anything else?

Functional analysis: the ABC of behaviour management

Cognitive psychology

Cognitive psychology is the study of the mind and its patterns, and has to do with memory, perception, formation of language and the roles of various brain functions. Cognitive psychology focuses on conscious rather than unconscious thinking processes. It is used to help people learn to notice and change their own thoughts with powerful emotional and behavioural benefits. The philosophy behind cognitive psychology is that what you choose to think determines what you feel and what you do. Specific thoughts create and control feelings, and thinking is largely within the realm of individual control.

Behavioural psychology

If learning in the coaching environment can be defined as the process that leads to potential behaviour change, then behavioural psychology is useful to us as it looks at how internal states and external stimuli influence our behaviour. Ultimately, the behavioural approach is useful because "frequently a powerful and successful person possesses one or two sets of dysfunctional behaviours that cause repetitive difficulties" (Peltier, 2001: xxiii). The underlying belief is that "if something happens to you repeatedly, you are probably reinforcing it in some way". In other words, behaviour is a "function of its consequences" (Peltier, 2001: 44).

The strength of the cognitive behavioural approach is that it encourages measurement (always welcome in any organization), and identifies when small behavioural changes can make an impact on executives in high positions. The flip side is that it can be problematic to identify and quantify specific behaviours to be changed, and it can be difficult to break down new behaviours into something that is measurable and easy to learn.

Functional analysis

Functional analysis is a two-stage question framework derived from cognitive behavioural psychology. The results from functional analysis help clients to learn about their own behaviours, the effect the environment has on how they think and behave, and which new behaviours may motivate change in themselves and others.

In functional analysis, the coach helps the client to clarify a specific behaviour that needs to change, and identifies what precedes the behaviour, and what are the consequences of such behaviour. This helps the client to decide which changes (if any) can be made to the **antecedent** in order to change the **behaviour** and the **consequences**. The antecedent is what precedes behaviour; behaviour is what behaviour the client wants to change; consequences refer to things that happen right after the behaviour to change. In this questioning process, the coach helps the client to think not just about their behaviour—but also about the thought process which impacts that behaviour.

Stage 1: Identifying the old behaviour

> **Antecedent**: What precedes the behaviour the client wants to change?
>
> **Behaviour**: What is the behaviour the client wants to change?
>
> **Consequence**: Which things happen right after the behaviour the client wants changed?

For example, one of my clients, a line manager, wanted to change the way she reacted with one of her direct reports who became defensive whenever questioned about unsatisfactory results in monthly team meetings. The line manager picked several situations, and we worked out the **antecedent, behaviour** and **consequent**. We identified the **antecedent**: the direct report would cross his arms, frown, look down, interrupt the line manager, and deny that the results were the result of his actions. The **behaviour** immediately triggered, on the part of the line manager, was an exclamation of disbelief that the direct report could even dispute his responsibility; this behaviour often took the form of raised voices, with both loudly interrupting each other and the line manager finally claiming seniority and ending the argument. She realized that she often seemed out of control. The **consequence** was a clear lack of respect from one to the other, with the direct report behaving passive-aggressively, and the line manager abruptly ending the communication.

Stage 2: Identifying the new behaviour

> **Antecedent**: What can the client do or say differently (i.e., changing behaviour) that will make a positive change to that behaviour?
>
> **Behaviour**: What will the new behaviour look like, sound like and feel like?
>
> **Consequence**: Which things may happen right after the new behaviour?

The projected **antecedent** was for the line manager to catch herself in the moment that she observed and experienced the direct report's aggressive body language and verbal refusal to accept responsibility for his actions. She planned to do this by pausing before answering, waiting to ensure the direct report had finished, asking him if he had anything more to contribute, then carefully setting out the boundaries for how the communication was to continue. She practised this with her coach by working out how to acknowledge the direct report's reply, and how to set boundaries; she practised making a link to what she wanted to say, giving direction for the way forward. She practised envisioning her behaviour as one of calm, being in control, breathing steadily, keeping her attention on the eyes of the direct report, and not in a hurry. The **consequent** she visualized was of being relaxed, in control of herself and the situation, finally resolving the situation with gravitas and respect for both individuals.

In our coaching sessions, we continued to work on "how" she could stay calm, relaxed and cool when triggered, and we began to work on the various disempowering assumptions that she had embraced as the manager of this particular individual.

Action learning approach

Action learning is used by hundreds of companies around the world. These companies employ action learning for strategic planning, developing managers, creating high performance teams and becoming learning organizations. Action learning is a dynamic process to solve problems while focusing on what needs to be learned and how learning can benefit the individual, the team and the organization overall.

Action learning helps you respond more effectively to change. Developed by Professor Reg Revans in England, action learning took off when adopted by Jack Welch at General Electric in the USA. Action learning is an experience-based approach to developing people that uses work on meaningful problems as a way to learn. Action learning typically comprises the following activities: experiential learning, creative complex problem solving, acquiring relevant knowledge, and co-learning group support.

Stage 1: The problem

When the client has a problem to identify, understand and resolve, ask them to work through the following questions:

1. Why does the problem exist?
2. When does it happen? When is it worse?

3. Which other problems does it cause?
4. Why is it difficult to solve?
5. Who is responsible?

Stage 2: The solution

Working with the client, take the same problem and only talk about the solution:

1. How would you like the situation to be?
2. If the problem were solved, which things would be happening?
3. What are parts of the solution happening now?
4. Which resources do you have?
5. What are some ways you can use the resources to help bring about more of the solution?

This is a very useful question framework to use with group coaching. The teams work in small groups, first with the problem questions, followed by the solution questions. The two stages are important. For clear thinking to happen, the problem and the solution stages need to operate separately. It is a useful two-stage process, as individuals often need to articulate what is wrong before being able to think through possible alternative options or solutions. For example, in one of my media client organizations, the leadership team found this a very useful framework to help resolve situations that went awry with customers. Rather than having an "inquiry" into what had happened, how much money was lost, whose fault it was—the team began to use this as a thinking process. It moved them away from a "blame" culture to a solution-seeking, collaborative culture.

Three-stage frameworks

Contracting

There are a variety of question frameworks available to the business coach, and I refer to some of the better known ones to help you use them creatively, referring to those I don't explore in depth but which may be useful to you. These are valuable for coach practitioners, and for managers who prefer to use a coaching style with their direct reports. A practical three-stage framework to use during the contracting session follows.

Stage 1: What does the client need to change and do?

The coach and client meet to decide the potential for a coaching relationship. Coach and client also meet with the sponsor (i.e., the line manager, HR or OD department) to agree on the basic parameters of the coaching relationship (timing, fees, objectives and confidentiality agreements).

Stage 2: How will the client go about changing?

The coach, client and sponsor contract together on the methods they'll use to improve the client's capabilities, and the performance measures that they'll use to assess progress.

Stage 3: How do we make the learning stick?

The coach and client agree how they will embed new behaviours, highlighting the impact of such behaviours on the individual, team and organization. Also agreed is the structure of the development plan to be created that will visibly show up results achieved as part of the coaching journey.

What needs work?

A simple three-stage question framework will assist you as coach/manager to understand the power of asking questions as opposed to telling. This emphasizes the importance of developing active listening skills and opens up the coaching conversation to the client's key concerns in their job and life as a whole.

These questions open up the individual's thinking on a subject where they are stuck, or where they cannot see a situation clearly, as well as helping the client to identify the core issues the coaching journey will tackle:

1. What is working?
2. What is not working?
3. What (if anything) can you do differently?

CASE STUDY: WHAT NEEDS WORK?

A recent experience has led us to re-evaluate the balance between the simple "use of questions" by the coach, and the importance of the "relationship" between coach and client, and the way that relationship develops. One of my students and I demonstrated this elegantly simple coaching process in front of a larger group of 20 students. I asked the student the three simple questions:

- What's working?
- What's not working?
- What, if anything, can you do differently?

The purpose of the demonstration was for observation and feedback on what had worked and what had not worked between coach and client, and to learn how important specific questions are in the process.

As it turned out, how the questions were asked, and how attentive and focused the coach was on the client, and the coach's ability to "sit" with the client in her thinking space, proved to be the most powerful parts of the process. I interrupted the process several times to turn back to the group to discuss where coach and client were in the process. As long as the client knows explicitly during teaching demos what is to happen (i.e., that the coach will stop and turn to the audience periodically), the client will go right on thinking until the coach turns back to the conversation.

In this three-question process, the client's core values started to be uncovered. The question process allowed a key value, "health", to pop up. As it turned out, it was the crucial value. What allowed the client to explore this value (which had been held internally but which was never made explicit or articulated in action, commitment or taking responsibility) courageously was the non-judgemental focus and complete attention of the coach on the client through the most difficult moments in the coaching conversation.

So, the integration of the question framework with the key components that help to build the relationship seems fundamental to the success of the coaching intervention. The coach helps to create the space for the client to feel safe, even when surrounded by 20 fellow students.

Four-stage frameworks

Whitmore's GROW model

GROW and CLEAR are models, as they **metaphorically** represent a coaching process. GROW indicates growth through goal setting, and CLEAR signifies clearing the client's presenting issue. However, because both models allow you to design a framework of questions in preparation prior to the coaching conversation, they both embody useful question frameworks to describe in this chapter.

John Whitmore's GROW model is a basic four-stage coaching process which easily structures a goal-setting session with the client, and adds greater depth to the coaching conversation. It is useful for learner coaches who need to understand the importance of structure, deep listening and how to ask questions. Although it is primarily a goal-setting tool, it can be used in many different formats. The basis of Whitmore's four-stage question framework is his definition of the essence of coaching: "Coaching is unlocking a person's potential to maximize their own performance. It is helping them to learn rather than teaching them" (Whitmore, 2002:8). The GROW question framework is structured as follows (adapted from Whitmore, 2002:54–55;173–176):

Stage one: What is your **G**oal?
Stage two: What is the **R**eality?
Stage three: What are your **O**ptions?
Stage four: What **W**ill you do?

Although many master executive coaches think the GROW model is very simplistic, its importance derives from the fact that Whitmore identified three essential concerns of coaching: developing self-awareness, taking responsibility for learning, plus the use of questions as the coach's primary tool. The questions that can be used in each of the four stages are useful, not just for setting goals, but also for developing an understanding of the fundamental structure of a coaching question framework. The rationale behind the GROW model is fundamental: to build awareness and responsibility in the client through the effective use of the right questions (Whitmore, 2002:14–19;32–38;44–46).

Stage one: What is your goal?

Outline the client's key goals for the year, their overarching goals, and then the goal for this particular coaching conversation. GROW is about working with the elimination of external and internal obstacles to goal achievement. Furthermore, help the client to identify the type of goal, i.e., performance goal, end goal, dream goal (Whitmore, 2002:59):

- What would you like to get out of the session?
- Where do you want to be by the end of our time together?
- What would be the most helpful thing for you to take away from the session?

Stage two: What is the reality?

Here the coach invites the client to tell their story—in other words, to say what is currently going on for the client as it relates to this goal. The coach should invite self-assessment, and the question could be, "What is happening for you right now as it relates to this objective?" At this point, the coach may take the client back to redefine the goal if it is not specific enough, then to clarify the current situation. Whitmore (2002:67–74) suggests that the reality questions provide the most straightforward means of self-assessment. He suggests rarely using "how" and "why" because they invite analysis and opinion. Asking "why" invites defensiveness and keeps the client in the conscious thinking process. Whitmore (2002:74) suggests reality questions that emphasize the value of action and the difference between action and thinking:

- What action have you taken on so far?
- What were the effects of that action?
- What are the internal obstacles?
- What are the internal blocks?
- What assumptions could be limiting your thinking?

Stage three: What are your options?

This focuses on what the client could do. This will encompass possible action plans and strategies, a development of some alternative perspectives, and brainstorming options. What could the client do, from realistic to fantastic thinking? The options stage of GROW is not about finding the right answer; it is about creating as many courses of action as possible. Whitmore (2002:81–82) focuses on the implicit assumptions that people carry around with them—again the arena in which I prefer to work with clients. Examples of implicit assumptions are:

- I can't do it.
- We've never done it like that before.
- I will never get permission to do it like that.
- They won't give me the budget to spend.
- No one in the team has the time to fix it.
- I expect the competition have already thought of it.

The options phase is to stop the client from finding reasons why not to do something. It is to encourage the brainstorming of options without judgement and to eliminate assumptions that stop the client from achieving what they want to achieve. Some alternative questions for the options phase are:

- What if you had a large enough budget?
- What if you had more staff?
- What if you knew the answer? What would it be?
- What if that obstacle did not exist? What would you do then?
- What do you really want?
- What are all the different things you could do to achieve it?
- What else?
- What are you willing to commit yourself to?
- What are the advantages and disadvantages?

Stage four: What will you do?

Step four refers to what clients will do. What did they learn? What are they going to do differently? What can change? This is the practical, summing up and writing down of the action steps to be taken to achieve the goal set originally under "G". This stage moves the client into decision mode with precision and detailed timelines (Whitmore, 2002:89–90). It is about "will"—what **will** the client do? Hence the questions:

- What are you going to do?
- When are you going to do it?

- Will this action meet your goal?
- Which obstacles might you meet along the way?
- Who needs to know?
- What support do you need?
- How and when are you going to get that support?
- What other considerations do you have?
- Rate the percentage of certainty you have that you will carry out the actions as agreed.

O'Neill's "executive coaching with backbone and heart"

Mary Beth O'Neill (2000) focuses on patterns of behaviour and coaching conversations with leaders to develop their business goals. Her style is action-focused and systems-oriented. She makes many suggestions about the framework within which the executive coach works and suggests a sequence of questions to help the coach intervene successfully with the client.

O'Neill describes the essence of coaching as "helping leaders get unstuck from their dilemmas and assisting them in transferring their learning into results for the organization". She has coined the term "signature presence" (O'Neill, 2000:xiii–xiv). Signature presence means "using one's presence in the moment at the time of intervention".

A four-question sequence

According to O'Neill (2000:5–7), the coach's question framework needs to embrace four essential ingredients with complementary questions:

1. **Which business challenges are you facing? How much time have you got?**
   How can you be results-oriented in relation to a leader's problem?
2. **What keeps you from getting the results you want?**
   What do you need to work or do to be a partner to the leader?
3. **What is challenging for you about this situation given the disappointing results?**
   How can you develop an ability to engage the executive in specific leadership challenges?

4. **What specifically do you expect from your team that would directly lead to higher results; and what will be required of you to produce those results through your team?**
Here, link team behaviours to bottom-line goals, pointing out the need to set specific expectations for their teams.

The journey of the individual executive and the coach are parallel journeys. You are helping that individual to find more of their own signature presence; at the same time you are being clear, objective and staying aligned with their issue.

Five-stage frameworks

Framework for change

Peltier (2001) states that one of the reasons people feel they cannot change is that they would have to acknowledge they were previously wrong. He mentions the components of emotional intelligence (self-awareness, self-regulation, motivation, empathy, social skills) and uses Goleman's definition of emotional intelligence: "the capacity for recognizing our own feelings and those of others, for motivating ourselves and for managing emotions well in ourselves and in our relationships" (Goleman, 1996:317). I have rephrased an intervention, suggested by Peltier (2001:139) and based on Silberman's (1986) model for change, as a coaching question framework:

Stage 1:   What is the situation now?
Stage 2:   What is the situation as you want it to be?
Stage 3:   What will keep the situation from changing?
Stage 4:   What action steps can you take?
Stage 5:   What resources are needed to help you make the change?

Working for change

Stage 1: What is the situation now?

One of my female executive clients, Patience, was working in a male-dominated engineering environment. She realized that it would be difficult for her to accelerate her learning and development without the mentoring or sponsorship of a senior executive. Although she had been put forward for several leadership development programmes, she was not making progress within her own division of this large corporate.

Stage 2: What is the situation as you want it to be?

The situation that Patience aimed for was not necessarily a promotion. She had attended several of the leadership and management development programmes offered within and outside the organization; however, she did not have any direct reports other than those with a dotted-line responsibility. She wanted to practice the skills that she had learned on the various programmes, but had no way to build her competence or capacity. Those who had a dotted-line responsibility to her were about 10 to 15 years her senior. She had worked two years in the organization, and her direct reports had each completed up to 10 years.

Stage 3: What will keep the situation from changing?

We spent an entire coaching session on this question. As Patience developed in self-awareness, she realized that she was the only one who could effect change. She was waiting for something to be offered to her, based on merit and her good work during the previous two years. However, unless she built alliances, and communicated her management development aspirations, nothing would happen. There was another difficulty: her line manager was ineffectual and not particularly interested in her achievements or developmental aims. As far as he was concerned, she was in a coaching relationship, and he needn't do anything further for her except increase her salary year after year.

Stage 4: What action steps can you take?

She decided to put together her own leadership development plan, making sure that it was aligned with divisional and organizational values. Part of the plan was to build her network within the organization, which was sizeable and international. As we devised the plan, working step by step, she identified the skills and competences that were areas for improvement; and she identified her skills and competences that were not being utilized. As a business analyst, she realized that she needed to find a mentor outside the organization to help with her development. She wanted to move into an international position eventually, so began to build her network in the international office. She continued to work on her management and interpersonal skills to manage her tendency to "introversion", and began taking classes in a foreign language to improve the possibility of eventually moving into that market.

Stage 5: What resources are needed to help you make the change?

The resources she required were:

- finances for the various programmes which she personally funded;
- a sponsor for the organization's upcoming management development programme;
- time and energy to apply herself to learning a foreign language on a weekly basis; and
- a health and fitness programme to begin to achieve a greater work/life balance.

Finally, she realized that her networking and alliance building skills were most useful to her, catapulting her into greater "visibility" within the environment. This paid off, and she was offered responsibility as project manager on a sizeable project. This would give her the chance to build her contacts across diverse organizational functions and to "project manage" a team of people. This framework moved the client from frustration, to a sense that she was in control of her own career path.

Working with the CLEAR model

CLEAR metaphorically represents a process to help the client "clear" a presenting issue. CLEAR is an acronym for contracting, listening, exploring, action and **review.** CLEAR provides a slightly different perspective on what to focus on in a coaching session, providing a sequence of questions to help the coach move progressively from contracting to reviewing learning, actions and decisions made. This is a very useful and straightforward framework for managers to use with direct reports.

Stage 1: Contracting: Opening the discussion, setting the scene, establishing the desired outcomes, and agreeing the ground rules

CLEAR looks not only at the goal of the session but allows for wider contracting issues such as time available for both parties as well as specific ground rules to be observed, such as confidentiality. Questions to ask are:

- How would you like me to coach you today?
- What helps you learn?
- What blocks your learning?

Stage 2: Listening: Active listening as a catalytic coaching intervention helps the client develop their understanding of the situation and generate personal insight

- What am I hearing in the content of the words?
- What am I hearing that isn't being said?
- What isn't being heard or said?
- What could I ask that would help the client to reflect?

As a guideline, **listen** 75 per cent of the time and **speak** only 25 per cent of the time in your coaching session. Rather than focusing on your next response, concentrate on what the individual is trying to communicate through the content of their message: their non-verbal signals, metaphors, stories and limiting assumptions. In this context, you can paraphrase or reframe the client's words to clarify understanding and to avoid your own assumptions.

Stage 3: Exploring 1: Helping the client to understand the personal impact the situation is having on them and Exploring 2: Challenging the client to think through possibilities for future action in resolving the situation

All behaviour is driven by what we think or feel, and it usually has a wider implication than the specific incident or event. Exploring can be used to help the client understand their own assumptions about other people's behaviour as well as their own:

- Has this happened before? Has anything similar happened before?
- What was the outcome/result?

- How did your behaviour/reaction affect the situation?
- What did you feel when so-and-so said ... or did ...?
- What outcome would you prefer?

Stage 4: Action—supporting the client in choosing a way ahead and deciding the next step

In Stage four, the client should ideally figure out the next steps for themselves. Be careful not to advise an action or behaviour that worked for you in similar situations. Your experience might be invaluable and useful, but it does not necessarily mean that your way is the best way for the client to learn or change behaviour. In experiential learning, the client's insight is the best indicator of change:

- What do you think you can do?
- Is there anything else you could possibly do?
- How will this (action step) help you achieve your goal?

Stage 5: Review—closing the intervention, reinforcing ground covered, decisions made and value added. The coach also encourages feedback from the client on what was helpful about the coaching process, what was difficult and what they would like to be different in future coaching sessions

This stage adds reflection, which is a missing ingredient in the wrap-up stage of GROW. Summarize what was discussed and agreed and ask the client to reflect and review the process:

- What worked for you in this session?
- What did not work?
- What else would you have preferred either of us to do or say?

Six-stage frameworks

Nancy Kline's Thinking Partnership®

Nancy Kline's question framework comprises a six-stage process underpinned by ten components or behaviours, positive philosophical choice, and incisive questions. One of the key theories which determines how we work with clients in the "coaching conversation" is that of "positive philosophical choice". Kline's Thinking Partnership® is based on the "chosen philosophical view that human beings are by nature good: intelligent, loving, powerful, multi-talented, emotional, assertive, able to think through anything, imaginative and logi-cal". Kline says that "behaviour to the contrary is seen as the result of assumptions generated over a lifetime by events, conditions and attitudes in a person's environment" (Kline, 2005:4). The Thinking Partnership® model is based on positive philosophical choice and ten thinking components:

1. **attention** (listening with interest and without interruption);
2. **equality** (treating the other as a thinking peer; keeping agreements and boundaries);
3. **ease** (offering freedom from internal rush or urgency);
4. **appreciation** (a 5:1 ratio of appreciation to criticism);
5. **encouragement** (moving beyond internal competition);
6. **feelings** (allowing sufficient emotional release to restore thinking);
7. **information** (supplying facts; managing organizational denial);
8. **diversity** (welcoming divergent thinking and diverse group identities);
9. **incisive questions** (removing assumptions that limit ideas); and
10. **place** (creating a physical environment that says to the other, "You matter").

Six-stage Thinking Environment® coaching process

In Kline's Thinking Environment® sequence, the crucial work is to identify and replace limiting assumptions with a more powerful worldview by choosing one core limiting assumption at a time that is relevant to the presenting issue. Kline's framework is based on six stages of questioning (Kline, 2005:4–21):

1. **Exploration** (What do you want to think about?)
2. **Further goal** (What would you like to accomplish in the rest of this session?)
3. **Assumptions** (What are you assuming that is stopping you from [insert goal])?
   - What is the key assumption?
   - Is that assumption true?
   - What are your reasons for thinking that? (Look for alignment with positive philosophical choice, logic and information).

Transition question:
- (If it is true or possibly true): That is possible, but what are you assuming that makes that assumption hold you back from [insert goal]?
- (If it is not true): As [insert untrue assumption] is not true, what are your words for what is true?

Invitation question:
- Given that that assumption is stopping you from achieving your goal, what could you more credibly assume that would help you achieve your goal?
- Would you be interested in choosing that view for a few minutes?
- So, it is not true that (restate the untrue limiting assumption). What would be your words for what is true (for a liberating alternative to that assumption)?

4. **Incisive question** (if you knew [insert true liberating assumption] how would you [insert goal]?)
5. **Recording** (client records incisive question and action to be taken).
6. **Appreciation** (key component: what quality do you respect/admire in each other?)

According to Nancy Kline (1999/2004:100–1), team effectiveness depends on the calibre of thinking the team can do. Yet most teams do not operate within a thinking environment with the ten components necessary to enhance quality thinking and decision making. Teams are the most strategic place to begin organizational change, but the limiting assumptions of each team member and the limiting assumptions of the group as a whole need to be identified and replaced with empowering assumptions.

Although this is one of the purest coaching question frameworks I have encountered, its ultimate success in the coaching context is in the client's implementing the goals that are set as a result. This question framework helps us to understand the process of identifying limiting assumptions and replacing them with more empowering assumptions. This is a transformative process for the individual client.

In the Thinking Environment® question framework, awareness and insight is the context within which the coach works with the client to identify, understand and change those limiting assumptions that are most getting in the way of the client's taking responsibility, setting goals, taking action, growing and learning.

Eight-stage frameworks

Well-formed outcomes (NLP)

NLP is a cognitive behavioural representation system. **Neuro** refers to the nervous system (the mind), through which our experience is processed via five senses: visual, auditory, kinaesthetic, olfactory and gustatory. **Linguistic** refers to language and other non-verbal communication systems through which our neural representations are coded, ordered and given meaning. This includes pictures, sounds, feelings, tastes, smells and words (self-talk). **Programming** refers to the ability to discover and utilize the mental programmes that we run (our communication to ourselves and others) in our neurological systems to achieve our specific and desired outcomes.

NLP interventions are based on the NLP communication model and can include third-position thinking, circle of excellence, rapport exercises and setting well-formed outcomes. NLP is based on the clinical practices and research of Alfred Korzybski (General Semantics 1930–40); Paul Watzlawick (Linguistics 1950s); levels of language and theory of logical types (logical levels); Richard Bandler (Computer Linguistics); John Grinder (Gestalt Linguistics); Milton Erickson (hypnosis); Gregory Bateson (syllogism); Fritz Perls (Gestalt Therapy); and Virginia Satir (family therapy) (McLoughlin and Stout Rostron, 2002).

Well-formed outcomes: Practical exercise

NLP can be defined as how to use the language of the mind to consistently achieve our specific and desired outcomes. The various ways to achieve a well-formed outcome are well documented in the NLP literature. The following question framework will assist the coach in setting well-formed outcomes with the client.

1. **Stated in the positive:**
   • What specifically do you want?
2. **Specify present situation:**
   • Where are you now?

3. **Demonstrable in sensory experience:**
   - Evidence procedure.
   - How will you know when you've got your outcome? Imagine you have it now:
     - What are you seeing having got it?
     - What are you hearing having got it?
     - What are you feeling having got it?
     - What are you doing having got it?
     - What will others be seeing, hearing and feeling that lets them know that you've got it?
4. **Is it congruently desirable?**
   - What will this outcome get for you or allow you to do?
5. **Is it self-initiated and self-maintained?**
   - Is it only for you? (You cannot set goals for others. You can only set goals for yourself.)
6. **Appropriately contextualized:**
   - When, where and with whom do you want it?
   - When, where and with whom do you not want it?
   - For how long do you want it?
7. **What resources are needed?**
   - What do you have now, and what do you need to get your outcome?
   - Have you ever had or done this before?
   - Do you know anyone who has?
   - Act as if you have it.
8. **Ecology check:**
   - For what purpose do you want this?
   - What will you gain or lose if you have it?
   - Is it worth the cost to you?
   - Is it worth the time it is going to take?
   - Is this outcome in keeping with your sense of self?

An alternative well-formed outcomes exercise

Here is a version for setting well-formed outcomes advocated by Peter McNab (2005):

1. **What do you want?**
   - (Is it stated in the positive? Is it initiated and controlled by you? Is it sensory-based?)

2. **Where, when and with whom do you want it?**
   - Have you considered different contexts? Is it ecological? Is it sensory-based?
3. **How will you know that you have it?**
   - Is it sensory-based, appropriate, and timely?
4. **What do you get out of your current behaviour?**
   - What will you lose? How will you maintain this in your desired state?
5. **Ecology #1**
   - How will your outcome affect other aspects of your life? Who and what else will it affect?
6. **Ecology #2**
   - Under which conditions would you not want to implement your goal?
7. **What (if anything) stops you having your desired state already?**
   - If so, what additional resources do you need?
8. **What are you going to do? When are you going to do it?**
   - Give appropriate detail with the first step precisely defined.

Ten-stage frameworks

Business Best Year Yet®

Best Year Yet® is both an individual and a team coaching process. Business Best Year Yet® works with a ten-stage coaching intervention to create aligned individual and team plans by identifying and replacing limiting paradigms, creating a new vision, aligning organizational strategy with the team's top ten goals.

The coach helps the individual or team to set goals and develop new guidelines, new values and a new empowering paradigm or vision. Not dissimilar to the Nancy Kline Thinking Environment® process, the central focus is on the moment of change (transformation of a disempowering paradigm to an empowering one). The ten questions help the coach to focus the client first on the past 12 months, and second on creating a new vision for the next 12 months. This is a useful one-on-one coaching tool, as well as a tool for a team coaching process. As coach, you can use the ten questions developed by Jinny Ditzler (1994), which follow, as a question framework to help the client to set goals that will reflect their new paradigm or mindset.

Having worked with the Best Year Yet® process for nearly ten years, I have described each of the ten steps for you to use in an individual coaching process. For those who want to use the team coaching process, you will need to contact Best Year Yet®. For more information on this process developed by Jinny Ditzler, refer to her book, *Your Best Year Yet: The 10 Questions That Will Change Your Life Forever* (1994).

Best Year Yet® coaching exercise

1. **What were your accomplishments over the last 12 months?**
   - What was the secret of your success?
   - What worked?
   - Why were you able to achieve what you did?
2. **What were your biggest disappointments, frustrations and unmet expectations in the last 12 months?**
   - What didn't work and why not?
   - What would have worked better?
3. **What did you learn?**
   - What can you learn from your own excellence?
   - What can you learn from the things that didn't work?
   - Pick three and turn them into **guidelines** for your next 12 months.
4. **In what way do you stop yourself from achieving your best, and how can you change?**
   - What is it that you do and say that stops you from achieving?
   - What do you say to yourself (write it down!) to justify these reasons or excuses?
   - Pick the most powerful one or two that would create the greatest change if they worked for you rather than against you. Now brainstorm the words that would turn it into a future-oriented, powerful, positive way forward.
5. **What is it that gets you up in the morning, motivated and ready to go?**
   - What is important to you about work? About home? About life?
   - Choose those unmeasurable intrinsic drivers: such as achievement, recognition, health, being loved, giving something back—these are the intangibles that are really driving you from within.
   - Which ones most represent who you are?

6. **Which key roles do you play, i.e., what hats do you wear, professionally and personally?**
   - i.e., owner, manager, boss, employee, partner, peer, husband, wife, mother, father, son, daughter, sister, brother, friend.
   - Choose the top eight.
7. **Which hat (or role) needs to be your major focus to make the next year your best one yet?**
8. **Write down three goals for each role.**
9. **From your list, choose the top ten goals which will make the difference for you.**
10. **Now, what will most help you to achieve them?**

Developing your own question frameworks

In this chapter, I have introduced you to a range of question frameworks that help structure the business coaching conversation. It is useful for you to begin to develop your own range of questions as they relate to your coaching model. At the end of each session with a client, write up your reflections on the conversation, making a note of the overall structure of the conversation and the sequence of questions that you used. In the next chapter, we explore various coaching models available in the business environment today, and coaching question frameworks that are specific to those models.

Question frameworks are simply tools for you to structure the coaching conversation. As you develop your work with your clients, choose question frameworks that are suitable to your personal style of working and the needs of your client. Gradually, as you begin to refine your own coaching model, it will become clear which questions are most useful to you.

One of the core skills of the business coach is the ability not just to ask questions but to ask incisive questions that will help the client to explore their own attitudes and assumptions about themselves and others in the workplace. Having done so, they are better able to develop an awareness of self and others, which in turn allows them to manage relationships more successfully.

What is shown to be transformative and to create the greatest change in the coaching conversation is the identification and transformation of limiting assumptions into empowering assumptions through the use of a question process.

Change happens when the client transforms limiting assumptions into empowering ones—and then commits themselves to action as a result. The coach's job is to understand this process and to help the client create empowering assumptions—and thus a new attitude or mindset—which could be the beginning of a new paradigm or worldview. This can take place at any stage of the coaching process.

However, there needs to be a high degree of trust between the coach and the client. The relationship needs to be strong. It is in the safety and confidential nature of the coach/client relationship that the client will feel free to be challenged by their limiting thoughts, feelings or behaviour (Stout Rostron, 2006c:225).

During the coaching conversation, the process of asking questions has to be done from a point of no prejudgement or assumption, really clarifying and understanding the thinking of the client. This is difficult, as each individual operates within their own worldview and limiting paradigms, and each coach approaches the coaching conversation with their own assumptions and biases, and must therefore learn to bracket such assumptions and biases and put them aside. This is a core skill for a coach: to learn to bracket their own assumptions and biases (Stout Rostron, 2006c:147). For example, if as a practitioner you are going to reframe or say something about the client's process, just describe it, do not impose your assumptions on what they are saying. This is a difficult but crucial point for a coach.

The coaching conversation, ultimately, seems to be less about the mechanics of the coaching intervention than about the art of integrating pure, sheer presence and non-judgmental attention on the client, combined with the skill of asking the right question at the right time. It is the development of awareness that leads to knowledge and action. The coaching intervention is simply the bridge between reflection, awareness, learning, knowledge and action.

Coach's library

Bandler, R. and Grinder, J. (1992). *Reframing and the Transformation of Meaning*. Moab, UT: Real People Press.

Ditzler, J. (1994). *Your Best Year Yet: The 10 Questions That Will Change Your Life Forever*. New York, NY: Warner.

Kline, N. (1999/2004). *Time to Think: Listening with the Human Mind.* London: Ward Lock.

Kline, N. (2004). Keynote address. In: *Coaching in a Thinking Environment.* Wallingford: Time to Think.

McDermott, I. and Jago, W. (2001). *The NLP Coach: A Comprehensive Guide to Personal Well-Being and Professional Success.* London: Piatkus.

McNab, P. (2005). *Towards an Integral Vision: Using NLP and Ken Wilber's AQAL Model to Enhance Communication.* Crewe: Trafford.

O'Connor, J. and Seymour, J. (1990). *Introducing NLP.* London: Aquarian/Thorsons.

O'Neill, M. B. (2000). *Coaching with Backbone and Heart: A Systems Approach to Engaging Leaders with Their Challenges.* San Francisco, CA: Jossey-Bass.

Revans, R. W. (1983). *The ABC of Action Learning.* Bromley: Chartwell Bratt.

Whitmore, J. (2002). *Coaching for Performance: Growing People, Performance and Purpose.* London: Nicholas Brealey.

CHAPTER FIVE

Exploring and understanding coaching models

Listening and observation are key skills for the business coach. Developing the skill of observation is partly to develop the ability to be 'inside' the coaching conversation, and to be 'observing' the conversation. It is to take up a meta-position, while never leaving the micro level of being present for the client (Stout Rostron, 2006c:152).

CHAPTER OUTLINE
- Models
- Coaching tools and techniques
- How many models to use?
  - Purpose, Perspectives, Process model
- The coaching conversation and the coaching journey
  - Nested-levels model
  - The expert approach
  - "You have all the answers" approach
  - Learning level
  - Ontological levels—being and becoming
  - Learning

113

- Learning conversations
  - Three levels of intervention—behaviour, underlying drivers, root causes
- Four-quadrant models (Hippocrates)
  - Insights four-colour model
  - Domains of Competence model (Habermas)
  - Ken Wilber's four-quadrant Integral Model
  - Questions in the four quadrants
  - GROW and CLEAR models
  - EQ model
  - Kolb's Experiential Learning Model
  - Using Kolb's four modes of learning
  - Hudson's Renewal Cycle model
- Other circular models
  - I-T-O (Input, Throughput, Output)
- The U-process
  - Scharmer's U-process
- In conclusion
- Coach's library

Models

Today, coaches are trained in an eclectic range of coaching models. This chapter explores a cross-section of models that influence the work of business and executive coaches worldwide. I highlight the work of Daniel Goleman, John Whitmore, David Lane, New Ventures West, David Kolb, Frederick Hudson, Thomas Cummings and Christopher Worley, and Ken Wilber.

Coaching models help us to understand the coaching intervention from a systems perspective, and to understand the need for "structure" in the interaction between coach and client. Models help us to develop flexibility as coach practitioners. They offer structure and an outline for both the coaching conversation and the overall coaching journey—whether it is for 20 hours, six months, a year or more. However, although models create a system within which coach and client work, it is imperative that models are not experienced as either prescriptive or rigid.

The coaching conversation is about the client, not the coach. If the model is too prescriptive, it means the coach has their own agenda to fulfil, rather than attempting to understand the client's issues. In this chapter, I discuss four-quadrant models, circular and U-process models. I explore the flexibility you have to combine models and to construct your own if you so wish.

A model represents a system with an implied process. It is a metaphor or analogy used to help visualize and describe the journey. Models systemically visualize or represent a process that cannot be directly observed. In other words, a model represents more than what you are looking at. If you can develop a model that encompasses the coaching conversation and the entire coaching intervention, you will begin to work with considerably greater ease within your practice. This is how we will look at models in this chapter.

A coaching model is representative of what happens, or will happen, in the coaching conversation (micro) and in the overall coaching intervention or journey (macro). I recommend here simple models that can represent both the micro and macro coaching interventions.

Coaching tools and techniques

What is a coaching tool and what is a coaching technique? A **tool** is an instrument used to produce certain results; the tool is what you engage with as a coach inside the coaching conversation. For example, a hammer and nails are tools used to build a house; the tools you work with in the coaching conversation are profiles, assessments, questions, reframing statements, listening, question frameworks and models. A **technique**, on the other hand, is the technical skill, ability or competence you have developed to use that tool. For example listening is a tool, and active listening is a technique. This is where your experience, expertise and hours spent coaching come into effect. Often your tools and techniques fall into a specific part of your model's process.

The model is the process you use to work with your client. It embodies all of your tools and techniques, including the question frameworks I discussed in the previous chapter. Although you might be dying to explain your model to your client, they might not be particularly interested! They might be more interested in the tools and techniques that they will directly observe and experience with you. Often, if you are coaching other coaches, they will want to be debriefed on which tools, techniques and models you have used when working with them.

So, a model is a simple representation of the journey which can encompass the skills, experience and expertise coach and client bring to the coaching conversation. Part of the model may include the actions the client takes as a result of your coaching conversations when they go back into the workplace, and their own inner work throughout the entire coaching journey as they develop greater self-awareness and adaptability.

How many models to use?

There are varying degrees of thought when training coaches. Some schools train their coach practitioners to use only one coaching model. Other coach training schools teach a variety of models and advocate choosing one of them, or learning how to flexibly integrate a few models to develop your own.

The key purpose of this chapter is to introduce you to a variety of models (not all) for your own learning and development. If you prefer one particular model that is taught in the marketplace, it is essential to go through the training to ensure you have a depth of understanding in its use. Eventually, you may want to choose whether to work with one model, an integration of several models or to develop your own. That is not for us to prescribe. There are many valuable and useful models available to you.

Whatever you decide, I believe that knowledge is power, and the more understanding of available models you have, the more intelligent your choice will be. When I teach coach practitioners in models and question frameworks, I look at how to integrate different models to construct your own. However, my purpose in this chapter is simply to explore a variety of coaching models and to give examples of how to facilitate a coaching conversation with each one.

Purpose, Perspectives, Process model

The key principle I want to convey is that it is essential to adopt a structured approach to your coaching conversation. This does not mean that you cannot let the conversation grow and be explorative—I mean structure in a big-picture way. That is the beauty of any model:

having the freedom to explore within each part of the model. The Purpose, Perspectives, Process model (see Figure 1) was developed by David Lane of the Professional Development Foundation (PDF) and the Work-Based Learning Unit at London's Middlesex University (Lane and Corrie, 2006).

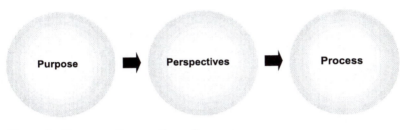

Figure 1. Purpose, Perspectives, Process.

Source: Lane and Corrie (2006).

Purpose (where are we going and why?)

What is the purpose in working with the client? Where are you going with this client? What does the client want to achieve? Where do they want to go in their overall journey with you as their coach?

For example, one client working in the telecoms industry said in our first session together, "I need your help because everybody in the organization distrusts me and I'm in a pretty senior position. What can I do about it? I'm highly respected by those subordinate to me in position and disliked and mistrusted by those superior or equal to me in position." As coach, your questions will relate to client purpose, i.e., "Where are we going, and what's the reason for going there?" It is usually better to ask a "what" question rather than a "why" question. For example, "Why are we going there?" sounds intrusive and can create a defensive posture on the part of the client. "What" questions help to create a bigger picture of the journey; "what" creates perspective. This client's purpose was to "build alliances and trust with peers, colleagues and superiors throughout the organization".

Part of the client's purpose will be aligned with the questions they bring to the coaching process. Their questions are often related

to "why" they want to go where they want to go, and they are test-
ing you to see if you can help them to arrive at their final destination. Your job is to understand what is motivating them, what is
driving them. For example, I worked with a group of people whose
underlying purpose was to build a business partnership together in
the field of leadership development. They peppered me with questions as to how they could achieve what they had set out to achieve
as their overarching strategic purpose. My job was to understand
their vision and the driving interests underlying their vision. With
the telecoms client for example, his purpose was to develop better
relationships with his peers and colleagues, and building alliances
became his overarching theme in the work we did together.

Perspectives (what will inform our journey?)

What perspectives inform the journey for both coach and client?
What informs our journey, i.e., what informs the client and what
informs the coach? Both coach and client come in with their individual backgrounds, experience, expertise, culture, values, motivations
and assumptions that drive behaviour.

Not so long ago, I had a call from a potential client within the
energy industry. He was a general manager and asked if we could
just chat. We chatted about his perspective on his background, experience, career and his current job. We discussed his perspective in
terms of his position within the organization, his style of leading and
managing his team of people, the impact and influence of his age on
his career prospects, and finally he said, "I have got as far as I can get
with what I know now—and I need to know more, somehow".

We then discussed my perspective, i.e., what informs the way I
work with clients, what informs my experience and expertise and,
based on our mutual perspectives, he asked, "Would we have some
kind of synchronicity or a match in order to work together?" He
wanted to understand what models, tools and techniques I used as
he wanted to create his own leadership development toolbox for his
senior managers. He also wanted to understand how to handle mistakes: did I make them and what would my education, training and
work experience bring to our conversation?

One of the things I am very careful of with clients is never to
"over-talk" my perspective; and it's also important for clients to

understand that you are constantly learning from your mistakes. The coaching intervention is about **them**, not you. Perspectives are informed by both the client and the coach's cultural and structural interpretation of the world—defined by their family, education, learning, qualifications, faith, spirituality, experiences, expertise, personality traits, values, feelings, motivations, assumptions and behaviour. In this first contracting conversation, we worked through the model beginning with perspectives:

Perspectives—how we might bring our two worlds together;

Purpose—what he ultimately wanted from the coaching experience; and

Process—how we would work together to achieve his outcomes.

The process (how will we get there?)

Using this model helped me to begin to understand the above client's needs, to develop rapport, and to identify not just his overall outcomes but a way to begin working together. At this stage of the model we contracted, set boundaries, agreed confidentiality matters, outlining the fee paying process and the development of a leadership development plan. We also agreed on timing (how often we would see each other and the individual client's line manager). What assessments would be useful for the individual client to complete? How would we debrief those profiles? We also discussed potential coaching assignments and timing for the overall contract (including termination and exit possibilities if either party was unhappy) and explored how to obtain line manager approval. Finally, we set up a separate meeting to agree the process with the line manager and the Group HR Director.

A model is a metaphor for the journey and embodies a structured process. This model can help you in three ways: to contract with the client, to structure the entire coaching journey, and to guide your coaching conversation. Out of the specific conversation about process emerged the client's purpose, the way our perspectives fit together to help him to achieve his purpose, and the process within which we would work to achieve the outcomes desired.

This model can be used for the regular coaching conversations you have with your client. The client arrives and brings into the conversation a possible "menu" of topics to be discussed, or even just one particular topic. One of my clients in the media came to me one day saying, "My purpose today is to understand why I am sabotaging my best efforts to delegate to my senior managers" (purpose). As the coach, I wanted to understand all of the perspectives underlying the client's aim for this conversation (perspectives), as well as identifying the various tools or techniques that could be used in the process.

In this instance, I suggested that we use the Nancy Kline six-stage Thinking Environment® question framework to explore his goal (process). After an hour of exploratory thinking, my client identified a "further" goal for the session. The questions in this process led him to articulate assumptions never actually voiced before. We moved eventually from a disempowering assumption to a liberating assumption that allowed him to identify action steps to delegate skilfully and artfully in a format that he would adhere to.

The coaching conversation and the coaching journey

This model can represent the process for just one coaching conversation, but it can also represent the overall journey. For example, the client comes in with their **purpose**, "I would like to work with you; no one else will work with me as they find me too difficult". This client's purpose became to find a coach who would work with him, to help him to identify how he could not just develop the interpersonal skills to work successfully with others—but to demonstrate his new learning through visible behaviour change at work. The coach's and the client's **perspectives** will be unique and different. In working with the client, you bring not just perspective, but your observations as to how this client seems to be working within the organizational system.

In terms of process, the coach may ask the client to do a range of assessment profiles, or you may shadow the client at work to experience how they facilitate meetings, and interact with customers, subordinates, superiors and colleagues. This way you can make observations (your perspective), being careful not to interpret as a therapist would, and to ask questions that would enable the client to develop self-awareness and self-management skills and competences that will ultimately lead them to interact more successfully with others in the workplace.

Nested-levels model

The next model was developed by New Ventures West (Weiss, 2004). This model introduces the concept of horizontal and vertical levels in coaching models. It is a "nested-levels" model. Although somewhat different from the U-shape model, which I discuss later in this chapter, it is based on a similar idea of depth. The nested model works first at the horizontal level of "doing", eventually moving into deeper "learning" one level down; reflecting about self, others and experience at a third "ontological" level where new knowledge emerges about oneself and the world (Figure 2).

In her web article, Pam Weiss talks about the two different camps of coaches. In jest, I call them the New York versus the L.A. camp. The New York camp says, "I'm the expert, let me fix you". The L.A. camp says, "You are perfect and whole and have all of your own answers". Joking aside, each of these camps falls short, even though coaches often fall into one or the other. The role of coaching is actually about developing human beings. It is not really about "expertise" versus "you already have all your own answers".

The expert approach

Clients are not broken and do not need fixing as the experts might think. Clients may be anxious, stressed, nervous, overworked and even narcissistic—but they don't need fixing. They are mostly healthy human beings going about their jobs and lives, experiencing their own human difficulties. Your job as coach is to help the clients to "learn" for themselves so that when you are no longer walking alongside them, they have become "self-directed" learners (Harri-Augstein and Thomas, 1991) and do not need you anymore.

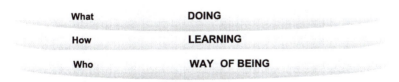

What	DOING
How	LEARNING
Who	WAY OF BEING

Figure 2. Nested-levels model.

Source: Adapted from Weiss (2004).

The second view about "expertise" also has limitations. The role of expertise is that, as coach, you are an expert; but coaching is not about the coach giving all the answers; that tends to be the role of the consultant, i.e., to find solutions for the client.

"You have all the answers" approach

The "you have all the answers" assumption is partially true; but there are several limitations according to Weiss. The first one is that we all have blind spots, and it is your job as coach to help the client to identify their blind spots. Secondly, it's perhaps a bit of "mythical" thinking that the client has all of the answers already; the flip side of that argument is that, if it does not work out, the client assumes blame and fault. In other words, "If I have all the answers, I should be able to do it myself without help". If that is not the case, they could feel, "Oh dear, if I am not able to do it myself, then perhaps I'm a failure".

Both of these approaches are "horizontal"; in other words they skim the surface of the work you can do with the client. Both help people to maintain the lives they currently have. The expert "New York" approach helps the client to do it better, faster, more efficiently, and the "L.A." approach may withhold the coach's insights and observations, which could help to build the client's awareness of their blind spots. What is important, rather than "fixing" the client, is the skill of "observation" on the part or the coach. There is no problem in helping the client to **do** it better, faster or more efficiently—that is often what the organization hopes for in terms of performance improvement. However, it is important for the client to gain the learning they need to address blind spots and to build their own internal capacity and competence.

Learning level

If you continue to help people to accomplish tasks, achieve goals and to keep on "doing", they risk falling into the trap of being "busy" and possibly overwhelmed. They may, however, not necessarily get the "learning" they need to develop self-awareness and self-management. I know all too well about this trap of being excessively busy. If we keep "doing" without reflection we eventually burn out. To keep individual executives performing better and better, they need to work at one level lower—at the level of learning. They need to **learn how** to "do the doing" better. As soon as an executive begins to work with a coach, they begin the possibility of working at one or two levels deeper.

As coach you will be asking questions to help clients reflect, review and gain useable knowledge from their experience. In this model, the higher levels don't include the lower ones, but the lower levels include the higher ones. So, we need to help clients address their purpose one level down, at the level of learning. At this level you may ask questions such as, "how are you doing; what are you doing; what are you feeling; how are your peers/ colleagues experiencing you/this; what is working and what isn't working; what is useful learning for you here; what needs to change and how?"

Ontological levels—being and becoming

The third and fourth levels of coaching intervention are that of who the client **is** and who the client **wishes to become** in terms of thinking, feeling and behaviour (I have added the level of "becoming"). Your questions move from "what do they need to do", and "how do they need to do it" (**doing**), to "how does their style of learning impact on how they do what they do; what do they need to learn in order to improve thinking/behaviour/feeling/performance/ leadership" (**learning**); to questions about "what do they need to understand and acknowledge about themselves, who are they, how do they be who they are, and what needs to change (**being and becoming**)?"

CASE STUDY: LEVELS OF LEARNING
My client, working in the field of IT technology security, wanted to lead and manage his team more effectively, and to build trust not just with team members but also with colleagues, superiors and clients (**doing**). In order to do so, he needed to identify what the interpersonal skills and competences were where he already had "unconscious competence", and which new skills and competences he needed to learn in order to build alliances

and develop better relationships (**learning**). Even more so, he needed to understand who he is, what his essence is, what do people sense about him, how do others perceive him, and how does he behave when perceiving others (**being**), as well as who he wanted to become (**becoming**) in terms of his thinking, feeling and behaviour.

We agreed to do a range of assessment profiles, including a 360° feedback, for him to gain a sense of how others experienced him in the workplace. He was surprised to learn that he was experienced negatively as someone who barked orders, was impatient to the point of intolerance, and seemingly had no empathy for real feelings and people's individual lives. This helped him begin to identify who he was perceived to be and who he needed to become in terms of his behaviour if he was to achieve his goals (**doing**).

One of the ways we began to identify how to go about changing (**learning**) was from my observations of him in the workplace, at social business occasions, and inside the coaching conversation. Gradually, this executive client began to take a greater interest in others, beginning to articulate his assumptions about his team's capabilities and learning to understand how his assumptions were sabotaging the process of learning for his direct reports. Although the process took over a year, this executive became clear about his own style of learning and those of his team. He slowly began to engage differently with others at all levels in the workplace. Although trust cannot be easily built, his behaviour enforced the perception that he was proactively trying to change. This encouraged his direct reports, peers and superiors to be confident that his "being different" was something he was working on even if it was not perfectly embodied.

CASE STUDY: DOING

Another client, a senior leader in the financial sector, was an authoritative, but gentle giant, whose size was somewhat alarming to his subordinates and direct reports. He embodied a sense of self-assurance and exactitude, which kept people at a distance. On top of that, he lost his patience with fair regularity. The original purpose of our work together was to help him begin to manage his "short fuse"; in fact, our goal in working together was to help him develop "a longer fuse" that would impact on how he behaved (**doing**). We first identified how his short fuse impacted on his performance and on that of his team, and we looked at quite a few specific examples to identify what triggered his short fuse and loss of temper. Once we had identified the triggers, we could begin to look at how to change them.

So, what assists people in getting things done? Above all, it is about clarifying goals, creating action steps, taking responsibility and being accountable. In order to perform more effectively, we need to help clients shift down a gear to learn how to work with competence (a set of skills) rather than just learning a specific new skill.

Learning

Your job as the coach is to help the client be open to possibilities of learning something new, and to help them relate to themselves and others at a deeper level. With my financial client, at the level of "learning", we identified his need for a greater sense of self-confidence. It was important for him to feel that he could deal with ineffective behaviour and performance at work. His effective handling of difficult situations would be visible to the more senior authorities upon whose recognition he depended if he was to move upwards in the organization. He needed to know that he had the skills and competence to get people to perform at their best. Executives in the corporate world usually know how to play the game of politics, but they often don't know how to win over the people who drive results for them.

This client began to develop a greater set of interpersonal skills and competences. These helped him to build a bond with his direct reports and their subordinates. They began to trust that he was bringing change to the division and gradually, due to his hands-on style, they began to trust their new perceptions of him. He grew in leadership competence, managing team forums and regional road shows for the staff. As he developed leadership competence in his direct reports, he also gradually built bridges with staff. He was willing to understand the challenges faced by employees in the field.

CASE STUDY: ADDRESSING THE PERSON VERSUS THE ISSUE
Another client, employed on the technological side within the energy industry, was working about 60 hours a week, driving two hours a day, and doing an MBA part-time. On weekends, he had to find time to study and to be with his family. He and his wife had a new baby. On Sundays, he refereed a football team for disadvantaged adolescent boys. How high were his stress levels? We identified his need to learn how to create balance in his life, and to find a way to bring exercise, diet and nutrition into the equation—just thinking about it made him more stressed! He also needed to learn to let go of control. Eventually he found an entrepreneurial young man who was willing to drive him back and forth to work during the week. This freed up two hours a day when travelling that he could devote to study, sleep or emails.

On the football field, he took to running with the boys. He and his wife also bought an exercise bike, which everyone in the family began to use. They worked out an economic way to add fresh vegetables and fruit to their diet. For the client, it was about learning how to "do the doing" better; at a deeper level becoming the more balanced person he wanted to be. This shifted the gears in the coaching relationship. It was a move from simply addressing the **issue** to addressing the **person**.

To use this model, you could ask questions such as:

1. What is it that the client wants to **do**? What is their aim or purpose in working with you?
2. What do they need to **learn** in order to make the change? What in their thinking, feeling and behaviour needs to change in order to do the doing better? How can they use their own experience to learn what is needed?
3. How do, and how will, their thoughts, feelings and behaviour impact on how they "**be** who they are" and "who is it that they want to **become**"? In this way, we work at horizontal and vertical levels. At the end of the day, the client's new attitudes, behaviours, motivations and assumptions begin to impact positively on their own performance and their relationships with others.

What is our aim with this model? Is it to shift any limiting sense of who they are so that they can interact and engage with the world in new ways? As the client begins to shift, it has an impact on others with whom they interact in the workplace. It also means addressing issues systemically, from a holistic perspective, whether it revolves around health, stress, anxiety, performance or relationships with others. Our task as coaches is to widen the circle, enlarge the perspective of the client, and help them to learn from their own experience to reach their potential.

Learning conversations

One of the core areas where coaches work with clients is that of learning. If you are guiding, directing and giving your clients all the information they need, it will be difficult for them to ever be free of you. From your first conversation as a coach, you should be trying to work yourself out of a job—in other words, to help your clients learn to be without you. Harri-Augstein and Thomas (1991:27–29) define learning as follows: "From birth each person strives to understand; grows and develops; reaches for greater awareness; constructs personal worlds; achieves at least some needs and purposes; invests new patterns of thoughts and feelings; acts to validate these; builds new personal worlds, habitations into stable routines; survives; declines; lives through personal and social crises ..."

At the end of each coaching session with my clients, we complete a learning contract to fully integrate the learning with goals set and commitment to action:

1. **Vision**—Refine their vision: where is the client going?
2. **Strategy**—Outline the strategy: how is the client going to achieve their vision?
3. **Outcomes**—What are the specific outcomes that need to be accomplished in the next few weeks in order to work towards achieving the vision and putting the strategy into action?
4. **Learning**—Help the client summarize what was gained from the session in order to help underline self-reflection, continuing to help the client understand that they are responsible for their own thinking, their own doing, and their own being.

The learning contract is adapted from Learning Conversations, which are based on research into learning conversations and self-organized learning developed by S. Harri-Augstein and L. F. Thomas (1991:24).

If **learning** "is the conversational construction, reconstruction and exchange of personally significant, relevant and viable meanings with awareness" (Harri-Augstein and Thomas, 1991:23), then **meaning** and **experience** inform our learning. Individuals learn something, take two steps forward, three back, and a few more forward. Although learning is an uncomfortable space until competence is developed, it is critical that learning is significant and relevant to the journey. It is helpful if the client embodies new learning personally and physiologically. It is about helping them to reconstruct their own thinking and feeling to gain perspective and become self-directed learners.

The conversation with your client centres on what is meaningful to them. If significance and relevance are to emerge from your coaching conversation with them, your conversation is going to be around what they need. It has nothing to do with what you need or think they need. What do they need to learn; what is significant and relevant to **them**? It doesn't matter what is relevant to you; it matters what is relevant to them. So, it is important to be aware of your own assumptions in the coaching conversation.

Three levels of intervention—behaviour, underlying drivers, root causes

This concept is introduced in the *CCL Handbook of Coaching* by Ting and Scisco (2006:19–21). The coaching framework of nested levels with which we worked above identified **doing, learning** and **being**. This framework can be adapted in another way for the coaching conversation. Instead of looking at **doing, learning** and **being/becoming,** we can look at **behaviour, underlying drivers** and **root causes**. It is important to be careful here due to the mistaken impression that coaching is therapy. Coaching is not therapy, although it can be therapeutic. Often when things go wrong it is due to poor practice on the part of the coach, perhaps from not setting proper boundaries (Ting and Scisco, 2006:19). The coaching waters deepen gradually, moving from the behavioural to the underlying drivers and root causes (Figure 3).

Behaviour

If we work at the level of behaviour, we look at observable actions: what the client says and does, what they don't say and do and their verbal and non-verbal language. Typically, the questions to ask are "what's working, what's not working, and what could you do or say differently?"

Sometimes behaviour is connected to difficult life experiences. Or, perhaps there is a family history of psychological disorders, such as addiction or chemical abuse. We need to differentiate between these behaviours and those associated with intrinsic drivers. This will be apparent through the ease and degree of consciousness with which these behaviours can be discussed.

Underlying drivers

If we work at the level of underlying drivers, we are looking at the client's personal style, orientation (introvert or extravert), culture, worldview, assumptions, values, beliefs, core needs and life experiences. Remember the two-stage exercise we did in Chapter 2? The question was "What is important to you about your professional and personal life?" You may spend the entire coaching journey helping clients to be aware of their underlying drivers and assumptions which impact on behaviour. It is at this level where it is useful to look at any assessment profiles your client has completed, which may identify conscious and unconscious thinking, feeling and behaviour.

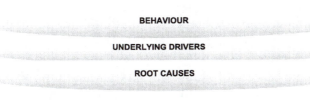

Figure 3. Levels of coaching intervention.

Source: Adapted from Ting and Scisco (2006:20).

Root causes

If we look at root causes, we begin to work with the client's life experiences, most often their experiences in the workplace. However, they may bring into the conversation traumas they have experienced. There may even be the presence of a psychological disorder, and it is therefore critical for a coach to know when to refer a client to a therapist. Ting and Scisco (2006:23) suggest a few guidelines: (a) when the client needs to delve into past life experiences, and (b) when the client needs to relive and heal past wounds. It is at the level of root causes that coach and client may start to identify repetitive patterns of behaviour that need to change for the client to be successful. For example, a history of losing one's temper, taking things personally, or creating conflict in the workplace.

A great way to start any coaching intervention is to ask the client to tell their life story. The coach begins to understand some of the client's current issues and presenting challenges, and begins to observe the client's patterns of thinking, feeling and behaviour. Because we work with Kolb's theory of "understanding experience in order to transform it into useable knowledge", this model helps us to determine the context in which the person is operating, where the individual and systemic problems may be occurring, and how the organizational values and culture impact on individuals and teams. It is at this level that the coach's ability to observe, challenge and ask appropriate questions can be most transformational.

Four-quadrant models (Hippocrates)

It is thought that the first quadrant model was Hippocrates' Model of the Four Humours. Although today medical science has moved on from the diagnostic aspect of Hippocrates' theory, his behavioural observations remain so relevant that many modern personality studies are based on Hippocrates' theory of the four humours: sanguines, cholerics, melancholics and phlegmatics (Stout Rostron, 2006c:A40–A41). The model equates the liquids in the body with the four seasons and four elements: black bile, earth and autumn represent melancholics; phlegm, water and winter represent phleg-matics; blood, air and spring represent sanguines; yellow bile, fire and summer represent cholerics. Before exploring other four-quad-rant models, it is useful to understand the model of the four humours (Figure 4).

In terms of temperament:

Cholerics: appear to be tough-minded natural leaders (choleric refers to the bile, which Hippocrates thought controlled anger). Chol-erics are known to have a short fuse and are referred to as A-types.

Sanguines: are outgoing, optimistic, high energy and fun-lov-ing (sanguine means blood and is related to optimism and high energy).

Phlegmatics: observe from the sidelines and tend to comply with other's demands (the term originates from bodily phlegm, which was thought to make a person steady, peaceful and passive). This profile is seen as the cool dude, very laid back.

Melancholics: like orderly lives and are prone to mood changes (melancholy represents black bile and melancholics therefore have a tendency to depression). Melancholics are considered to have depth of intelligence; this profile is sometimes noted as that of a typical artist.

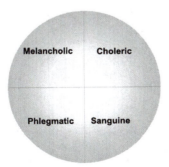

Figure 4. Hippocrates' four humours.

Source: Stout Rostron (2006c: A40–A41).

Insights four-colour model

The Insights model is based on the four colour quadrants of the Insights profile (blue, red, yellow and green). The four colours are used to represent "energies" that interact with the personality, and the subsequent archetypes (observer, reformer, director, motivator, inspirer, helper, supporter, coordinator) are an aid to understanding oneself (see Figure 5). The Insights profile is the result of extensive psychological research, particularly Jung's work on the personality. In 1921, Carl G. Jung published *Psychological Types,* and the Insights Discovery profile (with some similarities to MBTI®) is based on this aspect of Jung's work (Insights, 2008).

The colour energies on a good and a "not so good" day are:

UR Fiery red: Positive, affirmative, bold, assertive (Upper Right quadrant): (bossy, aggressive on a bad day).

LR Sunshine yellow: Cheerful, uplifting, spirited, buoyant (Lower Right quadrant): (idealistic, feet not on the ground, over-enthusiastic on a bad day).

LL Earth green: Still, tranquil, calming, soothing (Lower Left quadrant): (sickly sweet, needy on a bad day, over-sentimental, over-sensitive).

UL Cool blue: Showing no bias, objective, detached (Upper Left quadrant): (Lacking empathy and compassion on a bad day).

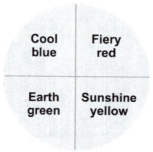

Figure 5. Insights Jungian model (circularity and quadernity).

Source: Stout Rostron (2006c: A40–A41).

We can also represent Hippocrates' model using the colours of the Insights framework (Figure 6):

Our system of knowledge and beliefs can be seen as a set of **paradigms**. In the coaching conversation, we are often looking to identify and shift disempowering paradigms. This profile looks at conscious and less conscious personas; **introversion** and **extraversion**: Jung's attitudes/orientations; **thinking** and **feeling**: Jung's rational functions; **sensing** and **intuition**: Jung's irrational functions. This profile identifies eight archetypes within the circle, and four energy colours in the over-laying quadrants (Figure 7). These archetypes and the profile itself is only one of many useful assessment tools, which can be used as an assessment tool at the beginning of a coaching intervention.

In this chapter, we explore coaching with models structured in a specific way. The four quadrant models are based on the Jungian Insights model, with "interior" on the left, i.e., what is not visible individually and collectively; and on the right, what is made visible through behaviour, i.e., what is external individually and collectively. In the Insights model above, the "thinking" function is in the top two quadrants (blue and red), the "feeling" function in the bottom two quadrants (green and yellow); the left-hand quadrants represent the interior, and the right-hand side the exterior of the individual and the collective.

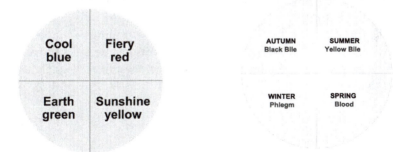

Figure 6. Hippocrates' quadrants with Insights colours.

Source: Adapted from Insights (2008) and Stout Rostron (2006c).

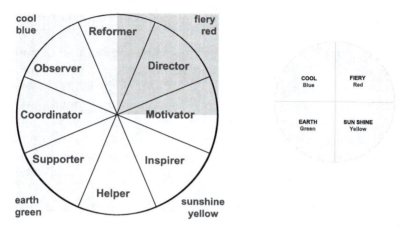

Figure 7. Insights Jungian model (circularity and quadernity) showing the eight primary Insights types.

Source: Adapted from Insights (2008) and Stout Rostron (2006c).

Domains of Competence model (Habermas)

Part of a coach's discipline is to be able to use and understand models to structure the coaching intervention, helping the client to develop self-awareness and to change behaviour. Habermas's Domains of Competence model (Figure 8) is a precursor to understanding Wilber's four-quadrant model. Habermas' model defines the "general structures of communication" that enable clients to engage in successful interaction (Wilber, 2000b:82–83). Habermas defined three domains of reality in the world that exist concurrently: I, We, It (see Flaherty, 2008 for an excellent detailing of Habermas' domains of competency). The right-hand drawing below is the original example in James Flaherty's *Coaching: Evoking Excellence in Others* (Flaherty, 1999:83). I have adapted it to a holistic model for our use on the left.

I: The domain of the individual

This domain relates to the subjective world of the individual who sees the world through their own eyes. Access to this domain is through self-observation and the development of self-knowledge.

Domains of Competence

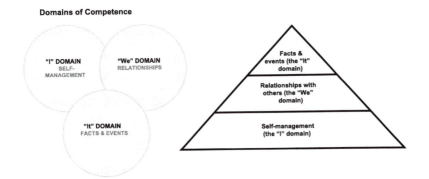

Figure 8. Habermas' Domains of Competence.

Source: Adapted from Weiss (2004) and Flaherty (1999).

The skills required are those of self-observation, self-knowledge, self-management, self-remembering, self-consistency and daring. The competences are purpose, self-knowledge, self-correction and persistence. The basis of this domain is subjective and the qualities are those of vision, passion, integrity, trust and curiosity.

We: The domain of the collective or the community

This is the collective view of how we see the world. This view is embodied in social practices, roles, rituals, meaning, narratives and values that determine what is possible. Access to this domain is through dialogue, conversation and relationships. The skills required to access this domain are listening, speaking, setting standards, learning and innovating (Braaten, 1991). The competences are relationship, communication, leadership and inspiration. The basis of this domain's reality is "subjective". The qualities of this reality are empathy, reliability, openness, and faith.

It: The domain of the external or objective world (Wilber, 1996)

This domain is that of science and technology, objective nature, empirical forms and processes. It deals with objects, and access to this domain is by becoming observant, analyzing, predicting and building models. The competences of this objective domain are processes, technology, measurement and statistics, and the qualities of this domain are rigour, objectivity, persistence, creativity and focus.

Ken Wilber's four-quadrant Integral Model

Ken Wilber has written prodigiously about the evolution of his model, and various adaptations of his Integral Model are taught in South African coach training institutions. Wilber's Integral Model is an elegant way to map the essentials of human growth and development—socially, psychologically and spiritually. Wilber integrates five factors essential to facilitating human growth which he calls **quadrants**, **levels**, **lines**, **states** and **types**. However, in this book, we are going to work only with his four quadrants, which

---

PRACTICAL EXERCISE

Our clients operate in all three of these domains, and we can devise questions in each to further client development. As an exercise, devise questions that you could ask, relevant to each domain. These questions are to help your clients understand the lens through which they see the world, and to help them begin to think about, experience and see the world through others' eyes. James Flaherty says this model represents the essential domains of life in which a "leader must be competent" (Weiss, 2004). Examples of possible questions:

I Domain: How can you continue your own self-development? What are your short-term and long-term goals? How can you balance both work and personal life? What are your blind spots and how can you work with them?

We Domain: How can you use your skills of communication and persuasion to inspire people to action? What is your value to the team? How can you build competence in the team having lost a valued member? What are the values and goals of your team?

It Domain: What are the processes that are working in the organization? What technical processes need to be written up for your training, learning and development manuals? What processes are not being strictly adhered to and how can you best apply them?

refer to the subjective and objective realities within each of us (Figure 9).

Wilber's (2006:17) philosophy is that "every level of interior consciousness is accompanied by a level of exterior physical complexity". In other words, the more consciousness we have in the interior, the greater our corresponding understanding of the complexities of the exterior world. If as coaches we are helping clients to learn from experience, then it is important that we understand the **I** (inside the individual), the **we** (inside the collective), the **it** (outside the individual), and the **its** (outside the collective) (Wilber, 2006:20–21).

My purpose is to help you design coaching questions that emerge within each of the quadrants, to develop your client's growing consciousness in their interaction with "self" and the "world". All four quadrants can show growth and development. Wilber explains that the unfolding four quadrants can "include expanding spheres of consciousness ... Self and culture and nature can all develop and evolve" (Wilber, 2006:25). All four quadrants need to be taken into account if we want to work as integrally as possible with our clients, helping them to integrate perspectives and awareness.

Initially, to use this as a coaching process, we can look at the types of questions you might ask clients within each quadrant to build perspective on themselves and their own issues. This is a very complex model

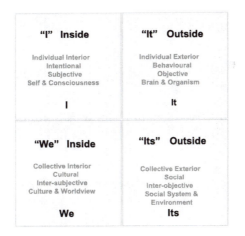

Figure 9. Ken Wilber's model.

Source: Wilber (2006:36–39).

and we are working with it in its formative stages. We can devise questions from a macro and a micro perspective, whether for contracting, for the overall coaching journey, or the individual coaching conversation. Try to devise your own questions before looking at the examples listed after the following descriptions for each quadrant (Figure 10).

Upper Left (UL)

I (UL) is inside the individual, i.e., self and consciousness; the individual's values, vision, their purpose, their culture, their norm. In this model, the upper left (UL) is **interior, individual** and **intentional**. The internal you is represented by your values, your beliefs, your morals, your feelings, your emotions, your self-confidence and self-assurance. The UL represents what goes on inside of you and is not visible to the external world.

Upper Right (UR)

It, the UR quadrant is described as **exterior, individual** and **behavioural**. The UR shows how your values, beliefs, feelings and emotions show up through your behaviour and interaction with others in the external world. It is outside the individual, i.e., to do with the

Figure 10. Ken Wilber's Integral Model.

Source: Adapted from Pampallis Paisley (2006).

body, brain and behaviour. This is how the individual shows up in their behaviour with another individual out in the world; it is their interpersonal skills, competences, what they say and do; what they don't say and do. Once this behaviour is visible, i.e., what you say and do, and what you don't say and do, this behaviour is represented in the upper right quadrant (UR).

Lower Left (LL)

We, the lower left, is **interior, collective** and **cultural. We** is inside the collective, i.e., culture and worldview of the organization or the society; the values, culture and beliefs of the team, organization, society, nation of which the individual is a part. This is represented by an awareness of your relationships with others, with the values and beliefs of the collectives in which you operate.

For example, your organization (superiors, subordinates, peers) or family, or within the communities of your spiritual life—these collectives all share similar values. Your organization may, for instance, be underpinned by family values or health or may be capitalising on consumer needs with which you are in alignment.

Lower Right (LR)

Its (LR) is outside the collective, i.e., the social system and its environment. This is represented by the systems, rules, regulations and procedures within the corporate environment and society within which the client works. The lower right quadrant (LR) is represented by the **exterior collective** and the **systems** within which you live and work, i.e., the rules, regulations, processes and procedures that operate within your family, society, workplace, region, nation and the world. The shared values and the shared relationships meet each other in harmony or conflict in this quadrant.

Teams or companies within the system are, for example, able to work collaboratively. Or on the other hand, due to gender inequalities, an organization may only pay lip service to the development of women in leadership, pulling candidates from training and development programmes without understanding the negative impact it might have on women wishing to move into management roles within that organization.

According to Wilber (1997), these four quadrants enable us to map every phenomenon, every interest, every area and every process in life according to internal and external processes. As coaches, we can use this model to help clients to understand themselves, developing self-awareness and a conscious awareness of their interior life. Coaches can also use this model to help clients understand the impact of their interactions with others in the external world, and the way they manage themselves and their relationships within the cultures and systems (family, community, organization, society and nation) within which they live and work.

CASE STUDY: HOW THE QUADRANTS ARE REPRESENTED —IN THE WORKPLACE

Recently, I have been working with an executive, Ben, in a retail manufacturing industry that has a history of success. Ben's divisional performance (LR) and his individual performance (UR) have always been rated as excellent. However, in the last two years, Ben has suffered an extreme loss of self-confidence and worrying health problems. This was due to working with a destructive line manager whose behaviour was extremely negative over a two-year period. This line manager undermined Ben constantly, shouting and humiliating Ben in meetings (LR), as well as displaying constant aggressive behaviour one-on-one (UR).

Eventually, the constant undermining of Ben began to impact negatively on his performance (UR). The work between coach and client (UR) has been to rebuild the confidence and self-esteem of this individual by increasing his levels of self-awareness (UL). The coach instituted a 360° feedback (LL) and discovered that Ben was highly thought of throughout the organization (LL). However, the organization was very concerned about Ben's mental and physical health (UL). Gradually, through a combination of one-on-one coaching conversations between coach and client with Ben and various senior executives to whom he reports (UR), and coaching conversations in the collective team (LR), Ben has begun the process of working on his confidence and his health by learning new interpersonal skills and competences (UR), developing greater self-awareness of his own and others' assumptions (UL).

Questions in the four quadrants

What are the questions we can ask in each of the four quadrants to use Wilber's model in the coaching process? Devise your own questions before looking at the examples below (Figure 11).

Upper Left (UL):   What is going on for you; how are you thinking and feeling?

Upper Right (UR): Where are you in relation to the other?

Lower Left (LL):   How would you describe the culture, values and relationships in your organization?

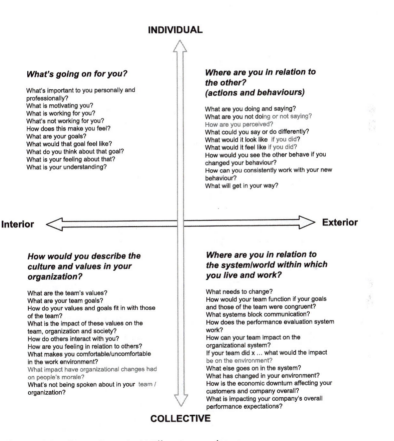

Figure 11. Questions in Wilber's quadrants.

Source: Questions devised by author to fit Wilber's four quadrants.

Lower Right (LR): Where are you in relation to the system/world in which you live and work?

CASE STUDY: HOW THE QUADRANTS ARE REPRESENTED
—IN SOCIETY

In May 2008 South Africa experienced a flood of violent, xenophobic behaviour. It had been brewing on the individual interior level (UL) for many years among individuals who felt discriminated against in society. As Jonathan Faull wrote in the Cape Times: "Many poor, urban citizens of South Africa's cities feel under- or unrepresented, buffeted by the tides of poverty, subsistence, criminality and the desperate competition for resources and opportunity ..." (Faull, 2008). In poorer areas, foreign nationals have grouped together by nationality to protect themselves and to continue to live within a semblance of a culture that they understand (LL). Locals, nationals and foreign nationals have managed to co-exist with each other with the odd external flare-up or demonstration of conflict at an individual level (UR) and between cultures (LR). The xenophobic attacks have been at a systemic level (LR): mobs and criminal gangs have instituted an array of violent attacks against poorer, isolated foreign nationals. The attackers' sense of frustration and discrimination shows up in the attacks on individuals (UR) and on groups of foreign nationals (LR). The sense of despair is due to a lack of jobs, housing and the continuing poverty within which many continue to live (LR).

EQ model

We can relate this model to the four quadrants of the EQ model. In the upper left is a developing self-awareness, which people do not see. That self-awareness shows up in your behaviour. In the upper right are your interactions with other individuals (self-management). In the lower left is your developing awareness of values, beliefs, feelings and culture (relationship awareness), and in the lower right, managing relationships at a systemic level (relationship management), i.e., how teams or companies interact within an organization, and how families work together in a family system.

The EQ (Emotional Intelligence) model developed by Daniel Goleman (1996) provides fuel for investigation inside the coaching conversation, usually starting with questions about self-awareness and self-management, moving at a later stage to develop relationship awareness and relationship skills (such as interpersonal communication, managing people, and handling conflict). I have overlaid the EQ model with the Insights and Ken Wilber's (2006) four quadrants (left side for intrinsic, right side for extrinsic; individual in the north, collective in the south) (Figure 12). This EQ model can represent the journey you and the client engage in together. The coach uses the EQ model to help the client learn how to manage themselves and relationships. The coaching journey begins with developing the self.

As clients develop **self-awareness**, they become more aware of what they say and do, and how they engage with others (**self-management**). As they begin to engage differently with others they gain an understanding and awareness of the culture, values and beliefs that exist within that organization, and the diverse relationships operating concurrently in teams (**relationship awareness**). As their awareness grows, they also become more aware of how the system operates, how teams cooperate with each other or not, and how units, divisions, staff, customers and stakeholders interact with each other (**relationship management**) (Table 1).

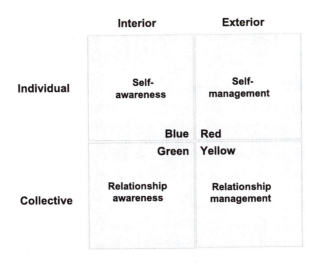

Figure 12. EQ model, a four-quadrant adaptation.

Source: Adapted from Goleman (1996), Wilber (2006) and Insights (2008).

Table 1. Emotional intelligence: competences and associated skill.

Self-awareness →	Self-management →	Relationship awareness → (Team awareness)	Relationship management → (Team management)
Knowing self	Interpersonal behaviour	Organizational culture (values, beliefs, feelings)	Team behaviour; Client management
Resistances	Communication skills	Environment	Conflict management
Purpose	Management skills	Politics	Systems integration

Source: Stout Rostron (2006c).

GROW and CLEAR models

John Whitmore (2002) developed the GROW model, which we explored in the previous chapter, as an excellent goal-setting process. GROW is confusing as it has been described as both a model and a question framework. It actually is a model which is useful to structure the coaching conversation, i.e., it is a metaphor for the growth which you hope your clients will experience in the overall coaching journey. It is a model representative of the process of that growth using a goal-setting framework of questions that hopefully leads to awareness, responsibility and change. GROW can be used as a goal-setting process: identifying a goal, discussing the client's current reality, exploring the client's options, and summarizing outcomes and what the client will actually do differently.

CLEAR as a model implies a contracting process, identifying the rigour of listening, exploring the client's issue at depth, asking questions throughout the coaching process, and finally reviewing where the client is at the end of the coaching conversation. In the previous chapter we explored the sequence of questions that can be thought about prior to the coaching conversation using CLEAR. However, the general rule with models, is that questions emerge during the conversation itself as they relate to the context, complexity and situation of the client.

Kolb's Experiential Learning Model

The coaching conversation is essentially reflecting on experience. Coach and client reflect the client's experience and behaviours, devising new thinking, feeling, behaviours and actions. Kolb says that learning is not just an active, self-directed process, but also a process where knowledge is created through the transformation of experience (Kolb, 1984:42). Sometimes you just cannot get the learning on your own, which is where the role of a coach or mentor comes in. The coaching conversation helps to transform their experience into workable knowledge; learning then becomes an "emergent experience" within a cycle of continuous learning.

Below is my adaptation from the original Kolb model, showing the learning modes and integrated learning styles. However, for the four-quadrant models we are practically working with in this book, I have positioned "thinking" in the top right and left quadrants; "feeling" in the bottom two quadrants; "interior/intrinsic" on the left, and "exterior/extrinsic" on the right. Thus, following Kolb's original model (Figure 13), is the version of Kolb's model to be used in the coaching process (Figure 14).

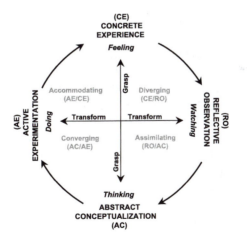

Figure 13. Kolb's original Experiential Learning Model.

Source: Adapted from Figure 3.1 in Kolb (1984:42).

Figure 14. Kolb's Adapted Experiential Learning Model.

Source: Stout Rostron (2006c).

Using Kolb's four modes of learning

This is a very useful coaching model, as all clients come into the coaching conversation with their concrete experiences. Coach and client reflect and observe, think and theorize based on the client's observations, and agree what new thinking, feeling and behaviour need to take place back in the working environment (Figure 15). If the client stays in doing, action and concrete experiencing (e.g., if we coach continuously without reflection, observation and evaluation) it would not be possible to gain new learning (for both coach and client). Many businesses get stuck because they create business plans, put them into action and complete them but do not take enough time out to review and evaluate. The integration of the quadrants into learning styles is explored in depth in Chapter 6 on diversity, culture and gender.

The basis of this learning process in coaching is to integrate the four adaptive modes of Kolb's learning model (concrete, abstract, reflective and conceptual). Kolb (1984:41) insists that knowledge is the result of "grasping of experience and transforming it into divergent, assimilative, convergent and accommodative knowledge". A further definition of the coaching conversation could be "an integration of reflection and thinking on action and experience". Kolb's definition of each of his experiential learning quadrants is particularly helpful:

CE (concrete experience) is about feeling and experiencing;

RO (reflective observation) is about observing and watching;

AC (abstract conceptualization) is about thinking and conceptualizing; and

AE (active experimentation) is about doing and being in action.

Kolb's model can be used to structure the coaching conversation and the coaching journey overall. We gain knowledge through our own experience; each individual filters their worldview through their own experience. In reflecting on our concrete experiences, we can transform experience into some kind of useable knowledge. Some people prefer to step into the experience itself; others prefer to watch, reflect and review; some like to conceptualize, hypothesize and theorize; others like to experiment with doing something new. All four work in conjunction with each other. Essentially, each one of us integrates all four learning modes, but we tend to have a preference for one or two.

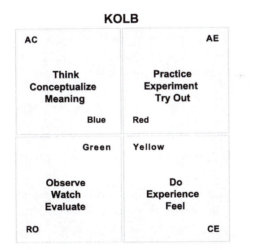

Figure 15. Coaching with Kolb's Experiential Learning Model.

Source: Stout Rostron (2006c).

What Kolb's four learning modes indicate

Concrete experiencers: adopt a receptive, experience-based approach to learning that relies heavily on feeling-based judgments. CE individuals tend to be empathetic and "people-oriented". They generally find theoretical approaches to be unhelpful and prefer to treat each situation as a unique case. They learn best from specific examples in which they can become involved. Individuals who emphasize concrete experience tend to be oriented more toward peers and less toward authority in their approach to learning. They benefit most from feedback and discussion with their coach and peers.

Reflective observers: adopt a tentative, impartial and reflective approach to learning. RO individuals rely heavily on careful observation in making judgments and prefer learning situations such as lectures that allow them to take the role of impartial objective observers. These individuals tend to be introverts and require a typically greater reflective approach to the coaching session. Coaching needs to be very reflective for them to access the learning needed to move forward.

Abstract conceptualizers: adopt an analytical, conceptual approach to learning that relies heavily on logical thinking and rational evaluation. AC individuals tend to be oriented more toward things and symbols and less toward other people. They learn in impersonal, authority-directed learning situations that emphasize theory and systematic analysis. They are often frustrated by, and benefit little from, unstructured "discovery" learning approaches, such as activities and role-plays. The coach needs to be able to provide a structured thinking approach to the session, and could use the Kolb model to help the client to access the other learning modes.

Active experimenters: adopt an active, "doing" orientation to learning that relies heavily on experimentation. AE individuals learn best when they can engage in such things as projects, homework, developing new techniques inside the coaching conversation that they can take back out to the workplace, and in group discussions. They dislike passive learning situations such as lectures, and tend to be extraverts. AE clients can be active and noisy and may require focused energy in the coaching environment.

Case study—Using Kolb's learning modes as a coaching process

In the case study below, the coach's comments are in italics; the clients are in standard type. The coach determined during a previous coaching session that it would be useful with this client (who was a coach) to work with a specific concrete "coaching" experience, as the client had had trouble using the Kolb process as a coaching model with his client.

The aim of the coaching conversation below was to help the coachee to understand how to use the four modes of the Kolb experiential learning process in a coaching session with his own clients. Having read the definitions of each learning mode and the following case study, think about how you can use this model in certain coaching situations.

What is your goal? To build my confidence in the coaching process and to pay attention to structure; and to do so I want to try to understand how to use the Kolb model as a coaching process.

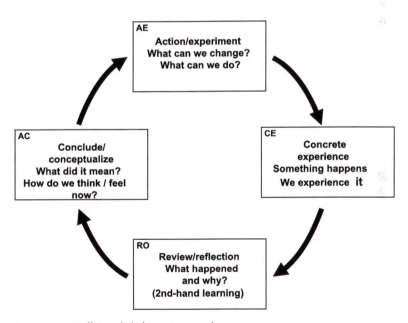

Figure 16. Kolb's adult learning cycle.

Source: Adapted from Kolb (1984:42).

OK, so would you like me to use the Kolb model for this conversation, and then we can reflect back at the end to understand how we moved through the four modes, from concrete experience, to reflective observation, abstract conceptualization and active experimentation? Yes, and would we always start with concrete experience?

Not always; it depends on what the client needs. You said that you have a specific experience that you wish to start with, so I am suggesting we begin with your specific concrete experience. Okay, let's go.

Concrete experience (CE)

Can you tell me a little more about this goal, sharing your experience so that I can understand the issue? I want to explore the triggers that prompt me to be too hasty when I am coaching. Usually, as I end the coaching conversation, I find that I have been very judgemental of the client, and I always rush to close. In other words, I make way too many assumptions. I want to understand what I can do to guard against rushing.

So tell me a little more about what happens that makes you rush in this coaching session. If you like, tell me a little about both your thoughts and feelings, as well as what you feel physically in your body as you coach. I feel helpless, frustrated, with a huge sense of urgency and anxiety that sits in my gut, yet I still feel that I need to get it done at a high level. And I start to concentrate more on what I am feeling and tend to stop focusing on my client. In other words, I am more aware of a sense of myself than I am of my client.

Anything else? It's useful to look at what you are thinking and feeling, whether it's anxiety or a sense of urgency. Looking at this one specific instance may be a really useful way for us to look at what happens, not just in this instance, but also when this has happened to you in previous coaching sessions. Yes, it's a similar experience in all of my coaching sessions. And one of my assumptions is that it's both a sense of urgency underpinned by some kind of anxiety about getting it done.

This is the second time you have spoken about your "assumptions". Yes. I think I'm making too many assumptions.

Can you remember any of the things you are assuming as you begin to feel that anxiety? Can you visualize or feel yourself back in that situation and describe how you are experiencing it? Yes, some of the assumptions are that I might not be able to help; that I should already know the answers; that this is too difficult already.

Ok, and what was your goal during the coaching session for yourself?
I want to complete the Kolb coaching process and give value to the client.

Reflective observation (RO)

So we've explored your experience a bit and identified some of the assumptions that may take your focus off of the client. Rather than sitting inside the experience as if it's happening now, let's look back at this experience as something you've experienced in the past. When you were in the coaching session, what triggered your assumptions? I cannot recall; only that **time** seemed to be one of the triggers.

So when time became a trigger, what kinds of things were you assuming? That I should jump in with answers for the client; that I should make suggestions about what they should do; and that perhaps I'm not the right person to do this; and also I sort of feel like they "need fixing". *When you got to the end of the session what did you assume?* That I hadn't completed stuff and that I hadn't really acknowledged them, or something about them.

So, as we reflect on this, it seems that you actually had some clarity on your own thinking and feeling which can be useful for us to learn from. Is there anything else about your assumptions that got in your way? Just that I spend so much time thinking about my own thoughts that I am not listening effectively to the client.

And what would you prefer to do? I want to focus on the client. I want to let go of my thoughts.

Okay, so what can we learn from this that will help you learn next time? I think that I need to find a way to centre and focus before I start the coaching conversation, so that I am entirely focused on them throughout.

You spoke earlier about having your attention in several areas at once, identified as the three streams of attention described in Nancy Kline's Thinking Environment® [Kline, 1999/2004].

I would like to do that; be focused on them, know what my responses are and still create an environment conducive to coaching.

If you are able to do that, will you experience the coaching conversation differently from your current experience? Yes, I will feel that I can add value to the client, which is what I want. And I feel that this process may be perfect for me to use.

What do you mean by perfect? I think it is structured yet has flexibility, and I think I can trust the process.

And so if you were to have faith in this process, how would that help you? I would calm down, and let go of my anxiety and that sense of urgency. Anything else, now that we are reflecting? What else do you think you need to learn from this specific experience? I think it's about self-balance.

Can I just check that I understand what you mean by "self-balance"? For me, self-balance forges self-respect and respect for others.

So self-balance in the coaching relationship is self-balance for the coach as well as self-balance for the client? What I'm going to suggest is that we move from reflection on this specific conversation to think about and conceptualize what the conversation may look and feel like if there is self-balance for both coach and client? Great, I'm happy with that. I think that if I have dealt with some of the assumptions that we have discovered then that will help, but also I need to feel centred and balanced before entering into the conversation.

Okay, shall we explore and perhaps transform or overturn some of these disempowering assumptions before moving on? Yes, please ...

[Coach and client identify the key limiting assumptions, and the coach helps the client to identify if they are true or false, identifying several more empowering assumptions and constructive ways of thinking. They then move into the next phase, continuing to use the Kolb experiential learning process.]

Abstract conceptualization (AC)

Do you mean, noticing and observing what you think and feel, and letting go of assumptions that might disempower both you and the client? Yes, I need to focus on the client, knowing that if I just listen that that in itself is empowering and gives some space for thinking together.

So, you want to refocus and give attention back to the client. What else? I need to find some way to ... create a sense of groundedness, like being rooted but still flexible.

Some of the language you use is sometimes reflective of NLP [neurolinguistic programming—see Chapter 2 for a discussion of this approach]. *So I wonder if it is "anchoring" you are thinking of?* Yes, I need some sort of physical anchor to move me out of my head to be able to create a focus on listening and being present for the client at all times. That will help me shift some of these assumptions. Can you help me with that?

Sure, tell me what would work best as an anchor for you? A question, a thought, something you do physically with your hands? That would be the simplest and not distract the client.

In other words, you need to use something physical and tangible to take the focus off your own disempowering thinking? Yes, that would be perfect. I don't want to get up and pace up and down as that would be distracting. I want to do something that calms both my mind and my body.

Okay, so that would help you to refocus; sounds useful. [Coach and client agree on the anchor, and the coach helps the client to create an anchor that will work in every coaching conversation to create focus. "The process of anchoring involves linking a specific sight, sound or touch with an experience that is present. For example, a situation in which you are associated. This process enables you to use the anchor to re-access the same experience" (McLoughlin and Stout Rostron, 2002:48)]. *Anything else that would help you to refocus on the client?* No, that is perfect.

Do you think that this one gesture will be enough to help you anchor and refocus on the client? Yes.

OK, so in the coaching conversation, this will help to manage self-balance; what else would be useful to think about in terms of self-balance for the client? Well, actually it was an assumption to think the client needs self-balance. It's actually me who needs it, so I think this is a start!

What else might be valuable—to think about how you use your self-balance and refocus back on the client? I don't know.

It's a tough one. My observation is that if this has happened once it may happen again. So in what way could you work going forward? It's something about being present for the client in the way I frame questions and reflect back what they are saying. If I am "anchored" I will easily be able to do it because I know that I have done it before.

Great, so essentially to refocus and give attention you would need to fire your anchor. In the same way, if self-balance continues to come up, will the other reflective practices that you have prepared help you? Definitely, and this is how I will use them ...

Anything else that when you conceptualize the coaching conversation would be helpful to you? Yes, I will ...

Anything else that would be helpful for you to focus on the client?

Active experimentation (AE)

Ok, so we've been working on conceptualizing and moving away from your disempowering thinking. Shall we think about how you actually could do it differently, and think differently, when coaching? Yes, let's try it.

So now we will actively think about how you would do it. Let's start by thinking about how you would have done the old conversation differently ... I would be so focused on the client that I am hearing what she has to say, and I am actually thinking about where we are in the process, in terms of structure, in the coaching conversation.

Can you think of something coming up to think about how you would do it differently? Yes, in fact I am going to practice this at home first, focusing on the kids as they tell me about their school day. I'm going to fire my anchor and listen to my wife. Usually I just interrupt and don't let any of them finish what they have to say. I guess I'm fixing them too! I think it's a practice that I have to begin at home in order to make it something that begins to come naturally.

That sounds great—it's always hardest to do any kind of new thinking and behaviour at home. Also, I think I need to use my anchor to put on the "pause button". In other words, I need to pause before I say anything. This is something I need to experiment with.

Pushing the pause button sounds like a great anchor. How will you reflect how effectively you are in pressing the pause button? Perhaps I should make a few notes ...

Would you like to write down some of these new active practices, and in our next session, we can reflect on what has worked for you? These are useful new practices. [Client makes notes]. *Is there anything else you would like to accomplish to actively experiment with doing something differently?* No, I think this will do and I am already developing some awareness of myself that will help with self-balance. I think actually that I may keep a small journal at the end of the day that will help me to adopt these practices. I have several coaching sessions with new clients before I see you again, and I will reflect on what's worked and what hasn't when I see you next.

Fine, anything else that comes to mind that would be useful going out into the world and doing it differently? No, I like this process and just want to reflect a few minutes on how we went through the four modes of the Kolb process, and how I might use it and my anchors in my next coaching session. If we could do that, then I think I'm all set. Thanks.

Great, let's finish with that. Okay, let me think it through with you. We seem to have stepped into the "concrete experience" itself when you asked me to think about how I felt, what I was thinking, and what I was assuming in that one specific coaching conversation with my client. We then moved into a reflective space, as I reflected on those thoughts, feelings and assumptions and we thought about what I had learned from that session in reflection. We then talked about the coaching conversation in a kind of thinking manner, i.e., we conceptualized a different way forward, and in fact we moved into active experimentation as we developed anchors. So, in fact, we already have begun to experiment. Then we worked with anchors and talked about how pause buttons can best be put to use at home and in my next coaching session. I have an action plan and will report back on how I do in our next session. I think it's about more self-awareness, focusing on the client, and thinking about new behaviours as I am beginning to think and feel differently.

Is there anything else you need from this conversation? No thanks.

Can I ask what you gained from working with this process? I think that I understand the Kolb model better, particularly the conceptualization stage, and I feel quite comfortable to try it in a coaching session for myself.

Reflecting on the case study

In the above coaching conversation, the coach first helped the client determine his goals for the session, and structured the conversation using the Kolb model. The coach made sure that she constantly clarified the way forward with the client, not moving before he was ready. Furthermore, she tried to mostly use the client's words. Once or twice she reframed what the client had said to check whether she had understanding. The coach referred to thinking, feeling and assumptions right through the conversation, having picked that up from the client. And, to end the conversation, the client reviewed the cycle, reiterating the **experience**, what was **reflected**, what the new **concept** was to work differently in the coaching conversation, and how they **experimented** with a way forward. Using this model, the coach was able to help the client articulate how he experiences the world, and where his levels of discomfort were in the coaching process. The coach also confirmed that NLP was part of his experience before they worked to develop new anchors; previously, disempowering assumptions were his anchors. In all of these ways, the coach was able to safely create an environment to use the Kolb model, which the client wished to learn as a coaching structure. Finally, the coach moved from the specific situation to create anchors and an understanding of how to use the Kolb model in a coaching situation i.e., she moved from the specific to the general.

Hudson's Renewal Cycle model

Frederick Hudson's (1998:79) model is useful in order to understand an adult's experience of life and change. Hudson's renewal cycle can be used to structure the coaching conversation and the overall journey. I have placed Hudson's four quadrants where they are most aligned with the Insights four colours (Figure 17). The quadrants integrate relatively well with the Insights four colours: yellow for "getting ready" to go back into the world, red for actively "going for it", blue for the "doldrums" and green for "cocooning". Often

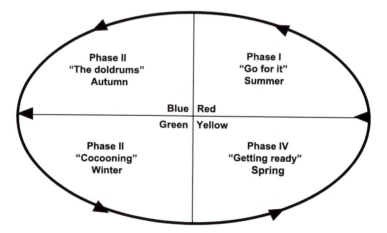

Figure 17. Hudson's four stages.

Source: Adapted from Hudson (1999:106) and Insights (2008).

when you overlay one model over another, it is not always a perfect match.

As a coaching model, the coach can start wherever is most useful for the client, and in whatever sequence is needed (Stout Rostron, 2006c):

1. **Go for it (summer)**—In phase one, the individual is purposeful, active, busy, committed, optimistic, and energized as a team player.
2. **Doldrums (autumn)**—In phase two, the individual is bored, restless or feeling stuck, reactive, in denial, angry, sad, pessimistic, low in energy, a loner, and resistant to change.
3. **Cocooning (winter)**—In phase three, the individual is turned inward, meditative, experimenting, exploring, disorientated, healing, quiet, deconstructing and reconstructing the self, tapping into core values, tapping resilient emotions, spiritual, and doing inner work.
4. **Getting ready (spring)**—In phase four, the individual senses a new purpose, searching, networking; this phase is creative, free and uncommitted, naively optimistic, recovering perhaps forgotten childlike and spontaneous abilities.

We can create an analogy for each of these phases with the seasons of the year. As in autumn, the client is in the **doldrums**, in the dark and resistant to change. **Cocooning** is like winter, where the client is deconstructing, reconstructing, doing some inner work, meditative. **Getting ready** is like spring, and the client is seeking new purpose, searching, maybe looking for that new job, the inner child is at work. **The going for it** phase is like summer, where the client is busy with a new sense of purpose, committed and optimistic and energized.

CASE STUDY: USING HUDSON'S MODEL FOR COACHING

The doldrums

A young woman who wanted to change careers, Shannon, came to me for coaching. Shannon wanted to work with someone who could understand the passion she had for her AIDS NGO work, and she wanted someone to help her think through the next steps to develop her career. Although qualified as a law-yer, Shannon was working in marketing and promotions rather than on the legal side. She was in the doldrums, working about 12 hours a day, exhausted, not feeling that she was working at a senior enough position to make a difference. She was highly committed to the work she was doing. In some ways, I was also a mentor for her. One aspect of a mentor's job is to introduce the client to their own network to help the client to build alliances and relationships. This moves them the next step in their career. In our first session, we talked about the doldrums, which is how she described her current thinking and feeling, and what was different to when she first began her work in this NGO.

Cocooning
In our next few sessions, we talked about her need to do a bit of **cocooning**, to sit back and reflect, using the coaching sessions as a space to do so. We agreed she would **cocoon** as long as it took. We thought about the following questions:

- What do I really want to do?
- Shall I stay or leave my job?
- Do I want to leave South Africa to pursue my studies?
- Would that be the right thing to do?
- Can I grow my skills and education by staying in South Africa?

Eventually Shannon realized she thought she was ready to begin to think about making a move from her current job, but she was not yet willing to leave the projects in which she was immersed.

Getting ready
We met a few times, and gradually she began to articulate a possible way forward. As we moved into the **getting ready** phase, she looked at her options and decided that she would first begin to build her network, and create relationships that could open doors for her. She attended a few courses, including a master class in the Thinking Environment® with Nancy Kline, and participated in several business breakfasts on Leadership Skills for Women. She made contact with the two NGOs with whom I had contact, searching for opportunities to continue her education by studying and working abroad. She was clear that her ultimate aim was to return to South Africa with new skills that could be applied to the AIDS organizations. I knew two people in the NGO world who

were potential employers. Shannon met with these two international NGOs who had offices in South Africa although their head
offices were in the States.

After a period of about six months, Shannon thought she was
ready to move into action. This would normally be the **go for it**
phase. However, was she ready to go for it? She applied for a
scholarship to study further at Georgetown University in Washington DC. When she was accepted, her words were, "I don't
understand why I am not jumping for joy. It is an incredible
opportunity, I am going to get a visa for four years. I am going
to study in the States. I am going to have a research job. What is
wrong with me? It's right there." The question always worth asking is, "What does the client need now?" Here she was ready for
a change but, although a marvellous opportunity was within her
grasp she could not understand why she didn't just "go for it".

Going for it
We talked about what she needed in order to get back into action.
She decided to stick with her current NGO job. There were projects
still to complete before she could move out of the country and
take up the scholarship. She felt she could not let her colleagues
down by not implementing her current programmes. In this way,
she revitalized her passion for her current job. We discussed ways
to create boundaries to manage her working hours. In speaking
to her several months later, I learned that she was on track to take
up the scholarship the following year. Her intention was to return
to South Africa when she was qualified, looking then to accept a
new and more empowering role.

Other circular models

I-T-O (Input, Throughput, Output)

Models in coaching are very useful to us as a way to structure the
entire coaching intervention, and the individual coaching conversation. However, all models must provide flexibility, not rigidity. The
following model is an open systems model developed for change management by Thomas G. Cummings and Christopher G. Worley (2004).
It is used by i-Coach Academy, Middlesex University, London and is

taught in their Masters in Coaching degree in the UK, USA and South Africa. This model can easily be used to structure the coaching conversation, or to structure the overall coaching intervention (Figure 18).

Input (Why)

As a coach (and for the client), where do you come from and what are you **informed** by? This is the **input** part of the coach's framework, the **why** (i.e., why you're working together as coach and client). It assumes the "input" or beginning stage of the coaching conversation between coach and client. Input is what informs you as a coach, the underlying theories you are working with, your experience and expertise, your philosophy and values, and the constructs that underpin your worldview. Questions you might ask the client in the input stage are:

- What is on the menu for our conversation today?
- What do you want to think about?
- What are your key issues or challenges?
- What are your priorities?

Throughput (How/What)

The **process** the coach uses in the coaching conversation is the **throughput** of the coaching framework. It is the **how**, in other words, what the coach actually does in the coaching conversation. This second stage, throughput, is represented by the tools, techniques, models, processes, mechanics and systems the coach brings into the coaching conversation. Typical questions you could ask may be:

Figure 18. Input, Throughput, Output.

Source: Cummings and Worley (2004).

- What are your observations about your thinking?
- What are your questions about your thinking?
- What can you learn from your thinking?
- What are you assuming that is stopping you/limiting you/ holding you back?
- What makes that stop you?

Output (What for/purpose)

The third stage is the purpose (**what for**) in the coaching process and relates to the client's **outcomes**. **Output** represents the actions, goals, results and measurements expected from the coaching conversation, including an outline of what the client has learned, will do differently and goals set.

Output is represented by the results, objectives and outputs which the client gains from the coaching conversation. It is represented by the client arriving at their desired outcome. Output relates to where the client is going, how results can be measured and what has changed as a result of the coaching. Typical questions might be:

- What action are you now going to take?
- What has changed in your overall vision, strategy and goals?
- What is the overall learning this session?
- What will you do differently as a result of today?

Contracting with I-T-O

To contract the overall journey, coach and client discuss what each brings to the relationship, and the overall aim of coaching for the client (**input**). Coach and client then discuss how the coaching will take place: timing, boundaries, fees and the tools and techniques to be used by the coach, and the way the client would prefer to work (**throughput**). They also discuss the overall results and outcomes the client hopes to achieve from the coaching intervention, results that need to be visible to the organization, and thinking, feeling and behaviour that the client would like to change (**output**).

As a rule, when using this model, I start the coaching conversation with **input**: "Where are you now?" "Where do you want to get to by the end of this conversation?" "What do you want to talk about?" "What's on the menu for today?" Once we have identified what needs to be worked on, I move into throughput: using whichever question frameworks, tools or techniques are relevant to the process. For **output**, we summarize actions, learning and outcomes from the conversation.

CASE STUDY: I-T-O

Input

With one of my current executive clients, Rosalyn, coach and client chatted for an hour about where Rosalyn was in her personal and professional life. She felt that she was somewhat chaotic in her approach to her new position as Director of Transformation for her organization. After an hour's thinking, she identified her goal for the coaching session: "I'd like to create a transformation workshop that can be facilitated throughout the entire organization. So, I need to do some thinking around how I can do it and who can do it for me, and whether I should subcontract you, another external consultant, or facilitate myself. I'm thinking about creating a series of national transformation workshops. What do you think?" Coach and client agreed to work on an outline for the workshop as a start.

Throughput

The coach asked the questions that would help Rosalyn to think through a framework for the one-day programme. Coach and client identified the assumptions that were stopping Rosalyn from thinking she was the person to facilitate the transformational workshops. We discussed who might be the facilitator, and it emerged that she was the right person: she had the relevant skills, organizational knowledge, experience and an understanding of diversity and empowerment in South Africa. She also had a better understanding of organizational culture than an external consultant might have. We agreed that, as her coach, it was more constructive for her if I simply helped her to design the programme.

Output

To conclude, we reflected on what she had gained from the session. She concluded that she felt empowered to be both designer

---

and facilitator for the pilot session with the board. She decided to think during our next session about how to develop other facilitators for the process. She wanted to be the trainer of the facilitators. She also decided to put forward a proposal for a deputy who would help her with administration and policy-making. She came to the conclusion that transformation needed to start at the top, otherwise the complexity of transformation would not be fully embraced. We summarized her action steps, finished the outline for the programme, and explored how she could present her ideas to the board.

The U-process

The U-process is sometimes known as the process of transition, while many have also experienced it as similar to Kübler-Ross's cycle of grieving, or as a mid-range change theory. Kübler-Ross's stages of death and dying are denial and isolation, anger, bargaining, depression and acceptance. This stage theory has been controversial, primarily because the theory denies the individuality of human beings and other needs of the dying, such as having some control in their own treatment and destiny, the role of culture, religion, personality, family dynamics and so on (Gorle, 2002). Although the staging theory has experienced limitations in its interpretation, in the coaching field this U-process is more typically represented in Scharmer's U-process.

Scharmer's U-process

In the process of transition, the client can move from anxiety, through happiness, fear, threat, guilt, denial, disillusionment, depression, gradual acceptance and hostility to moving forward.

The change process

The U-process is considered a mid-range change theory with a sense of an emerging future. Scharmer's process moves the client through different levels of perception and change, with differing levels of action which follow. The three main elements are sensing, presencing and realizing. These represent the three basic aspects of the U (Figure 19).

Sensing
observe, observe, observe
become one with the world

Realizing
act swiftly with the
natural flow

Presencing
retreat and reflect
allow the inner knowing to emerge

Figure 19. Scharmer's U-Process Model.

Source: Adapted from Senge, Scharmer, Jaworski and Flowers (2005:88).

This process helps the client to work at different levels of perception and change, and allows different levels of actions to follow. All three are extensions of the learning process. As the coach and client move into the U, **sensing** is about observing and becoming one with the world; **presencing,** moving to the bottom of the U, is about retreating and reflecting and allowing an inner knowing to emerge, and **realizing** as you move out of the "U", is about acting swiftly and with a natural flow from the knowledge and understanding that has emerged.

The U-theory suggests co-creation between the individual and the collective—i.e., the larger world. It is about the interconnection or integration of the self with the world. At the bottom of the U, as described by Scharmer, is the "inner gate" where we drop the baggage of our journey, going through a threshold. The metaphor used here is that of "death of the old self", and "rebirth of the new self", the client emerges with a different sense of self. On the Web is a lovely dialogue between Wilber and Scharmer where they discuss the seven states and the three movements in this one process (Scharmer, 2003).

Superficial learning and change processes are shorter versions of the U-movement. In using this as a coaching process, the client moves downwards into the base of the U, moving from acting, to thinking, to feeling, to will. This is to help the client to download with the coach, to let go and discover who they really are, to see from the deepest part of themselves, developing an awareness that is expanded with a shift in intention.

Otto Scharmer, in an executive summary of his new book, *Theory U: Leading From the Future as it Emerges,* describes the U-process as

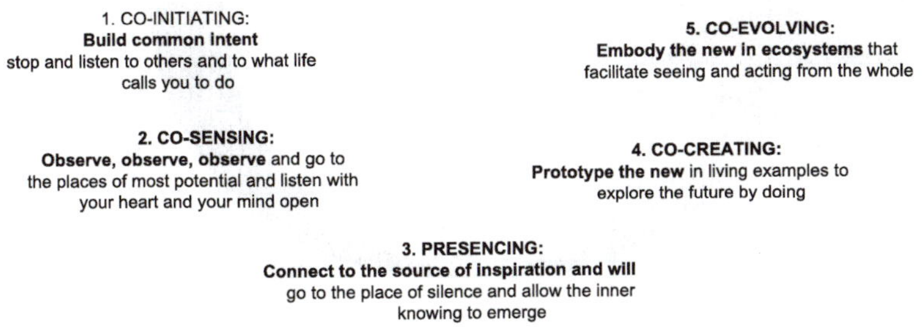

1. CO-INITIATING:
Build common intent
stop and listen to others and to what life
calls you to do

5. CO-EVOLVING:
Embody the new in ecosystems that
facilitate seeing and acting from the whole

2. CO-SENSING:
Observe, observe, observe and go to
the places of most potential and listen with
your heart and your mind open

4. CO-CREATING:
Prototype the new in living examples to
explore the future by doing

3. PRESENCING:
Connect to the source of inspiration and will
go to the place of silence and allow the inner
knowing to emerge

Figure 20. U-process case study.

Source: Scharmer (2007:6).

five movements: co-initiating, co-sensing, presencing, co-creating and co-evolving (Scharmer, 2007:5–8). Scharmer describes this as moving "first into intimate connection with the world and to a place of inner knowing that can emerge from within, followed by bringing forth the new, which entails discovering the future by doing" (Scharmer, 2007:6). The following case study demonstrates the five-step process.

Case study: The Global Convention on Coaching (GCC)

From July 2007 until July 2008, Marti and I took part in the Global Convention on Coaching. I was chairperson of the GCC's Working Group on a Research Agenda for Development of the Field, and Marti participated in the Working Group dialogue process. The GCC was originally established to create a collaborative dialogue for all stakeholders in coaching worldwide, with the ultimate aim of professionalizing the industry. Nine initial working groups were formed by the GCC's Steering Committee to discuss critical issues related to the professionalization of coaching, producing "white papers" on the current realities and possible future scenarios of these issues. These white papers were presented at the GCC's Dublin convention in July 2008. This case study summarizes the working group process of the research agenda, which comprised a 12-month online dialogue process, with the addition of monthly telephone conversations, during 2007–2008. The white papers for all nine working groups (plus the new tenth group, Coaching and Society) are available at www.coachingconvention.org.

1. Co-initiation

Co-initiating is about building common intent, stopping and listening to others and to what life calls you to do. In the Working Group for the Research Agenda, the group built common intent by first setting up the group, defining their purpose and beginning to discuss the process that they wanted to use for their dialogue. It was agreed that the chairperson and facilitator would invite specific individuals to join the Working Group, and those members would suggest other individuals who might have a key interest in the research agenda for the field (i.e., the emerging coaching profession). The group began their online dialogue, once all had accepted the invitation and received instructions on how to use the online GCC web forum. It was agreed that there would be three communities working together: the Working Group and the Consultative Body for the Research Agenda, and the Steering Committee who were responsible for the leadership and management of the other groups.

2. Co-sensing

Observe, Observe, Observe. Go to the places of most potential and listen with your mind and heart wide open. The chairperson and the facilitator of the Working Group had to learn to co-facilitate, observing each other's skill and competence. They had to be willing to listen to each other, observing each other's style in facilitating an online dialogue. They needed to create the group, and to facilitate the way forward with the group, learning to take constructive criticism and appreciation from each other, guiding the group forward without being prescriptive. Both chairperson and facilitator agreed to co-chair the process, remaining mentally and emotionally open to each other's divergent opinions, ways of being and styles of interpersonal communication, whether working with the group online or by phone.

3. Presencing

Connect to the source of inspiration, and will. Go to the place of silence and allow the inner knowing to emerge. Each individual in the process read, reflected and regularly added their thoughts and feelings to the online forum. Debate, conflict and agreement emerged—with chair and facilitator taking responsibility to keep the group on track without being prescriptive. The chair and facilitator had to connect, each one to their own individual source of inspiration and to bring that together as one voice to guide the group.

4. Co-creating

Prototype the new. In living examples to explore the future by doing. This entailed harnessing the energy of the Working Group to draft a current reality document of their online and tele-conference dialogue; this document was revised four times. They brought in a facilitator for the Consultative Body who entered the Consultative Body dialogue at stage 1 (co-initiating), but entered the Working Group dialogue at stage 3 (presencing). Trying to move forward with their own Working Group process, yet move the Consultative Body from stage 1 to stage 2 (co-initiation to co-sensing) was a complex, parallel process. The chairperson and facilitator enlisted the help of a copywriter and editor to manage the writing process of the white paper during the Working Group's co-creation (or stage 4).

5. Co-evolving

Embody the new in ecosystems that facilitate seeing and acting from the whole. The final stage of the process was the physical gathering at the Dublin convention. This took place in three stages: pre-convention, during the convention and post-convention (post-convention work has just begun). Several months prior to the convention, all nine working groups began to work together online and by telephone to share their own varied stages in the U-process; in this way they learned from each other as they gathered momentum moving towards Dublin which was to be the culmination of their year-long project. Some groups had lost participants during the 12 months through disagreement; others managed to harness the energy to move through each of the stages together. The three processes were:

- **Pre-convention**: Preparation for the presentation of a white paper by nine committees; this was for their committee's current global reality and future possible scenarios for their topic, with the addition of a tenth committee four months prior to Dublin.
- **Convention**: Physical presence, dialogue and debate in Dublin with each of the working groups. This was paralleled with virtual online

feedback on a daily basis from those not able to attend the convention (however, there were difficulties with this process which frustrated some who could not access the virtual dialogue during that week).

- **Post-convention**: Continuation of the process with a new format. The work to take place in diverse groups regionally and nation-wide, to proceed to the next step building the emerging profession of coaching. Post-convention, a Transitional Steering Group (TSG) has begun work to harness the energy of those wishing to continue. The new GCC sees its role as an organic one, continuing to facilitate a global dialogue, rather than forming another coaching organization. The GCC Transitional Steering Group (TSG), with representatives from the USA, UK, Australia Argentina, Singapore and South Africa, have designed a web-based networking platform for the 17 000 GCC members who have signed up to the *Dublin Declaration on Coaching* (GCC, 2008 g). (Those wishing to take part in this ongoing worldwide dialogue can access it via the web on gccweb.ning.com.)

This U-process is applicable to large innovation projects where the unfolding takes place over a long time; a year in this instance. The team composition in such projects as this will change and adapt to some degree after each movement: in the GCC process the working group for the Research Agenda had lost and added new members, whereas the consultative body was a looser entity with only certain members playing a strong role. This was a process of discovery, exploring the future by doing, thinking and reflecting. As Scharmer explains, it facilitates an opening. Facilitating an opening process involves "the tuning of three instruments: the open mind, the open heart, and the open will" (Scharmer, 2007:8–9).

At any one time there were three U-process journeys taking place for the Research Agenda: within the working group, the working group interacting with the consultative body, and the working group interacting with the steering committee.

In conclusion

Coach practitioners have a great deal of flexibility when working with coaching models. In this book, we work from an experiential learning premise because the client always brings their experience into the coaching conversation. The client's experience is underpinned by a range of factors, including culture, education, life experience and personality.

This chapter has explored a few models that hang on a framework of circularity, quadernity and the U-shape. As it is not possible to work with every coaching model available in the marketplace, we have not delved into Maslow's triangular model, Beck and Cowen's spiral dynamics model, Ned Herrmann's four-quadrant, wholebrain business model, or Will McWhinney's Paths of Change model. I leave those for you to explore, and hope that you have gained a sense of the flexibility models can offer the coach practitioner, as well as the elasticity in overlaying one over another. Simplicity is the prerequisite.

I hope that this chapter has introduced some new learning and the curiosity to experiment with new structures within your coaching conversations. It may be that you add one or two of these models into your coach's toolkit; or that you register for a coach training programme to learn to work with a new model for your own continuing professional development.

Coach's library

Cummings, T. G., and Worley, C. G. (2004). *Organization Development and Change*. Mason, OH: South-Western College Publishing.

Flaherty, J. (2008). *Detail of: Habermas' Domains of Competency*. Webpage: coaching.gc.ca/documents/coaching_essential_competences_for_leaders_e.asp.

Goleman, D. (1996). *Emotional Intelligence*. London: Bloomsbury.

Harri-Augstein, S., and Thomas, L. F. (1991). *Learning Conversations, Self-Organised Learning: The Way to Personal and Organizational Growth*. London: Routledge.

Hudson, F. M. (1999). *The Handbook of Coaching: A Comprehensive Resource Guide for Managers, Executives, Consultants, and Human Resource Professionals*. San Francisco, CA: Jossey-Bass.

Insights (2008). *Insights Model*. Webpage: www.insights.co.uk.

Kline, N. (1999/2004). *Time to Think: Listening with the Human Mind*. London: Ward Lock.

Kolb, D. A. (1984). *Experiential Learning: Experience as the Source of Learning and Development*. Upper Saddle River, NJ: Prentice Hall.

Lane, D. A., and Corrie, S. (2006). *The Modern Scientist-Practitioner: A Guide to Practice in Psychology*. Hove: Routledge.

Scharmer, C. O. (2007). *Addressing the Blind Spot of Our Time: An Executive Summary of the New Book by Otto Scharmer: Theory U: Leading from the Future as it Emerges*. Theoryu.com. Webpage: www.theoryu.com/execsummary.html.

Senge, P., Scharmer, C. O., Jaworski, J., and Flowers, B. S. (2005). *Presence: Exploring Profound Change in People, Organizations and Society*. London: Nicholas Brealey.

Ting, S., and Scisco, P. (2006). *The CCL Handbook of Coaching: A Guide for the Leader Coach*. San Francisco, CA: Jossey-Bass.

Weiss, P. (2004). *The Three Levels of Coaching*. San Francisco, CA: An Appropriate Response. Webpage: www.newventureswest.com/three_levels.pdf.

Wilber, K. (2000a). *A Theory of Everything: An Integral Vision for Business, Politics, Science and Spirituality*. Dublin: Gateway.

CHAPTER SIX

Diversity, culture and gender

by Sunny Stout Rostron, Marti Janse van Rensburg and Daniel Marques Sampaio

- Marti Janse van Rensburg writes
  - Background and similarities
  - Race
  - Gender
  - Communication styles
  - Language and linguistic patterns
  - Religion
- Cultural differences in the workplace
  - Individualism versus collectivism
  - Context
- Bringing it all together
- Coach's library

This is a general introduction to a vital subject with which all business coaches need to get to grips. It is neither an academic assessment nor designed for those who are already experts in the field. This is for the general practitioners who need to reflect on their own levels of awareness and their personal approach to diversity, culture and gender differences.

Today we all coach within diversity, and our clients operate in diverse environments. People assume "diversity" is only about gender or race, but diversity is both about the differences and the similarities between individuals and groups. Any form of power exacerbates difference and influences how we perceive and react to behaviour. This is true in any area of life, and nowhere more so than in the business context, specifically due to the hierarchical nature of organizational systems.

In the business environment, the coach needs to become aware of and manage their own responses to questions of diversity, before they can begin to coach a client on similar issues. This chapter focuses on raising the business coach's awareness of these crucial diversity issues, both within themselves and within their individual and organizational clients.

In this chapter Sunny Stout Rostron introduces the subject of diversity and power relations, looking at how assumptions limit individuals and groups. Power relations not only have deep roots in our cultural matrix—our shared ways of doing things, of making sense of the world—but they can often also inform our personal views, choices, and actions. Daniel Marques Sampaio then explores the challenge to worldviews and cultural understanding based on power relations, privilege and binary opposites. Finally, Marti Janse van Rensburg examines and analyzes in practical terms issues of race, gender and linguistics which may influence and impact on the work of the business coach.

Sunny Stout Rostron writes

Some years ago when I was facilitating a programme in London, I walked into the conference room and heard: "Oh my goodness, look ... it's a woman", I heard one of the executives whisper behind my back to a colleague. "Good morning everyone", I said with a smile, choosing to ignore this rather coarse chauvinism. "And, even worse, she's a bloody American", he groaned.

It was not clear whether this man, highly placed in his organization, intended me to overhear his comments. He probably did. Like many competitive executives who climb the corporate ladder, he was almost certainly flexing his muscles and trying to intimidate me from the outset. Instead, however, he'd given himself away. So, rather than confront such prejudice openly, I now knew who was likely to be somewhat difficult during the seminar. It would be my job to demonstrate that his assumptions were entirely misplaced, and were in all likelihood one of the reasons why his organization was experiencing personnel difficulties and considerable internal conflict. And so it proved.

In my work, it constantly amazes me what assumptions people immediately draw from the fact that I speak with an American accent. Frequently, without asking me any questions, some feel entitled to lecture me about the ills of this or that facet of American policy, or assume that they know how I think or voted—even though I have lived and worked outside of my own country for nearly 40 years now. But it does frequently remind me of the assumptions that we all constantly make upon meeting another person. It is this sensitivity to diversity that coaches need to be acutely aware of at all times—and they can do so only by beginning to work on their own unconscious or unquestioned attitudes and personal responses first.

With globalization, as the world increasingly "shrinks", diversity becomes an ever more pressing topic, one we are faced with every day. Too often, however, I feel that the discussion of diversity can take on a slightly patronizing tone: one that subtly suggests we must be nice to people who are in some way different to us, and graciously allow them to sit at our own table. Diversity, if it is to mean anything of real significance, must surely mean that there is an absolute assumption and acceptance of equality.

Diversity comes in many shapes, sizes and sounds. As I currently work in South Africa, the most easily identifiable mark is that of skin colour. But there are, particularly in this country, many variations and subtleties; these can include language and even food.

I have been involved with companies where diversity-related problems seemed intractable. In one instance, although colleagues from different cultures within the same organization finally felt that they had the freedom to talk openly, their sense of resentment, even bitterness, came down to the fact that one individual in a team would often talk socially, without even thinking, in a language that was not easy for other colleagues—even though they could have easily switched to a language which everyone understood. In another instance, a facilitation which had gone well, and had unblocked many misunderstandings within an organization, nearly blew up into a walk-out at lunch time. The food on offer was common daily fare for one social group, but not familiar to the minority of delegates, who felt they were being slighted.

"Oh, but they shouldn't be so sensitive," wailed the manager who'd organized the event. "That's what we always order for corporate events. I didn't even think about it!" His words, alas, proved exactly what the disgruntled participants most feared: they simply hadn't been catered for. The organizer didn't even think about it: he just arranged for what seemed "normal" to him, and expected everyone else to conform. This wasn't meant maliciously. But it reflected exactly the pattern of unawareness that was causing all the problems within that particular company. It wasn't overt attitudes or easily identifiable prejudices that were undermining the smooth running of the business. It was all those commonplace, everyday, unconscious assumptions—social, linguistic, culinary—that constantly made the minority feel that the majority were simply bulldozing over their personal feelings and collective sensibilities. In this case, it was an absolute revelation to those senior executives who had been causing offence—without exception white, male South Africans. Most were appalled and upset to discover how their behaviour had been perceived and experienced, and were extremely anxious to learn how they could develop from this experience—and broaden their own hitherto limited horizons.

Such unconscious attitudes are, mostly, the privilege of power. In many ways diversity is, ultimately, about power and the lack thereof: who has power, and who does not. This can take many forms. In another instance, I facilitated a team forum at a major organization which all the senior women managers were about to leave. They were of different ethnic backgrounds, languages and ages; the only common factor among them was that they were women. It soon became clear that the male culture in that company—and this included those men who in South Africa would be considered "previously disadvantaged" from the apartheid past— tolerated an aggressive and even open disrespect for women, even to the types of crudely sexist jokes which were told in front of them. Such was the atmosphere that not even the most senior women executives dared to speak up. Instead, they chose to leave the institution. When all this eventually spilled out at the facilitation, the men expressed amazement and shock. They had never considered that their behaviour was unacceptable: it just seemed "normal" to them. This was another manifestation of the unthinking exercise of power.

So diversity can take many guises. This is why I felt it was appropriate to tackle the subject from three very different perspectives: mine, as an American woman who has lived and worked in the United Kingdom, Europe, USA and South Africa; Dr Daniel Marques Sampaio, a Brazilian from Rio de Janeiro whose first language is Portuguese, but who now lectures at two British universities; and Marti Janse van Rensburg: female, white and Afrikaans, who is working within the complex diversity of modern-day South Africa, speaking English and Afrikaans on a daily basis.

Diversity

Diversity is about difference: in equality, power, and worldview.

Equality and power are in many ways related. Power creates its own self-justifying worldview. This often becomes an unexamined rationalization for the dominant group's power. The mirror image of this is that it negates the view of those without power. Thus it can be very difficult to get those with power to see the prejudiced limits of their bias—particularly their limiting assumptions about the powerless—because it is precisely that which justifies their monopoly of power. On the other hand, to achieve full equality— politically, professionally and personally—those without power also need to come to grips with their own limiting assumptions (often dictated by those who have had power over them). In both cases, for the powerful and the powerless, being able to discard such limiting worldviews is liberating.

On an individual level, many problems are also fuelled by our own self-limiting assumptions. We see through the filters of our own worldview, as we are all products of our personal histories, language, culture, experience, education, gender and social conditioning.

Having worked for many years with Nancy Kline in the Thinking Environment®, I have come to understand how important it is for us as business coaches to first help ourselves, then our clients, by exploring the roots of our own discriminatory attitudes and behaviours. We do this by starting to examine "untrue" limiting assumptions that society and organizations make about people on the basis of their "group" identities and their place in the hierarchy of work and society (Kline, 1999:88–89).

Although people live and work in a diverse world, we have become suspicious and mistrusting of our differences. In doing so we discriminate against, and disempower, others on the basis of their difference, rather than welcoming these differences and encompassing other worldviews to enhance our own.

When working with a client in the coaching conversation, it is useful to help them learn to remove the limiting assumptions they hold about themselves, others and the systems in which they live and work. We actually need diversity in order to approach difficult situations with fresh thinking. Only true, liberating assumptions can free individuals and groups and help them to reclaim their self-esteem and influence. This of course means developing an awareness of our own prejudices, biases, limiting thinking and life conditioning.

Nancy Kline defines diversity as "difference and equality" (Kline, 1999:87). To truly honour diversity requires genuinely diverse thinking with an appreciation for difference, an elimination of punishment for difference, and crucially highlights authority issues (who has the power?) and the fundamental issue of individuals being encouraged and permitted to think for themselves.

In working with teams in the thinking environment we often ask, "do we think better if there is an amount of diversity, safety and openness; and if so, why?" (Kline, 1999). One answer is that diversity simply gives us a more complete picture of reality. Another question is, "if the norm is power in organizational teams and in societal groups, how can we create "safety" to help people to think clearly?" (Kline, 1999). An answer to this question is that, "we think best in the midst of diversity" (Kline, 1999). To appreciate the power of diversity, however, we need to operate from a foundation of really believing that people are created equal. We all need to work on developing an internal ease in the world of difference that we face everyday.

There is diversity in experience, race, ethnicity, background, education, culture, history, language, faith, belief, capability and disability. It is crucial in the working environment to help individuals become aware of all the groups they identify with—particularly the less visible. The circuits of discrimination are complex. Every day we witness (or experience) instances of prejudice or bias, driven by untrue limiting assumptions that everyone in some way carries with them; sometimes knowingly, often unconsciously. For example, my mother-in-law, who had been a well-known and very glamorous stage actress in her youth, used to comment that the older she got, the more invisible she became. "I can walk into a room full of people that I don't know nowadays," she'd say, "and no one will notice or bother with me. I'm just the little, white-haired, old lady in the room".

Cultural competency is awareness, cultural knowledge and understanding of our human differences that may affect our work relationships and our interpersonal relationships (Stout Rostron, 2006c:27). Our purpose here is to help business coaches begin to develop an awareness of the complexity of diversity, and through their own inner journey be able to identify and name all the diversity issues which face them and their clients on a daily basis.

TRANSFORMING LIMITING ASSUMPTIONS

This is a simple but powerful exercise that my colleagues working as consultants in the Thinking Environment® have learned working with Nancy Kline. The late, wonderful Margaret Legum and her business colleague, Dorrian Aiken, have been instrumental in taking this work to greater depths within organizations in South Africa. It is important to first identify your own untrue limiting assumptions; only then can you begin to help your clients to do so.

The following exercise is one used when working with diversity in a Thinking Environment® (Kline, 2005). Make a list of the groups with whom you identify, and about whom society makes assumptions that limit the power, confidence and dignity of each of those groups. Of those groups choose the three that you most identify with, and list the assumptions made about those groups that are most limiting to their power, dignity, happiness and influence. Choose the one assumption you believe is the most limiting; do you think it is inherently true for this group? What instead would be your words for what is a liberating, true alternative assumption?

Finally, ask yourself, "if you and the world knew that truth, what would change for you and the world?" The assumptions that we hold about ourselves are the most limiting. In working through this, and similar exercises, you can start to develop an acute awareness of the preconceptions, limiting assumptions and prejudices that you work with everyday.

What happens when it goes wrong?

How can we deal with the situation when diversity goes wrong in practical terms? Diversity mistakes can be emotional—and when any situation becomes emotional, individuals often lose perspective. If business coaches can help clients to develop greater emotional intelligence, particularly self-awareness and self-management skills, any diversity situation can be improved.

Working with diversity in business can also go beyond cultural differences, bringing in a range of other perspectives. For example, in business it is rare for the marketing and finance functions to see eye-to-eye, or to have the same intention of outcome. Marketers and accountants not only occupy different functions within the organization, they will have developed differences in personal and professional worldviews.

Working with the EQ model that we explored in Chapter 5 can be helpful. Questions to ask your client are: What are they thinking and feeling; what are they assuming, and is it inherently true; what is working; what is not working? How can they use their own self-awareness to bring perspective to the situation? How might they manage what they say and do differently, to create a better result and to manage any conflict that has arisen? How will their new behaviours impact on the values and culture of the team and the organization, and ultimately on the business and business processes?

Social and workplace transformation

South Africa

In *Using Experience for Learning*, Costas Criticos (1996) reflected on social and political conditions in South Africa, exploring how apartheid affected the experience and learning of all members of its society. Criticos writes about the challenges which South Africa faces as a result of the apartheid years. He points out that two of the most important South African institutions that actually challenged the apartheid government and created space for dialogue were the churches and the universities.

His description of apartheid describes a pathology of racist oppression. This pathology was created by the tension "between contradictory experiences and contradictory explanations of society" (Criticos, 1996:157). He explains that even so, "learning" can live inside the conversations and dialogues that are produced by these tensions. As Criticos explores the liberating nature of experiential learning in South Africa, it is clear that very different learning emerges from such dramatically divergent experiences as those of the powerful and those of the powerless. Whether privileged or previously disadvantaged, the nature of recent historical experience in South Africa is so momentous and all-pervasive that it must inform—whether consciously or unconsciously—many of the attitudes of both executives and coaches.

Although diversity in the workplace will continue to be an important topic for continued transformation in South Africa, affirmative action in business remains a controversial topic in both emerging markets and developed nations. Worldwide, issues of culture, gender, language and race remain an important arena for business coaching—continuing to require that executives and business coaches be skilled in managing all aspects of diversity.

This means being able to see through a multiplicity of lenses—experiencing the world not just through your own individual perspective, but beginning to experience and understand the worldviews of those whose experience, education, background, hopes and fears are very different from your own. The business coach also needs to see through the lens of the organization, the individual executive being coached, the society and community within which both operate—and to understand how their own limiting assumptions may prevent them from understanding other points of view.

Coaching across cultures

Argentina

In Chapter 2 we read about the development of coaching in Argentina. Organizations in Argentina are often influenced by the latest international management theory, without always taking into consideration the social and cultural factors that would make those management processes work well in a Latin American environment. For example, managers often share an understanding of participative leadership, but they do not necessarily manage their teams accordingly. This experience can be confusing for team members who might have been inculcated in participative discourse, yet continue to experience or be managed in a style of command and control. This creates a strong opportunity for executive coaching, even where cultural resistance to coaching may be the result of a power centric attitude. There is an assumption that coaching may show up certain managerial weaknesses; this creates resistance in a culture where even female executives tend to exercise a macho approach to business relationships (Kottner, 2008).

Asia

In *Leadership Coaching: Inspiration from Asia*, Elisabeth Legrain and Michael Fox (2008) foresee the need for leadership which accommodates cultural differences in the workplace. They look to Asian culture as a "source of inspiration to draw on," advocating that Asian culture may be the inspiration needed "for corporate coaching to develop transcultural leadership capacity". One of the paradoxes they bemoan is that, in our global society today, Asian people are adapting Western behaviours which may be considered "aggressive" in their own culture (Legrain and Fox, 2008:1). They suggest that organizations could seriously benefit from Asian "transcultural leadership" which takes its inspiration from a recognition of cultural differences. They look to Asia for its approach to self-awareness in martial arts practice, and propose that powerful coaching is one which, "like martial arts practice, takes the client on their individual journey to build deep awareness of their capacities, their culture, values, passions and motivations" (Legrain and Fox, 2008:2).

In "Asian perspectives in coaching", Foo See Luan emphasizes the diversity and strategic position of Singapore, "situated in the vibrant Asia-Pacific Region and home to some 6 000 multinational corporations" (Foo, 2004:7). Foo suggests that coaches keep in mind the difference between Asian and North American values. He describes Americans as more individualistic, with a less collective orientation; and Asians as more collective and less individualistic. Perhaps even more importantly, he explains that Asians tend to be reflective and less direct in their communication; while Americans tend to be action-oriented, and quite direct and assertive. Foo (2004:8) underlines the need for "mutual understanding, collaboration, respect and shared values". His suggestion to coaches is to learn to appreciate diversity and difference, and to develop an understanding of two diametrically opposed cultures: one a culture focused on performance and success (i.e., doing), versus another with a focus on quality and relationships (i.e., being).

Coaching Latinos

The following case study addresses several critical aspects of coaching in a cross-cultural context. It also reminds us that coaches need to equally balance the values and culture of the organization with the values and culture of the individual being coached.

COMPLEXITY IN CULTURAL DIVERSITY

In her article about *Coaching Across Cultures*, Francia Baez (2006), Vice President of Human Resources for a multinational organization in Latin America, talks about the cultural differences coaches need to be aware of when coaching Latinos. Her article states that Latinos are expected to "represent 25 per cent of the US population by 2050" (Baez, 2006:20). Due to the complexity of the cultural mix in the USA, Baez explains eight criteria that can help coaches working within this cross-cultural context.

1. Collectivism and relationships
It's important for coaches to understand the importance of establishing relationships that encourage openness and approachability, and to avoid being too directive. When coaching Latinos, being too directive may encourage submissive behaviour, as hierarchy and knowledge are culturally highly regarded (Baez, 2006:20–21).

2. Family and relationships
Baez (2006:21) indicates that Latinos may treat work relationships as extended familial relationships. She suggests that coaches and line managers should be aware of the cultural need for Latinos to discuss potential work decisions with family. This is because family and professional life are not separated in the same sense as within an Anglo-American context.

3. Religion
Although religion is usually excluded from the workplace in most cultures, Latino work behaviours are often guided by religious principles. The significance of this, according to Baez (2006:21), is the need for a more holistic coaching approach to management. An equivalent of this is being experienced in South Africa where organizations have begun to create an environment for prayers during the working day in accordance with the cultural rituals of their employees.

4. Time orientation
Baez (2006:21) explains that although time is a valuable and limited asset in business, Latinos tend to have a more relaxed view of time than Anglo-Americans. Importance is paid to small talk, and

the coach needs to "warm up" to the coaching conversation. This is comparable to African culture, where time spent in greeting is significant in building and maintaining relationships. This is often heard in radio phone-in programmes in South Africa; callers first greet the radio presenter and ask after their health before settling in to discuss the subject at hand.

5. Communication
Feelings play a major role in Latino communication, and the coach needs to be sensitive when a directive style is required so that the client does not feel diminished. Conversely, a Latino being coached may show respect to the coach/manager by agreeing with one of their suggestions, but may have no intention of following it up. Once the coaching relationship is established there may be more self-disclosure by the client than mainstream US culture is accustomed to, as Latinos are less sensitive to privacy issues (Baez, 2006: 21).

6. Body language and distance
The acceptable physical distance between individuals in interpersonal communication is different in every culture. Baez (2006:21) indicates that a "Latino may inadvertently decrease interpersonal space to the point of causing discomfort in someone of a different cultural background. Latino culture is a contact culture." It is also important that the coach understands the cultural background to relatively intense and prolonged touching, eye contact and facial expressions, which are generally meant to be signs of sincerity.

7. Gender Issues
All cultures have defined gender roles. Baez (2006:22) indicates that "Latino men are typically raised to be dominant, paternalistic providers and protectors", while Latinas are socialized to show "nurturing behaviour expressed by playing a supporting role". These are important cultural factors for any coach to be aware of.

8. Problem-solving and linguistic styles
One of the difficulties Baez shares is that Latinos may avoid confrontation, choosing to "protect relationships by being indirect. Although some may demonstrate authority by adopting an aggressive style, this approach is viewed negatively" (Baez, 2006:22).

In any culture, the coach needs to understand the meaning of indirect linguistic signals and body language, which could easily be misinterpreted in a business environment where issues may be addressed in a direct manner.

Stepping into Africa

Below is an interview with Marilyn Johnson, General Manager for Africa of an international engineering corporation with a US head office. Johnson is an African American who grew up in the southern USA with civil rights issues at the fore. Johnson shares her experience of living and working in South Africa for three years, managing plant facilities and sales managers in a variety of African countries, as well as managing cultural and skills diversity within the workplace. She shares how she has learned to adapt to a variety of cultural environments, with all of the challenges that this encompasses.

CORPORATE INTERVIEW

People

Can you give us your perspective on living and working in Africa?

From my personal perspective, Africa has millions of people who are multilingual. They speak more languages than any other people in the world. They are creative and innovative—but Africa has been stereotyped, like many other communities round the world. The perception of Africa is that Africans suffer from extremely high crime and poverty, with a high degree of illiteracy and an enormous lack of education. Seen though the eyes of prejudice, they are seen as dumb.

Yet if one takes a wider look at Africa, African people can be seen as among the most capable, if not the most versatile, people in the world. They are highly multilingual, with some speaking eight to 12 languages including English. Africans are also the poorest of people, with large numbers living in informal settlements in homes that are simply one- to two-room shacks. There are men and women selling their crafts on street corners in all African cities, albeit that they are often excellent craftsmen and artisans. Although I travel all over the African continent, I live in South Africa which is renowned for its sophisticated banking system, excellent wine and the healthiest food I have ever experienced in my work and travels around the world. That certainly bucks the stereotype!

The culture of the corporation

As an African American female executive, how did you end up in Africa?

The corporation for which I work had identified Africa as the next emerging market; growth potential for the corporation is expected to exceed US$200 billion by 2020. I was selected for my ability to turn around difficult markets. Yet for political and stereotypical reasons the new thinking and priority is to move to Eastern Europe. The perception is that Europe is safer, and the thinking is that European markets will not only outperform developing markets, but that it is easier to do business there—primarily because of the northern hemisphere bias of white versus black. White cultures are perceived to be First-World, consumer-oriented, capitalistic, educated and sophisticated. In reality, corporations face onerous labour regulations, and self-oriented, individualistic cultures, versus the African collective and communalistic culture which supports a workplace that is team-oriented, supportive and loyal. Based on these aspects, objectively, the corporation should continue to opt for African cultures and countries.

Working on a daily basis in the business

How does diversity affect what you are trying to do?

Being the first black, female, American General Manager for the corporation has brought its challenges and rewards. The successes during my tenure have been "extraordinary" to say the least. We have exceeded expectations, accomplishing tasks ahead of schedule, working cross-functionally across other business divisions in the corporation. We have also made profound contributions to the community, donating more than 500 000 rands (approximately US$50 000) to the local community. This includes building a Habitat for Humanity Home for children suffering from AIDS; making grants to Children's Day Care Centres; funding homes for the elderly; sponsoring gardening projects; and opening an on-site health clinic for employees from the local community.

Although the South African location was an existing division of the corporation, it had not received any capital investments during the years prior to my arrival, of either capital or people. Asked to take this position, I was tasked with making improvements to bring the entire African operation and staff into alignment with all of the other divisions in the corporation. In addition to business growth, my role also includes integrative training, skills development and coaching initiatives to introduce and develop a culture that will allow the African countries where we are located to be in alignment with the other First-World cultures who operate within the corporate entity.

With the assistance of a colleague who moved to South Africa during the same time period as me, we exceeded Head Office expectations by making the required changes and providing the "right" working environment for employees. Our plant was awarded the organization's "Safety Award" for being one of the safest facilities.

Personal experience in South Africa

What are the contradictions experienced in your work in South Africa?

Candidly, the main problems and contradictions that I have experienced in South Africa are as a direct result of the secrecy, lack of transparency and various internal corporate intrigues taking place at Head Office in the USA. Quite frankly, the behaviour at corporate headquarters is in contradiction to the views they espouse: the behaviour that they typically attribute to the African continent is in fact a mirror of their own failings.

What did you do to coach your team?

As the leader-coach, I used coaching and mentoring as an integral part of management training, customer care programmes and talent development. In spite of the corporate politics and the challenges, the business has grown 29 per cent in sales revenue, and 19 per cent in profit over the previous year. This was achieved through continuous communication across all functions, staying customer-focused, and individually coaching the manufacturing team members. The aim of coaching was to help each individual focus specifically on customer care and open-door relationships with both customers and employees. Most important of all, I worked with an executive coach to keep my motivation levels high, and to have a thinking partner for strategic thinking and difficult decisions.

As General Manager, I maintained an open-door policy, making frequent visits to the plant, and implemented safety "star reward" and service recognition programmes which had never before existed. We implemented a variable compensation bonus programme to encourage all shop floor employees to work collaboratively to achieve company targets. Their efforts would be rewarded by them participating in the company's performance bonus programme.

What are the lessons learned from your hands-on strategy?
I've learned to trust myself and my intuition, being willing to build trust in a diverse group of people across geographical plants, actively encouraging employees to participate in management decisions. I and my management team facilitated focus group meetings, and provided mentoring and coaching programmes to develop people throughout all of our markets. Taking the time to develop people is one of the key lessons I have learned, and it has provided the leadership development, success and fulfilment that I have achieved personally while working on this assignment.

What, if anything, would you do differently next time?
My best advice to an executive stepping into a new culture and new marketplace is to first visit the country several times for extended periods to become familiar with the laws, culture and environment before accepting the position. Prior to stepping into the position my visits to South Africa were minimal. Nor had I visited the other African countries where the corporation was already established. More and/or more extended visits would have given me a broader perspective on the work required, and would have enabled me to better understand the different labour regulations, as well as the significance of the project.

HOW TO USE THIS

Self-awareness and practice

What lenses do you see through based on your background, culture and gender? Use first-, second- and third-position thinking to step into the other's shoes and to see from a new perspective. This is an NLP coaching technique (discussed in Chapter 4). The coach helps the client to identify their lenses from three individual positions (first position/their own; second position/the other; third position/themselves as coach seeing with a new perspective). Physically stand in first position (the client's own position); second position (the other's position); and third position (that of coach) in order to resolve a conflict or see the other person's point of view.

Use this for yourself and your clients. I use this technique frequently when the client has an issue or difficulty with another party and needs to hear, see and feel perspectives from all points of view. When coach and client enact it, the client actually verbalizes what they think, feel and see—it helps you (or the client) to understand the assumptions that influence the lens through which you (or they) see the world, and helps to determine what needs to change in your (or their) behaviour in order to interact more effectively with others.

Daniel Marques Sampaio Writes

In this section, Daniel Marques Sampaio challenges the assumptions that inform our views of the world—assumptions about ourselves, our cultures and our identities. He examines how we can engage with difference, and looks at the historical use of dualities or binary opposites to make sense of the world. In setting out the challenge of putting equality into practice, he argues the need to create a new map of the world.

Something I hear all the time is: "But you don't seem very Brazilian!" If, like me, you are from Rio, a lot of people seem to expect you to be a football fan, or a walking/talking carnival parade, your every entrance announced by a "ta-dah!"

After nearly 20 years in London I still don't know how to respond, or even if I should say anything at all. That's because such comments come not only from people in Britain, but also from other Brazilians, who seem to think that I am not "like them", or at any rate not like what some believe both they and I ought to be like. Of course, most people don't mean to be malicious. They may be simply expressing surprise that someone who was born so far away is not that different from them; or, conversely, that someone who grew up "with them" might behave, even think, in a way they consider "foreign".

Born in Rio de Janeiro, I moved to London two decades ago. Most of my adult life, therefore, has been spent in the UK, where I studied, and where I live and work. Mine is not an experience of exile, a forced departure from the homeland, but a personal decision: a "rational choice". Yet this doesn't mean that I am not constantly questioned about my origin and about my allegiances: "So, do you often go back home?" No, I want to say, my home is in London!

As a university lecturer, I am immersed in an environment thoroughly defined by diversity. My campus sometimes resembles one of those intergalactic bars in films like *Star Wars*, with a multiplicity of accents: a mix of national, cultural and social backgrounds and styles. There are students in ethnic dress, members of subcultures, fashion-conscious students, even the occasional corduroy-jacket-with-elbow-patches type. Despite worldwide developments in education policy that seem to be turning universities everywhere into skills factories, it is still for many a place to discover themselves, to expand their minds and unlock their potential. In this sense, being an education professional has much in common with coaching: both lecturers and coaches are concerned with questioning the assumptions that we make about the world, about our place in it. More fundamentally, both professions take that questioning further, by reconsidering the way we act, so as to chart new paths of action that steer clear of limiting worldviews.

Accepting diversity and equality is about probing many things, including the way we think about identity—especially our own. It is about examining models of identity based on a defensive, even reactionary, antagonism towards what lies "outside"—models such as certain types of nationalism, or forms of identification based on a rejection of "the Other", with all the negative connotations that term carries. It is about questioning the perception of what is foreign: of what originates elsewhere, or of those who view the world differently. This need to re-evaluate our limiting worldviews is what I wish to examine here.

Worldview

> Leading in a multicultural and diverse environment is like
> playing several instruments. It partly calls for different atti-
> tudes and skills: restraint in passing judgement and the abil-
> ity to recognize that familiar tunes might have to be played
> differently. Our natural tendency is to watch the world from
> behind the windows of a cultural home and to act as if people
> from other countries, ethnicities, or categories have something
> special about them (a culture) but home is normal. Awareness
> means the discovery that there is no normal position in cultural
> matters (Hofstede, 2005:ix).

In recent decades significant changes have taken place in the way
the world is organized, thought about, and represented—none
more so than in the area of, and increasing sensitivity to, cultural
diversity. After two world wars, countless local conflicts, and following a century that was arguably packed with more radical
social, cultural, scientific and technological change than any previous one, we seem to be living in a world where old certainties
and assumptions no longer apply. Many old power relations, relating to imperialism and collectivism, have been swept away by
the "march of history". This image of a whirlwind carrying away
worldviews is, however, by no means new. As early as 1848, Karl
Marx and Friedrich Engels had already noted in the *Communist
Manifesto* (with a rhetorical stridency to match Marx's famously
dishevelled hair and beard) that with capitalism, "All fixed, fast-
frozen relations, with their train of ancient and venerable prejudices and opinions, are swept away, all new-formed ones become
antiquated before they can ossify. All that is solid melts into air, all
that is holy is profaned, and man is at last compelled to face with
sober senses his real conditions of life, and his relations with his
kind" (Marx and Engels, 1848:4).

One such old certainty that finds itself continually questioned
concerns our personal place in the world, and the primacy of our
worldviews. The contemporary, globalized world is one in which
everything is in flux. This process involves the flow of material
goods—everything from foodstuffs to furniture, as well as all kinds
of technical artefacts; financial and trading flows; and, particularly

important for any debate on diversity, flows of information, of people, or worldviews.

To understand how deeply these flows touch us in our everyday lives picture, for instance, the writer of this chapter, a Brazilian-British university lecturer in London, typing these words on a laptop, and as soon as a draft is ready, it is emailed to his colleague, a British-American who was born in California, and now lives in South Africa. This immediacy of communication—an email sent from London to Cape Town in a matter of seconds—encapsulates the changes that executives and managers face on a daily basis.

Communication might be relatively unproblematic in a situation where we both have similar education, and where we both inhabit broadly similar linguistic, social and cultural worlds—a professional and intellectual world that seems to have taken to globalization like fish to water. But even in this exchange there are areas fraught with misunderstanding and confusion—linguistic and cultural. Nothing can be taken for granted. Imagine, for instance, a situation in which language is a means not only of expressing and sharing ideas, but also of preserving our identity. How would these changes—in the immediacy of connections, in the availability of communication channels, in the sudden geographical closeness between people who previously lived so far apart—impact on us?

These are questions that coaches must ask not only their clients, but also themselves: what would our relationship with the world be like if we were in that position? How would we respond to it? We must be aware of the need to differentiate between those who benefit from globalization, and those for whom all that mobility, all that interconnectivity, represents at best a challenge to their world, and at worst its undoing.

Some years ago I attended a conference on globalization in which a researcher gave a paper on economic aspects of migrations. After the presentation, answering a question from the audience, he made a throwaway remark about youngsters in the *favelas*, the shanty towns of Rio de Janeiro; he bemoaned their inability to escape their lives, which he attributed to their "closed minds", and said that those kids were, in economic terms, a "dead weight".

Now, I grew up in Rio de Janeiro, and like many *cariocas*, I have first-hand experience of the wild social, cultural and economic disparities of that city. I am fully aware of how difficult it is to break out of poverty, which perpetuates itself in a vicious circle; but I am also aware that the residents of the *favelas* are anything but closed-minded. These are people who have produced some of the world's best footballers, and who every year put on the greatest street party in the world—who have, in short, made a significant contribution to a global culture. Far from being a "dead weight", they are responsible for a great deal of global interest in Rio that in economic terms translates into tourism revenue. Yet they are also imprisoned by the very social, cultural and economic situation from which their contribution to globalization springs. So, maybe the researcher made that particular comment through ignorance rather than through malice. Yet the argument remains valid, that to engage with diversity in a meaningful way, we need to be open-minded to the changes brought about by global processes, changes that manifest themselves both in the opening up of new avenues for action, and in the shutting down of others.

Assumptions

What these changes mean is that all the assumptions that inform our views of the world—assumptions about ourselves, our cultures and our identities, as well as about the cultures and identities that we experience through distance and unfamiliarity—have to be reconsidered. It is precisely those filters of distance and unfamiliarity that ensure these assumptions are maintained in the first place. It is through the safeguarding of distance and unfamiliarity, that certain qualities and characteristics can be ascribed to some customs and cultural practices, and can be marked as **different**—these people who share the same customs, who define their cultures through these practices, are seen as the bearers of **difference**.

As soon as what is distant becomes **near**, as soon as the once unfamiliar is found in everyday life, we then experience a sense of dislocation so aptly described by Hofstede in the above opening quote: the impression of an upset in the "normal" ordering of our world. For many this appears to be a destabilising experience, which can be dealt with by retreating into one's own sense of identity, by drawing a clear distinction between those with whom we do belong, and those with whom we don't—to the "cultural home" mentioned by Hofstede. However, to anyone concerned with exploring, questioning, and overcoming limiting assumptions and worldviews (especially coaches and other professionals), this sense of dislocation presents both major challenges and exhilarating opportunities.

The challenges are those derived from engaging with cultures, ways of being, and practices that are different from our own. On the one hand we shouldn't fall into the trap of pretending that such differences do not exist: the "benevolent" attitude which says that "we all belong to the same family", to "humankind". This attitude, often well-intentioned, fails to acknowledge that sometimes people **do** define themselves precisely through some of those markers of difference: i.e., race, gender, sexuality, culture, language, religion, and so on. These differences may form the very core of who they are, and should not be erased by a desire to include all others into an all-encompassing category—**us**—this may be insensitive to their specificity.

This sensitivity to the elements that go into the making of an individual is crucial to coaching practice. It is also something that coaching shares with other professional activities. For example, some years ago I conducted some research on a Brazilian novelist, Clarice Lispector. Her novels had fascinated me since my teens, even though I was not sure what it was that attracted me so much: something to do with her oblique (some would say obscure) style. Yes, but more than that—it was a sense that this showed me not only another way of thinking, but also a different way of being. In the course of attempting (ah, the innocence of youth!) a translation of one of those novels, I came across a comment by the French philosopher, Hélène Cixous, who put the finger right on the root of that fascination: for Cixous, Lispector's entire work was "a book of respect, a book of the **right distance**".

It is this respectful understanding of the "right distance", this ability to perceive someone in all their individuality which is the problem—and is one of the most important attributes of a good coach. This is, ultimately, the ability to see and accept equality. On the other hand, the great Nigerian novelist Chinua Achebe (1977), in "An Image of Africa", writes critically of the classic Joseph Conrad novel, *Heart of Darkness*, set in the Congo: "Quite simply it is the desire—one might indeed say the need—in Western psychology to set Africa up as a foil in Europe, as a place of negations at once remote and vaguely familiar in comparison with which Europe's own state of spiritual grace will be manifest" (Achebe, 1977:782). This is the danger for the coach. It is critical to see where the power relations reside.

Crucially, one must also avoid the trap of defining people through such differences in a way that locks them into the role of "representatives" of their gender, race, culture, religion: as if a particular woman "represented" what "being a woman" could mean, or a Muslim person could be seen as a "spokesperson" for the whole of Islamism, regardless of their individual histories, desires, and choices.

Here again, Chinua Achebe is an acute observer. For anyone from a dominant culture, or even in a dominant position, there is always the temptation (even subconsciously) to assume they know best. It is a potentially fatal trap for coaches. This is how Achebe puts it: "To the colonialist mind it was always of the utmost importance to be able to say: 'I know my natives', a claim which implied two things at once: (a) that the native was really quite simple and (b) that understanding him and controlling him went hand-in-hand—understanding being a precondition for control and control constituting adequate proof of understanding" (Achebe, 1988:48).

Engaging with difference

Yet if the challenges are great, so are the opportunities. Engaging with difference provides us with the imperative to question some of our most deeply held assumptions about who we are, and the limits of what we can think and do. On the one hand, the technological and social possibilities associated with globalization, such as the transmission across the world within seconds of images of one culture to another, linking people geographically far apart, can help to break down rigid ideas of cultural stereotypes. Personal experiences of globalization seem to indicate that we now live in a world where difference can no longer be safely ascribed to things **far away** from us, and therefore easy to ignore. If we live in a world of continuous contact and interchange, then all that which was previously put into a black box and safely consigned to being "other" and "different from us", can now be experienced in our daily lives. This everyday contact with difference shows us that there is no single true way of seeing or understanding the world—there are many different and potentially valid ways of making sense of the world.

On the other hand, globalization can just as easily help reinforce old stereotypes and even build up new ones. The popular media provides some of the most powerful voices of globalizing forces, and often reinforces such stereotypes. The Kenyan novelist and essayist Ngũgĩ wa Thiong'o, one of Africa's most prominent intellectuals, has made the important point that crass racial stereotypes portrayed in the hugely popular novels of nineteenth- and twentieth-century writers like Rider Haggard, Elspeth Huxley and Robert Ruark (to which we could add some of the works of "airport" novelists such as Michael Crichton, or the popular sprawling sagas of a Wilber Smith), helped to create and shape the template for images currently shown on TV. In his seminal essay, *Decolonizing the Mind*, Ngũgĩ writes: "Thus imaginative literature had created the necessary racist vocabulary and symbols long before the TV and the popular media had come to dominate the scene" (Ngũgĩ, 1986:93).

Ngũgĩ makes the vital point that African children, who encountered literature in colonial schools, also learned to see the world as Europeans did: "the entire way of looking at the world, even the world of the immediate environment, was Eurocentric. Europe was the centre of the universe. The earth moved round the European scholarly axis" (Ngũgĩ, 1986:93). This is what he calls the colonization of the mind. Yet how much more alluring are such easy Eurocentric assumptions, replete with lazy clichés, for the former colonizers today? This is precisely the pitfall which coaches must avoid. The key is that we are all, in different ways and in varying degrees, shaped by our cultural background—therefore our way of making sense of the world is culturally determined.

Binary oppositions

Within Western cultures it has been noted that one of the key ways of making sense of the world is through binary oppositions. This is, indeed, one of the key theoretical models propounded by Structuralism, in particular within the works of Claude Lévi-Strauss (1908-) in Anthropology, and Ferdinand de Saussure (1857–1913) in Linguistics—see Sturrock (2003) for a summary. It involves the idea that people construct meaning through the recognition of "opposites"—that people can only define what something **is** by knowing what it **isn't**: we know what being *rich* is because it isn't the same as being **poor**, we know that being **masculine** is different from being **feminine**, we know **white** is not **black**.

Binary oppositions put the world into clearly defined categories— "this" and "that", "self" and "other"—and these categories can be helpful, reassuring, convenient. Moreover, "common sense" seems to tell us that there are basic differences: between rich and poor, between white and black, between masculine and feminine.

However, upon closer examination, what we assume to be "common sense"—i.e., the "basic difference" between two opposites— turns out to be an expression or way of seeing the world that is formed by unexamined assumptions. One such unexamined assumption is that these binary opposites, helpful and convenient though they may appear, actually correspond to human experience of meaning. In fact, we experience meaning in much more subtle and complex ways, which suggest not so much an "either/or" distinction but more a sliding scale of values and qualities. For example, what we think of as the distinction between "masculine" and "feminine" is an extreme simplification of a wide range of social and cultural perceptions of masculinity and femininity. These perceptions underpin the attribution of certain roles, identities and characteristics to men and women. In this sense, categories such as "masculine" and "feminine" are **socially constructed**; they depend on perceptions of gender which are contingent on the social or cultural beliefs of a particular society (see Abizadeh, 2001). In many societies, characteristics such as assertiveness, initiative and leadership are seen as masculine, whereas obedience and a concern for the domestic sphere are seen as feminine qualities. Thus, men and women whose behaviour does not match those roles, identities, or characteristics, may be considered less masculine or feminine.

Binary opposites are often experienced as levels of intensity within a sliding scale of values and qualities. As noted by feminist critic Joan Scott, in an article discussing equality and difference: "Fixed oppositions conceal the extent to which things presented as oppositional are, in fact, interdependent—that is, they derive their meaning from a particularly established contrast rather than from some inherent or pure antithesis" (Scott, 1994:286).

This division of experience into binary oppositions also reflects a particular structure of power: one side of the opposition has traditionally been privileged (and often exercised that privilege) over the other: men (and masculinity) have traditionally been privileged over women (and femininity); whites over blacks; rich over poor.

Historical experiences of shifting power relations helped solidify these privileges—practices of colonialism during the last two centuries is a case in point, affirmed by one side dominating or enjoying greater privileges over the other. The colonizer was privileged over the colonized, a practice supported and consolidated in layers of other power relations based on race, class, culture, etc., Conversely, the overthrowing of many oppressive political and social systems has often retained some forms of discrimination based on a "turning the tables" mentality (the oppressed becoming the oppressor), which kept the context of unequal power relations unchanged.

However, where hierarchies are challenged, or the cultural comfort zones are bypassed, the results can be socially disturbing. In *Tipping Point: How Little Things Can Make a Big Difference*, Malcolm Gladwell (2007) discusses moments of anomaly, upheaval, and social disturbance which are triggers for change in society. His discussion of these disturbing moments is significant for coaching practitioners, who must consider both the **macro** scale of historical processes, and the **micro** scale of personal transformation.

Taking his cue from the biological sciences, Gladwell seeks to explain some of the changes that mark everyday life. He notes that "ideas and products and messages and behaviours spread like viruses do", describing **tipping points** as "moments of critical mass, the threshold, the boiling point" in which change takes place (Gladwell, 2000:7;12). As an idea, a message, or a specific behaviour tips over a certain threshold, it can trigger change. In looking at diversity historically, it is interesting to think about those moments when an idea went from being important to a specific minority group (even if that minority group is statistically significant) to being a new basis for a fundamental way of understanding the world. For example, the actions, life and philosophies of Mahatma Gandhi—virtually unknown in Britain until after World War II. But now, Gandhi is an almost universally recognized name and ideal; most people can articulate his fundamental beliefs of non-violence.

In historical, as well as personal terms, these are the moments where difference strikes us with its full potency: as the entire edifice of unexamined power relations has its arbitrary foundations exposed, values and worldviews borne out of the experience of privilege have to be reconsidered. This can be seen in both small-scale (social rituals) or large-scale (political reform) events. Thus, when thinking about gender, individual concern and desire for change and equality increases in tandem with large-scale events such as women's suffrage and feminism. In relation to race and ethnicity, consciousness of diversity appears as part of a series of events that includes the abolition of slavery, decolonization, and civil rights movements.

The notion of diversity has arisen from challenges to those worldviews based on power relations considered "normal" for long periods of time; for some, these power relations have become the very foundation-stone of human relations (e.g., apartheid)—as attested, in its most extreme fashion, by the Hobbesian image of "the war of all against all". These power relations have deep roots in our cultural matrix, i.e., our shared ways of doing things, of making sense of the world—but they can often also almost unconsciously inform our personal views, choices, and actions. It is at this level of assumption, particularly with regard to a cultural way of understanding the world, that coaches need to work with their clients in order to understand how to manage diversity in the workplace.

Dualities such as masculine/feminine, white/black, rich/poor, etc., divide the world into easily manageable categories. Such divisions also solidify these opposites, making them inflexible or totemic. However, as argued above, experience seems to suggest there are stages between conditions, rather than being complete polar opposites; the very division of the world into binary opposites underlines the accepted hierarchical foundations for power relations that inform our most unexamined worldviews.

The challenge of putting equality into practice

In a professional context, the limiting effect of such worldviews can be felt in particularly acute ways. Discrimination on the basis of gender, for instance, is a fact of life in most countries in the world. Many women experience occupational segregation because of cultural and social attitudes towards what might be considered "female" versus "male" jobs. In her 2004 update of *Breaking Through the Glass Ceiling: Women in Management* (Wirth, 2001), Linda Wirth supplements research conducted by the International Labour Organization in a sample from 63 countries with the most recent international statistical data.

Despite representing over 40 per cent of the global labour force, women still have lower labour market participation rates, higher unemployment rates, and significant pay differences compared to men. Gender segregation in the workplace tends to manifest itself in two main ways: (1) on the concentration of women in traditionally "feminised" jobs such as nursing, teaching and administration; and (2) on the difficulties in rising to senior positions or higher paid job categories in comparison with men. Despite such segregation, Wirth's report provides evidence that women are breaking into fields such as law, science, engineering, and information and communication technology (ICT), which have been traditionally male-dominated. That progress is, however, balanced by the constraints that many women face in the workplace, such as sexual harassment or isolation.

A further difficulty experienced by women in the workplace is that women are more likely to have shorter careers than men, because they might leave full-time employment in order to fulfil family responsibilities, which leads to slower promotion and lower salaries (Wirth, 2004:1–3). At the root of this dilemma is the inflexibility of labour practice in public policy and business; this practice makes few concessions to women's traditional job of raising children and managing a family. This inflexibility, although affecting women most acutely, also poses problems for men, who can be reluctant to take advantage of paternity leave or similar opportunities for time with family, for fear of being passed over for promotion, or of being seen to be lacking in commitment to the job.

Interestingly, Wirth observes that, as employers start to recognize that family-friendly policies can have benefits not only to male and female employees but also in helping to increase overall business productivity, "personal characteristics of integrity, diligence and sincerity, traditionally attributed to women, are increasingly viewed as qualities that can enhance a company's image in a world riddled with corporate misconduct" (Wirth, 2004:18).

A growth in self-employment among women has also been observed in recent years. This is explained in two arguably interrelated ways: one explanation may be that women have been attracted to self-employment by a desire for autonomy and flexibility, as well as to escape the constraints encountered in large organizations, i.e., the "glass ceiling". The other explanation might be that the rise in entrepreneurship is due to the erosion of jobs in public and private sectors, caused by restructuring and downsizing. This is a phenomenon that particularly affects women who tend to occupy non-strategic positions in these sectors—another form of gender segregation. In many countries, such as the United States, Great Britain, and Denmark, women have reported high levels of satisfaction with their new working lives (Wirth, 2004:33–36).

This growth in entrepreneurial activity among women can also be interpreted as a contradiction to the standard stereotyping of women as passive and timid, and as lacking traits considered to be "masculine", such as initiative, competitiveness, and decisiveness. However, by focusing on the professional experience of "women" generally, Wirth's report does not address a number of aspects of women's relationship to the workplace. "Women" do not constitute a generic, universal, undifferentiated category; a woman's experience of work and other aspects of life depend on many other variables, such as race/ethnicity, age, class, culture, religion, etc.,

This meeting point of gender and other diversity variables is the subject of another important comparative study, *Gender Equality, Cultural Diversity: European Comparisons and Lessons* (Dustin, 2007). Although its focus is on cultural and religious factors, rather than on social and economic aspects of diversity in relation to gender, this study offers important insights on the roots of power imbalance and institutionalized discrimination which afflict members of minority communities. Bearing in mind that the study considers challenges to diversity specific to Europe, these power imbalances include the continuous portrayal of members of religious and cultural minorities in homogenising and often negative ways. The study also makes a related observation that individuals or groups, without a prior history of interest in women's rights, have on many occasions used the concept of gender equality to pursue anti-immigration and Islamo-phobic agendas—by, for instance, equating the use of the *hijab* with oppression of women, despite many Islamic women's assertions that their decision to wear it was based on free will (Dustin, 2007:1–3).

Many countries have passed legislation specifically designed to stamp out racial discrimination. In Britain, the Race Relations Act 1976 (amended by the Race Relations Amendment Act 2000), makes racial discrimination and harassment unlawful, and provides the right to challenge negative discrimination in the courts or at an employment tribunal. However, it has also been widely noted that social inequality caused by discriminatory practices cannot be tackled simply through preventive or punitive jurisdiction: formal, legally recognized equality may not be enough to provide all with equal opportunities.

This recognition of the limits of the use of law as a neutral tool for the means of resolution of social disputes informs the policies of affirmative action (also known as "positive discrimination"). Marc Bossuyt, an expert in international law and a judge in the Constitutional Court of Belgium, defines affirmative action as "... a coherent packet of measures ... aimed specifically at correcting the position of members of a target group in one or more aspects of their social life, in order to obtain effective equality" (Bossuyt, 2002:3).

However, policies of affirmative action can also encounter resistance. Objections have been made from an ideological point of view, claiming that the liberal "ideal" of equality of opportunity is to create the conditions for equality, such as equal access to education and jobs, while leaving individuals free to pursue their own personal betterment within those conditions. Policies designed to address inequalities through positive discrimination can therefore have a jarring effect when confronted with such an ideal notion (for a review of these objections, see Krstić, 2003). It has also been noted that it is the most fortunate segments of the groups designated as beneficiaries of affirmative action who seem to get the most out of such policies: middle-class white women, for instance, will often benefit more than lower-class women of other ethnicities (Bossuyt, 2002:4).

Affirmative action in business is a controversial topic, although the statistics often tell their own story. According to the September 2008 Employment Equity Commission report in South Africa, there is still "gross under-representation of Africans, Coloureds [i.e., people of mixed race], and people with disabilities in key areas of the labour market" (Johwa, 2008:4). There are fluctuating, sometimes even regressive figures for black representation according to Jimmy Manyi, President of the Black Management Forum (BMF) and Chair of the Employment Equity Commission. Manyi points out that the number of blacks decreased 8.7 per cent to 41.3 per cent of the total in professional and middle management level, while black Africans experienced the largest decline, falling 14.9 per cent to reach 24.1 per cent (Johwa, 2008:4).

Apparently, white women had made the largest gains in the corporate marketplace, which has led the Commission's Chair to recommend that white women be removed from the definition of affirmative action's "graduation principle" as the "prejudice against white women cannot be compared to that suffered by black women" (Johwa, 2008:4).

At any rate, what this indicates is the importance of considering diversity in its many facets. The stratification of gender with racial/ethnic, religious, and cultural perspectives is a particularly critical configuration for most countries at this historical juncture—in which processes of globalization create a stimulus greater than had ever existed for the transnational mobility of individuals, both male and female. The cultural challenges brought about by these processes are experienced in daily life. Expressions of gender, sexuality, ethnicity and culture—such as dress, behaviour and language, once considered private matters of choice—are now contested ever more publicly. What is the position of coaching professionals, then, in such a configuration? Where is the coach placed in this newly emerging map of the world?

A new map of the world

The argument being made here is not simply that coaching practitioners should acknowledge the hierarchies and effects of inequality which are produced by dividing the world into binary oppositions, or that they should make themselves familiar with diversity legislation relevant to the particular culture and nation within which they are working. What is important, is for coaching professionals to question their own views of the world, including their own place in the "map" of that world.

As noted before, our world is becoming more and more interconnected due to the processes of globalization. Cultures, ethnic groups and customs that once were separated by vast distances now find themselves in close contact, experienced as a matter of routine in everyday life. A walk in cities like London, Paris, New York, São Paulo, Dubai and Shanghai is enough to demonstrate this. These are no longer simply national cities, but international meeting points.

The contemporary city offers more than a metaphor for diversity; its very physical structure is a manifestation of change in the ways that the world is reorganizing itself. Medieval cities used to be enclosed by walls. In the contemporary, global city, what matters are roads, airports, railways—installations designed to open up the city, to ensure that it remains diverse, to facilitate the movement of people and ideas. Similarly, for the coaching professional, engagement with diversity offers the opportunity to tear down the walls that enclose us within our own limited personal views, to open up new mental roads, to travel through new intellectual and personal paths, to develop and explore hitherto neglected tracks for action and imagination.

It is therefore not simply that diversity—as a set of policies within the public realm but also as a way of viewing the world—is here to stay, but that it can provide us with exciting opportunities to move **beyond** our habits of thinking, behaving and ways of organizing our worlds. Because living with diversity gives us a much more complete picture of reality—one that takes into account the plurality of experiences that compose the world—it can function as a catalyst for an expansion of our capabilities at both personal and collective levels.

This, however, is not achieved without a personal commitment to self-examination. We need to examine our idea of where we are in relation to others. If we think of our own view of the world as a kind of map, then we have to think about where we place the centre of this map—and who designed the map in the first place.

This is something most of us take for granted. But it would be a salutary exercise for all coaches to re-think their own ideas of the world map—and their personal place within it. Professor Mahmood Mamdani, of Columbia University, writes:

> When the sixteenth-century Italian missionary Matteo Ricci brought a European map of the world—showing the new discoveries in America—to China, he was surprised to find that the Chinese were offended by it. The map put Europe at the centre of the world and split the Pacific, which meant that China

appeared at the right-hand edge of the map. But the Chinese had always thought of China as the 'Middle Kingdom', which obviously should have been at the centre of the map.

To please his hosts, Ricci produced another map, one that split the Atlantic, making China seem more central. In China, maps are still drawn this way, but Europe has clung to the first type of map. The most commonly used map in North America shows the United States at the centre of the world, sometimes even splitting the Asian continent in two ... today, the most widely used world map has Western Europe at its centre. Based on the Mercator Projection, it systematically distorts our image of the world: even though Europe has approximately the same area as each of the other two peninsulas of Asia—pre-partition India and Southeast Asia—Europe is called a continent, whereas India is a subcontinent, and Southeast Asia is not even accorded that status; at the same time, the area most dramatically reduced by the Mercator Projection is Africa (Mamdani, 2004:28).

In other words, maps are not the simple objective records that most people take them for. They are loaded with presuppositions and omissions. Maps broadly reflect power relations and cultural assumptions—and in this sense, maps also reflect our own unconscious attitudes and inherited cultural assumptions. "We" tend to see ourselves as occupying the centre of the world, while other cultures are satellites orbiting around us on the periphery. This is an accurate image of precisely what coaches must avoid: they are not the centre of the universe, with the clients—particularly if from different cultures—merely drawn in by the coach's gravitational power. They must be galaxies of equal measure.

It can be hard, even unsettling, to adjust life-long held assumptions. The Peters Projection Map, for example, was created in 1974 in order to redress the traditional imbalance created by the projections first set out by the sixteenth-century cartographer Gerhard Mercator, which are still largely in use today. While necessarily creating other distortions, the Peters Projection more accurately reflects the correct size of the continents, particularly restoring Africa to its rightful size.

To these representational changes in the way spaces are located on maps, we must add also technological ones. When looking at a map printed on a piece of paper, for instance, we usually approach it in the traditional way, locating North, South, West and East by following the conventional "top, bottom, left, right" direction. So, Europe, North America and parts of Asia are seen in the North, while the remaining areas of the world are seen in the South. But think of a map as seen on a computer screen, in an application like Google Earth, for example. In a map like that, the relationship between the person and the charted territory takes on an entirely new dimension, as the points of reference are not fixed—we can see, and "enter", the map from any direction.

Maps using the Peters Projection have been used in Leadership Development seminars in the United States to demonstrate that there are indeed other ways of conceptualizing the world, and that our own "space" may actually be smaller and less central than we had always assumed. To this we can add that our points of reference—our bearings—may also need to be reconsidered. Our understanding of North, South, West, East, as well as top, bottom, left and right, with all the symbolic associations that these points of reference imply, may also need to be reconfigured. Fascinatingly, some facilitators have reported that a variety of clients, faced with these new perspectives, have reacted with disbelief or even anger.

The centre has long been seen as the West, with the periphery consisting mostly of the West's former colonies. In his important work *Orientalism*, the scholar Edward Saïd deconstructed the long history of Western scholarship which purported to portray "the Orient," but which was frequently not only patronising, but as much an instrument of colonial control as of scholarship. Saïd wrote:

> Orientalism was ultimately a political vision of reality whose structure promoted the difference between the familiar (Europe, the West, 'us') and the strange (the Orient, the East, 'them'). This vision, in a sense, created and then served the two worlds thus conceived. Orientals lived in their world; 'we' lived in ours. The vision and material reality propped each other up, kept each other going. A certain freedom of intercourse was always the Westerner's privilege; because his was the stronger culture, he could penetrate, he could wrestle with, he could give shape and meaning to the great Asiatic mystery, as Disraeli once called it (Saïd, 1991:43–44).

This does not differ so greatly from some of the images served up today by much of the Western media, particularly TV, especially when fashionable notions such as a "clash of civilizations" have been widely aired. In his later work, *Culture and Imperialism*, Saïd argues that the huge changes that occurred in the post-colonial era and a shift in the balance of power have led to a sense of unease in the West: "The sense for Europeans of a tremendous and disorienting change in perspective to the West-non-West relationship was entirely new, experienced neither in the European renaissance nor in the 'discovery' of the Orient three centuries later" (Saïd, 1994:237).

Today such uncertainty can lead to entirely fresh possibilities. "History and geography are transfigured in new maps, in new and far less stable entities, in new types of connections", wrote Saïd (1994:384).

In the context of diversity, it is precisely such "connections" which coaches must strive to create or facilitate. New roads and pathways must be cut out of the walled cities of our minds. But coaches, too, must "decolonize" their minds. They must rethink their understanding of what constitutes the centre and what comprises the periphery, so as not to place themselves as the symbolic centre of a relationship in which the client occupies, even if only temporarily, the outer edge. This requires commitment and constant vigilance on the part of the coach, as well as an awareness of the complex processes—social, cultural, economic, personal—that go on to make us what we are. Only then can they help create the new, more realistic and equitable maps that clients need to chart.

Marti Janse van Rensburg writes

Marti Janse van Rensburg discusses other diverse influences such as race, language and gender in order to help coaching practitioners work with greater knowledge, understanding and wisdom with their clients in an increasingly complex business environment.

I recall going to school when I was five years old wearing built-up boots to correct a knee problem and being teased mercilessly by a group of kids, the same age, same colour and speaking the same language as me. For all intents and purposes we were the same. I was also teased for not being able to read as my parents thought that learning to read in school was soon enough. I was a relatively happy child, the first-born grandchild on both sides of the family and well-loved. This was a shock to me, and it did not get easier. I learnt to read very quickly, and six months into my first school year I had read all the prescribed books for the first five years of primary school. This made me more of a freak.

Throughout my 12 years of school, I often felt the odd one out in spite of the fact that in apartheid South Africa I was in a school with hardly any recognized diversity. The kids were uniformly white, Afrikaans-speaking, and all linked to some version of a Protestant Christian church. The fact that at 14 years old, I suddenly grew to be six feet tall didn't help. I made friends with the other odd kids at school, and even though we had our differences, I found that they were more tolerant and understanding than the so-called "in-crowd".

Later I studied chemical engineering at a conservative Afrikaans university; the engineering faculty being even more conservative. I was the first female ever to sit on the engineering house committee. Even at university, I found I was drawn to the "strange ones" with whom I could explore odd thoughts and philosophies.

This is not a sad story. I learnt from an early age to try and understand what motivates people, what are their rules, and how they are different. I wondered if there was something in their difference that might be useful to me. This process started a life-long journey where diversity for me was not about race, gender or religion—but rather how we are similar in values and beliefs, as well as how we are different. I wondered, where did these values and beliefs come from and should they be questioned? In this way, I began to question the underlying assumptions the people around me were operating from, and I have continued to explore these in my work on myself and in my coaching and facilitation work with others.

Origins and similarities

We can all trace our ancestry back to Africa about 150 000 to 200 000 years ago when we shared a common ancestor or mother (Kaessmann and Pääbo, 2002). During an ice age approximately 80 000 years ago, a group of early humans left Africa for Yemen. These people, an estimated 250 of them, created all the other races in the world today. About 70 000 years ago some of this group moved to the Indian sub-continent, and continued into Indonesia and Australasia. With the thawing of the ice age, humans moved into the interior of Asia and Europe and only arrived in Europe approximately 42 000 to 43 000 years ago from India and the Middle East (Olson, 2007).

The final migration was roughly 15 000 to 35 000 years ago during another ice age, when some of the hominids inhabiting the Arctic went into North and later South America (Olson, 2007). This means that the entire population of Europe, Asia, Australasia and the Americas are descendants from an estimated 250 people who left Africa all that time ago. This is why among rugby players, Lote Turquiri (a Melanesian from Fiji) is more closely related to Stephen Larkham (a white Australian) than George Gregan (who was born in Zambia).

Given our common ancestral lineage, how did we develop our obsession with difference? How we appear to each other has become more important than how we feel, taste and smell. We have become acutely sensitive to small differences which we use to evaluate and judge others. We create groupings around these differences in order to belong—whether to race, gender, a religious group or even the book club we join.

Unfortunately, in the process, we also create assumptions about other groups and their relative hierarchy to our group. We tend to associate power with other groups, as an aspiration ("I want to belong to that group"), or because we fear that our choice might be incorrect. This often leads to judgement, for example, that the other group is "wrong" or "inferior". This habit has sparked many religious and ethnic conflicts and wars.

To understand and manage diversity we need to look at the various elements that constitute difference, looking in some detail at race, gender, language and religion.

Race

Although skin colour is a surface adaptation to climate conditions, it still makes a huge difference to how we see people ... and how we see ourselves.

Ramphele (2008:73) defines racism: "Racism is essentially the use of the concept of 'races' to establish a hierarchy of power relationships by assigning value to categories of people defined as inferior or superior. It is a socio-economic and political mechanism that justifies treating fellow human beings as 'others'." As Ramphele states, we assign value either inferior or superior to the "other".

Race differentiation is particularly pertinent in South Africa due to its history. I once gave a client an article, "Dear White Boss" (Caver and Livers, 2002), which he said he could have written himself. A compilation of the experiences of African Americans in the USA, the article expressed feelings of alienation, and how some felt they could not trust their white colleagues or bosses to support them when they made mistakes. As a result, these individuals did not feel they could contribute fully at work. One African American manager said: "The executive team saw me, not as a seasoned strategist, but as an authority on race relations" (Caver and Livers, 2002). Another story, told by an inebriated white colleague over dinner, was that blacks get too many breaks and are not smart enough to be in executive positions. This is not dissimilar to what I hear from my black clients in South Africa, comments such as: "If I am quiet, I am told I am not assertive enough—and when I speak up, I am told I am too aggressive".

In *Our Separate Ways*, Bell and Nkomo (2001) talk about the experiences of white and black females in the USA. They talk about the journey of women with ambition and armed with degrees: working hard, contributing to the bottom line, proving themselves, putting in excessive time, often at the expense of their personal lives, only to be told to wait for opportunities, while the ones who decide not to leave often find that the rewards are not in line with the costs. They talk about what is different for black and white women, and how black women more readily find their authority questioned. These are worldwide issues.

Differences can concern eye contact, greetings and apologizing. Westerners view lack of eye contact as offensive or shifty, whereas Africans cultures regard it as a sign of respect. Loud conversation between Africans is a sign that no secrets are withheld, while Westerners regard it as bad manners. Generally speaking, greetings with Europeans are a simple habit and carry little meaning. The person who asks you "How are you?" expects a superficial answer. In African culture, it is a ritual that has to be done with respect and attention. One student told how he walked through his village as a child. He stopped in front each person, asking about all the family members and their well-being. This was done every time he walked through the village, even if several times a day.

Deborah Tannen, the well-known American socio-linguist, in *The Power of Talk* (1995:142) mentions that "we speak in ways our culture has conventionalized and expect certain types of responses. Take greetings for example. I have heard visitors to the United States complain that Americans are hypocritical because they ask how you are but aren't interested in the answer. To Americans, How are you? is obviously a ritualized way to start a conversation rather than a literal request for information. In other parts of the world, including the Philippines, people ask each other, 'Where are you going?' when they meet. The question seems intrusive to Americans, who do not realize that it, too, is a ritual query to which the only expected reply is a vague 'Over there'."

Differences can be even more obvious in language. Africans generally say "sorry" to indicate that they witness your discomfort or pain; "sorry" does not indicate an apology for it. A few years ago, I worked with an American colleague who tripped over a wire on a conference room floor. The technician setting up the computer equipment said "Sorry". My colleague turned around in surprise and said, "It wasn't your fault" and the technician, who was black, just shook his head.

It is no secret that the ethnic debate in South Africa is complex, but it is not the only nation facing similar issues. On a daily basis, there are media stories about people from other African countries who complain that they are badly treated by ordinary citizens and the police in South Africa. As I write, the dominant story in the news is the ethnic violence in townships in Johannesburg and Cape Town. Dr Mamphela Ramphele in *Laying Ghosts to Rest* references ethnic chauvinism, and the way different ethnic groups in South Africa "experience their sense of belonging in different regions in South Africa" (Ramphele, 2008:98). She cites the example of President Julius Nyerere of Tanzania, who abolished the formal role of traditional leaders in the interest of national unity. This allowed Tanzanians to see themselves as Tanzanians first, in contrast to South Africa where tribal leaders and ethnicity are recognized by the Constitution. "Indigenous laws and practices can only enrich our democracy if they are properly reviewed and aligned with the values we aspire to in our national Constitution. Otherwise tradition will continue to be a source of disadvantage and division" (Ramphele, 2008:98).

HOW TO USE THIS

Self-awareness and practice

Developing self-awareness and personal wisdom only translates into changed behaviour when we decide what we may need to do differently, practising changes first in ourselves and then being observant inside the coaching conversation. This exercise is taken from Nancy Kline's work for coaches and consultants in the Thinking Environment® (1995).

- List your assumptions about your own race versus other races; which if any are inherently true?
- What assumptions do you make about the different types of power of your race versus other races?
- What assumptions do you make about your clients, their abilities, their habits and potential?
- Which assumptions are stopping you from seeing the potential of your clients?
- Ask your clients' how their racial experience affects their view and behaviour towards others, both at work and in their personal lives?
- How is your racial experience impacting the way you coach, and what might be a more liberating alternative view for you to enhance your success as a business coach?

Gender

> We know that many women and men diverge in interests, abilities and desires. But is this a problem that should be fixed? (Pinker, 2008:255).

In this section, we explore gender, choices women and men make, and the different ways in which men and women communicate. We also look at how both parties are affected in a business context, and what this would mean for the coach.

South Africa is regarded as one of the most progressive countries in terms of gender representation. Gender equality is written into the South African Constitution. Nevertheless, "Women are still treated as lesser beings in the name of culture. They are considered minors, possessions of their patriarchal families in many settings, and they can be denied the right to inherit. Pride in the distinctiveness of African customs is cited as a reason for continuing practices that are in conflict with our constitution" (Ramphele, 2008:75). In addition, South Africa is reputed to have one of the highest incidences of violence against women in the world, including rape.

In general, most women with whom I work do not want to be treated differently. What they want is choice and equal opportunity, equal responsibility and equal pay.

Aiming for balanced representation might not be the ideal solution, even if it seems to be the obvious one. Pinker (2008) wrote about research on this issue in the USA, Canada and Europe. Pinker says that her book is about what women want and why they want it, and asks whether it makes sense to use men as the base model when we talk about women at work. She shows distinct differences in the psychological profiles of men and women: learning problems, attention deficit disorder, and autism spectrum disorders are four to ten times more likely to occur in boys, whereas anxiety and depression are twice as likely in girls. Despite learning disabilities, boys tend to be successful in adult life, while the girls, despite forging ahead of the boys in social skills and learning, usually choose different paths from those that would give them lucrative careers and status.

Pinker (2008:10) points out that "Equal opportunity doesn't necessarily lead to equal results". Currently women outnumber men at universities throughout the developed world. Women far outnumber men in veterinary science, pharmacy, law and medicine. In the awarding of business degrees, the numbers are equal, while more degrees are awarded to men in architecture, physics and engineering. Added to this, in spite of the percentage of degrees awarded, there are far fewer female than male physicians and lawyers practising. As much as this might be due to current incumbents coming from years when the degrees obtained were more skewed to males, Pinker shows that women often start their chosen careers and subsequently leave to take up alternative options.

What is this about, then? Grouzet *et al.* (2005) researched this topic via a survey of nearly 1 900 people in 15 countries regarding intrinsic versus extrinsic goals. Intrinsic goals were defined as making a difference and belonging, whereas extrinsic goals were defined as the search for financial reward and status. The research showed that the goals are in conflict, and that people seldom pursue both. The research study also indicated that women are more likely to be motivated by intrinsic goals, where men are motivated by extrinsic goals. Further research indicates that these results vary from more affluent or developed countries to less affluent or developing countries.

Communication styles

We also need to consider how men and women differ in their styles of communication. Tannen's (1995) research indicates that men talk about "I" and women talk about "we". In US businesses, men's speaking style, as the majority voice, dominates. Women tend to be ignored and interrupted. Women in a business environment say "we" even when they do the work themselves. Pinker (2008) indicates that men tend to blame externally when something goes wrong, yet accept praise internally. Pinker indicates that women do the opposite, and are more inclined to attribute their success to chance and to their own failure or inability.

If we consider confidence, women tend to minimize their certainty and men their doubts. This may create the impression that women lack confidence. This can be due to their tone of voice, hesitancy in speech or use of language. Some of this, especially in South Africa, might be due to speaking in a second or third language. As women are more inclined to feel they must know everything before speaking, and men are often happy to know 50 per cent and fake the rest (Pinker, 2008), women tend to ask more questions. Again, although not necessarily an indication of a lack of confidence, it could create that impression. Studies show that women are more likely to downplay their certainty and men more likely to minimize their doubts. One study provides evidence that, what comes across as lack of confidence on the part of women, may actually reflect not one's actual level of confidence but the desire not to seem boastful (Tannen, 1995:142). However, in business, and particularly in the USA, the style of interaction that is more common is the assertive style used among men.

Often men and women in the same position end up being paid unequally. Usually, we attribute this to gender discrimination and injustice, but there may be an alternate reason. Babcock and Laschever

(2003) showed in several studies that women do not negotiate for more money. Even women trained in negotiation skills do not negotiate salaries and perks for themselves. Men tend to strongly negotiate on salary, position and authority; women are often more concerned about whether they are qualified enough to do the job.

HOW TO USE THIS

Self-awareness and practice

- How do you experience discrimination against your gender, and what are your views on the opposite sex?
- How does this influence the way you experience your clients' issues and their choices?
- Think of a time when one of your clients had an opposing view to yours; how did that affect your ability to be objective and to coach the client without judgement?
- Think of a difficult experience a client has experienced with a boss or direct report of the opposite sex? How did this affect their thinking and behaviour? What would they have done differently if the person in question was of the same sex?

Changing behaviour, fundamentally and transformationally, requires you as a coach to help yourself and the client to reflect on assumptions that cause specific behaviour, and to review the belief systems that underlie those assumptions. Identifying and transforming limiting assumptions to empowering ones can in itself lead to behaviour change.

Language and linguistic patterns

As I live and work in a country with 11 official languages, it is necessary to view language as a diversity issue. Although the standard business language is English, it is sometimes forgotten that for many of us English is not our first language. Although an Afrikaans-speaking South African, I speak English most of the day and tend to think and dream in English. I recently facilitated a group session where I noticed that a black man was frowning. I asked him if I had said something with which he disagreed. He spoke fluent and beautiful English, and his answer surprised me. He explained that he was translating my words into his own language, and that one word did not have a direct translation. He clarified that he tends to think in his own language, and when he goes home on Friday he leaves English in his car, picking it up again on Monday when back in the office. I was astonished that two people who, in spite of not having English as a first language, speak it fluently all day long yet have such different experiences. It made me aware of how easy it is to make incorrect assumptions about people's use of language.

Often I find myself coaching in English, my second language, with a client who is also speaking English; but for them, English may be their second, third or fourth language. One observation made by a colleague in a supervision session recently, was that because she speaks, thinks and works in a second or third language as a coach—it heightens her focus, attention and being present for the client.

Other than language, how we say what we say is learned behaviour and differs from one person to the other. We all, including our clients, have probably had the experience of speaking to a group of people, realizing later that the interpretation of what we had said varied from person to person. Similarly, in talking to individuals, we may have experienced one person being overly sensitive to criticism or feedback, and another hardly noticing it at all. We often think that what we say is easily interpreted and understood, but that is not necessarily so. It is said that one should treat people the way you would like to be treated, but there are subtleties to this rule. Your view of how you would feel if spoken to in a certain way, is not necessarily the same as that of the person being spoken to. In African tradition, for instance, when you lend something to a friend or neighbour, you may not ask for it back. If you want your lawnmower back, you need to ask to borrow it back from the same neighbour.

As a socio-linguist Tannen (1995) discusses how linguistic style determines our view of people and ideas, and how our assumptions can be mistaken. She explains that there is a visible difference between the way men and women communicate. We assign meaning to linguistic behaviours, such as apologizing, questioning, being direct or indirect, and in the process we can easily misjudge others. In the fast-changing business world, success often depends on recognizing good ideas and implementing them. However, should an executive miss an idea because it was not voiced confidently enough, it could have serious repercussions for the business. Table 2 shows the rationale behind various styles of talking, the assumptions behind each style, and the unintended and potential consequences due to misinterpreted stylistic differences.

As coaches, we should be aware of our own linguistic behaviour when coaching executives, and be able to help them to become observant, recognizing their own and their team's style and behaviour.

Taking turns to speak is at the centre of any conversation or meeting, yet knowing when it is appropriate to speak depends on reading signals. Often meetings deteriorate because some feel it is acceptable

Table 2. Style of talking and possible consequences thereof.

	Style of talking	*Unintended consequences of style*
Sharing credit	Uses "we" rather than "I" to describe accomplishments. Why? Using "I" seems too self-promoting.	Speaker doesn't get credit for accomplishments and may hesitate to offer good ideas in the future.
Acting modest	Downplays their certainty, rather than minimizing doubts, about future performance. Why? Confident behaviour seems too boastful.	Speaker *appears* to lack confidence and, therefore, competence; others reject speaker's good ideas.
Asking questions	Asks questions freely. Why? Questions generate needed knowledge.	Speaker appears ignorant to others; if organization discourages speaker from asking questions, valuable knowledge remains buried.
Apologizing	Apologizes freely. Why? Apologies express concern for others.	Speaker appears to lack authority.

Giving feedback	Notes weaknesses only after first citing strengths. Why? Buffering criticism saves face for the individual receiving feedback.	Person receiving feedback concludes that areas needing improvement aren't important.
Avoiding verbal opposition	Avoids challenging others' ideas, and hedges when stating own ideas. Why? Verbal opposition signals destructive fighting.	Others conclude that speaker has weak ideas.
Managing up	Avoids talking up achievements with higher-ups. Why? Emphasizing achievements to higher-ups constitutes boasting.	Managers conclude that speaker hasn't achieved much and doesn't deserve recognition or promotion.
Being indirect	Speaks indirectly rather than bluntly when telling subordinates what to do. Why? Blatantly directing others is too bossy.	Subordinates conclude that manager lacks assertiveness and clear thinking, and judge manager's directives as unimportant.

Source: Tannen, D. (1995).

to interrupt or to finish a colleague's sentences. Some people have a rather long thinking pause and might feel left out if not given time to speak; alternatively they might choose to not participate at all. Kline (1999/2004) advocates a meeting process where everyone speaks once before anyone speaks twice. This is helpful if everyone is to be heard, and Sunny and I use this methodology to great effect. I have found that when teaching groups, individuals who pause, taking longer to speak, find this process very useful and contribute well. Extraverts or very vocal participants find it frustrating as they cannot speak as often as they would like to.

HOW TO USE THIS

Self-awareness and practice:

- What is your home language or mother tongue, and are the two different?
- What is the home language or mother tongue of your client? If there is a language differential, how does this affect both of you?
- Are any of the language patterns shown in Table 2 true for you? How does this affect you in your communication with people around you, and especially with clients?
- How does your client gauge their effectiveness in communicating with colleagues, direct reports and more senior people in the organization?
- Are any of the language patterns in Table 2 useful for your client?
- How can you help your client to be more aware of their linguistic patterns, and what can they change in order to have a greater impact or influence in the workplace?

Ask your client to keep a journal observing when their linguistic patterns are successful and when not in the workplace. Once your client is aware of the effectiveness of their communication and the cause of potential ineffectiveness, you can agree goals and an action plan to create substantial change.

Religion

Religion comes into play in South Africa as well, although not as radically as in other parts of the world where wars are fought over religious differentiation. It is possible that with the variety of races in South Africa, and given the country's history, religion is not as critical a point of differentiation as elsewhere. Freedom of religion is entrenched in the South African Constitution, Clause 15 of which provides that "Everyone has the right to freedom of conscience, religion, thought, belief and opinion". This is similar to the First Amendment of the US Constitution, which includes the provision that "Congress shall make no law respecting an establishment of religion, or prohibiting the free exercise thereof".

Coach practitioners need to have an understanding of religion, without letting their own views on religion and spirituality cloud how they work with their clients. When conducting research a few years ago on the status of coaching in South Africa, I spoke to a coach who was a devout Christian. He insisted that Christianity be brought into his coaching practice with all of his clients. My view is that if clients are aware of this, and choose him accordingly, that is fine. If not, it is inappropriate. With most of my clients, I respect their beliefs and endeavour to gain enough understanding of their religion to coach them within their belief system.

This view is supported by Barney Pityana, chairman of the South African Human Rights Council (HRC), in his foreword to *Clued-up on Culture: A Practical Guide for South Africa* (2001). He indicates that religious freedom is found where a group observes its rituals without infringing on the rights of others. It is therefore important to understand the basics of other beliefs and cultural practices. Pityana says, "Religion cannot be confined to the performance of ritual; it is pre-eminently a lifestyle as well."

It is also important to note that religious belief is not necessarily evident, and people do not always adhere to the religion associated with their race or cultural group.

HOW TO USE THIS

Self-awareness and practice

- What are your religious or spiritual beliefs?
- How do they impact on your view of other religions?
- What religion, if any, does your client practice?
- If so, how important is it in their life and how does it impact on their business environment?
- How much do you understand about your client's faith? Should you learn more?
- If the client's religious beliefs fundamentally differ from yours, should you consider not taking the contract?

Cultural differences in the workplace

It is important to consider how culture is defined, particularly within a business context, including classifications and dimensions of culture, and how these may be applied to business coaching.

Culture may be defined as a collective programming of the mind that shows in the values, symbols and rituals to which we hold fast (Hofstede, 2001). **Values** may be defined as people's aspirations of how things should be done, and **beliefs** as practices within the culture (Javidan and House, 2001).

Rosinski (2003) advocates understanding different cultures as necessary for a coach to broaden their understanding and be better equipped to assist the client. He talks about professional or organizational culture versus national culture, and indicates various groupings of diversity such as geography and nationality (including region, religion and ethnicity), discipline, profession and education, organization (including industry, corporation, union and function), social life (including family, friends, social class and clubs), and gender and sexual orientation.

He compiled a Cultural Orientations Framework of seven categories, and within each of these categories are several dimensions:

- a sense of power and responsibility round the question, "Do you control nature or does nature control you?" (Rosinski, 2003:51);
- time-management approaches;
- identity and purpose;
- organizational arrangements;
- territory;
- communication patterns; and
- modes of thinking.

This work creates understanding between people who work together, and helps coaches understand the clients with whom they work, as well as the environment within which their clients operate. Robbins (2001) attests that a flaw in most organizational behaviour research is that it is chiefly (80 per cent) conducted by Americans in the USA. Hofstede's original research included South Africa, but because the respondents were primarily English-speaking white males, the research is hardly representative of the population.

Although strongly Eurocentric, Hofstede's dimensions are internationally acclaimed as descriptive of regional, ethnic and religious cultures (Schneier, 1998). In 1998 Schneier conducted qualitative research in South Africa to determine whether these dimensions are relevant and sufficient to describe South African ethnic culture. Her research is based on the premise that an overarching imperative in cross-cultural research is the issue of meaning. She argues that quantitative calculations of dimensions may be similar or equivalent but that this does not necessarily imply their similarity or equivalence in terms of meaning. "The effective communication of meaning requires an awareness of how others view their world" (Schneier, 1998:3).

Schneier's (1998) results indicated that, although relevant, Hofstede's five dimensions are not sufficient to describe South African ethnicity. Values that are distinctly African emerged in two main areas: communalism and procedure-driven, time orientation. Communalism is described as implying an interdependence of a uniquely African kind; it stands separate from individualism and collectivism. Hofstede's reference to time in his fifth dimension links time to entrepreneurialism. He does not refer to a past, present and future orientation nor to a linear, circular or procedural perspective of time. Schneier (1998) argues that acknowledging an African procedural-traditional time orientation may play a role in focusing on the quality of an experience or intervention and its results in addition to maintaining efficiency within the traditional Western linear time orientation.

Relevant is the finding that management effectiveness is independent of culture and race, and that ethnically diverse management will not inhibit corporate competitive performance (Thomas and Bendixen, 2000:516). This confirms our view that the purpose of any of these studies is to assist our clients in becoming global managers.

It also confirms that research is needed in all countries where coaching is taking place that will help both coaches and organizations to understand the cultural implications of their work with senior managers and executives. For example, in Indonesia, a series of ten local culture research projects was aimed at researching regional cultural values with the aim of making "local cultures national", and "connecting the Republic of Indonesia together with cultural diversity through the state-slogan, 'Unity in Diversity'" (Jones, 2005:278). For coaches in our global economy today, and particularly for those who may be coaching by telephone from another part of the globe, it is important to understand the culture of the country, as well as the culture of the organization.

As Percy Barnevik, the CEO of the Swedish firm Asea Brown Boveri, put it, "Global managers have exceptionally open minds. They respect how different countries do things, and they have the imagination to appreciate why they do them that way ... Global managers are made, not born" (Javidan and House, 2001:292). As coaches, we can assist in the "making" of global managers if we have open minds and have a deep understanding of our own individual worldview.

HOW TO USE THIS

Self-awareness and practice

- How aware are you of the cultural differences within your client's organization?
- How do these differences influence their style of communication and how do they inhibit clear communication?
- As a coach, how can you communicate across the differences between your culture and that of your client?
- If your client operates in a multi-national organization in a variety of countries, how does this impact on their behaviour?
- What needs to happen to broaden understanding for the client?
- How can you help your client to change their communication style and behaviour?

Example: For example, Sunny is working with a female client who has a humane and very gentle orientation. The client is working within what the client feels to be an aggressive, male dominated multi-national. One of the areas with which she is helping her client, is to develop a style of assertive intervention to get her point across, while at the same time proposing a communication strategy behind the scenes with her line manager to change the aggressive culture of meetings. Sunny is working with her client on style of communication, i.e., linguistic patterns that do not serve the client's ability to communicate assertively, and body language that will be influential rather than submissive. She is also working with her client to help her to identify the benefits and consequences of changing her style of speaking and presenting.

In any multi-cultural or multi-national organization, it is useful to conduct a survey to understand how individuals view managing people, resolving conflict, taking decisions and solving problems differently. Once differences are identified and understood, the individual or group can aim to create agreed guidelines for behaviour towards colleagues and in teams.

Individualism versus collectivism

One of Hofstede's five dimensions (Robbins, 2001) is individualism versus collectivism. Hofstede defines individualism as the degree to which people act as individuals rather than members of a group, and collectivism as the opposite. Hofstede (1999) also defines individualism as something that occurs in a society where the ties between individuals are loose. Everyone looks after themselves and immediate family only. The Thomas and Bendixen (2000) study indicated a strong score on individualism for all the groups that participated.

In a collectivist society, people are part of a cohesive unit from birth and this continues throughout their lifetime with unquestioning loyalty. Rosinski (2003) has a similar definition. Countries like Japan and South Korea have become more affluent, tending to take care of their elders less than in previous decades; however, they are by no means as individualistic as Western countries.

According to Allik and McCrae (2004), Asia and Africa are predominantly collectivist, and Europeans and Americans individualist. Peterson (2007) describes common values in collectivist cultures as group achievement, harmony, keeping relationships over time, contributing to the well-being of the group, and being friendly, agreeable and sympathetic. Values associated with individualist cultures are personal achievement and advancement, dominance, autonomy and self-reliance, openness to new experience, and having fun.

Hofstede (1999) also points out that, according to his research during the 1960s and 1970s, this dimension has seen the biggest change in 30 years, and there is a correlation between a shift to individualism and economic affluence. He stresses that this is not a radical shift but rather a gradual movement. In South Africa, we have noticed the tendency in black cultures to be more collectivist, where it is assumed that elders will be taken care of. My godfather, a judge, tells the story of an old man in KwaZulu-Natal who came to see him in circuit court pleading with him to help. He had spent his money providing his children with a good education; however, once educated, they moved away and were not interested in providing for him in his old age. They said he should have provided for himself.

Javidan and House (2001) distinguish between an *institutional* emphasis on collectivism and *in-group* collectivism:

- **Institutional collectivism**: People are encouraged to belong to larger groups within society. This belonging is encouraged through incentives for such societies and groups. The society or institution decides how resources, such as the provision of childcare facilities, should be allocated. Group membership is highly valued. The group makes the important decisions, and group goals are more important than individual goals. Countries such as Greece, Italy and Argentina score low and value their individual freedom and autonomy. Self-interest is more important than the collective good. By contrast, countries such as Sweden, South Korea and Japan value group harmony and cooperation and score high in this dimension.
- **In-group collectivism**: This dimension measures the level to which people value and take pride in belonging to small groups such as family and a close circle of friends or the organization they work for. There are strong expectations of these close-knit ties, such as being favoured for positions and rewards. It is accepted and often expected to use these ties to get doors opened. Countries such as Sweden, Denmark and New Zealand score low, and favouritism and cronyism are unacceptable.

Senghor (1965) describes African collectivism as "communalism", where individualism is not in contrast to but co-exists with communalism. I have found that my clients often grapple with these apparent dichotomies. I have several clients who take care of families or even extended families, understanding that this is expected of them. Some are drawing a line as to the extent to which they are prepared to continue to do this. A few clients believe that their organizations and/or government should take care of them; others believe that they need to do it themselves.

The distinctions between individualism, collectivism and communalism, and how these are experienced by ourselves and our clients, raise interesting questions with regard to the values under-pinning the different relationships between the individual and the collective in society. In her research, Schneier (1998) presents an argument that dominant forms of European thought, such as those that gave rise to the dimensions of collectivism and individualism, are based on materialist values while communalism has humanism as its value base.

HOW TO USE THIS

Self-awareness and practice

- Do you have a tendency to be more collectivist, individualistic or communalistic?
- What are your clients like: individualist, collectivist or communalistic?
- How do they manage the expectation of behaving one way at work and another at home?
- How does their being either individualist, collectivist or com-munalistic affect them and the organizations within which they operate?
- How does this influence their aspirations and goals?

Context

Peterson (2007) points out that executive coaching is about the indi-vidual, and the coach works with the individual. Diversity, or in his definition culture, plays a different role in a group setting, espe-cially in multicultural environments. Should the coach deal with a diverse group, as in a team-coaching situation, the various cul-tures represented need to be taken into account. When the coach works with an individual, culture plays a different role. It becomes one of various factors that shape the personality and values of the individual—and assumptions about the culture should not "inter-fere with coaching the individual" (Peterson, 2007:262). Peterson cites an instance when working with a group: the Americans in the group were the most vocal, and the Japanese in the group were the least vocal. However, the individual who dominated the session was Japanese, contrary to the group norm. He states, "The deeper a coach's insights into how culture has shaped their own beliefs and values, the more sensitive they can be to how their assumptions shape their reactions and advice to the people they coach" (Peterson, 2007:262).

What is the context within which you coach? The client with whom you work might not fit the norm of their culture; but what is the norm for the organization within which the client operates? The Japanese in the above example might have a different experience working in an American company as opposed to a Japanese company. Wilber (2000a) points out that the individual works within a system. We should consider all of the systems within which an individual works, from the family, community and organization and how all of these influence the client's views, values and beliefs.

An important context in South Africa is Black Economic Empowerment (BEE) and its implications. Ramphele says of the exodus of skills, "South Africa is inflicting a double injury to itself. It is losing sorely needed skills in engineering, medicine and the humanities. It is also throwing away the significant investment made by taxpayers in educating these young people. We behave like a person who is limping from an injured foot who then shoots himself in the other foot to even the score" (Ramphele, 2008:86).

People who are part of the dominant culture of any organization or country are often unaware of culture, as it is their norm. It is the minority who tend to be more acutely aware of their own culture and the way it differs from the norm which surrounds them. For example, if we take the experience of a white man versus a black female, what are the power and rank issues that arise? The white male in most organizations in South Africa represents the dominant group, and represents authority and therefore sets the norms of behaviour. On the other hand, the white male is today's marginalized voice; white men could be angry about BEE and are the ones who often choose to leave the country.

The experience of a black woman could be entirely different as she tries to unpack the nature of power relationships that happen between people in the workplace. For example, her experience in a predominantly white, male dominated, large corporate could be different to working in a government ministry for a democratically elected black government.

HOW TO USE THIS
Self-awareness and practice

- Overall, as a coach, what is your experience of context—and how do the various contextual settings affect how you view yourself and your ability to function at your best?
- Just as cultures have a dominant leadership style, so do companies. What is the dominant leadership style of the company or corporation within which your client operates and how is that different from your client's view on leadership and their dominant leadership style?
- What contrasting experiences has the client had in other companies with different teams, and more particularly with other line managers who demonstrate contrasting styles of leadership that perhaps conflict with that of your client?

What is acceptable in one context is not necessarily acceptable in another. Some organizations value aggressive and assertive behaviour, whereas others prefer a more humane orientation. Understanding that these differences are not about right or wrong, but more about assisting the client to build their capacity to discern and adapt to difference, helps to build sustainability for clients developing new skills and competence.

Bringing it all together

> The great organization must not only accommodate the fact that each employee is different, it must capitalize on these differences (Buckingham and Clifton, 2002:5).

Diversity is a universal theme. It is important in a fast-changing and ever-diminishing world for everyone—organizations, leaders, managers as well as coaches—to understand and embrace diversity. "No matter how highly skilled, well trained, or intelligent you are, if you are making wrong or culturally inappropriate assumptions, you will not be accurate in your assessment, meaningful in your understanding, or appropriate in your interactions as a leader" (Connerley and Pedersen, 2005).

We like to ask clients to tell their life story as a start to building the relationship. Rosinski (2003) supports this when he states that in the beginning of a coaching relationship he sets aside several hours to hear the client's story. The goal here is to understand, not judge. Their story will bring out some of the themes we have discussed in this chapter. It is important to note, however, that the client may not initially share much more than superficial facts. Over time, as trust is built, this should improve, leading to more information being offered at deeper levels.

In Malcolm Gladwell's *Outliers: The Story of Success* (2008:19), he says that "People don't rise from nothing. We do owe something to parentage and patronage ... It makes a difference where and when we grew up. The culture we belong to and the legacies passed down by our forebears shape the patterns of our achievement in ways we cannot begin to imagine". His research shows that we "are products of our history and community, of opportunity and legacy" (Gladwell, 2008:285), and that "cultural legacies **matter**" (Gladwell, 2008:231).

If the coach ignores the cultural background of a client and all the subtleties that entails, the coach will almost certainly end up being prescriptive, interpreting the client's needs and experience through the coach's own lens and unconscious bias. At the worst, this could end up being invasive rather than reflective. In this sense, it is the coach's role to try to see the client's world, upbringing, background, culture and work experience through the client's eyes, helping them to reflect on how that may impact both their business practice and perspective on the world.

The various diversity themes mentioned in this chapter are a starting point, not an end destination. Although understanding diversity in all of its facets is relevant to building self-awareness, we should not underestimate its complexity. Human beings are not unlike a five-billion piece jigsaw puzzle. Coaching assists the client in starting a lifelong journey to discover those pieces, realizing that they may change over time; some may fall away and new ones be taken on.

Connerley and Pedersen (2005) suggest that multicultural aware-ness can be learned but not taught. They emphasize that training can provide the knowledge and skills necessary to cultivate bet-ter interaction and the growth of awareness. Their recommended framework for dealing with multicultural environments is a process that:

- cultivates awareness;
- acquires knowledge; and
- practises and applies the required skills.

They also indicate that the reasons why most training programmes fail are because of an overemphasis on one of three components while neglecting the other two; in coaching we should be aware of all three. **Awareness** is the first level which starts by beginning to understand your own culture—and in particular how it influences your worldview. The second level is to find the information and **knowledge** that will help you to understand how and why people are different from you. The third level is to start acquiring and practising your newly acquired **skills**, competences and behaviour that will help you to manage diversity.

In this chapter we have explored various themes of diversity, culture and gender issues. It is up to you to cultivate self-awareness, continuing your own professional development and applied practice when working with diversity, culture and gender issues in an organizational context. An integrated understanding of this chapter's core themes can only enhance your success as a business coach.

> Regardless of the amount of cultural knowledge a coach has, the best coaches will always be those who coach with an open attitude of curiosity and interest, who meet people where they are, who accept them for what they are, and who project a genuine desire to be helpful to each person on their own terms (Peterson, 2007).

Our aim is to deepen your understanding and to provide helpful pointers on which to reflect. It is strongly recommended that you enhance your understanding through your own personal development and diversity work. Every practitioner needs to expand their own ability to work with business clients who may well see the world through not just a different perspective, but through multiple lenses. For those who wish to study further there are recommended resources at the end of the chapter.

Coach's library

Babcock, L., and Laschever, S. (2003). *Women Don't Ask: Negotiation and the Gender Divide*. Princeton, NJ: Princeton University Press.

Baez, F. (2006). Coaching across cultures. WABC *Business Coaching Worldwide eZine*, 2(4)20–23. Webpage: www.wabccoaches.com/bcw/2006_v2_i4/edge.html.

Bell, E.L.J., and Nkomo, S. M. (2001). *Our Separate Ways: Black and White Women and the Struggle for Identity*. Cambridge, MA: Harvard Business School Press.

Caver, K.A., and Livers, A.B. (2002). Dear White Boss. *Harvard Business Review*, 80(11):76–81.

Connerley, M.L., and Pedersen, P.B. (2005). *Leadership in a Diverse and Multicultural Environment*. London: Sage.

Eriksen, T.H. (2001). *Small Places, Large Issues: An Introduction to Social and Cultural Anthropology*. London: Pluto Press.

Foo, S.L. (2004). Asian perspectives in coaching. *Tomorrow's Life Coach*, 3(5):7–8.

Gladwell, M. (2000). *The Tipping Point: How Little Things Can Make a Big Difference*. Boston, MA: Little Brown.

Javidan, M., and House, R.J. (2001). Cultural acumen for the global manager: lessons from Project GLOBE. *Organizational Dynamics*, 29(4):289–305.

Kline, N. (1999/2004). *Time to Think: Listening with the Human Mind*. London: Ward Lock.

Lévi-Strauss, C. (1958). *Race and History*. Paris: UNESCO.

Ngũgĩ wa Thiong'o (1986). *Decolonizing the Mind*. Oxford: James Currey/Nairobi: EAEP.

Peterson, D.B. (2007). Executive coaching in a cross-cultural context. *Consulting Psychology Journal: Practice and Research*, 59(4):261–271.

Pinker, S. (2008). *The Sexual Paradox: Men, Women and the Real Gender Gap*. New York, NY: Scribner.

Rosinski, P. (2003). *Coaching Across Cultures: New Tools for Leveraging National, Corporate and Professional Differences*. London: Nicholas Brealey.

Tannen, D. (1995). The power of talk: Who gets heard and why. *Harvard Business Review*, September–October.

UNESCO (1950). *The Race Question*. Paris: UNESCO. Webpage: unesdoc.unesco.org/images/0012/001282/128291eo.pdf.

Wirth, L. (2001). *Breaking Through the Glass Ceiling: Women in Management.* Geneva: International Labour Office. Webpage: www.ilo.org/public/libdoc/ilo/2001/101B09_102_engl.pdf, January 2009.

Wirth, L. (2004). *Breaking Through the Glass Ceiling: Women in Management: Update 2004.* Geneva: International Labour Office. Webpage: www.ilo.org/dyn/gender/docs/RES/292/F267981337/Breaking%20 Glass%20PDF%20English.pdf, January 2009.

CHAPTER SEVEN

Existential and experiential learning issues

In a nutshell, what leadership coaches offer their clients is independence. True independence means being free from the domination of one's unconscious needs and desires and being courageous enough to choose one's own destiny (Kets de Vries, 2006:272).

CHAPTER OUTLINE
- Freedom—an existential moment
- What is existentialism?
  - Being versus doing
  - Existential dilemma: meaning and purpose
  - Four ultimate existential concerns
- Existential themes at work
  - Management culture
  - The coach/client relationship
- Coaching for meaning
  - Decision making
  - Past versus present versus future

- Human systems
  - Relationships and systems
- Using experience for learning
  - Discovering barriers to learning
- In conclusion
- Coach's library

In this chapter, we explore existential and experiential learning issues that confront the coach and client at every stage in their coaching conversation, as well as the impact of psychological research in these areas. The relationship between coach and client is crucial to the successful conclusion of whatever the coaching process is seeking to accomplish. The coach's intent is not always outcomes-based; it can also focus on **learning, development, meaning** and **transformation**. The complexity of these issues is often influenced by the three-way intervention between the organization, the client and the coach.

Existential philosophy regards human existence as unexplainable, and emphasizes freedom of choice and taking responsibility for one's acts. Within the business coaching context, the coach helps the client to articulate existential concerns such as freedom, purpose, choice and anxiety, and to identify and replace limiting paradigms with empowering paradigms, thus leading to positive change.

These existential issues are relevant to the coach too. For example, if you look at purpose, the coach might be tempted to confuse their own individual purpose with that of the client, and in the process be seduced to use their position or power to influence the client. The coach often holds "guru" status, especially in the beginning of the relationship, and it is therefore important for the business coach to be aware of their own existential issues as well as those of the client.

As in existentialism, the "relationship" comes up as an important factor in learning from experience. According to Boud, Cohen and Walker (1996:11), experience is created in the "transaction" between the individual and the environment in which they operate—in other words, it is relational. More is often lost than gained by ignoring the uniqueness of each person's history and ways of experiencing the world.

In existential terms, the meaning of individual experience is not a given; in coaching, it is subject to interpretation by the individual client. In the coaching conversation, experiential learning is viewed as an active process in which the individual executive works with their own experience again and again to appreciate the meanings associated with it. In other words, the coaching client learns to actively reconstruct their own experience, attaching their own meaning to events, and yet understanding commonly accepted interpretations of their world.

Freedom—an existential moment

This exercise is adapted from an audio CD by Dr Michael Wetzler (2000).

"Imagine yourself in a field or a meadow at the base of a mountain. It is quiet, peaceful and safe. You're going to climb this mountain, wearing comfortable boots. When you're ready, begin to climb. Observe the scenery and the woods as you move. Feel the shade of the trees. You come to a stream. Listen to its soothing sounds. It is fresh, and you drink from it. Perhaps you freshen your face and your hands in its cool waters. You go further and, in due course, you reach the tree line where there are no more trees. As you look back over the valley, the view is unobstructed. It is a view of your everyday life: your comings and your goings; your struggles and your victories; your relationships with others and with your own everyday self.

"Now, you resume your journey. In front of you is a large abyss, spanned by a bridge. The bridge is strong and safe. You begin to cross the bridge and eventually you reach the other side. It is good to be on the mountain once again with your feet on solid ground. You climb on, up steeper and steeper rocks, going higher and higher until you reach the top. Here the view is breathtaking and the air is thinner. You feel that you are on top of the world, so rest here for a few moments. Not far from the top, you can see a small shelter made out of wood or stone. It is beckoning to you. You move towards it, and once inside you find a haven, a place of peace. To your surprise, as you are resting here, a figure enters. You are not afraid. You realize this figure is a guide, a mentor, of great wisdom. This being looks at you and knows you. You feel loved, known, understood and recognized. You may have a question that you need to ask about any area of your life. So ask it and listen to the response. Is an answer forthcoming, a gesture, or even a look? Allow yourself to hear the response, even if you hear it with your own voice. Or, perhaps, you even just hear a semblance of what the response might be.

"If anything else needs to be said, by you or your mentor, now is the time. When you're ready, your mentor hands you a gift. What is it? You acknowledge and receive it with gratitude. You begin to take your farewell, whether it be with a hug, a handshake, a look or a gentle parting. You leave the shelter, taking another look at the breathtaking view as you turn to walk down the mountain. With your comfortable boots you soon find yourself by the bridge. How do you feel now? You cross the bridge. Once again, you look out over the valley and behold your life.

"You have returned with your gift. Is there any way you sense that this image of your life is changing for the better? You move on down the mountain, through forest and glade, crossing the stream, till once again you find yourself in the meadow at the bottom of the mountain. For a moment you reflect on the journey you have taken. Now gently, very gently, you become conscious of being where you are in the room, in this place, listening to the sounds, conscious of your breathing, conscious of your body, and conscious of your own self and your entire life right now, today. And, you know that in future, you can always return whenever needed, to that place of peace and wisdom within you."

This concern with change and the client's journey through life is a core component of the coaching process, and combined with the question of "who am I", can present various dilemmas for coach and client within an organizational system. We explore several of these dilemmas in this chapter.

What is existentialism?

Much confusion surrounds the terms "existentialist" and "existentialism". Existential concerns have been discussed from the beginning of philosophical debate about the human condition, encompassing thinkers such as Socrates and his dialogues. The literary, philosophical and artistic response to modern cultural crises has also massively influenced existentialism. Yet existentialism remains elusive to define, and consequently today there is no cohesive school of existential therapists or coaches.

Existentialism displays a concern with individuals in crisis. The term "existence" refers to coming into being or becoming. It derives from the Latin root *ex-sistere* which means to "stand out or emerge". Existential psychology has grown out of the awareness that serious gaps exist in our way of understanding human beings. It sought to analyze the structure of human existence to "understand the reality underlying all situations of human beings in crisis" (May, 1983:44).

Basically concerned with ontology, or the science of being, existentialism is based on the underlying fact that "you and I alone must face the fact that at some unknown moment in the future we shall die" (May, 1983:51). Existential vocabulary includes terms such as **being, choice, responsibility, freedom, death, isolation, mortality, absurdity, purpose in life, limitations** and **willing**.

Rollo May (1983:49) describes existentialism as the "unique and specific portrayal of the psychological predicament of contemporary Western man". Jean-Paul Sartre is the philosophical and literary figure most associated with existentialism, although he represents an extreme and is more known for expressing many of his themes through plays and novels rather than psychological analyses (May, 1983:55).

In the United States, there was an initial resistance to the existential movement for various reasons. Firstly, it was assumed that all major discoveries had been made in the fields of psychology, psychotherapy and psychiatry. Secondly, existentialism was considered to be a philosophical encroachment into psychiatry. The third area of resistance to existentialism in the USA was the most crucial, according to May (1983:13). He describes it as the pragmatic tendency to be preoccupied with technique and an active concern in helping and changing people.

The existential movement in the fields of psychology and psychotherapy developed in a fashion that was more, rather than less, empirical, but it also crucially acknowledged that "human beings reveal themselves in art and literature and philosophy and by profiting from the insights of the particular cultural movements which express the anxiety and conflicts of contemporary man" (May, 1983:45).

Being versus doing

Ernesto Spinelli, previously existential professor of psychology at Regent's College London, noted in a lecture in Cape Town in February 2005 that:

At the moment, we inhabit a culture which places tremendous importance on expectations. A group is growing in numbers, who are seen as 'experts-in-living' and who are working with clients. We need our clients to see us as experts, but if someone asks 'What is your expertise?', our tendency is to translate expertise in terms of skills, competences, specialist knowledge, certain forms of personality tests. Our primary focus is 'doing'—experts do.

Existentialism challenges the notion of expertise as 'doing' and reconsiders expertise from the point of view of 'being'. The question then becomes, 'How is it that I am with other human beings, with other living beings, with living and non-living objects?'

The basic idea is this, that the way I reveal myself with other beings or the world in general exposes not only that moment of being, but gives a sense of totality—that individual's general stance towards reality. How I am with you reveals how I am, not only to you, but to myself, to others and to the world in general (Spinelli, 2005).

Being emphasizes the activity rather than the goal. **Being in becoming** emphasizes **who** the person is rather than **what** the person can accomplish. But it still emphasizes the concept of development. The **doing** orientation emphasizes accomplishments that are measurable by standards outside of the acting individual (Yalom, 1980:121). If we are to transform organizations—culturally, socially, emotionally and cognitively—then the ultimate goal of coaching is seeking transformation of self.

Culture plays an important role in the shaping of individual values. Florence Kluckholm, who pursued research in cultural value orientations, suggested three anthropological value orientations for the individual human: **being, being in becoming**, and **doing** (Kluckholm and Stroedbeck, 1961:15). There is constant discussion in contemporary coaching circles about which comes first, being or doing; but little mention is made about "being in becoming". This may, in fact, be the existential category where coaches most often work with their clients (McWhinney et al., 1993:28).

Existential dilemma: meaning and purpose

> If you want to build a ship, don't drum up the men to gather wood,
> divide the work and give orders. Instead, teach them to yearn for
> the vast and endless sea (Antoine de Saint-Exupéry, 1900–1944).

Often in the business coaching environment, the client will state
that one of their objectives is to determine meaning in their personal and professional life. The client may be questioning why they
do what they do. The start of this personal philosophical thinking
tends to originate from questions such as, "What motivates you?"
and "What is important to you?". One well-known example concerns two stone masons who were asked what they were doing.
One answered, "I am cutting a stone"; the other said, "I am building
a cathedral". To ask your client, "What is the meaning and purpose
of your work?" can be the beginning of a quest of self-discovery. A
surgeon in India wanted to make cataract operations very inexpen-
sive for the poor. Rather than tell his team that this was the ultimate
aim, he explained that their real vision was to "cure blindness".

Faith or spirituality speaks to our underlying values and drivers,
often being a search for something greater than we are. "Who am I and
why am I here?", is ultimately a search for meaning and purpose in life.
Often, individuals turn to faith or a spiritual journey with these questions. From a coaching perspective, a client may ask questions about a
possible change of career, or even start to think about unfulfilled challenges. Typically, these questions evolve to "Who are they?" and "How
do they be who they are?". Although coaches love to work with existential questions, such questions present a dilemma. If the organization
pays the coach's fees, and the aim of coaching is performance-related,
yet the client focuses on an inner search for meaning and purpose,
this may present an ethical challenge for the coach. Some clients are
lucky and the organization contracts the coach to pave the individual's
road to self-discovery. This, however, is not the norm! It is useful to
build this possibility into the contracting process. One way to manage
this process can be to contract with clients that those individuals who
undergo the coaching process sign an agreement to stay for one year
from the end of the coaching intervention—but I have yet to see this
implemented by the organizations with whom I work.

"The belief that one's life is controlled by external forces is associated with a sense of powerlessness, ineffectualness and ... can lead to low self-esteem" (Yalom, 1980:163). This is particularly relevant for clients who work within a large family-dominated organization with a legacy to fulfil, or a large bureaucratic corporation hampered by policies and procedures. It is here that Yalom defines anxiety: "Anxiety is a signal that one perceives some threat to one's continued existence". Coaches consistently work with anxiety, although most clients tend to label this "stress" originating from external sources.

Yalom (1980:188) states that death anxiety exists at the deepest levels of being, is heavily repressed and is rarely experienced in its full sense. He says anxiety is a guide to point the way to an authentic existence, and that life cannot be lived nor faced without anxiety.

A framework for coaching (in Yalom's view) may be a synthesis of the business belief system, the coach's model with its theoretical underpinnings, plus the development of the relationship. Spinelli, in his Cape Town supervisory session in April 2004, indicated that the "relationship" is the core factor in any therapeutic, coaching, supervisory or counselling session and perhaps even for research. My work and research have examined this and underlined, time and time again, that no matter what level the coaching intervention, it seems that the fundamental work of the coaching intervention establishes the importance of the relationship.

As Yalom puts it (in the context of psychotherapy):

> I am convinced that the surreptitious 'throw-ins' made all the difference ... I believe that, when no one is looking, the therapist throws in the 'real thing'. But what are these 'throw-ins', these elusive, 'off the record' extras? They exist outside of formal theory, they are not written about, they are not explicitly taught ... Indeed, is it possible to define and teach such qualities as compassion, 'presence', caring, extending oneself, touching the patient at a profound level, or—that most elusive of all—wisdom? (Yalom, 1980:3–4).
>
> Existential psychotherapy is a dynamic approach to therapy which focuses on concerns that are rooted in the individual existence ... it is the relationship that heals (Yalom, 1980:5).

According to May, in the Western world, we have managed to dominate nature, but in the process we have repressed the sense of being—the ontological being. Robert Hargrove (2003) says a coach is something that you "be". He asks whether the coach is "being" or "doing" when helping clients inside the coaching conversation. Hargrove promotes the idea of "Kokoro", i.e., perfecting one's inner nature. "One must not only master the technique but also perfect the way of being consistent with the discipline, having a calm and centred inner spirit; to be able to teach people; one must perfect his/her own nature" (Hargrove, 2003:44).

Hargrove (2003:48), who often brings in an existential point of view, says we have the power to choose who we are being. Choice is one of the existential concerns in the coaching process and is related to the process of setting goals and taking action. He says the coach can help the client declare new possibilities for themselves through the power of language, and that the power to choose who you need to be exists in your conversations, in your speaking and listening, and not in grappling with your history. This emphasizes the performance model versus a psychological model.

Within the coaching conversation, the coach is not necessarily looking for the psychological paradigm, but listening more to what underpins language and linguistic patterns. This resonates with my linguistic background, which predisposes the coach to analyze the context, content, structure and meaning of language when working with clients, either when shadowing them at work or in the coaching conversation.

DOING	Accomplishing tasks and goals
LEARNING	Developing competences
BEING	Understanding meaning
BECOMING	Transforming self

Figure 1. Becoming—transforming self.

Source: Adapted from Weiss (2004).

THE RABBIT HOLE STORY

One of my clients wanted help to structure the way she approached her daily life and business. I helped the client to translate her actions and her way of thinking into meaningful experience. The client discovered that she thinks linguistically and kinaesthetically, but it did not help her to structure her day using words and feelings. She decided that she needed to interpret her world differently, i.e., visually, in order to have more meaningful experiences and make life work better for her.

When the coach and client constructed a learning contract at the end of a first session, the client had as her **purpose**: to learn to structure her thinking differently; as her **strategy**: to use the new way of thinking to manage her life and her business more effectively; and as **specific outcomes**: (1) to work daily with visual thinking and visual language, and (2) to journal daily from words into pictures into visual language.

Previously, the client had constructed a kinaesthetic view of the world and had ascribed meaning to it kinaesthetically and linguistically. She needed to bring in visual thinking to make more sense of her world and to be able to "see her day". The coach and client focused on her limiting assumption that she could not think visually. That changed on the day when client and coach "went down a rabbit hole" in the coaching conversation. The client discovered herself visually by describing her journey down the "rabbit hole"; she came out into the light of the natural world with a visual rather than a kinaesthetic reconstruction of her experience.

In the light of these coaching conversations, the coach was helping the client to interpret her own reality and to see how she constructed meaning within that reality. The client achieved her goal at the end of the "rabbit hole" session—i.e., to identify her avoiding behaviours when trying to think visually (Stout Rostron, 2006c:167).

According to Hargrove (2003), masterful coaches make an existential choice to make a difference in the life of an individual, a team or an organization. He says that it is important to introduce powerful ideas into the client's thinking because that is what has the capability of shifting paradigms. Hargrove mentions the importance of questions. In the coaching process, the purpose of questions is to create insights, shift limiting assumptions, and help decisions to be made and goals to be set.

Interestingly, Hargrove (2003) insists that, if the relationship is to be powerful or profound, it is important for the coach to provide information that could possibly be difficult or threatening or embarrassing, but which is necessary for growth and learning. This is contrary to how we see the coach's role, i.e., as one of teasing out the thinking of the client. Rather than being the active agent, the coach's role is to make observations that are challenging, but which are neither judgemental, directive, nor interpretive (a therapist might choose to be analytical, directive or interpretive). I would suggest that, if Hargrove is recommending that the coach as "guru" provide answers, this could set up a relatively disempowering relationship that renders the client more passive in the thinking process. It is more valuable to focus on the empowerment of the client as an "active" agent and thinker which encourages personal responsibility.

Personal responsibility and awareness

One of our first areas of focus is awareness: helping the client to grow in awareness and to accept personal responsibility to create change for themselves. How the client takes up responsibility for change emerges from the coaching conversation.

"Locus of control" measures, at a superficial level, whether an individual accepts personal responsibility for their behaviour and life experiences, or whether the individual believes that what happens to them is unrelated to personal behaviour and is therefore beyond personal control. Individuals who accept responsibility are considered to have an "internal" locus of control, and those who reject it have an "external" locus of control (Yalom, 1980:262).

A question arises: how directive should the coach be, and what is required by coaching clients with an internal locus of control versus an external locus of control? Does your coaching process account for both? In the coaching process, the assumption of personal responsibility is a key step towards growth, achieving professional goals and creating desired individual change—personally and professionally.

Existentially, choice and change offer a way of taking responsibility and defining one's own self. Sartre also wrote, "authenticity versus self-deception is the absolute personal responsibility" (Peltier, 2001:157). "We cannot make life deliver what we want, but we can control what we think and desire; rigorous self-disciplined thought is the key" (Olson, 1962:11, cited in Peltier, 2001:158). Not specifically an intervention, but ten existential guidelines are offered for the executive coach by Peltier (2001:164–167):

- anticipate anxiety and defensiveness;
- clients must figure things out in their own way;
- commit to something;
- create and sustain authentic relationships;
- encourage choice;
- get going;
- honour individuality;
- manage conflict and confrontation;
- value responsibility taking;
- welcome and appreciate the absurd.

Coaching guidelines could advocate: reflection, developing insight and awareness, setting goals, using language appropriately, making choices and taking action. Peltier (2001:168) says, "authentic individualism requires extensive self-examination and the willingness to live with the decisions one makes as a result". This may be in contrast with other belief systems or cultural values, such as the principle of *ubuntu* in African cultures, where it is not so much individualism that is important, but relationships within the community.

Ubuntu

The African notion of *ubuntu* can be defined as "morality, humaneness, compassion, care, understanding and empathy. It is about shared values and humanity" (Boon, 1996:31). In *ubuntu* terms, you are only who you are in relation to others. In other words, *ubuntu* is about interaction within the community. *Ubuntu* sends you as an individual on a journey where you will find out who you are when you meet the people in your life. It is about life, relationships and values, and in many ways, this is a very existentialist philosophy. Northern European individualism is a very different philosophy from *ubuntu*, which experiences existence in relation to others, and within a sense of community.

The term *ubuntu* is important in the South African context as it refers to an African view of life and worldview. *Ubuntu* powerfully suggests that man is essentially a social being and that "a person is a person through other persons" (Devenish, 2005). Justice Yvonne Mokgoro of the South African Constitutional Court says that *ubuntu* is the basis "for a morality of co-operation, compassion, community (spiritedness) and concern for the interests of the collective, for others and respect for the dignity of personhood; all the time emphasising the virtues of that dignity in social relationships and practices" (Devenish, 2005).

Ubuntu is more aligned with the second of the two famously assumed existential states of being: being-for-itself and being-for-others. *Ubuntu* requires the "right balance between individualism and collectivism and is made possible by taking seriously people's need for dignity, self-respect and regard for others. Its emphasis is not on differences, but on accommodating these" (Devenish, 2005).

Four ultimate existential concerns

Yalom (2001:xvi) defines existential psychotherapy as "a dynamic therapeutic approach that focuses on concerns rooted in existence". In its technical sense, "dynamic" is rooted in Freud's model of mental functioning, assuming that "forces in conflict within the individual generate the individual's thought, emotion, and behaviour". The importance of this definition is that "these conflicting forces exist at varying levels of awareness; indeed some are entirely unconscious". These inner conflicts are not just from the individual's struggle with suppressed instinctual strivings or from traumatic memories, but are also "from our confrontation with the 'givens' of existence" (Yalom, 2001:xvii). These, "givens" or "ultimate concerns" are the "deep structures of experience". The four most closely aligned with psychotherapy are death, freedom, isolation, meaninglessness.

FOUR ULTIMATE CONCERNS: DEATH, FREEDOM, ISOLATION, MEANINGLESSNESS

The first concern is **death**. The existential conflict is the "tension between the awareness of the inevitability of death and the wish to continue to be". The second concern, **freedom**, is usually considered to be a positive factor in life. Existentially, freedom refers to each individual being responsible for their own individual worldview, life design, choices and actions. The existential tension is the implication of nothingness when human beings wish for groundedness and structure. The third concern is **isolation**, which is a fundamental, unbridgeable isolation from others. We enter the world alone and exit alone. The existential conflict is the tension between our "awareness of our absolute isolation and our wish for contact, for protection, and our wish to be part of a larger whole". The fourth concern is **meaninglessness**. If we are ultimately alone in a meaningless or indifferent universe, what is the point of living? Without a preordained design for each individual human being, "each of us must construct our own meaning in life". The existential conflict is the result of another paradox; human beings who seek meaning are thrown into a universe with no meaning (Yalom, 1980:8–10).

Paradigms and the four concerns

What is relevant to us as coaches is the construct of paradigms or worldviews. Yalom (1980:26) writes that paradigms "are self-created, wafer-thin barriers against the pain of uncertainty". He talks about the importance of meaning, how important it is for the individual human being to construct meaning in their life. He says that the existential paradigm assumes that anxiety emanates from the individual's confrontation with those four ultimate concerns in existence: death, freedom, isolation and meaninglessness.

EXISTENTIAL DILEMMA: INDIVIDUAL VERSUS COLLECTIVE PURPOSE

An interesting dilemma is the client whose family's political purpose was not aligned with the career choice that she made. She began working for an NGO, which made her family happy, as she was brought up in a family with strong socialist values. She completed her studies, moving into a helping profession where she became very dissatisfied. With great difficulty, she made the decision to fulfil her entrepreneurial talent by starting her own business, even though she knew it was against the principles of her family. She has subsequently become financially successful, showing that she has the ability and capacity to be a success in the commercial world. However, her family continues to disapprove of her newfound capability, and vociferously lets her know of their disappointment. Her dilemma is: should she continue in business or move back into the NGO environment to please her family? Will she be desperately unhappy if she cannot align her own vision for her life with that of her family? Does she need their approval to have meaning in her life, and how isolated will she be without it?

The question for executive coaches is how do these four ultimate concerns affect coaching? How do these ultimate concerns affect the client in the workplace? Is it more about purpose because people want to be doing a job that is meaningful? We know that human beings want meaningful work, and often the workplace is a major contributor to human purpose and significance. And where does their job and career fit into the rest of their life, and how does it impact on their sense of meaning, purpose or isolation?

May (1983) talks about the "organization man", i.e., the corporate executives who live, eat and breathe their work, deriving their identity from their position, power and status inside the organization and society at large. May calls this the "outer-directed man" who conforms and disperses themselves to such a degree, and participates and identifies so much with others that their own being is emptied.

Closely related to the "workaholic" executive are individuals who have always strived "for competent effective power and control ... getting ahead, achieving, accumulating material wealth, leaving works behind as imperishable monuments". These driving pressures can become a way of life that effectively conceal the questions about our ultimate concerns (Yalom, 1980:120).

Death, freedom, isolation, and meaninglessness

Yalom (1980) says that death is only one component of the human being's existential situation, and that anxiety can be understood by understanding death. According to Yalom, freedom helps us to understand the assumption of responsibility, commitment to change, decision and action; isolation illuminates the role of relationship; and meaninglessness turns our attention to the principle of engagement with ourselves and others.

The assumption of personal responsibility has a parallel with coaching. It plays a major part in any business coaching conversation: what is, and what will be, the commitment and responsibility that the executive will undertake as a step towards achieving goals. The coach is ultimately trying to help the client take responsibility for their actions, to become aware of their actions, and to be conscious of how their behaviour impacts on others. In order to look at these existential concerns as they relate to coaching, it is useful to look briefly at the research in existential psychotherapy, as well as some findings from sports coaching.

Lessons from sports coaches

What has emerged from the success of athletic coaches is the importance of dreaming and setting goals: aligning everything and "going for it". Athletic coaches introduced the concept of "balance" in one's life: where does work fit into your life and dreams; how driven do you want to be? On the other hand, "positive mental health and self-esteem are greatly enhanced when a person is excellent at something" (Peltier, 2001:170).

Failure can set up a sense of loss and isolation. One fundamental underpinning of success is to be able to make mistakes and to learn from failure: the coach needs to be able to empathize with the client and to discern how the client views failure, and help the client to see where failure can be a turning point. The client then makes the decision to change, looks at how to view things differently and learns something completely new, which is put into practice. A crucial component to learn from failure is awareness.

Existential isolation

Yalom (1980:357) gives a definition of existential isolation: "Existential isolation refers to an unbridgeable gulf between one's self and any other being; the separation between the individual and the world, separation from the world". In freedom, there is existential isolation, and the paradox of relationship is the problem of isolation. "One must learn to relate to another without giving way to the desire to slip out of isolation by becoming part of the other, but one must also learn to relate to another without reducing the other to a tool" (Yalom, 1980:359).

Yalom mentions the encounter group as a means of self-expression, but suggests they are simply monologues disguised as dialogues. If the coach is not careful, we can simply be listening to a monologue (with no room for awareness, introspection and reflection) on the part of the client. This also flags the necessity for awareness in group coaching. Unless the lead coach is trained in a methodology to include all voices, and to have all voices heard, the group process will simply be that of various individuals' solo thinking.

Very often in the first half hour of a coaching session, I find that I am listening to a monologue—so, eventually and when appropriate, I step into the labyrinth of the monologue with interventions such as clarifying questions. I would suggest that in coaching, the coach turns toward the client with the same "listening intensity" as is developed in psychotherapy.

A very interesting question is always: how many other people are there in a room, even if it seems it is just coach and client? Yalom suggests that all other people must be swept away before an authentic relationship between client and therapist can be developed. In coaching, it is essential to explore the system. In other words, the client's relationships with others in the workplace, as well as personal relationships are to be discovered. Although Yalom (1980:401) says that the "encounter itself is healing" and that "a positive relationship between patient and therapist is positively related to therapy outcome", in business coaching it is somewhat different. Although the relationship between coach and client is one key relationship, there is also the relationship with the organization.

As a consequence of coaching, the organization will be looking for visible results. These results could be made visible in a number of ways, depending on how the outcomes are defined. In the business world, it is necessary for the client to make change visible, often in behaviour or some kind of tangible results. Often the client is developing in self-awareness, and may be grappling with various existential issues. However, unless the learning is made visible in the workplace, the organization will wonder what it is to which they are contributing. If results are not forthcoming, there could be a physical (if not existential) isolation opening up for that executive!

The importance of relationship

The key concept of Yalom's research and writing is that the relationship heals. And he says that the "throw-ins" in psychotherapy, the off-the-record contributions, help to build that relationship. He asks, "How does a therapeutic relationship heal?" He answers it firmly and finally by saying "There is much evidence for the argument that it is the relationship that heals and that the real agent of change is the relationship" (Yalom, 1980:404).

The basis of my own research has been to establish if it is the relationship that determines the success of the coaching intervention. Although relationship is in fact one of the key parameters for success, there are other components that need to be in place for the intervention to be successful. For example (Stout Rostron, 2008):

- assessing qualitatively and quantitatively what has shifted during the coaching intervention;
- being coached yourself;
- being flexible;
- creating a development plan with goals;
- developing EQ;
- identifying which new client behaviours are visible and how performance has improved;
- learning from experience;
- making your ethical code explicit;
- measuring coaching results; and
- understanding the roles of others.

Sartre (Russel, 1978:38) says that engagement is the ultimate meaning. However, the difficulty is that actually one must invent one's own meaning, and then permit oneself to fulfil that meaning. Maslow (1968:21) says we live in order to fulfil our potential. The Austrian psychiatrist and creator of logotherapy, Viktor Frankl, believed that three categories help to determine life meaning:

- what one accomplishes or gives to the world in terms of one's creation;
- what one takes from the world in terms of encounters and experiences; and
- one's own stand towards suffering, and towards a state that one cannot change (Frankl, 1946).

Frankl (1946) emphasizes the uniqueness of each person's individual meaning, and that engagement emerges as an answer to meaninglessness. A core concept from Yalom (1980) and Spinelli (1989) is that it is the relationship that helps the client to move on. My work shows that the development of the relationship emerges from engagement and intervention.

Existential themes at work

Of course, coaching is very different from psychotherapy. Hargrove picks up an existential theme, quoting Peter Senge: "I believe we suffer every day; in every single business meeting we go to". He mentions the despair that many managers experience: "they feel they are unable to have authentic communication where they discuss the un-discussable, talk about problems openly, and overcome the game playing" (Hargrove, 2003:174).

Coach practitioners often explore the client's values, ethics, meaning of life, life's purpose, significant and challenging work, choice, will, action, responsibility, decision, relationships, building alliances, self-creation and desire for self-actualization.

EXISTENTIAL DILEMMA: VALUE SYSTEMS CLASH
Another potential dilemma develops when the client feels that their underlying value system clashes with that of their organization. People often have a strong sense of ethical, moral or faith-based values. When they voice their concerns inside a coaching assignment, they are reflecting on whether their value system is in

conflict with the values of the organization. The issues frustrating them may not be clear-cut, and more often than not are complex. The issues raised could be related to performance ratings, recruitment procedures, or even whether the organization's actions are in alignment with its public claims—i.e., whether they are "walking their talk".

One of Marti's friends, for example, started a new job and questioned several of the organization's business processes, indicating that they were unethical. The answer offered to him was that the company was not involved in illegal activities; their business reaped enormous capital return, and they did not plan to change their business model.

An organization's value statement may recommend specific rules and regulations, yet the leadership team might not follow or act in accordance, even behaving unethically or inappropriately. Other examples are organizations who do not adhere to environmental laws, or who pay lip service to corporate social investment for marketing purposes. Although there have been changes in corporate governance worldwide, there is still room for "massaging the numbers" or flexible management.

Management culture

Whitmore (2002:28) defines management coaching as "the management style of a transformed culture". The key existential themes to emerge from his model are responsibility demands choice, and choice implies freedom. He says because stress has reached epidemic levels worldwide, and because people are allowed little personal control in the workplace, this has impacted heavily on self-esteem. "Self-esteem is the life force of the personality, and if that is suppressed or diminished so is the person" (Whitmore, 2002:30). Whitmore's argument is that coaching for performance is a means to obtain optimum performance, but that it demands fundamental changes in attitude, in managerial behaviour and in organizational structure.

Existential therapy takes a different view of the specific forces, motives and fears that interact within the individual. The existential view emphasizes a different type of basic conflict: the existential conflict stems from the individual's confrontation with the "givens" of existence—those ultimate concerns that are inescapably part of each individual existence in the world. The four existential "concerns" do arise in the coaching context, and, although not explored as deeply as in a therapeutic context, it is important for the coach to be sensitive to them.

The coach/client relationship

"Relationship" is a key variable determining the coach's expertise. Spinelli's (1989) analysis is that we need to move away from "doing" to an authenticity which will take the coach straight to the "heart" of the relationship between the coach and the client. This is of particular significance to coaches because no matter what model or methodology a practitioner uses, it is, according to Spinelli, "the relationship" that affects the outcome of the coaching or therapy. It is the "quality" of the relationship that is of importance.

The coaching discipline worldwide has only recently begun to research the importance of the relationship in the coaching process, although psychotherapists have been analyzing the skills needed in the therapeutic environment for over 100 years. The fields of existentialism and psychotherapy are very useful to us in terms of their research into the "encounter" and the "relationship" between practitioner and client.

Whitmore's (2002:20) focus is on the question of relationship: "the relationship between the coach and coachee must be one of partnership in the endeavour of trust, of safety and of minimal pressure". To develop the relationship effectively, Peltier (2001:68) looks at the principles and concepts of the Rogerian, person-centred, relationship-oriented and experiential approach. This grew out of the existential philosophical tradition, and has an underlying humanist vision. Peltier describes it as particularly American, i.e., pragmatic, optimistic, and believing in the unlimited potential of the individual. Similar to the approach suggested by Yalom and Spinelli, Rogerian theory requires that the therapist listen with acceptance and without judgment if clients are going to be able to change.

The core skills of the client-centred approach are active listening, respecting clients and adopting their internal frame of reference. The structure of the coaching intervention needs to be framed by the ability to listen and to actively intervene only when needed. However, the coach/client relationship is based on equality. This is different to the therapist/patient relationship, which is often not considered to be an equal relationship. In a coaching relationship, one is not superior to the other; both are travellers on the client's journey. A "safe thinking environment" is built through the development of the relationship, and the relationship is what can help with the onset of change.

A vital aspect of the coaching intervention is the value of positive support of coach to client. Not only does it build trust in the relationship; it may be one of the few places where the client is unconditionally supported in their personal and professional life. The three essential characteristics identified by Carl Rogers for effective therapy are unconditional positive regard, genuineness and accurate empathy (Rogers, 1961:281–283).

This is aligned with the "appreciation" component of Nancy Kline's Thinking Partnership® in her six-stage coaching process. Giving support means a willingness on the part of the coach to give, but it also models the giving of support. I see this as a very important aspect of coaching. It is also important that both coach and client change as the relationship grows. "I urge you to let your patients matter to you", wrote Yalom (2001:26–27), "to let them enter your mind, influence you, change you—and not to conceal this from them".

The throw-ins

Yalom mentions the "throw-ins" that make all the difference in successful therapy. These "throw-ins" are just as relevant in business coaching. Yalom (1980:3) believes that, when no one is looking, "the therapist throws in the 'real thing' like a chef". These throw-ins, or off-the-record extras, are not written about, studied or even explicitly taught. Therapists and coaches may not even be aware of them. Most therapists, according to Yalom, cannot explain why many patients get better. This is why, in the emerging discipline of business coaching, it is critical that practitioners begin to develop a body of knowledge through research—to begin to identify what works, and what does not work, with the organizational coaching intervention.

The critical "throw-ins" or ingredients exist outside of formal theory. They are not written about, and are qualities such as "compassion, presence, caring, extending oneself, touching the patient at a profound level, or—that most elusive one of all—wisdom" (Yalom, 1980:4).

The existential approach helps us, as coach practitioners, to ask questions about relationships, e.g., how does your client relate to themselves and to others? As we know, participation involves risk, and interacting with others to develop relationships, the core of any business, involves personal risk and vulnerability. The question of relationships, building alliances with others, is a common thread in business. The old adage, "people do business with their friends" is relevant here. This influences the individual's journey or search for personal values and purpose.

EXISTENTIAL LIFE-CHANGING DILEMMA

What about taking on an assignment when the client has no understanding of how the coaching may change their life? Marti once turned down a potential client, who, in his initial conversation with her, revealed that he had never experienced an equal partnership in any of his relationships. He tended to fall into the role of parent or child. In marriage, he played the role of parent. He had married a much younger woman and mentored her through her academic studies. Once she was qualified, he helped her to start her professional career—then she left him. At the time of the conversation, he was in a similar relationship.

A friend had recommended that he find a coach, but he did not have a particular aim for the assignment; he said he was happy with life as it was. Marti surprised him by saying that she would rather not enter into a coaching engagement. She explained that, although he was very comfortable with his life the way it was, it did not fit the norm of a rounded or balanced set of relationships. Working on a "relationship" because society indicated he should, would require a lot of work, which could cause major personal upheaval, and it was possible that therapy was more relevant. He agreed and they parted.

Marti addressed her own concerns with the client, and would have referred him to another coach had he insisted. Her usual approach to any potential client who asks existential-type questions, is that the client needs to be prepared to question everything in their life and be committed to the process. A recent client, on completion of a long coaching intervention, said that although she had warned him, he hadn't really internalized what was going to happen. He also said he wouldn't have engaged for so long if it hadn't been so fundamentally life-changing for him. The coaching helped him to realize that it's important to be able to understand the choices available to you; in that way you can move on.

My work has examined this and underlined, time and time again, that no matter at what level the coaching intervention, it seems that the fundamental work of the coaching intervention is to establish the possibility for the relationship. It is from this position that change is possible.

The encounter

The integration of questions with the components that help to build the relationship seems fundamental to the success of the coaching intervention. The coach helps to create the container or space for the client to feel safe, even when surrounded by 20 fellow students. When compassion, presence, caring, extending yourself, touching the client at a profound level (Yalom, 1980:4) begins to open the client up to the core issues of existence such as freedom, choice, purpose and values, only then will the coaching process begin to deepen.

So, the professional encounter can cause both joy and anxiety, but it is essentially a creative experience. According to Jung, change must occur in both client and practitioner otherwise the therapy will not be effective (May, 1983:22). May suggests that the phenomena of the encounter must be studied as "it is not possible for one person to have a feeling without the other having it to some degree also" (May, 1983:23). In some ways, there is a case here for all coaches to have a theoretical understanding of cognitive behavioural psychology as well as systems theory (including family systems theory) in order to understand some of the mechanics of "relationship" that happen within the helping professions.

QUESTIONS TO DEVELOP THE RELATIONSHIP
A recent experience has led me to re-evaluate the balance between the "use of questions" by the coach and the "relationship" between coach and client and how that develops. One of my students and

I demonstrated a very simple coaching process in front of a larger group of 20 students. I, as the coach asked the student three simple questions: what's working; what's not working; and what if anything can you do differently? The purpose of the demonstration was for the other students to observe and give feedback on what worked and what didn't work between coach and client, and to identify how important the questions were.

As it turned out, how the questions were asked, and how attentive and focused the coach was on the client, and the coach's ability to "sit" with the client in her thinking space proved to be the most powerful part of the process. As coach, I interrupted the process several times to turn back to the group to discuss where we were in the process. What I have learned from working with Nancy Kline, is that as long as the client knows explicitly what is going to happen (i.e., that you will stop and turn to the audience periodically), the client goes right on thinking until you turn back to the conversation between the two of you.

In this three-question process, the client's core values started to be identified, with a depth of understanding of self. The question process allowed a key value, "health", to pop up. As it turned out, this was the crucial value. What allowed the student (as client) to courageously explore this value (being held internally but never made explicit in actions, commitment or taking responsibility) was the non-judgemental focus of the coach on the client and staying with the client in the most difficult moments.

Coaching for meaning

> Man's search for meaning is the primary motivation in his life (Victor Frankl, 1946:105).

Reconstruction of meaning is one of the most important levels in which practitioners work with their coaching clients. In coaching today, clients raise the issue and often focus on the meaning and purpose in their professional and personal lives. Whitmore (2002:119) mentions that one of the goals of humanistic psychology is the fulfilment "of human potential through self-awareness".

Elisabeth Denton defined spiritual intelligence as "the basic desire to find ultimate meaning and purpose in one's life and to live an integrated life" (Whitmore, 2002:120). Zohar and Marshall (2001) in *Spiritual Intelligence* say that in business today people are facing a real crisis of meaning. This theme is being carried forward in most of the contemporary coaching literature. Many coaches work and integrate meaning in all four quadrants (Wilber, 1997) and work at the levels of IQ, EQ and SQ (rational, emotional and spiritual intelligence) with their clients inside the coaching relationship.

Whitmore (2002) says coaching can help people to clear away their defensive shields and self-imposed blockages, often coaching their clients through various crises of meaning in their lives. He makes a salient point that maybe it is better for some businesses to steer away from the complexities of meaning and purpose. For the coach, this has an impact in how they work with the client.

FAMOUS PARENT DILEMMA

One particular executive is the daughter of famous parents, and feels that she never quite measures up to their expectations. Marti experienced this to a certain degree with her scientist father and fashion designer mother. Being interested in both fields, she studied science at the university where her father was well known. Whenever she gained high marks it was said, "Well, no wonder, look who her father is, he probably helped her", and when she did not do well the comment was, "Do you know who her father is? He must be so disappointed." Similarly, when Marti entered the fashion industry, she was always her "mother's daughter", and the whispers suggested that this was the reason she was hired, or asked to design clothes for fashion shows, or gained media publicity: was because of her mother. And, her parents were not necessarily famous, simply well-known. What must it be like to be the great-grandson or great-granddaughter of Sigmund Freud, Pablo Picasso, or a child of Nelson Mandela?

This is a real dilemma for children of famous parents. They often struggle to find themselves in a world where they are in the first place someone's child, and in the second themselves. Marti attended a lecture by Richard Olivier, son of Lawrence Olivier and Joan Plowright. He tells how he thought he would go into the family business—acting—and then realized that with a father who is regarded as one of the best actors in the world, it would be too difficult to be the best actor even within his own nuclear family.

Decision making

Decisions are a skill and an art for the business executive. Decisions are a lonely act; they not only force the individual to face the limitation of possibilities, but force "one to accept personal responsibility and existential isolation" (Yalom, 1980:319). Yalom describes a decision as a boundary situation, not dissimilar to an awareness of death as a boundary situation: "To be fully aware of one's existential situation means that one becomes aware of self-creation" and "decision, insofar as it forces one to accept personal responsibility and existential isolation, threatens one's belief in the existence of an ultimate rescuer; decision is a lonely act, and it is our own act" (Yalom, 1980:319). Decision forces one to accept personal responsibility and this existential isolation creates anxiety.

For an executive in a senior position, the importance of the decisions taken, based on the data collected, can often either represent a risk to the business that may catapult the executive to success—or be a comfortable decision that keeps the business on a safe track without embracing the executive's or the team's creativity and innovative thinking. Ultimately, all decisions impact on the business; this is the existential dilemma for the executive.

The exact relationship between decision to change and insight is hard to define. "Insight" is defined by Webster's (1983) as "an instance of apprehending the true nature of a thing, especially through intuitive understanding, or penetrating discernment". In its broadest sense, Yalom (1980:339) says that insight refers to self-discovery, an inward sighting: "Once having made a decision ... one has constituted one's world differently and is able to seize truths that one had previously hidden from oneself". Insight is a tool or a catalyst for change used by both therapists and coaches.

Past versus present versus future

Yalom argues that "psychotherapy is successful to the extent that it allows the patient to alter their future. Yet it is not the future but the past tense that dominates psychotherapy literature" (Yalom, 1980). According to Yalom, psychotherapists often believe that to provide insight the therapist must relate the present event to some past situation. The therapist may explain a patient's behaviour by examining conscious and unconscious motivations which currently affect that individual. Yalom incisively asks, "Where does the ability to change come from if we are determined by the past?"

Most therapists take the position that the client's circumstances were beyond their control when a child, and that paradoxically therapy sessions offer release from the past, yet appeal to the client to take responsibility for the future. Yalom suggests existential therapists tend to focus less on the past and more on the future than other therapists; and, although it is important to learn to forgive oneself, many individuals take on too much responsibility and guilt for the actions and feelings of others. Finally, Yalom (1980:350) reiterates that "the real agent of change" is "the therapeutic relationship ... and the past is explored in order to facilitate and deepen the present relationship".

Coaching, different to therapy, more often explores the present in order to go into the future. This is one of the reasons that coaches focus on creating a professional development plan which defines the client's overarching purpose for the coaching, the strategy required to achieve it, developmental objectives which relate to competence and capacity building, and finally actions agreed during the coaching conversation. The past can be touched on for insight but is not probed in the same depth as in a therapeutic relationship. However, it is critical that the coach is trained to recognize when the client should be referred for therapy. Bruce Peltier (2001:xix) defines counselling as "personal" and "aimed at personal problems," and he appropriately indicates that coaching carries a more positive implication in the corporate world.

However, as Peltier indicates, contemporary psychotherapy literature is relevant and invaluable for executive coaches because it is systems-oriented; it draws from the models of humanistic, existential, behavioural and psychodynamic psychology to help executives develop themselves and become more effective (Peltier, 2001:ix–xx).

Human systems

In recent years, "systems thinking" has become an increasingly useful and popular approach to understand how organizations, businesses and groups of people behave, and how change comes about within those structures. "Systems thinking" teaches us about the interconnectedness of people, professions, disciplines and other "structures" within a team, organization, business or family.

Family system therapies developed to explain individual behaviour "arising from the behaviour of the family system or of the immediate family plus other relevant people and institutions" (McWhinney *et al.*, 1993:45). Systems theory, although originally developed to work with the nuclear family, is seen to be very relevant to organizations, teams, other work groups and communities, i.e., work, social, cultural and religious.

In coaching, we are particularly concerned with "human and organizational systems" (rather than mathematical or economic structures) and the way these function and change. "Human systems" take into account the various components of human nature, i.e., thinking, feeling, and attitudes, thinking patterns and the behaviours that impact on performance within the working system.

All the components of a system have an organized, consistent relationship to one another. These components interact in a predictable, organized fashion with one another and are interdependent on one another. A complex model contains smaller subsystems that make up the larger "super-system". Within each of these subsystems, different levels of power are exercised, different skills learned, and different responsibilities are assigned. It is also possible to belong to more than one subsystem at a time, which may imply a different set of relationships, responsibilities or levels of power. An example in the business world is the tiered hierarchy of executives, managers, supervisors and employees.

When dealing with human systems one is always and ever concerned with the relationships between the people in the system. In a coaching conversation, it is the immediate relationship between coach and client; in the larger system it is the others to whom the client relates—the tiered workplace or the family or social system. Relationships can include conscious and overt relationships as well as the unconscious and covert relationships between members of the system.

Within my client coaching conversations, we talk a lot about building alliances with others (colleagues, customers, suppliers) in order for them to build personal and professional credibility in the workplace. We also discuss the necessity of understanding which alliances, coalitions and triangles already exist that could be threatening to the individual executive.

People need symbols and coherent systems of belief to manage meaning and purpose in their lives. Systems help us to understand the interrelationships that articulate a cultural worldview, and as McWhinney *et al.* suggest, it is time to choose "the elements of a new world-view", or, as Thomas Kuhn expresses it, to participate in a "paradigm shift" (McWhinney *et al.*, 1993:2).

The coaching conversation is an important factor in helping business clients to develop self-awareness and an understanding of their own perceptions (or lenses) through which they view the world. First, by understanding all of the systems in which they play a part; i.e., family, team, organization, community and society. Second, the experiential nature of the coaching conversation helps them to "shift", not just their worldview, but their behaviour. This often relates to a shift in the limiting assumptions they hold about themselves, or the systems within which they operate, and the groups with which they identify or to which they are resistant.

Relationships and systems

May (1983:17) defines "anxiety" as the "patient's fear of his own powers, and the conflicts that arise from that fear". May looks at "transference", another psychological mechanism which refers to the relationship between two people (for our purposes between client and coach).

As May describes it, the patient brings into the consulting room previous or present relationships with others (mother, father, partner, children, work colleagues, friends) and perceives the practitioner as similar to those beings; thus building their world with the practitioner in the same way. From a systems point of view, the practitioner can simply become another part of the system within which the client exists.

This is an important concept for the business coach who often works with clients in a corporate environment. The coach needs to stay aware at all times of the system within which the client works, so that the coach does not simply become part of that system. Freud emphasizes how deeply we are bound to each other: "We live in others and they in us" (May, 1983:18). The concept of transference can undermine the entire experience and "rob the client of the sense of responsibility" (May, 1983:18–19).

SYSTEMS DILEMMA

I encountered this recently at a group coaching supervision session in which I am not the lead supervisor. The coaches had recently started to discuss their own blind spots—and where they, within the group supervision process, were parallel tracking the system of the clients within the organizational system. The coaches realized that they were beginning to interact with each other in a way not dissimilar to the way their organizational clients were behaving, and that they needed to look at their own behaviour and thinking processes to ensure that they were not simply re-enacting an already existing dysfunctional system.

Using experience for learning

> 'Construction of experience is never-ending' because experience of life is never-ending (Boud, Cohen and Walker, 1996:12).

The basic approach in my research project and in this book is that the coaching intervention helps to build the rapport and the relationship between client and coach, which leads naturally to the success of the coaching conversation. Throughout this book, I have assumed the base of the coaching conversation to be the concrete experience of the client. The conclusion by Boud, Cohen and Walker (1996:8) in *Using Experience for Learning* is that experience is the foundation and the source of learning, and that every experience is potentially an opportunity for learning.

In studying existential philosophy, it is clear that there are certain universal themes. Experience is not simply an event that happens, it is an event with meaning, or it could be said that experience is a meaningful **encounter**. However, because experience is so "multifaceted, multi-layered and so inextricably connected with our experiences ... we must take account of, and build on, the unique perceptions and experiences of those involved, for without this we are dealing with only the most superficial aspects of learning" (Boud, Cohen and Walker, 1996:7).

In *Using Experience for Learning* (Boud, Cohen and Walker, 1996), a wide variety of writers share their research in using experience for learning, asking, "How do we learn from experience; how does experience impact on individual and group learning; what is the role of personal experience in learning; and do emotions have a vital role to play in intellectual learning?"

When I began my research project I thought I would search for the perfect template of coaching interventions, and very soon began to realize this was not realistic, and that, due to the unique life experiences of all clients, there would be no such thing as the perfect template. In other words, question frameworks need to be tailored to the client. Below are the five propositions that Boud, Cohen and Walker (1996) make about learning from experience.

1. Experience is the foundation of and stimulus for learning

It is meaningless to talk about learning in isolation from experience. Learning can only occur if the experience of the individual is engaged, at least at some level, and every experience is potentially an opportunity for learning (Boud, Cohen and Walker, 1996:8). In other words, learning always relates, in one way or another, to what has gone before. This means that the effect of all experience influences all learning, which further implies a seeking of new meanings from old experience. We do not simply see a new situation afresh, but we see it in terms of how we relate to it and how it resonates with what past experience has made us.

2. Individuals actively construct their experience

Individuals attach their own meaning to events, and reach commonly accepted interpretations of the world. This suggests that experience is always subject to interpretation. As in existentialism, the meaning of experience is then not a given.

It is interesting that "relationship" comes up as an important factor in learning from experience. According to Boud, Cohen and Walker (1996), experience is created in the "transaction" between the individual and the environment in which they operate, in other words, it is relational. How learners construct their experience is what Boud, Cohen and Walker (1996:11) term the individual's "personal foundation of experience".

3. Learning is a holistic process

The authors make a common division between **cognitive, affective** and **conative** learning. Cognitive learning is concerned with thinking, while affective learning is concerned with values and feelings. Conative or psychomotor learning is concerned with action and doing, as "conative" pertains to the nature of conation, or expressing endeavour or effort—conation is the part of mental life having to do with striving, including desire and volition (Webster's, 1989). Learning is cognitive, affective and psychomotor; therefore learning involves feeling and emotions (affective), the intellectual and cerebral (cognitive) and action (conative).

4. Learning is socially and culturally constructed

Individuals do not exist independently of their environment, and learning does not occur in isolation from our social and cultural norms and values. While individuals construct their own experience, they do so in the context of a particular social setting and range of cultural values. Other considerations are language, social class, gender, ethnic background and our own learning from an early age. The most powerful influence from the social and cultural context on our learning occurs through language. This is critically important for those coaching in multi-cultural contexts.

5. Learning is influenced by the socio-emotional context in which it occurs

Denial of emotions leads to a denial of learning. There are two key sources of influence in learning: past experience and the role of others in the present that support our learning. Furthermore, different kinds of learning occur depending on whether the context is perceived as positive or negative. "The way in which we interpret experience is intimately connected with how we view ourselves" (Boud, Cohen and Walker, 1996:15–16). This determines how we develop confidence and self-esteem, which are necessary to learn from experience.

AN EXISTENTIAL AND EXPERIENTIAL LEARNING DILEMMA
One of my financial sector clients recently discovered that he was not to be promoted into the top executive position in his organization. His dilemma became one of "now what?"—"Do I stay or do I go?"—as everything he had been working towards had been aimed at taking over this particular position within his organization. Coach and client looked at the pros and cons of all the possibilities. We used his experience in building, maintaining and running the business as the base point to answer the question: "Where do you have freedom of choice?' We identified three potential scenarios: (1) accepting the new reporting structure, in the short term, to sit on the new Board; (2) accepting the status quo of his position yet influencing the continued independence of the business unit; or (3) looking elsewhere in the financial sector for a new position. As coach and client reconstructed the client's experience, it became clear that he had many possible scenarios for action that would enable him to continue to create change and build relationships internally and externally, which was his forte. We identified what the current position gave him in terms of: freedom of movement, integration of activity within the organization, and being able to manage his 700 people in a relationship-oriented way. His key learning that would ultimately influence his final decision was that he was not observant of the politics which had influenced the choice of his new line manager. Coach and client began to reflect on the areas where the client was resistant to identifying how and when to play the game of politics within the organization, and how he would choose to learn to do so, or not.

Discovering barriers to learning

With a focus on the client, practitioners need to identify what are the barriers for their clients in beginning to learn from their own experience. How does experience transform their perceptions? What is the relationship between their personal experience, and their ability to reflect and learn? As coaches, do we provide enough time for reflective activity? Reflection on experience leads to awareness and an ability to identify what is working, what is not working, and what needs to change.

Finally, how can you as a business coach use your coaching model to help the client reflect on and learn from their experience? Whatever else we do as reflective practitioners, it is important that we help the client to consider their entire experience as relevant and not be too surprised when critically reflecting that they make connections which previously they were unable to see.

In conclusion

In the context of the coaching conversation, when the client talks about their experience, they are creating a story. Storytelling constructs meaning in a different way than merely describing an experience. There is power in the client's use of language and in the content of their story, and the significance which comes from the interpretation and structure of the story.

But, if clients do not see themselves as learners, or as learning from experience, or even see their stories as reconstructions of their own reality, then we need to ask how we can use the coaching conversation, and especially coaching interventions, to help clients to learn, change and achieve their outcomes. Learning, and particularly learning from experience, seems to be a major component of the coaching conversation.

In existential philosophy, all human beings must create meaning for their own lives. Existentialism emphasizes freedom of choice and taking responsibility for one's actions. Existential issues that arise in the coaching conversation, such as "freedom", "meaning and purpose" and "choice", are aligned with anxiety. Working with the client in the coaching conversation, from this point of view, is about coming to a new way of understanding ourselves and our interaction with the world and all of the systems of which we are a part.

Spinelli's analysis is that we need to move away from "doing" to an authenticity which will take the coach straight to the heart of the relationship between the coach and the client. This is of particular significance to coaches because no matter what model or methodology a practitioner uses, I agree with Spinelli that it is "the relationship" which affects the outcome of the coaching or therapy. However, it is the **quality** of the relationship that is of importance.

The relationship which develops as a result of the coaching conversation is to shift or move the client from the level of "doing", to developing competence and capacity through "learning"—ultimately "becoming" and living out their full potential as a human being. This then provides us with some serious reflection for thought, research and debate as we continue to explore the dynamic of experiential learning, the development of the relationship, and the existential concerns which arise as a result of the coaching.

Coach's library

Boud, D., Cohen, R., and Walker, D. (Eds.). (1996). *Using Experience for Learning*. Buckingham: SRHE and Open University Press.

Frankl, V.E. (1946). *Man's Search for Meaning*. London: Hodder and Stoughton.

Hargrove, R. (2003). *Masterful Coaching: Inspire an "Impossible Future" While Producing Extraordinary Leaders and Extraordinary Results*. San Francisco, CA: Jossey-Bass/Pfeiffer.

May, R. (1983). *The Discovery of Being*. New York, NY: Norton.

McWhinney, W., Webber, J.B., Smith, D.M., and Novokowsky, B.J. (1993). *Creating Paths of Change: Managing Issues and Resolving Problems in Organizations*. Venice, CA: Enthusion.

Peltier, B. (2001). *The Psychology of Executive Coaching: Theory and Application*. New York, NY: Brunner-Routledge.

Rogers, C.R. (1961/2004). *On Becoming a Person: A Therapist's View of Psychotherapy*. London: Constable and Robinson.

Whitmore, J. (2002). *Coaching for Performance: Growing People, Performance and Purpose*. London: Nicholas Brealey.

Wilber, K. (1997). An integral theory of consciousness. *Journal of Consciousness Studies*, 4(1):71–92.

Yalom, I.D. (1980). *Existential Psychotherapy*. New York, NY: Basic Books.

Zohar, D., and Marshall, I. (2001). *Spiritual Intelligence: The Ultimate Intelligence*. London: Bloomsbury.

CHAPTER EIGHT

Supervision, contracting and ethical concerns

- Supervision as a form of empowerment
- Developing a professional approach
• Coach's library

T
hroughout the world, coaching supervision is still in its infancy. It is influenced by the role supervision plays for psychologists, who are required to be in professional supervision throughout their training and years of practice. This chapter examines how supervision is defined and practised internationally, and explores how you should go about being supervised and/or play the role of supervisor.

The chapter then looks at the role of ethics in business coaching, and ethical codes that have been developed in recent years through professional bodies such as the Worldwide Association of Business Coaches (WABC), European Mentoring and Coaching Council (EMCC), International Coach Federation (ICF), Chartered Institute of Personnel and Development (CIPD), and Coaches and Mentors of South Africa (COMENSA). Ethical dilemmas are as important as the professional codes themselves, and the author explores some of the potential dilemmas that arise during a coaching intervention period.

A third corporate governance issue for business coaches is the standard contract they draw up for agreement with the client. This chapter makes recommendations for key areas to consider when contracting with a client, a client organization and a supervisor.

Throughout this book, I refer to **ethical** dilemmas that emerge during the coaching process, the need for **supervision** for all coach practitioners, and **contracting** with the client for the logistics of the coaching process. I discuss the context and guidelines for contracting, what is the importance of committing to an ethical code, and the rationale for coaching supervision. All three areas are related, and for this reason are all addressed within this chapter.

Contracting with the reader

What I would like to ask of you, the reader, is that we contract together as you work through this chapter. As you read, what types of questions go through your mind, particularly as you read some of the stories and incidents that are explored? For example, what are your thoughts, your assumptions, and do you wonder how you might address the dilemma? How conscious are you of information that comes into your awareness at any given moment? Are you always aware of the ethical and professional questions that might arise during the coaching conversation, or that might be overridden by your own emotional or belief system ... or perhaps assumptions that might be operating? This aspect of high-level professional awareness may need reinforcement—this would include the self, the other, and any systems that may need to be held in your awareness.

Contracting

Contracting the relationship

We contract in supervision with our coaching supervisor, and in coaching with our client. According to Spinelli, contracting is deeply challenging to our normal way of "being" in the world. We normally just "do" without agreeing the parameters of the relationship. The contract leverages the entire relationship, creating a set of conditions or framework within which the coach can work (Spinelli, 1989, cited in Stout Rostron, 2006c:38).

Developing the habit of both formal and informal contracting is one of the first steps in beginning to understand the dynamics of formulating a coaching relationship. The coach and client agree to conditions of time, space, fees, confidentiality and goals. In contracting, the business coach agrees to a specific set of conditions. For example:

- As your coach I agree to support you in achieving the results you want. In turn, I expect you to give your best. Your success and your results will be determined by the commitment and responsibility to which we both commit ourselves.
- I will always act with integrity, honesty and openness, and I will consistently take responsibility for my actions, communicating any concerns or issues I have.
- I will provide excellence in coaching, offering value and professionalism.
- I will respect the confidentiality and boundaries of our relationship at all times.

- The measure of my effectiveness as a coach will be in your success and achievements.
- I agree to respect the boundaries of the contract that we structure together.

The purpose of the contract is to open up the potential for trust between coach and client. This is essential if the client is to trust their own self-exploration. As the agreement lays the foundation for the relationship, it must be adhered to in action for trust to develop.

Contracting definitions

The contract between coach and client sets out which services have been agreed and delineates all fees as well as the outcomes and deliverables that can be expected. The contract sets out ground rules for the coaching relationship so that both parties are aware of their obligations. This helps prevent future misunderstandings and provides a firm basis to deal with disagreements. The contract describes the relationship between the coach and multiple parties, such as the individual client, the client organization, the HR unit, and line management. It is important for the contract to describe the difference between coaching and other helping disciplines such as therapy, counselling, mentoring and training. Objectives for the individual executive and for the organization need to be clarified, with boundaries made explicit in terms of confidentiality, fees, cancellation and termination of the contract.

Often in coaching, the contracting process is linked to the generation and fulfilment of outcomes. Contracting usually deals with the management of the process, roles played, evaluation of the process, learning and outcomes, and the exit clauses. As a function, contracting has emerged as a critical function of coaching supervision. "The contracting for therapy and coaching have similarities in their purpose, i.e., to provide safety, set boundaries, manage time, money and ethical issues—but what is contracted and to what end creates a distinction. The contracting and the relationship building are crucial to the outcomes of the coaching intervention and this is no different to that of supervision" (Pampallis Paisley, 2006:85–86).

Contracting is complex as it determines what areas, and how deeply, the coach can work with the organization at an individual, team and systemic level. A question raised in Pampallis Paisley's

(2006) research was, "How do you get change in coaching that is innovative and not superficial if you do not go deep?" This is a serious question for supervision, and needs to be considered in the contracting process.

Questions to ask when setting up the contract

1. What are the needs of the individual executive client versus those of the organization?
   - What is the organization looking for?
   - What are the goals for the individual client?
   - Which performance improvements are desired?
   - What are the organizational goals for the coaching programme?
   - What are the organizational conditions and are they conducive to coaching?
   - Are the line manager and senior management supportive of the process?
   - Is the individual ready for coaching and is coaching appropriate?
   - How do you know?

2. Coaches must be able to define their work in terms of outcomes and solutions:
   - What will be better as a result of coaching?
   - How will we know, and what difference will it make?
   - How will we measure success, effectiveness and value for money?
   - What will be the initial goals?
   - Which pre-coaching assessments are recommended?
   - Who will provide the feedback?
   - Will there be a specific action and development plan to achieve goals?
   - How is the coaching contract terminated?
   - What follow-up and monitoring will occur after the coaching has been completed?

3. Coach and client need to discuss and agree the structure of the coaching sessions:
   - How many sessions will there be?
   - How often should they take place?
   - How long will they last, depending on the individual needs and breadth and depth of the client's issues?

- Where will the coaching sessions take place?
- Will the sessions be face-to-face, by telephone, or a combination of both?
- Will there be any contact by telephone or email between sessions?

Contracting for change inside the bigger picture

Bruce Peltier (2001:xxiii–xxiv) defines the coaching intervention as a four-step process:

1. **Get things started**: coaches must define their work in terms of outcomes and solutions, confidentiality, recording relationships, dimensions of the project and contracting (i.e., time, money and methodology).
2. **Gather information and make a plan**: with executives, it is important to develop a clear plan that includes measurable outcomes (executives work best to a development plan with clear goals and end points).
3. **Implement**: it can take from three months up to two years to produce results, develop skills and achieve objectives. The implementation may include work shadowing when the coach walks alongside the executive in the workplace and observes the client in action.
4. **Lock in the changes**: the coach should arrange for ongoing improvement and support, for short-term behaviours to be translated into long-term behaviours. (This author has changed "gains" to "behaviours".)

Common pitfalls

For the business coach, a common pitfall can be to mistakenly assume that the relationship between coach and executive happens in isolation from the dynamics of the executive's team, or outside the organizational dynamics. In other words, the coaching relationship is set within the context of the team and the organization. It is part of the overall system within which the executive works. This has huge implications for the coach's interventions with the executive. "If the prevailing organizational culture is one of blame and fear, then perception of learning needs and opportunities is likely to be correspondingly low" (Parsloe and Wray, 2000:35). Grayson and Larson (2000:121) define the six most common pitfalls as:

- failure to commit;
- unrealistic expectations;
- defensiveness;
- passive role in the coaching process;
- playing it safe; and
- failure to involve others.

It does not help that you are potentially the best coach in the world if you cannot recognize these and navigate the relationship, i.e., say no to the coaching assignment or walk away. Noer (2000) states that there are three big derailment factors:

- lack of clarity as to who is the client;
- coaches using a single model or approach; and
- creating a dependency relationship.

In the coaching conversation, Mary Beth O'Neill advocates three core principles for the coach: (1) self-management, (2) a systems perspective and a methodology, and (3) the use of backbone and heart. She cites her four phases of coaching as using a systems lens to contract, plan, conduct live action interviews and debrief (O'Neill, 2000:xvii, 10).

The bigger picture needs to be part of the contracting process. It is important for the coach to recognize the larger systems at play and the "force field" that shapes and influences all the individuals working within the system. Therefore coaches need to hold a "bifocal" view, being able to see their client in the system, as well as seeing oneself in the system (O'Neill; 2000:xv). It is important to remember that contracting determines at which level the coach will work individually and systemically.

Another important aspect of contracting is the evaluation of the contract, including termination or renewal. In any business contracting process, it is important to draw up the "marriage" and the "divorce" papers at the beginning: a bit like a prenuptial contract. It is as important to specify the boundaries and parameters of the entire coaching intervention, i.e., how the process will proceed from beginning to end, and how to terminate the process, whether at the contracted termination point or sooner if required by either party.

Defining coaching in your contract

It is useful to include a definition of coaching within your contract, specifying how coaching differs from the other helping professions. For example, "the services to be provided by coach to client are coaching as designed jointly with the client. Coaching, which is not advice, therapy, or counselling, may address specific personal or professional projects, business issues, or general conditions in the client's life or profession".

Also to be included could be the following clause which we use in our own coaching contracts:

> Throughout the working relationship, the coach will engage with the client in direct conversation. The client can count on the coach to be honest and straightforward in asking questions, making interventions and facilitating the setting of goals. The client understands that the power of coaching is in the relationship between client and coach. If the client or the coach believes the coaching is not working as desired, either client or coach will communicate this.

Client questions in the contracting phase

The contracting phase of the intervention is about building the relationship, identifying the executive's goals, determining the boundaries for the coaching relationship, and setting up expectations for coach, client and the organization. Your contract needs to make explicit to the client what will happen within the entire coaching intervention. Here are several questions clients may ask you during the contracting phase:

- How quickly can you begin to understand my position, the environment within which I work and the pressures that I need to learn to negotiate?
- What can you understand about my needs and position?
- How practical and effective will you be in helping me to achieve my goal?

- How will you help me to work more effectively within the organization?
- How will we work together?
- What is the breadth and depth of your coaching experience?
- Share with me some of your successes and failures as a coach.
- How will you help me to become a more effective leader and manager?
- Here is one specific issue I have to deal with ... what would you advise or ask me?
- What could possibly get in the way of our coaching relationship that I might not have thought about?

Client commitment to the coaching process

During the contracting phase, the commitment of the client to the coaching intervention is vital. For example, the client may commit themselves to:

- being frank, open and honest with the coach at all times;
- communicating with the coach specific concerns about the client/ coach relationship;
- taking responsibility to communicate with the coach at all times;
- Understanding that the essence and strength of the coaching conversation is in the "relationship"; and
- agreeing to be "coachable" and considering the coach's observations on all issues.

Logistics: Fees, legality and subcontractors

The written contract needs to include the coaching commencement date and the agreed period of the coaching intervention. For example, the intervention could be for 20 hours, six months or one year, renewable after an agreed period. Built into the contract will be the agreed meetings between coach, executive and line management, and the structure of the coaching fees.

The legal contract may be overseen by a sponsor, an HR division, or another third party. Whichever, for your contract, we suggest a workable and flexible system for payment of fees. It might be on a monthly, hourly, or retainer basis, or paid in several tranches throughout the agreed period of the coaching intervention.

The contract will build in the supervision sessions with line management, or with the lead coach if the individual coach is subcontracted through a lead coach. If you as coach are subcontracted by a lead coach, ensure that you sign a legal contract that protects you for payment of fees, cancellation and for indemnity purposes. Many subcontractors build into the contract that you are responsible for your own coaching consultancy boundaries. Also, if you have been subcontracted, the client organization is not your client, but is the client of the lead contractor. Ensure that your contract includes details of how to handle future contracted work if offered to you.

It is useful to obtain samples of contracts from colleagues, coach training institutions and your professional body. Ensure that, if you supply the contract, an attorney approves that it will stand on its own as a legal document.

Managing cancellations and additional requests

Suggested clauses to include in your contract to handle cancellations and miscellaneous requests:

- We agree to provide one another with one month's notice in the event it is desired to cancel further coaching after the initial period of ...
- We agree to let each other know of any overseas or long-distance meetings or holidays at a minimum of two weeks' notice.
- The coach is available to speak on request by telephone, in addition to the normal face-to-face coaching sessions. Where the coach can, they will take the client's call. Failing that, client and coach will agree a time convenient to both.

The scope of the contract

The two most critical areas in contracting are possibly those of ethical issues and defining the scope of the overall coaching intervention. Both of these should be addressed in the coaching contract. Coaching processes often fail due to poor or insufficient contracting (Nowack and Wimer, 1997). As we have discussed above, contracting should include ethical issues such as the disclosure of personal and inappropriate information to a client's superior (Williams, 1996), and aligning the contract to corporate objectives in order to be credible (Olesen, 1996). Conflict of interest between the goals and expectations of the individual being coached, and those of the company, as well as the issues of quality standards and confidentiality can impact on trust between the individual executive and the coach (Janse van Rensburg, 2001b:24–25).

Success means contracting and goal setting. Outcomes and goals are typically discussed and reviewed at each subsequent session as agreed between coach and client. The contract needs to specify the parameters of the overall coaching period: for example, whether there will be the creation of a personal/professional development plan, and how outcomes will be measured from the beginning of the contract to the end. In terms of the coach's intervention, the underlying goal in the contracting phase is the development of the relationship.

FIRST MEETING WITH THE CLIENT

I include a "coachable moment" during the first meeting with the client. This is to introduce the client straight away to the "feel" of a coaching session and the beginnings of a coaching relationship. The client usually begins to talk about their issues in your first meeting anyway, and you will have characteristically asked what are their overall aims for the coaching intervention. If you contract in the first session without beginning the coaching process (if only to identify the client's aim for coaching, the possible strategy of working together, and overall goals) there is a risk that the client may remain confused about how the process is to work. The client begins to understand how you work and it helps the client to decide about the reality of working with you.

Husserl's (1962/1913) concept of "intentionality" would be important in many areas of coaching—and definitely in the area of contracting, i.e., what is the intention of all parties, coach, client and organization? This would be similar for supervision contracting.

What O'Neill (2000:93) terms "the partnership", I call the relationship. It begins when the executive actually begins to talk about their specific issues and where they are currently stuck. O'Neill's (2000:94) recommended coaching intervention questions in the contracting phase are:

- Which recurring patterns are present in this situation?
- Which patterns work well and which detract from the effort?
- How are you a part of these patterns?
- How have you responded to this issue?
- What is your knee-jerk contribution?
- Can you imagine a different pattern?
- How willing are you to develop the stamina required to stop your part of the pattern that is no longer effective?
- How will this help you get to your goal?
- How can I be useful to you?

O'Neill (2000:215–219; 97) suggests interventions at specific stages in her four-step model, and in alignment with certain themes (concreteness, empathy, confrontation, respect):

A. **Concreteness**—invite the executive to be more specific about their issue.
B. **Empathy**—make an effort to show you understand the leader's concerns.
C. **Confrontation**—point out discrepancies between what the leader says and what they actually do.
D. **Respect**—believe the executive has the ability to handle their situation.

Contracting interventions

Mary Beth O'Neill (2000) recommends other possible questions for contracting. Many of the questions O'Neill adapted and used, with the permission of Rob Schachter (1997), come from "Questions when contracting with leaders", from an unpublished document (Stout Rostron, 2006c: endnote 13–14):

- Which business challenges are you facing?
- Have you met this challenge successfully before?
- What is your best thinking about this issue?

- What are the gaps in meeting the same kind of challenge this time?
- What is keeping you from getting the results you want?
- How have you responded to this issue?
- Do you have any sense of your part in not meeting the challenge this time?
- How urgent are you?
- How much time do you have to achieve this?
- What do you find personally challenging about leading this effort, given the results you have to date?
- How do you think I could be useful to you?
- Do you have the authority to sponsor this plan, or do you need sponsorship from someone else?

Always build debriefing into the coaching contract. Here are four suggested categories to the debriefing session (Stout Rostron, 2006c:39).

1. celebrate achievements.
2. identify key recurring patterns.
3. assess the alignment of roles.
4. develop a personal and professional plan.

What should be in your written contract?

1. Ground rules and parameters such as confidentiality, reporting relationships, and dimensions of the project (people to be coached, timing and fees) must be established.
2. Include deliverables, explicit ways to know if and when you have accomplished your goals.
3. What will you deliver and how will you know when you have done so?
4. How will you make goals measurable and achievable?
5. Establish what will be different as a result of coaching.
6. Clarify your code of ethics and standards and the professional association of which you are a member. Clinicians use formal ethics codes and standards. As coaching is a new, emerging profession and formal structures are in the making, it is important to clarify to which code you are committed.
7. Negotiate explicit contracts that are fair to all parties.

8. Do you have a malpractice or liability carrier? Let them know that you are doing coaching as part of your professional practice. Check with other coaches to find out whom they are using.
9. Find out which contracts are currently in use and check the coaching literature (Whitworth, Kimsey-House and Sandahl, 1998:180).

Individual learning contracts

As well as the overall contract, which defines the parameters of the coaching relationship, you may develop learning contracts with your clients. These are "works in progress" throughout the entire coaching intervention period. Within my coaching process, at the end of a coaching session—to fully integrate the learning with goals set and commitment to action—we complete a learning contract to:

- Redefine the vision, where the client is going.
- Outline the strategy, how the client is going to achieve the vision.
- Identify the specific outcomes that need to be accomplished in the intervention period in order to work towards achieving the vision and putting the strategy into action.
- Identify the obstacles to achieving the goals identified, and the strengths that will enable the client to progress.
- Summarize what the client gained from the session in order to help underline self-reflection and continue to help the client to understand that they are responsible for their own thinking, feeling and behaviour.

The learning contract becomes the focus at the beginning of the next session with the client, and is the beginning of the client's learning or leadership development plan.

Supervision

When contracting with a client, ethical issues such as confidentiality and boundary management are critical to the success of the intervention. Key areas to be clarified centre on fees, boundaries and confidentiality. For the coach practitioner in supervision, ethical issues and dilemmas often emerge as core topics for exploration. I have tried to include some of the main issues that have arisen for myself and my colleagues, as coaching professionals, within our own practices, as well as those that have emerged with the founding and maintaining of our relevant professional body. There are consistent themes that have arisen in our own individual supervision, as well as issues that have emerged when supervising fellow practitioner coaches.

AN EARLY EXPERIENCE—WITH CONSEQUENCES

I often tell the story of an early experience in supervision. I did not clearly contract the parameters of confidentiality, or the ethical guidelines and boundaries for supervision in this instance. I was working from a set of assumptions with my supervisor, rather than a defined contract, because of a long-standing relationship with my supervisor. Even so, it demonstrates the consequences of not clearly contracting, verbally and in written form.

As a coach, I shared some of my uncertainty at how to best manage some of the difficulties I had recently faced with a client, whom I did not name. The supervisor listened, made observations, and even offered some advice about how to deal with the emerging systemic issue. At a later date, I was in a coaching conversation with this client, only to discover that the client knew all about the content of my conversation with my supervisor. How did that happen?

The coach and the supervisor had not clearly contracted the boundaries of confidentiality, including the ethical consequences of divulging client information. The supervisor somehow did not realize the damage that could be done in sharing this information with the client. So what was the damage? Essentially, the trust the client had in her coach was bruised, and it would take some time for it to be restored. Furthermore, the coach was dismayed, felt betrayed, and lost faith in her supervisor. What should she have done to clarify the situation?

We all make mistakes, and so it is important to be big enough to say, "Whoops, I really messed up here" and to take responsibility for one's own errors. The coach has done so with her client. However, her relationship with her supervisor also needs to be addressed. The coach needs to be clear with her supervisor about the consequences of broken confidentiality, the ethical dilemmas broken confidentiality can present, and what the boundaries in future should be. As we continue to discuss ethics and supervision in this chapter, it may be helpful to reflect back on this story.

What is coaching supervision?

The role of the supervisor is to support the development of the coach practitioner and to assess their competence. The term "supervision" describes the process by which the work of the practitioner is overseen and guidance is sought. The process may differ in significant ways from that undertaken in other professions, such as psychotherapy and counselling. Usually, both coach practitioner and supervisor will be bound by the Code of Ethics of their professional body. The purpose of supervision is to ensure that the coach maintains the highest standards of competence; best serves the needs of the client; is professionally trained and skilled in the practice of coaching; and is committed to a programme of continuing professional development throughout the years of their practice.

Within the emerging discipline of coaching, supervision has become a requirement for membership in many professional associations. However, if supervision becomes a monitoring function, it is possible that it might overstep the bounds of intention in the global environment of the developing profession of coaching.

Purpose of clinical supervision

The importance of the "coach being coached" or in supervision cannot be over-emphasized. While supervision has been a fundamental underpinning of therapy from the beginning, it is not yet a given for the coaching industry worldwide. The importance of coaching supervision is to ensure that the coach understands what the client goes through, and more importantly, to work through their own issues so that they do not become entangled with client concerns.

Some of the main themes that have arisen from research into executive coaching supervision are (Pampallis Paisley, 2006:76):

- boundary management;
- how to cope with the complexity of the supervisory system in which client, coach and organization were represented—i.e., the triangulations;

- the depth to which one should go in the coaching relationship;
- the importance of creating a space to think;
- whether supervision interventions needed to have a client-centred or coach-centred focus, or both.

As Yalom (2001:48) says, human problems are "largely relational" and an individual's interpersonal problems will ultimately manifest themselves in the here and now of a therapy encounter. The same is true of the coaching environment. The client's interpersonal issues will soon emerge in the relationship between coach and client. The client can trigger a coach's underlying drivers, even in a small way. For example, if coach and client are undergoing divorce simultaneously, it is important that the coach is able to maintain a "meta" position throughout the coaching intervention if divorce comes into the conversation. And, similarly, in my story, the next time I am in supervision, I need to be sure that I have cleared the air with my supervisor so as to be free of feelings of doubt or mistrust.

Caplan (1970) distinguishes between **supervision** and **consultation**. Supervision is an ongoing process of inspecting the work of the individual being supervised in a hierarchical power structure; consultation is a less formal, intermittent interaction between colleagues arising out of current work-related problems (Stout Rostron, 2006c:80). What coaching supervision refers to is more consultation arising out of the needs of the coach, individual executive and client organization.

Kadushin (1976) describes the three main functions of supervision as educative, supportive and managerial. He describes these functions as formative (namely educational), normative (which focuses on policies, organization and evaluation), and restorative (including a debriefing of both positive and negative feedback on practice). Hawkins and Shohet (2000) describe four categories of supervision, the fourth category being particularly relevant to coach practitioners:

1. **tutorial**—focusing on the educational function, but may include supportive and managerial aspects;
2. **training supervision**—where supervision is normative and managerial;
3. **managerial supervision**—which relates to hierarchical line management; and
4. **consultancy supervision**—for experienced practitioners.

Where does supervision originate from?

The origin of supervision within health and social care originates in psychological mental health care fields. The development
of counselling has had a formative impact on the creation of a
supervision model, and in occupational therapy, supervision has
been in practice since the 1970s. The UK Department of Health
defines clinical supervision as "a formal process of professional
support and learning which enables the individual practitioner to
develop knowledge and competence, assume responsibility for their
own practice and enhance consumer protection and safety of care in
complex clinical situations" (Jones and Jenkins, 2006:26).

The UK Chartered Society for Physiotherapy (CSP) guidelines
state: "Clinical supervision can be seen as a collaborative process
between two or more practitioners of the same or different professions. This process should encourage the development of professional
skills and enhanced quality of patient care through implementation
of an evidence-based approach to maintaining standards in practice.
These standards are maintained through discussion around specific
patient incidents or interventions using elements of reflection to
guide the discussion" (Jones and Jenkins, 2006).

The UK perspective positions "clinical supervision within service
quality and governance, and professional development and lifelong
learning". The USA perspective defines clinical supervision as a specific aspect of staff development dealing with the clinical skills and
competences of each staff member. The structure for clinical supervision is typically one-to-one or small groups who meet on a regular
basis" (Jones and Jenkins, 2006:23–24).

Why do coaches need supervision?

Due to the international growth and development of coaching and
mentoring as disciplines, most professional coaching bodies now
recommend an ethical code of conduct for their members; and, as
part of that code, a commitment to supervision on the part of the
practitioner.

The European Mentoring and Coaching Council (EMCC) states
in its *Code of Ethics* that "a coach/mentor must maintain a relationship with a suitably qualified supervisor, who will regularly assess

their competence and support their development" (EMCC, 2008b). The Chartered Institute of Personnel and Development (CIPD) in the UK cites guidelines for buyers of coaching and recommends that practitioners articulate what formal supervision arrangements they currently have in place (Jarvis, 2004).

In South Africa, COMENSA's policy on supervision is to "allow practitioners to reconstruct their experience, reflect, understand, design their professional reality, and develop new responses for future practice within the supervision context. Supervision can be described as a collaborative, co-constructed space in which coaching and mentoring competence and professional development are explored" (COMENSA, 2006b). The COMENSA (2007a) *Revised Code of Ethics* requires that all members have regular supervision with a suitably qualified supervisor who will regularly assess their professional development and competence. COMENSA's (2006b) *Interim Policy on Supervision* details the guidelines for their practitioner members, recommending a ratio of 1:15 hours of supervision to coaching or mentoring.

Supervision is useful as it ensures that the coach works to the executive's agenda, not to the coach's agenda. The need for supervision is something that international professional coaching bodies are recommending for all coaches in their continuing professional development (CPD).

A key component of a coach's personal and professional approach to their coaching practice is to work on a regular basis with a supervising coach, counsellor or therapist. The purpose of this is three-fold: first, and crucially, to deal with any unresolved issues of their own (an ongoing process for any coach), and specifically to learn not to bring their own personal concerns to the coaching conversation; second, to benefit from invaluable and ongoing supervision for the individual's coaching practice; and third, the supervision process provides the coach with an invaluable tool to understand the client/practitioner process from another perspective, i.e., from the client perspective rather than from the perspective of the practitioner. It provides an excellent alternate perspective on the coaching intervention (Stout Rostron, 2006c:14).

The structure of group supervision

An individual supervision session usually takes place in a one- or two-hour timeframe. Group supervision with anything up to ten practitioners usually lasts about three hours. One way to structure group supervision consists of:

1. A group check-in: what is going well with the client-coach relationship? This allows the group to break the ice, and to connect with each other within the coaching and the organizational system.
2. A "round" (where everyone speaks once before anyone speaks for the second time) to flipchart key issues and challenges each practitioner wishes to address in the supervision session. This includes emerging systemic issues, if the coaches are working for a specific organization. A subsequent round-table discussion about the specific issues and challenges highlighted. The group could break up into pairs to discuss and bring their thoughts back to the plenary session, or the discussion could be around the key topics highlighted from the previous round.
3. A demonstration with supervisor and an individual coach to work on one of their challenges. The other practitioners observe the conversation, making notes about what is happening in the coach-supervisor dialogue, what the supervisor is doing, and their own thoughts and feelings throughout the dialogue.
4. Feedback from coach and supervisor as to any learning gained from the dialogue; followed by a discussion bringing in the other practitioner observations, recommendations and questions. Questions help the supervisor to facilitate the next round of discussion. The supervisor and the participants encourage the supervisor to be aware of their own internal processes that are evoked when listening to the contributions from the practitioner participants. The discussion brings in any parallel processes that are occurring as a result of the supervisory dialogue and the subsequent discussion. Feedback is given to the supervisor on their own performance.
5. Subsequent coaching conversations with an observer. This could be done in triads, with coach/coachee/observer. At the end, the triads bring their learning and questions back into the round format. At each supervision session, it is important to vary who adopts each of the three roles.
6. Discussion in a "round" format. Each individual shares their learning from the process, blind spots they have noticed in themselves, and any queries that may have occurred. The process

allows lead coach and practitioner participants to learn from all perspectives.

The supervision session may also include feedback from the Lead Coach on surveys conducted since the introduction of the coaching intervention, and any feedback from the organizational Co-ordinator and line management.

What are the benefits of supervision?

There are multiple benefits for the individual practitioner in supervision, as well as for the team and the client organization. The coach practitioners have a chance to meet, with the supervising coach ensuring that all practitioners have a sound understanding of the organizational systems at play. Coaching supervision is an important regular meeting where the coaches can connect with each other, and can begin to understand the connections between their individual clients, particularly if they work within one organization. It is an important meeting where the individuals in the group learn from each other.

THE NEEDS OF COACHING SUPERVISION
In Pampallis Paisley's (2006:96–97) research into supervision for executive coaching, she identified a range of primary needs that emerged with a high degree of frequency. Her conclusion is that the coaching supervisor needs to empower the coach to:

- assess the level at which the client, the team, and the organization is working;
- clarify that what the coach identifies may indicate a need to refer for therapy;
- be ethically responsible and ask for permission; and
- be aware of outcomes. Is this the best option for this subject/issue/client? Or is it the coach's need?

There is a big question about the sustainability of shifts and the likelihood of "relapse" to old behaviours if the coach only works in the client's sphere of conscious competence and an emotional/

counselling component is not involved. Containment is important as the client needs to remain able to function in the world.
This can become an ethical issue when coaching in an organization, as the initial contract may have a time limit.

Supervision helps practitioners to grow their skills and
competence whether they are supervised individually or in groups.
The capacity of the coaches to facilitate learning for their clients is
also significantly increased. Other benefits are:

- ensuring that the client organization is getting a good return on
  investment (ROI) for their business;
- ensuring that a high value is placed on truly understanding clients;
- ensuring that the coach is as likely to enhance and develop self-
  awareness as the client; and
- the creation of a safe space to explore the heart of the practitioner's
  coaching practice.

There are some disadvantages to group supervision, and practitioners need to be particularly careful when managing client confidentiality. The advantages are the observations that the group can make
when observing each other. The 1:1 supervision encompasses more
intimate learning on the part of the individual coach with the time
to go into depth about the client situation and one's own individual
issues or concerns as a coach. It is almost inevitable that the coach can
become enmeshed in some of the organization's systemic dynamics.
It is helpful to have an observant supervisor who can help the coach
to step into a bigger picture position, looking at the client-coach-
system dynamics from a fresh perspective.

For the moment, there are no international guidelines to measure
the positive impact for clients and coach practitioners. This may be
considered as a possibility for future research; see Pampallis Paisley
(2006) for an example of doctoral research on supervision. Finally,
coaching supervision will observe the developmental stages of the
practitioners within their group forum. This type of supervision is
more collegial and consultative, encouraging the practice of self-
supervision. The lead coach or supervisor also needs to take note
of their own developmental stages in the profession as they gain in
expertise.

Managing the complexity of supervision

Supervision requires a tremendous amount of self-awareness and organizational awareness to meet the levels of complexity within which senior executives are working. This is to enable the depth of questioning and guidance that is needed in managing multiple levels and contexts.

The complexity of supervision is also noted when working with a diverse group of participants who embody a range of levels of awareness and competence. They will be in different stages of personal and professional development, and will exhibit a range of learning styles and interpersonal skills. This presents an enormous challenge for the supervisor.

Pampallis Paisley (2006) considered the nature of working within different contexts in her supervision research, while working with a group of coaches from widely diverse backgrounds. She says:

> All may be utilising different models and frameworks, and have varying levels of competences, training and consciousness, which impacts on what is brought into the supervisory room. Unlike therapeutic supervision for example, where an object relations therapist would work with a supervisor who is skilled in object relations theory and practice, this in-depth but narrow band—or what I call 'vertical depth of field' of specialisation may not be the domain of the coaching supervisor.
>
> There may be specialist areas that would require a mentoring process. With regards to the supervision of coaches working with leadership in complex organizations, coaching supervisors would need to have a broader focus, or what I call a 'horizontal depth of field'. It follows then that the supervision of coaching is in itself a complex discipline—one that requires levels of understanding and a comprehensive framework of knowledge and skills which cover both the horizontal planes and vertical depths that coaching encompasses (Pampallis Paisley, 2006:108–110).

How to find a supervisor

Within most professional coaching bodies today, supervision has become the number-one question to be addressed. The importance of coaching supervision is to ensure that the coach understands what the client goes through, and more importantly, to support the coach in working through their own issues so that they do not become entangled with client concerns.

The role of the supervisor is to support the development of the coach practitioner, and to assess the practitioner's competence. Coach training organizations are beginning to offer professional group supervision through their academic and practitioner training links. Your criteria when hiring a supervisor will include someone who:

- has knowledge of ethical, legal and regulatory aspects of the helping professions;
- is able to form a peer/collegial relationship as a supervising consultant;
- is sensitive to diversity issues of culture, ethnicity, gender, age, socio-economic and educational background;
- has knowledge of current research in the coaching supervision field;
- has competence and expertise as an executive/business coach; and
- has training in supervision.

Different types of supervision

In organizations and coach training institutions today, there are several ways to access supervision. There is one-on-one supervision, peer supervision, team supervision and group supervision. Many coach training institutes set up a peer supervision process for senior and junior graduates to work together in the supervision process, either individual, peer or group. We define the four specific types of supervision as educational, administrative, supportive and managerial.

Educational supervision is to assess the skills and needs and to facilitate the learning for practitioner coaches, and is usually in alliance with an educational development programme in coaching. **Administrative** supervision is to monitor the workload of the coaches within the group or the organization, ensuring that the purpose, vision and goals of the organization are met. **Supportive** supervision is to provide an environment for practitioners where their emotional needs are met, and where they are able to build skills and competence, whether in a one-on-one or group forum. **Managerial**

supervision is to ensure that individual client, coach and line manager meet regularly to ensure that the client is on track to meet the objectives set out for the coaching intervention.

What happens when supervision doesn't work?

In supervision, there are similarities with poor coaching practice. If conflicts arise in supervision sessions, it is often due to the lack of skill on the part of the supervisor and facilitator. It is important for there to be open, transparent dialogue about what is working, and what is not working for supervisors and practitioners in any session. For example, I have experienced poor supervision when the supervisor, or even one of the practitioners, has been operating from a lack of awareness of their blind spots. Also, if the practitioner begins to "advocate" for the supremacy of their "client" versus another "client", it is often a demonstration of the practitioner having become part of the systemic dynamics of the organization. The parallel processes and complexity of supervision require skill and self-awareness on the part of the supervisor and practitioners alike. The parallel processes are frequently where the greatest learning lies.

Ethics

> Ethics can be defined as 'a set of moral principles'. Ethics are most often recognized as the rules of conduct in respect of a particular group or culture, or the moral principles of an individual. Ethics is known as the branch of philosophy dealing with values which relate to human conduct (Webster's, 1983).

What ethical codes for coaching are in existence?

All professional bodies define the values, standards of competence and ethical benchmarks to which their members are held accountable.

The Worldwide Association of Business Coaches (WABC) requires members to adhere to its *Code of Business Coaching Ethics and Integrity*, which includes WABC's "Business Coaching Definition", "Principles", and "Safe Harbour Conciliation and Adjudication Process". The code tries to address the diverse range of business interactions faced all over the world by members, and has established a process to handle ethical dilemmas and issues (WABC, 2008a:1–4). (The WABC *Code of Business Coaching Ethics and Integrity* is available at www.wabccoaches.com.)

The European Mentoring and Coaching Council (EMCC) has been established to promote best practice and to ensure that the highest possible standards are maintained in the coach-mentor/client relationship. This is requested by the EMCC's Complaints and Disciplinary procedures. The EMCC's (2008b:2–4) *Ethical Code* defines five key ethical areas: competence, context, boundary management, integrity and professionalism. (The EMCC *Ethical Code* is available at www.emccouncil.org.)

The International Federation of Coaching (ICF) defines its *ICF Code of Ethics* explicitly in terms of professional conduct at large; conflicts of interest; professional conduct with clients; and confidentiality/privacy (ICF, 2008b:2–3). All members acknowledge and agree to honour the ICF Pledge of Ethics (ICF, 2008b:4). (The *ICF Code of Ethics* is available at www.coachfederation.org.)

The purpose of COMENSA's *Code of Ethics* (COMENSA, 2006c:1) and *Revised Code of Ethics* (COMENSA, 2007a:1) is to "set the ethical standards for South Africa in the fields of coaching and mentoring". It is agreed among members that this is an "organic" code which will evolve over the years as the discipline of coaching continues to emerge and gain recognition as a profession (COMENSA, 2007a:1). The proposed new COMENSA (2007b) *Membership Criteria and Standards of Competence Framework* recommends that all members commit to the ethical code as a foundation for their coaching practice. The COMENSA *Revised Code of Ethics* defines its "core values" as autonomy, beneficence, non-maleficence and justice, and its "guiding principles" as inclusivity, dignity, competence, context, boundary management, integrity, professionalism, and principles for the handling of breaches of the code (COMENSA, 2007a:2–5). (COMENSA's *Revised Code of Ethics* is available at www.comensa. org.za.)

To whom does a coach owe loyalty?

In business coaching, the question often arises, "To whom does the coach owe loyalty?" To the individual client, or to the organization who is paying the coach's fee? In fact, it is to both, which can some-times create an ethical dilemma. For instance, what if your client asks you to coach them out of the organization and into a new job? The question then arises, what are you bound to in your contract with the client organization in terms of client confidentiality and boundary management?

A coach must be able to understand the point of view of the organization with whom they have a coaching contract, and must find a way to synthesize the two interests: cooperative and competitive. Peltier (2001:222) appropriately quotes Robert Solomon (1997): "the search for excellence, whatever it may be, begins with ethics". Peltier explains that executive coaches have to navigate two types of cultures: the business culture, which is a proprietary culture based on market enterprise; and the individual client culture, which culti-vates the ethics of care, where looking after the client's best interests engenders a cooperative culture.

In clinical practice, clinicians look after their client's interest. These interests are the hub of the contract, and the arrangement is a **cooperative** one. However, in business there is a proprietary cul-ture based upon a **competitive** market philosophy. Both providers and buyers of coaching compete for the best deal they can get, and each party expects the other party to behave competitively. One party does not expect the other to look out for them or their inter-ests. Coaches need to navigate these two cultures. One is a business culture, where profit is the motive, and the other is the ethics of care for individual clients. A coach needs to understand the point of view of the organization and find a way to integrate the cooperative and the competitive points of view. This can often present a coach with dilemmas that challenge their ability to be loyal to both the organi-zation and the individual client.

In terms of client intervention, Peltier (2001:224) suggests three overall steps:

1. Develop clear written contracts—with clarity from the beginning of the relationship about confidentiality and boundary issues.
2. Whistle-blow when colleagues behave poorly or are found to be incompetent.
3. Know your limits and practice within those limits with supervision.

Peltier's main message is to focus on the single thing that one does best as a business coach, creating sustainable competitive advantage and being exceptional. His second step, to whistle blow, is something most coaches would be reluctant to do, not wanting to damage their image or a colleague's in the marketplace. However, without legislated ethical guidelines (unlike psychotherapists), coaches need to establish their behavioural norms through their working practices and commitment to their professional body's ethical code. Furthermore, if there is a definite dilemma regarding a colleague, the first step is **always** to speak to the person in question; second to speak to the lead supervisor confidentially; finally if unresolved to speak to the Ethics Committee of your professional association in complete confidence. However, any communication must be done having informed the colleague in question.

Human behaviour is always complex. In my supervision story earlier in this chapter, the coach only discovered the broken confidentiality in a subsequent coaching session with her client. She needed to first clear the situation with her client, then to clear the air with her supervisor. In this case, it did not need to be brought to anyone else's attention. One of the key difficulties with an emerging profession is that there are not necessarily precise guidelines for ethical behaviour, which is what all the international coaching bodies are gradually trying to build into their coaching guidelines for members.

Who is the client?

Coaches often forget to consider who the actual client is. Is it the organization that hires and pays the coach's fees to help with a business need? Or, is it the individual who is seeking to grow, develop and move forward in their career? The question is essentially answered when the executive personally pays the coach's fee. However, what happens when the company pays the bill? To whom does the coach owe loyalty?

ETHICAL DILEMMA
What happens if the client decides to focus on skills that the organization clearly does not condone, or skills that the client wishes to use in a future job or career? It is important to clarify

the parameters of capacity building in your contract so that you do not find yourself in this situation.

What happens when a client is angry, contemplating legal action against the organization, or is plotting their next move to a new organization. How can the coach work with this client? What information needs to be shared with the organization? When does it become unethical for the coach to continue to work with the individual client?

In this situation, once again, it is important to have stipulated in your contracting process, how you will handle a conflict of interest between the individual client and the organization. In this instance, you have several choices. You can advise your client to speak with the appropriate superiors within their organization, or you can advise your client that you and the client should possibly meet with the line manager, HR or OD, and that you will facilitate the discussion. Or, if those two scenarios are unacceptable to the client, you can withdraw from the contract letting the client know you can no longer work with them as they are unwilling to address the issue in a manner appropriate to the situation. If it is stipulated in your contract that you are facing an inappropriate conflict of interest between client and organization, only then would we advise taking it to the appropriate superiors in the organization. However, it is important that, if you are unsure of what to do, your first port of call may be to discuss it with your supervising coach.

Confidentiality issues

Another issue is that of confidentiality. It is often said that the rules for content confidentiality are up for grabs when it comes to coaching. To what extent is the relationship between coach and client confidential? In clinical practice, the counselling relationship and the content of that relationship are confidential. The only relationship that is legally protected in terms of confidentiality is that between lawyer and client, and we are aware of at least one case where a psychologist was subpoenaed to testify in court.

Many organizations insist that coach and client work in an organizational meeting space for their sessions. Often coach and client work in public spaces such as hotel foyers, coffee shops, and organizational canteens. What is the impact on privacy and confidentiality in these situations? How do you introduce your client when someone you know enters and interrupts your meeting? Have you agreed in advance how you will introduce each other when you meet other individuals you already know? How will interruptions influence the coaching conversation?

Coaches and clients must establish, in their contract and working arrangement, how they will manage the boundaries of confidentiality. For example, some clients are happy to introduce you as their coach; others will not introduce you at all, and others will introduce you as a colleague. Furthermore, the coaching relationship is not as strict as the therapeutic relationship. For example, coaches can be invited to product launches, media presentations, business and social events with their clients. It is important to address the boundaries of these events with your clients. How will you be introduced; what behaviour and feedback is expected from you?

HONOURING THE CLIENT'S AGENDA

A few years ago, a colleague had a client who was uncomfortable with being in the limelight and wanted to be coached on dealing with all the social and networking requirements of her new role. She invited her coach to join her at one of these events to observe her behaviour. Coach and client agreed that the coach would be introduced as a supplier, not as a coach. The coach played the role and to her surprise found herself introduced as "my coach". The client had changed her mind and was very comfortable with people knowing she had a coach. What is important is that only the client could make this choice, not the coach.

Part of a coach's code of ethics is to honour confidentiality in the coaching conversation. There will be a contracted agreement between client and coach about what is communicated to superiors in the working environment. This confidentiality must be agreed to and honoured at all times. The client entrusts the coach with confidences, and must feel safe to do so.

CONFIDENTIALITY DILEMMA

A question around confidentiality that needs to be addressed is to what extent does the coach owe the organization a confidential relationship, and take responsibility for the confidential boundaries defined in that relationship?

Coaches are consistently presented with confidential information about the company, its systems, processes, challenges and mistakes. For example, say you are working with a client organization about which there is much controversy in the marketplace and in the media. An example could be an organization responsible for media and communications, or for the supply of energy.

How do you handle information that, if passed on to the media, could expose your client's organization? What happens if you mention this piece of information in passing to a colleague, breaking the bounds of confidentiality, and this colleague, without thinking, then shares it with a journalist friend who reports it in the media, thus exposing your client's organization? What is your ethical responsibility in this instance? Should you confess your part? What bounds of confidentiality have you trespassed?

Firstly, in this instance, you have broken the bounds of confidentiality and are therefore in breach of contract with your client. Secondly, the person you spoke to who subsequently passed it on to the media, is in breach of confidentiality with you. However, there are no legal guidelines as coaching is only an emerging discipline. So, you have a problem. What should you do?

You may choose to speak honestly to your client, or your client organization, to let them know it came from you. Furthermore, you will need to clear it with your colleague who passed it on. If there has been any damage done to the client organization, you may face the consequences of your client losing trust in your services. It is for this reason that having indemnity insurance is critical in case the organization takes up legal proceedings against you. The moral of the story is to keep all confidences to yourself at all times; it is hard for most human beings to resist gossip.

What are ethical concerns?

Think about some of the ethical concerns that you have encountered as a coach. Examples may include fraud, broken confidentiality, three-party dilemmas, having a sexual relationship with your client, or seemingly coaching someone out of a job. For example, what do you need to have in place in your contract to ensure that, if your client is involved in some kind of criminal activity, such as embezzling funds, theft or fraud of any kind, you are protected if the client confesses to their organization and their organization chooses to inform the legal authorities? If this is the case, and you knew about the illegal activity and did not report it to the organization in question, the need for indemnity insurance may become an issue.

Other concerns centre on malpractice for coach practitioners, where "malpractice" is defined as "failure of a professional person to render proper services through reprehensible ignorance of negligence or through criminal intent, especially when injury or loss follows; or any improper negligent practice; misconduct or misuse" (Webster's, 1989). For example, what if a client organization sues you for failure on your part as a coaching professional to render services as contracted? How important is it to have insurance indemnity protection, i.e., "protection or security against damage or loss, or compensation for damage or loss sustained" (Webster's, 1989), in a similar manner to clinical psychologists? Do you have an arbitration clause in your contract about what the procedures are if conflict or misunderstandings arise?

These seem like abstract issues that may not concern you at present. But, as coaching continues to grow as a discipline, there will be claims against practitioners who do not fulfil contracts as promised. As an emerging profession, there is currently no legislated protection for practitioners. This is one of the reasons for setting up professional bodies such as EMCC, ICF, WABC and COMENSA. These organizations do not necessarily provide indemnity insurance as they consider that to be the responsibility of the individual practitioners. However, they can help practitioners to think about which types of protection are needed for them to practice with confidence and security. This is one of the key benefits of creating ethical guidelines, in parallel with an ethics complaint process.

How can you manage your ethical dilemmas?

Which ethical dilemmas have arisen for you in your practice? It is useful in your supervision sessions to discuss, on a regular basis, any ethical issues that arise. Here are several dilemmas a coach can face:

1. **It is recognized that there are circumstances where the coach may have two "clients", the individual being coached and the organization who may have commissioned the coaching.** How do you handle the giving of information to the senior manager and the organization? What needs to be in a written contract, and what do you need to verbally agree with your individual client? We tend to ensure that the written contract specifies the bounds of confidentiality between all parties, with agreed terms for reporting back to the organization. However, we also verbally contract with the individual client to ensure we are in agreement about how each of the coaching conversations will be held, and how we will handle written reports to the organization. We believe that any written communication to the third party needs to be seen and agreed to by the individual client before it is passed on to the relevant senior authority.

2. **What if you coach your client out of a job, and they leave the organization when under your coaching?** This may be a result of the client specifically asking you to coach them into a new job. Or, it may be that in developing self-awareness the client realizes that the job in which they are currently positioned is no longer suitable to their intrinsic drivers, values and career aspirations. What is your responsibility to the organization? Should you inform them? I experienced this recently. One of the senior executives I was coaching grew in self-awareness and decided to move out of his current position in the organization. There was no opportunity for him to do so within his current organization for at least a year, and he was bored. The discussion came up in the coaching conversations, and client and coach discussed the ethical difficulty under which this placed both coach and client. We agreed we would continue to work on his developing self-awareness and possibilities for growth—but the coach would not help him to leave the organization. The coach suggested that the client discuss his thinking with his line manager; he chose not to.

By contrast, another colleague had a coaching client where the client's boss, and therefore the representative of the company paying for the coaching, indicated that the individual client needed to figure out what they wanted—and if that meant that the client would leave the organization then that would be acceptable.

3. **Should you coach all the members of one team including the team leader or line manager?** This question often arises in supervision. Is it ethical in terms of boundary management for you to coach a team leader and one or more of their direct reports? What needs to be put in place in your contract to manage confidentiality? You will be in a very privileged position of knowledge, and you may lose the trust of one or more individual clients by simply carrying an individual's closely guarded secrets in terms of aspirations, personal conflicts, self-doubts and self-esteem issues. I and other colleagues have experienced lead coaches divulging information about team members to the entire team. In one instance, this led to the client organization refusing to hire external coaches in the future.

4. **How do you honour confidentiality when coaching a senior manager and their boss?** Is it ethical, and if not why not? How can you manage the boundaries of confidentiality? A typical scenario is that you are in the process of coaching a senior executive in an organization, and they recommend to their line manager that you would be suitable to coach them too. What are the issues of confidentiality that must be managed, and how do you go about it? Would it be useful to meet with both of them to discuss and agree the parameters, and what will, and will not, be disclosed to the organization as a result of the coaching? Usually, we agree that all conversations remain confidential, and the only results shared are those of the professional development plan i.e., vision, strategy, overall goals, obstacles to success and outcomes achieved. How can you ensure that individual clients are satisfied that their confidentiality will be respected and all boundaries honoured?

5. **Do you have a policy about meeting with the individual executive and line manager together?** Have you contracted this in written form so that it is open and transparent to the organization (i.e., HR, OD or line management)? Most importantly, how do

you manage the issue of confidentiality if you meet the line manager without the individual client? And, how do you manage confidentiality when the line manager, coach and individual client all meet together for the regular intermittent session? In our work, we often agree to meet several times during the contracted intervention period to align overall objectives on the part of individual client, line manager and the organization. How should you facilitate that session, and what are the parameters of what you can disclose to the line manager? We usually plan the session with the individual client, asking the client for their objectives of the meeting, and what is appropriate to be shared during the session. Once all three parties are together, the individual client facilitates the session, and brings into the conversation the overall objectives of the line manager for that session. What is important to be discussed, and what are the organization's expectations of both the coach and individual client for the duration of the coaching intervention?

6. **Ethical questions regarding a sexual relationship with a client.** In the field of psychology worldwide, this is strictly legislated against. However, in the fields of coaching and mentoring it is not necessarily defined as a part of ethical boundary management. It is important to understand what the professional conduct guidelines are for the professional body of which you are a member, and to be sure you understand the ethical conduct review process if it arises as an issue. It is essential to find out what the client's organizational policy is for colleagues/consultants working together, and many organizations have specified that it is or is not policy. The questions that arise are due to the consequences of such a relationship occurring. What are the implications for the success of the coach/client relationship, and how do the intimate boundaries created in a sexual encounter impact on the professional boundaries of coach/client? As a coach is always looking out for the client, a key question would be what the consequences for the individual would be if such a relationship occurs.

7. **Interference from the leading executive in the coaching intervention.** This is an interesting situation. An executive can readily see the benefits of coaching, and introduces coaching into their department. On perceiving the impact that they could

achieve on bottom-line results, this leader instructs the coaching supervisor to direct the team of coaches to work on specific business outcomes. However, this type of goal setting was not made explicit or agreed at the outset of the coaching intervention, or during the contracting process. The question is how coaches should manage the pressure of organizational demands from the sponsoring executive and yet confidentially hold the individual client's needs.

The complexity of supervision and ethics

It is critical that the coach develops self-awareness with the ability to self-regulate. Awareness of the ethical situations that arise is a first step; the second step is to manage them. Without self-awareness, integrity and the ability to manage complexity, ethical decisions may prove difficult or even remain in the unconscious. Personal lives, careers and organizations are often at stake and there is a high moral responsibility in this interpersonal journey. Bonds of trust, openness, fragility and honesty are developed at high levels and these need to remain honoured and deeply respected.

Supervision serves both the coach and their client, while also providing a place for learning. Supervision is a complex process, and in addition to the demanding aspect of this discipline, it needs to be in the hands of an experienced practitioner (Bluckert, 2008). The supervisor may be supervising a team of coaches and as such would have to be able to hold multiple perspectives and processes in consciousness and would therefore require a framework that would support this complexity.

Part of the complexity in executive coaching is its multiple triangular relationships. In business, coaches often work with an individual client, as well as other members of a board or team. This raises boundary and ethical questions as well as issues around managing psychological and systemic processes.

> The organization itself becomes a third party (the first triangle)— which forms a very powerful third force that can pull a coach into an enactment. The supervisory relationship is yet another triangle (the second triangle) that has to be negotiated, but one that can be extremely useful in highlighting parallel processes,

i.e., what happens in the supervision relationship may mirror a pattern that is prevalent in the organization or other individual relationships (Pampallis Paisley, 2006:26–27).

Supervisors contain and hold the stories told by the coach, the executive and the organization. Adherence to the highest levels of existing professional codes is paramount.

Developing a professional body for practitioners

One of the wider issues that became apparent during my doctoral research project (2002–2006), was the vital matter of ethics. When I commenced my doctorate, there was no accepted professional body in South Africa to represent or regulate the emerging disciplines of coaching and mentoring. This clearly led to the possibility, especially with a relatively new profession, of the abuse of standards and exploitation by opportunistic practitioners.

A core group of committed practitioners spearheaded and founded a professional body to discuss the creation of standards of competence, ethical guidelines and a recommended supervision framework, along with suggestions for the continuing professional development (CPD) of all practitioners. COMENSA has recognized the need to develop at the same pace as the disciplines of coaching and mentoring in South Africa. However, the body is creating organic frameworks for practice as needs arise, while remaining in alignment with international standards.

In other emerging markets there is a call for the founding of a professional body, for networking purposes and for creating a committed body of practitioners who can work together collaboratively to build the profession. In South Africa, COMENSA sought help from the European Mentoring and Coaching Council (EMCC) and the Worldwide Association of Business Coaches (WABC). Both continue to respond very generously. However, if a relatively developed country such as South Africa needed such help, COMENSA may have a role to play assisting sister professional bodies as they grow.

The Global Convention on Coaching (now the Global Community of Coaches or GCC) has acknowledged that, in the interest of the reputation of the coaching profession internationally, established bodies need to work together more proactively to promote the values and ethics of the coaching profession. The GCC was established to create a collaborative framework of stakeholders in coaching, with the aim of professionalizing the industry. Nine working groups were established by the GCC's Steering Committee to discuss critical issues related to the professionalization of coaching. All nine groups produced "white papers" across a 12-month working period (July 2007–July 2008) on the current realities and possible future scenarios of each area. These papers were presented at the GCC Convention in Dublin in July 2008. A tenth group, Coaching and Society, was added just prior to the July 2008 convention.

Because COMENSA was mentored throughout their process, it may be helpful for the organization to think about how to play a mentoring role to assist other African countries, where coaches may be operating in a similar vacuum and might benefit from their experience and expertise.

GCC Working Group on Developing a Code of Ethics

From July 2007 to July 2008, the role of the Global Convention on Coaching (GCC) was one of worldwide collaboration to bring the best thinking of coach practitioners and researchers together. At the end of the week-long convention in July 2008, the Working Group on Ethics published a statement. They stated that in their year-long dialogue it had become evident that a strong Code of Ethics is of paramount importance, and they believe that a Code of Ethics underpins the emergence of coaching as a profession—i.e., its status, education and development, and core competences. They stated they believed that a strong Code will help sustain the profession, and that it is evident that such a Code needs accountability mechanisms.

Ultimately, their aspiration is that by 2010 there will be a draft Universal Code of Ethics with regional tribunals made up of stakeholder representatives. The Code will be made up of the common features across the five available codes we have today (International Coach Federation, European Mentoring and Coaching Council, Worldwide Association of Business Coaches, Association for Coaching, Coaches and Mentors of South Africa, and European Coaching Institute). The Working Group on Ethics is inviting further contribution from parties not represented at the convention, making it clear that local codes will have their own accountability mechanisms. They envision it will be accompanied by a set of practical guidelines and tools to support ethical decision making and practice (GCC, 2008b).

Extending the social range of coaching

The GCC has made an effort to take into account the cultural world-views of the various nations which have taken part in the global dialogue. This is important in South Africa, for example, where the principles of empowerment and transformation influence the partic-ular social and historical conditions of the country. Many practition-ers' clients reflect the diverse facets of the South African community.

As currently practiced, however, coaching is usually a top-level man-agement or corporate activity. In the specific historical realities of South Africa, this often still means that previously privileged executives are the ones who chiefly benefit from the great riches that coaching has to offer. The irony is that many who would equally benefit are working in the same corporations, but are "previously disadvantaged" (i.e., black men and women who suffered under apartheid), and do not qualify for coaching within their organizations, as they are not yet employed in sufficiently senior executive positions. With coaching, they might be.

EXTENDING THE REACH OF COACHING

One of my female senior executive clients, Miriam, would not normally have had the luxury of a coaching experience had we not agreed to a collaborative *pro bono* coaching relationship. Miri-am's work in developing "previously disadvantaged" women highlights, for me, the fact that not only was my client a prime candidate for executive coaching, but other managers in her non-governmental organization (NGO) would have gained immeas-urably from such an experience. Sadly, the view of coaching is often that of an expensive "luxury" far beyond the financial parameters of the institution. This is an ethical dilemma in South Africa, which has been raised within COMENSA, but has yet to be resolved. Most practitioner coaches are keen to ensure that the coaching profession in South Africa does not appear "elitist" and exclusive. This dilemma may or may not apply, to a greater or lesser extent, in other countries, but could be something worth considering by other professional bodies.

The requirement for diversity could impact on the training of coach and mentor practitioners, looking at their gender and background. In the interests of being fully representative—particularly in South Africa—it is important that all facets of society be encouraged to join the coaching profession, to make it truly reflective of the community within which it works. For example, COMENSA has already begun to consider these important social issues. Steps are being taken by several COMENSA member coach training institutions to provide a system of learning and mentoring for coaches from disadvantaged backgrounds to ensure that the emerging profession becomes inclusive rather than exclusive. The creation and maintenance of this body is an important initiative which will have a long-lasting impact and influence on coaching and mentoring in South Africa.

The variety of perspectives and cultures involved in coaching worldwide, calls for a high level of sensitivity and awareness from coaches. One place to develop and refine this consciousness is in supervision.

Models of supervision

The Seven-Eyed Model of Supervision

There are many different models of supervision, but one of the most common models used today is the Seven-Eyed Model of Supervision. This framework is used in the supervision of coach and mentor practitioners, and in other helping professions. The model was developed by Peter Hawkins and Robin Shohet (2000). The seven modes of supervision are (Mike the Mentor, 2008a):

1. **The Client System**: The focus is on the coachee situation; the problem the coachee wants help with, how they represent the issues and the choices that they are making.
2. **The Coach's Interventions**: The focus is on the interventions the coach made, how and why they made them, and what else they might have done.
3. **The Relationship between the Coach and the Client**: The focus is on neither the coach nor the client but on the conscious and unconscious interactions between the two of them so that the

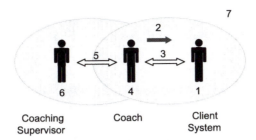

Figure 1. The Seven-Eyed Model of Supervision.

Source: Mike the Mentor (2008a).

coach develops a better understanding of the dynamics of the coaching relationship.

4. **The Coach**: The focus is on the coach's own experience as an instrument for registering what is happening beneath the coachee system.

5. **The Parallel Process**: The focus is on what the coach has absorbed from the client system and how it may be playing out in the relationship between the coach and supervisor.

6. **The Coaching Supervisor's Self-reflection**: The focus is the supervisor's "here and now" experience with the coach and how this can be used to shed light on the coach/client relationship.

7. **The Wider Context**: The focus is on the wider organizational, social, cultural, ethical, and contractual context within which the supervision is taking place.

The seven modes of supervision are illustrated in Figure 1.

To Practise the Seven-Eyed Model of Supervision

1. **Focus on the coach/client situation**. The practitioner identifies their problem or challenge, focusing on what actually happened in their sessions with clients, how the clients presented themselves, what was discussed, and any connections between issues.

2. **Explore the coach's interventions with the client.** The supervisor focuses on the interventions made, the coach's rationale, and helps in developing alternative strategies for interventions, and examines consequences now and for the future.

3. **Explore the relationship between coach and client.** The supervisor focuses on the dynamic between coach and client, at both a conscious and unconscious level. This step in the process can assist the coach to understand the deeper, underlying processes which could affect the outcome of the coach/client intervention. The aim of this mode is to help the coach gain greater insight and understanding of the dynamics of their relationships with clients.

4. **Focus on the coach practitioner's experience.** The aim of this step is to increase the capacity of the coach to engage with clients effectively. This offers the opportunity to develop self-awareness, deepening the learning about how to deal with conscious and less conscious assumptions and behaviours.

5. **Focus on the supervision relationship.** This is a parallel process to the coach/client relationship. This part of the discussion offers valuable perspective as to the dynamics present between coach/client that is played out in the supervisor/practitioner relationship. This process focuses on what is happening in the relationship between the supervisor and the coach and explores how it is playing out or paralleling the coach/client relationship.

6. **The supervisor self-reflects.** The supervisor observes and notes what they are experiencing in the supervision sessions. The aim of this step is for the supervisor to use their responses to provide another source of information to the coach. This is a very similar process to clinical psychology supervision.

7. **Focus on the bigger picture or wider context.** The supervisor and practitioner/s reflect on the wider client and organizational context. This brings in the ethical, cultural, systemic, organizational and social aspects of the coaching intervention. The aim of step 7 is to observe and understand the wider context to build capacity on the part of the practitioner.

The Double Matrix or Eight-eyed Supervisor Model

The Double Matrix or Eight-Eyed Supervisor Model is an adaptation of Hawkins and Shohet's Seven-Eyed Supervision Model discussed above. It consists of the following components (Jones and Jenkins, 2006:30) which I have adapted to the coaching conversation:

1. Reflection on the content of the coaching session;
2. Exploration of the strategies and interventions used by the coach practitioner;

3. Exploration of the coaching process and relationship;
4. Focus on the coaching process as it is reflected in the supervision process;
5. Focus on the supervisee's transference;
6. Focus on the here-and-now process as a mirror or parallel of the there-and-then process;
7. Focus on the supervisor's counter transference; and
8. Focus on the wider context.

Individual supervision

My model of individual and group supervision (Figure 2) is a précised version of the Seven-Eyed Model summarized above (although I also place it on a background of four quadrants with reflection on the UL; practice on the UR; and Observation split between LL and LR). Working with an individual practitioner, I will ask the practitioner for their reflections on the challenges currently facing them. Supervisor and coachee/s prioritize the issues to discuss, and work on one at a time. The supervisor leads the session in a coaching manner, by facilitating thinking on the part of the practitioner rather than thinking for them. However, the supervisor may share their observations and experience. The supervisor is helping the practitioner reflect on the content of a coaching session, as well as on their own internal dialogue and their response to the client. The supervisor will ask the practitioner to explain their processes and other interventions that might be useful or appropriate. The

Figure 2. Sunny's supervision model.

practitioner is adopting a meta position, looking at the coaching session in question from first, second and third positions; in NLP terms, this would be third-position thinking. In psychotherapeutic terms, the practitioner would be identifying any transference and counter-transference between client and coach. In third-position thinking, the practitioner can see themselves in miniature as if looking down from a corner of the ceiling. This reflective practice helps to develop self-awareness.

In the practice part of the session, the practitioner may coach the supervisor, with feedback from the supervisor at the end. At the end of this, the supervisor and practitioner move back into a reflective space to develop self-awareness, and identify what went well in terms of content, process and any parallel processes that might have been happening. It is important here for the supervisor to be aware of their own internal process; the supervisor is modelling coaching and self-awareness with the practitioner.

In terms of observation, the practitioner notices the learning gained overall from the session and any changes needed to their overall practice. Any steps for action or reflection are noted and the next session booked. Observation is about the wider context. How does the learning from this session impact on the overall coaching intervention with the client, and the overall coaching style of the practitioner? The supervisor needs to help the practitioner refer back to the context in which the coach, supervisor and client organization are working together, as well as the wider context of the practitioner's developing competence and capacity within their profession.

Group supervision

Reflection

With group supervision the facilitator begins a "round" asking a set of questions and hearing from each individual. Sample questions could be, "What's working for you in your coaching practice?" and "Which issues or dilemmas do you wish to work on today?" The facilitator elicits all challenges and issues and then breaks the group into pairs/triads. The pairs/triads select several issues to reflect on, creating strategies or recommendations for managing each issue. The group meets again in plenary and the facilitator takes thoughts and recommendations from each pair/triad. The issues that can be addressed in a reflective discussion are either answered here, or saved until the end of the supervision session.

Practice

The group prioritizes the issues and challenges that have been raised in the reflective session. A few practitioners volunteer to take part in a supervision demo. The lead coach, or supervisor, supervises a coaching conversation with the volunteer practitioner and coachee. The rest of the group gather round in a circle and observe, quietly taking notes. If necessary, the lead supervisor takes time out to speak to the group as part of the teaching. It is important that coach and client contract confidentiality and boundaries in this fishbowl situation.

Observation

At the end of the supervision demo, the facilitator solicits thoughts, observations and questions from the volunteer coach, coachee and the group, and facilitates a discussion on the questions raised. The group shares their learning from the session overall in a final round. If there has been no demo, but simply plenary rounds and thinking pairs/triads, the facilitator facilitates a discussion of learning gained from the session.

Supervision as a form of empowerment

In supervision, there is the cultural context of the organization and society as a whole to be aware of. Traditional models of supervision have been developed in Western consumer cultures, and more particularly in academic environments. These environments do not necessarily share the same assumptions as the developing coaching cultures in Argentina, China, East Asia, India or South Africa. We have discussed culture and diversity at length in Chapter 6, and the supervisor needs to be aware of the capacity and limitations of the practitioners under their supervision.

Coaching is fundamentally about empowering people, resulting in their ability to think through their challenges and issues successfully. In a very real sense, therefore, the role of supervision is to help empower the coach practitioner to think through all the perspectives that can impact on client issues and dilemmas. Supervision can be seen as both an empowerment tool as well as a commitment to best practice.

Developing a professional approach

Supervision may be the new and innovative context for coach practitioners to contribute to the development of self-reflective practice and practitioner research. In this way we may begin to move forward to being "professional".

The need to educate coaching supervisors, practitioners and managers in understanding the need for supervision is critical. The supervision relationship is a complex one, and the benefits from supervision are exponential for practitioners and client organizations. Developing an interprofessional approach is a sound one. Coaching can learn from the other helping professions until more research is undertaken worldwide. Whichever supervision model is worked with in the coaching context, it is important to develop a number of highly skilled supervisors who can help practitioners to work with greater knowledge, depth, skills and competence.

Contracting, supervision and ethical conduct are not new concepts. They have been practised in the helping professions for decades. However, they are not yet regulated and require understanding at all stages of development for practitioners. We have looked at each of the roles and functions of these three key areas and, although there are as yet no internationally agreed guidelines on the regulation of supervision, ethics and contracting, all of the professional bodies worldwide in alignment with the Global Coaching Community (GCC) are assessing and establishing what frameworks need to be in place for their member practitioners. Ultimately, these processes will benefit and protect coach, client and organization. The development of professional supervision, contracting and ethical codes is emerging as a vital function within the discipline of coaching.

Coach's library

Coaches and Mentors of South Africa (COMENSA). (2006b). *Interim Policy on Supervision*. Cape Town: COMENSA. Webpage: www.comensa.org.za/dotnetnuke/ProfessionalPractice/Supervision/tabid/79/language/en-ZA/Default.aspx

Coaches and Mentors of South Africa (COMENSA). (2007a). *Revised Code of Ethics*. Cape Town: COMENSA. Webpage: www.comensa.org.za/ dotnetnuke/ ProfessionalPractice/CodeofEthics/tabid/78/language/ en-ZA/Default.aspx

European Mentoring and Coaching Council (EMCC). (2008b). *Code of Ethics*. Webpage: www.emccouncil.org/fileadmin/documents/ EMCC_Code_of_Ethics.pdf

Hawkins, P., and Shohet, R. (2000). *Supervision in the Helping Professions*. Buckingham: Open University Press.

International Coach Federation (ICF). (2008b). *ICF Code of Ethics*. Lexington, KY: ICF. Webpage: www.coachfederation.org/about %2Dicf/ethics%2D%26%2Dregulation/icf%2Dcode%2Dof %2Dethics/

Jones, R., and Jenkins, F. (Eds.). (2006). *Developing the Allied Health Professions*. Oxford: Radcliffe.

Kadushin, A. (1976). *Supervision in Social Work*. New York, NY, Columbia University Press.

Noer, D. (2000). The big three derailment factors in a coaching relationship. In: Goldsmith, M., Lyons, L., and Freas, A. (Eds.), *Coaching for Leadership: How the World's Greatest Coaches Help Leaders Learn* (pp. 317–324). San Francisco, CA: Jossey-Bass/Pfeiffer.

Pampallis Paisley, P. (2006). *Towards a Theory of Supervision for Executive Coaching: An Integral Vision*. Unpublished DProf dissertation. London: Middlesex University.

Steere, J. (1984). *Ethics in Clinical Psychology*. Cape Town: Oxford University Press.

Worldwide Association of Business Coaches (WABC) (2008a). *Code of Business Coaching Ethics and Integrity*. Webpage: www.wabccoaches. com/includes/popups/code_of_ethics_2nd_edition_december_17_ 2007.html

CHAPTER NINE

Developing a body of knowledge— coaching research

One of the primary emerging disciplines in coaching is research. Its role is to determine the competences necessary to educate and develop coaches worldwide, as well as to create a definition of coaching that the global community will accept. Another way to describe it is "ongoing critical appraisal" of your own coaching practice. This chapter examines the current global thinking in terms of coaching research, stressing the importance of writing up your findings as you work within the business environment. This requires more than just being coached yourself and participating in supervision.

The work of the Research Agenda at the Global Convention on Coaching (GCC) in Dublin, July 2008, defined research as "the life blood of practice. It feeds our continuing development and brings fresh perspectives to our work. It can be the place to visit in our dilemmas and in our successes. In valuing research we are valuing our work, as one is the exploration of the other. Engagement in that exploration sustains our practice and fuels our own development" (GCC, 2008d).

The escalating demand for coaching has motivated a wide range of providers and consumers to advocate the professionalization of the industry in order to safeguard the quality, effectiveness and ethical integrity of coaching services. In turn, a growing awareness of the potential benefits to the industry of professional status has led to an interest in international dialogues, such as the Global Convention on Coaching (GCC), which was established with the explicit aim of exploring the professionalization of coaching.

The original role of the GCC was to research the rising profession of coaching worldwide, and to begin to build an international community who could share issues, concerns and ideas. What emerged was a prototype of a global coaching community, who have stated the need to develop a knowledge base for coaching through research, and the critical reflective practice of dedicated coach practitioners, in a global collaborative effort. In September 2008, the International Coaching Research Forum (ICRF), consisting of internationally recognised researchers, coaching professionals and other stakeholders, met at Harvard to produce 100 research proposal outlines to advance coaching as an evidence-based discipline. These papers are available online at www.coachingresearchforum.org.

What is research?

Research can be defined, in the traditional sense, as an academic investigation into the origins and developments of a given subject. However, it is not just academic research that is needed at this critical stage of the emerging profession of coaching. We are looking to encourage practitioner research, defining it as "specific critical reflection and evaluation" of your given practice.

The GCC defines research as "a 'search' for new knowledge and understanding, which can be undertaken in many different ways and from many perspectives. It becomes a continuum which includes individual critical reflective practice and goes through to distinct projects undertaken as teams" (GCC, 2008d).

A very new approach is to consider all practitioner coaches, in the local and global coaching community, as potential contributors to the emerging body of knowledge. This requires three specific sets of skills on the part of practitioners: a critical reading of research, an application of research to practice, and the capacity and ability to generate research. This should not in any way reduce the need or the requirement for quality. A body of knowledge has to be sustainable. At present, as is acknowledged by the GCC, academics and practitioners are responsible for both good and bad research.

What motivates research?

Organizations buying coaching services today are well informed about the business coaching process and the value of coaching for their executives and their business overall. They are asking for: (1) measurable results; (2) the evidence base that underpins coaching; and (3) the qualifications and experience of the coaches they employ. Many large organizations have begun assessment interviews to develop a bespoke bank of external coaches, and are looking to educate their internal coaches in quality coach training programmes with the appropriate credentials.

Although it is believed that coaching provides a positive intervention in building executive and management capability, there is very little empirical research into how the coaching relationship builds executive aptitude and impacts business positively. One reason for this lack of empirical research is that it has proved difficult to use longitudinal designs and control groups when evaluating coaching interventions. Rigorous evaluation historically is through randomized controlled trials (Grant and Cavanagh, 2007a). A second reason is that coaching is not yet a defined profession with regulated requirements for professional coaches.

Two other difficulties are that research often needs substantial funding and is not necessarily the domain of the newly "skilled" coach practitioner. The Research Agenda for the Global Convention on Coaching (GCC) has recommended that all coach training programmes internationally offer a basic module in research methodology and application. Other possibilities to build a body of knowledge are either for the supervision process to create a foundation for research into practice, or for a coach practitioner to work in conjunction with an academic student who is looking for a project. This idea is sound, particularly if your practice forms part of a coaching services business involved in large coaching interventions, and if you are interested in providing some kind of qualitative or quantitative benchmarking for your clients.

It has been previously assumed that coaches are scientist-practitioners, conducting research that ultimately informs and enhances their own practice. Another term applied to coach practitioners who critically appraise their own practice is that of the "scholar practitioner", i.e., someone who is a student of their own practice. However, research is expensive, and most coach practitioners are neither critically reflective of their own practice, nor do they research the outcomes of their coaching interventions. Research is needed to show a range of results: from the coaching process, to the skills and competence of the coach, the results of coach supervision, how organizations benefit from supervision, and the overall outcomes of coaching for the individual executive and the business.

Another possibility is to work collaboratively with other coach practitioners. This could be called a "partnership" model in which both full-time researchers and full-time practitioners work together, bringing their respective strengths to the research process (Green, cited in GCC, 2008c). However, partnership needs management. I recently spoke to a South African doctoral student at the University of South Africa (UNISA) who hopes to investigate core coaching competences being used by South African coaches. However, he has found it difficult to access coaches who are prepared to take part in such a research project. Although we cannot all spend time facilitating enquiry or research into our practice, it is crucial that we either facilitate or participate in building a body of knowledge for our discipline through critical reflection on our own coaching processes.

What research is available?

It has been recommended, as a result of the GCC process and the work done by the International Coaching Research Forum (ICRF) at

Harvard Medical School, that we need empirical evidence proving that coaching makes a difference for individuals, organizations, and society. Because there still remains a lack of clarity and consensus as to what professional coaching actually is, and what makes for an effective and reputable coach, it has been agreed that research needs to be conducted around the globe. The "Australian Research Council (ARC) has begun funding coaching research through Australian universities to encourage the development of the discipline (Grant, 2008:96).

A major question today is: what is the value of existing coaching research—particularly as there is no one existing database of research. Although a substantial body of coaching literature has emerged in the last few years, there are only a few academic coaching journals currently published, including a new Harvard coaching journal, *Coaching: An International Journal of Theory, Research and Practice*. The *International Journal of Evidence-Based Coaching and Mentoring* was established in August 2003, and the *International Coaching Psychology Review* in April 2006.

Fillery-Travis and Lane (2006) argue that those who wish to research whether coaching works are asking the wrong question. Their argument is that we first need to determine how coaching is being used and within which framework and only then can we analyze what is working. According to Baek-Kyoo (2005), "executive coaching has become increasingly popular despite limited empirical evidence about its impact and wide disagreement about necessary or desired professional qualifications".

In the last few years, there have been a number of business coaching, non-executive coaching, and life coaching studies. We list a variety of sources at the end of this chapter, including the compilation of research papers gathered by the GCC Research Agenda Working Group during their 2007/8 dialogue.

Building your knowledge base

A major reason to encourage practitioners to critically reflect and appraise their own practice, either in supervision, in partnership with other practitioner coaches or through academic research, is due to the need to build the knowledge base for coaching. A current definition of the knowledge base for coaching is that of competent practice, where competence drives the discipline and the knowledge base grows through the application of defined competences. In Chapter 3, we explored the competences required by various professional coaching bodies, and the GCC has recommended that a foundation of core competence be researched and accepted internationally by 2010.

However, if in future coaching is to emerge as a profession, key requirements include "identifiable and distinct skills; education and training to acquire proficiency; recognition outside the community as a profession; a code of ethics; public service by coaches; a formalized organization; evaluation of credentials and self-regulation; an established community of practitioners for networking and exchange of ideas; public recognition that coaching is a profession", and finally: "a coaching practice grounded in theoretical and factual research and knowledge" (Bennett, 2006:241–2).

In coaching, the knowledge base is multi-disciplinary, yet the field is undefined. Coaches are informed by various theoretical bases, including the following (GCC, 2008e:1):

- Learning theory (Kolb, Bloom, Bandura, Boud, Mumford);
- Change (Hudson, Batson, Kotter, Scott and Jaffee);
- Developmental (Kegan, Dubrowsky, Kohlberg);
- Ego (Loevinger, Cook);
- Communication (Wittgenstein, Watzlavick);
- Systemic thinking (Lewin, Senge);
- Social psychology (Izen);
- Organizational development (Ulrich, Smallwood, Schein, Beckhard, Burke);
- Process work (Mindell);
- Action learning (Revans, Board, Weinstock);
- Culture (Schein);
- Self-directed learning (Boyatzis);
- Leadership (Bennis, Jaques, Blanchard, Greenleaf);
- Existential theory and philosophy (Yalom, Spinelli);
- Chaos theory (Poncaré, Wheatley);
- Cognitive behavioural psychology (Beck, Ellis, Bandura, Skinner, Thorndike, Seligman);
- Emotional intelligence (Pert, Goleman); and
- Spiritual intelligence (Zohar).

At the moment, the knowledge base for coaching is driven by market forces, the momentum of its practitioners, and the different learning contexts for practitioners and commercial innovation. There is a growing interest in evidence-based and peer-reviewed coaching journals. This includes demands from clients to measure the return on coaching investment (ROI), with tangible proof of rigour and credibility in coaching as a developmental tool for business. More and more books are being written about coaching, and coach education programmes have a growing foundation in universities. The downside is that practitioners need money for research projects, and are not necessarily skilled in the rigour and techniques of research.

There is a gulf between practitioners with and without academic know-how who have the rigour to initiate practitioner research or to facilitate evidence-based work. Even so, what does the accumulation of evidence mean for the coaches themselves? Will they actually apply the findings of current research to their own practice, and crucially, how can they apply new findings if they themselves are not rigorously and critically reflecting on their own practice?

The majority of coaches are not necessarily trained in psychological science whose foundation of practice is its established knowledge base (Grant and Cavanagh, 2007a:241). Instead, coach practitioners tend to be trained in proprietary models with an unproven evidence base. Hence, the growing divide between psychologists and coaches not trained in psychological practice. In parallel with the Human Potential Movement (HPM) of the 1960s and 1970s, there is a strain of "anti-intellectualism" within the coaching community globally that reflects a strong desire among some "to liberate themselves from the bonds of socio-political systems that stifled individuality including science" (Spence, 2007b:259).

As a result, many coach practitioners do not see the value in researching evidence or outcomes from their practice. The consequence of this move could be towards a fashionable human development industry which is resistant to any mandatory professional training or accreditation. This may eventually result in the loss of freedom, so greatly sought after, due to inevitable future regulation and market demands. One of the emerging themes of the GCC was the need for coaching to regulate itself before someone else does, creating guidelines in ethics, supervision, core competences, and a research agenda in order to move coaching practice towards a robust, self-regulated, evidence-based, multi-cultural discipline.

Developing a new model of research

One of our recommendations is for coach practitioners to think about how they reflect on their practice, assessing and evaluating their skills and competence through supervision. One of the discussion points at the GCC was the potential for supervision to be a place for research and critical enquiry into practice. We recommend that coach practitioners begin to write up and publish case studies on their findings, but from a reflective and critical place of appraisal. The thinking that emerged from the GCC recommends that value be given to practitioner enquiry into practice as well as the high value given to academic and psychological research.

One possibility for non-academic coaching research could be from a supervision point of view. According to COMENSA, "Supervision allows practitioners to reconstruct their experience, reflect, understand, design their professional reality, and develop new responses for future practice within the supervision context" (COMENSA, 2006b).

Today, there is no widely recognized "non-academic" model of research for coach practitioners, which means doing a little "research" yourself to find e-zines, professional magazines, journals, and other media which will publish your findings. This is not about positioning or promoting your practice commercially. It is more about writing up discoveries, dilemmas and complexities to contribute to the growing body of knowledge for business coaching. The partnership model, working with a scholar or academic who will help you to research and write up your findings, is worth considering.

However, these suggestions may continue to be difficult until a new model for practitioner research is designed and tested. The author, in alignment with the GCC, recommends the development of a new model for coaching research that is "multi-disciplinary, multi-methodological and multi-cultural" (GCC, 2008d).

An emerging profession

Throughout this book, I have spoken about what is required for coaching to be recognized as a regulated discipline or profession.

Grant and Cavanagh (2006:3) have indicated that one requirement is that it should be done through peer-reviewed and accepted research. Spence concluded that the accepted foundation of a profession includes a requirement for members to have formal academic qualifications, that they adhere to an enforceable code of ethics, that licensed practice is only granted to qualified members, that members comply with applicable state-sanctioned regulation, underpinned by a common body of knowledge and skills (Spence, 2007b:261).

There is at present a gap between the criteria needed to develop a profession, and the current reality of coaching internationally. This gap presents a challenge to professional coaching bodies for several reasons. First, there is uncertainty about the role played by psychology in the development of the coaching profession. Spence (2007b:263) suggests, "psychologists have a unique role to play in securing the future of coaching and helping to establish it as a respected and credible sub-discipline of psychology". This point of view will never be popular with many practising coaches, and needs to be resolved in the current climate. What is greatly needed is for coaching-related research to be carried out "in order better to understand and refine the coaching process and hence coaching outcomes" (Linley, 2006:1).

The ICRF

In September 2008, a group of 40 internationally recognized coaching researchers, professionals and other coaching stakeholders came together in an historic meeting at Harvard. The International Coaching Research Forum (ICRF) had very specific aims. Firstly, to promote the field of coaching research worldwide by creating 100 coaching research proposals that could be disseminated to all coaching practitioners, academics and organizations; and secondly, to foster coaching research on a global scale to collaboratively advance this emerging profession.

While by no means inclusive, the ICRF participants met together with a third goal to build coaching research networks which would support coaching research at all levels. These individuals, who are considered to be at the forefront of academic coaching research and professional coaching practice, came from seven different countries. Collectively they publish books and peer-reviewed journal articles on coaching and coaching-related topics; lecture at academic and practitioner level; and work to facilitate positive change coaching professional clients and their teams.

A final aim was to communicate the message that practitioner and academic research is one of the primary ways to advance coaching as an evidence-based discipline, and to signpost that coaching is a powerful incentive to create positive change for both individuals and society. The document produced at the forum is available on the Foundation of Coaching's website (www.thefoundationofcoaching. org) and on the ICRF site (www.coachingresearchforum.org).

You can access the 100 coaching-related research proposals which the forum hopes will prompt new coaching research at all levels of practitioner and academic coaching worldwide. The ICRF was sponsored by The Foundation of Coaching, and The Coaching and Positive Psychology Initiative of Harvard University at McLean Hospital. The newly formed Institute of Coaching at Harvard (IC) is committed to sponsoring executive and life coaching research through their grant process to encourage the advancement of the field.

Key themes that emerged at the ICRF as important to coaching research are in: coaching specialities; modalities and process; outcomes and methodology; business coaching, politics, ethics and governance; training, development, and knowledge base; theoretical frameworks; definitions of coaching; coaching skills and core competences; coaching and society; and core diversity issues. One of the key questions to emerge from the ICRF for further consideration is how to most effectively mobilize and coordinate coaching research resources within each country and internationally.

The ICRF will also engage with other bodies including the GCC as it promotes research in important areas such as coach training, education and development; theoretical frameworks; selection of potential coaches; coaching sustainability; and methodologies for coaching research.

The need for collaboration

The GCC recommended that by 2010 research should be included as a core competence in all coach development programmes—with every practitioner taking responsibility to research their own practice, including coaching supervision as a fundamental research process.

If coaching is to emerge as a discipline with impact and a future, a series of difficult conversations still need to take place in forums such as the GCC, ICRF and other professional body events. How can we educate providers, buyers and stakeholders alike; where is the most useful coaching research to be found; and what are the barriers to individual practitioner involvement in research? Who will develop effective measures and outcomes to study the effectiveness of coaching, and who will undertake to develop a coaching research methodology for practitioners who are not academics?

Although we live and work in a diverse world, we still mistrust differences. We have just begun a global dialogue and collaboration to understand the status of coaching within each country and culture, acknowledging that our common needs are similar. However, issues of power and diversity may impact on how and which initiatives are taken forward. What are the issues of power that we need to address in order to be willing to listen to each other, and how can we move coaching towards becoming a more rigorous field?

In this chapter, we have sought to broaden the definition of research, and have identified possible contributing roles for coach practitioners, academic researchers and coaching psychologists. To cultivate the sustainability of practice through a growing body of knowledge, we believe that collaboration provides a dynamic and realistic way forward, meeting the needs of all coaching stakeholders.

A growing knowledge base is critical for the mature establishment of coaching. Worldwide, a principle is emerging, which is that every practitioner has the responsibility to research their own practice. The GCC recommends that practitioner and academic research equally be considered to be of value, and that education in research be included in all coach programmes at an appropriate developmental level. We believe that research is the vital component to grow the coaching profession. If it was a core competence for practitioner education, it would ensure the sustainability of coaching, whether or not coaching emerges as a defined profession.

Coach's library

Baek-Kyoo, B. (2005). Executive coaching: A conceptual framework from an integrative review of practice and research. *Human Resource Development Review*, 4:462–488.

Carter, A., Wolfe, H., and Kerrin, M. (2005). Employers and coaching evaluation. *International Journal of Coaching in Organizations*, 3(4).

Dagley, G. (2006). Human resources professionals' perceptions of executive coaching: Efficacy benefits and return on investment. *International Coaching Psychology Review*, 1(2):34–45.

Feldman, D.C., and Lankau, M.J. (2005). Executive coaching: A review and agenda for future research. *Journal of Management*, 31(6):829–848.

Fillery-Travis, A., and Lane, D. (2006). Does coaching work, or are we asking the wrong question? *International Coaching Psychology Review*, 1(1):23–36.

Kauffman, C.M., Russell, S.G., and Bush, M.W. (Eds.) (2008). *100 Coaching Research Proposal Abstracts*. International Coaching Research Forum. Cambridge, MA: The Coaching and Positive Psychology Initiative, McLean Hospital, Harvard Medical School and The Foundation of Coaching. Webpage: www.coachingresearchforum.org.

Laske, O.E. (2004). Can evidence-based coaching increase ROI? *International Journal of Evidence-Based Coaching and Mentoring*, 2(2):41–53.

Lawton-Smith, C., and Cox, E. (2007). Coaching: is it just a new name for training? *International Journal of Evidence-Based Coaching and Mentoring*, Special Issue.

Mackie, D. (2007). Evaluating the effectiveness of executive coaching: where are we now and where do we need to be? *Australian Psychologist*, 42(4):310–318.

Thach, E. C. (2002). The impact of executive coaching and 360 feedback on leadership effectiveness. *Leadership and Organization Development Journal*, 23(4):205–214.

Papers consulted by the GCC research working group

Bennett, J.L. (2006). An agenda for coaching-related research: A challenge for researchers. *Coaching Psychology Journal: Practice and Research*, 8(4):240–249.

Cox, E. (2007). *Collaborative Dialogue on the Research Agenda for Coaching*. Proceedings of a meeting of the Oxford Brookes Coaching and Mentoring Society on 14 December 2007. Mimeo.

Fillery-Travis, A. (2007). *Where's the Evidence? First Steps into the Literature.* Mimeo.

Fillery-Travis, A. (2008b). *Current State of Knowledge Production in the UK.* Mimeo.

Fillery-Travis, A., and Lane, D. (2008). How to develop your research interests. In: Palmer, S., and Bor, R. (Eds.), *The Practitioner's Handbook: A Guide for Counsellors, Psychotherapists and Counselling Psychologists* (pp. 176–192). London: Sage.

Grant, A.M. (2003a). The impact of life coaching on goal attainment, metacognition and mental health. *Social Behavior and Personality*, 31(3):253–264.

Grant, A.M. (2003b). *Keeping up with the Cheese! Research as a Foundation for Professional Coaching of the Future*. Keynote presentation to the International Coach Federation Conference Symposium on Research and Coaching, Denver, CO, November.

Grant, A.M., and Cavanagh, M.J. (2007a). Evidence-based coaching: flourishing or languishing? *Australian Psychologist*, 42(4):239–254.

Lane, D.A., and Corrie, S. (2006). *The Modern Scientist-Practitioner: A Guide to Practice in Psychology*. Hove: Routledge.

Linley, P.A. (2006). Coaching research: Who? What? Where? When? Why? *International Journal of Evidence-Based Coaching and Mentoring*, 4(2).

Salkovskis, P.M. (2002). Empirically grounded clinical interventions: cognitive-behavioural therapy progresses through a multi-dimensional approach to clinical science. *Behavioural and Cognitive Psychotherapy*, 30(11):3–9.

Spence, G.B. (2007b). Further development of evidence-based coaching: Lessons from the rise and fall of the human potential movement. *Australian Psychologist*, 42(4):255–265.

Whitmore, J. (2007a). *Corporate Coaching and Much More*. Mimeo.

Whitmore, J. (2007b). *Where Are We Coming From? Where Are We Going?* Mimeo.

CHAPTER TEN

Integration and synthesis

- Continuous reflection, learning and practice
  - The complexity of the coaching process
  - Coaching from a systems perspective
- Developing competence
  - Knowledge, wisdom and experience

How can you move to the next level in your practice? If we talk about adult stages of development, coaching as an emerging profession is currently journeying from adolescence into its adult phase. A danger is that it becomes a fashion to call oneself a coach, or to be a coach in training. In other words, rather than a respected profession, coaching becomes a passing bandwagon.

Although coaching in the USA, UK, Europe and Australia is moving into maturity in terms of its life curve—in emerging markets such as Argentina, China and East Asia, India, and South Africa, coaching is more in an adolescent stage, with "hormones racing up and down". Right now, coaching needs direction, and the continual building of a knowledge base, in order to begin to define its move towards professional practice.

Continuous reflection, learning and practice

I have based this book on my and my colleagues' research, teaching and business practice, emphasizing the need for continuous reflection and learning. The purpose of the book has been to integrate wisdom and practice with recommendations and suggestions for practitioner coaches, HR and OD professionals, and managerial leaders who want to fine-tune their business coaching skills and competence.

Throughout the book, I have endeavoured to provide a broad understanding of the business coaching process. Throughout the book we have looked at the origins and current reality of coaching, the influence of psychology, adult and experiential learning, existential and diversity theories as well as the theoretical and developmental underpinnings of coaching.

Coaching embraces a process of experiential and continuous learning for client and coach. Although I have explored how to use various question frameworks and models, these are not by any means all that is available to the business coach. In examining diversity issues that clients and coaches experience, we have identified diversity, cultural, linguistic and gender issues that require flexibility and the development of new competences on the part of the coach. We have endeavoured to share with you a broad range of business coaching approaches that will help you to identify gaps in your knowledge, but also to integrate new learning into your own practice.

The complexity of the coaching process

We have analyzed the complexities of the coaching conversation— the basic tool of the business and executive coach. Business coaching has a huge contribution to make to leadership competence inside organizations, and I have tried to take an in-depth, dynamic and integrative look at the coaching process, question frameworks, how to use current coaching models, examining current coach/client concerns such as ethics, contracting, supervision and the "relationship" between coach and client. The book's focus has been on the hub of the coaching conversation: learning from experience, which my colleagues and I believe is crucial for individual and organizational transformation.

The importance of experiential learning is that it emphasizes a client's individual, subjective experience. In existential terms, the meaning of experience is not a given, and is subject to interpretation. Coach and client use the business coaching conversation to actively reconstruct the client's experience, with a focus on setting goals that are aligned with the client's internal drivers, by which we mean their intrinsic values, beliefs and feelings. However, it is important that there is some kind of synthesis with the values of the organization within which they work.

Jaques and Clement (1991:xiv–xv) advocate that managerial leaders acquire qualities of cognitive complexity, appropriate knowledge and skills, and wisdom about people. Coaching is an egalitarian relationship, even if the focus is that of the coach on the client. Both individuals bring their experience, expertise and wisdom to the relationship. In coaching, the coach will adapt their style according to their model, but most important is the development of the relationship through the client/coach interactions.

Coaching from a systems perspective

Coaching models help us to understand the coaching intervention from a systems perspective, and to understand the need for "structure" in the interaction between coach and client. Models help us to develop flexibility as coach practitioners, offering structure and an outline for both the coaching conversation and the overall coaching journey.

Specific frameworks of questions are useful for the business coach, either as a way to get started with a new client, or simply as a tool to be used as part of their own coaching model. Common experiences which shape the culture of a society may impact on which frameworks are more useful to you than others.

Most cultures today embrace complexity, multiple cultures and diversity—yet within organizations there will be commonly shared values, beliefs and assumptions about leadership, management, responsibility, experience and language. We have looked at question frameworks simply as tools to structure the coaching conversation. Gradually, as you begin to refine your own coaching model, it will become clear which question frameworks are most useful to you.

In this book, we have explored a range of diversity themes: from personality traits to gender, race, ethnicity, language and linguistic patterns, as well as religion and styles of communication. In the business environment, the coach needs to become aware of, and to manage, their own responses to questions of diversity before they can begin to coach a client on similar issues. We have focused on raising the business coach's awareness to crucial diversity issues, both within themselves and within their individual and organizational clients.

Developing competence

Defined and benchmarked skills and competences serve a dual purpose. They give clarity in terms of how coaches are selected for an intervention, and they give the coach guidelines on client expectations and how to continually self-develop and improve. However, as coaching at this stage is very much an unregulated industry, skills and competence are basically defined by coaching associations as part of a philosophy or as a means to membership of their association.

We aim to help you identify your own level of skill and competence, recognizing your own strengths as well as targeting areas for development. We explained in detail the required skills and competences defined for business coaches by professional bodies, highlighting specific competences on which you should focus within your continuing professional development (CPD).

Although contracting, supervision and ethical conduct have been practised in the helping professions for decades, they are not yet regulated for coach practitioners. We have looked at each of the roles and functions of these three key areas, as ultimately these processes will benefit and protect coach and client. The development of professional supervision, contracting and ethical codes is emerging as a vital function within the discipline of professional coaching.

A very new competence under appraisal in the Global Coaching Community (GCC), and as a result of the ICRF, is that all practitioner coaches are potential contributors to an emerging and sustainable body of knowledge. This requires very specific skills from practitioners, including the ability to read and apply research and to generate critical enquiry into practice.

Knowledge, wisdom and experience

We see the business coaching process as one that helps business executives and leaders to develop a clear understanding of their roles and responsibilities. Business coaching, like sports coaching, is about high performance, but ultimately embodies sustained behavioural change and breakthrough performance.

Today, coaches need to understand human behaviour and human complexity. Within the business coaching context, the coach helps the client to articulate existential concerns such as freedom, purpose, choice and anxiety, and to identify and replace limiting paradigms with empowering paradigms, thus leading to positive change. Although existential philosophy regards human existence as unexplainable, it crucially stresses freedom of choice and taking responsibility for one's acts.

In a sense, you have been building your knowledge base, looking at how to transform your skill and competence into wisdom and experience as you work with individual executives and teams. Covey (1990) advocated that individuals need to change first if organizational transformation is to be sustainable. He inspired the dream that trust can be built within an organization, insisting that leadership begins with the individual. It is the same in business coaching—the work starts first with the individual coach to enable them to work with their executive clients.

Reflection and learning from experience must be applied by the coaching practitioner and professional in their own work. We attempt to model best practice, while at the same time helping the client to self-reflect and learn from experience. We hope this book will be of lasting value to you, and that you will take what you have learned here and turn it into practice. As coaches, we believe that we should always be striving for excellence.

APPENDIX: COMPETENCES IN BUSINESS COACHING

APPENDIX OUTLINE
- Competence frameworks
  - International Coach Federation (ICF)
  - Worldwide Association of Business Coaches (WABC)
  - European Mentoring and Coaching Council (EMCC)
  - Coaches and Mentors of South Africa (COMENSA)
- Specific competences required
  - Building the coaching relationship
  - Listening
  - Questioning
  - Self-awareness

Competence frameworks

This section outlines the structures of competence frameworks developed by four leading international and national professional bodies for coaches:

- International Coach Federation (ICF);
- Worldwide Association of Business Coaches (WABC);

- European Mentoring and Coaching Council (EMCC); and
- Coaches and Mentors of South Africa (COMENSA).

These bodies represent a valuable spectrum of international standards and requirements for business coaches today. There is considerable consistency among these professional bodies with respect to the skills and competences required for a coach, although coaching competences are yet to be empirically validated. Based on studies to date, these bodies recommend specific core competences to build your capacity as a coach.

International Coach Federation (ICF)

The ICF has definitions and related behaviours for each competency, distinguishing between behaviours that should always be present and visible and those that are called for only in certain coaching situations. The 11 competences are listed below in their four groupings, with the related behaviours omitted for the sake of clarity (ICF, 2008a:1–3)

A. **Setting the foundation**:
  1. Meeting ethical guidelines and professional standards.
  2. Establishing the coaching agreement.
B. **Co-creating the relationship**:
  3. Establishing trust and intimacy with the client.
  4. Coaching presence.
C. **Communicating effectively**:
  5. Active listening.
  6. Powerful questioning.
  7. Direct communication.
D. **Facilitating learning and results**:
  8. Creating awareness.
  9. Designing actions.
  10. Planning and goal setting.
  11. Managing progress and accountability.

The complete ICF competence framework can be found on the Federation's website at www.coachfederation.org.

Worldwide Association of Business Coaches (WABC)

The *WABC Business Coaching Competencies* are divided into three areas (WABC, 2008b:2):

- Self-management—knowing oneself and self-mastery;
- Core coaching skills base; and
- Business and leadership coaching capabilities.

The WABC business coaching competence framework is outlined as follows, with the illustrative examples for each competence omitted for the sake of brevity (WABC, 2008b:2–10):

A. Self-management—knowing oneself and self-mastery

1. **Knowing yourself: self-insight and understanding**:
   (a) Having ready access to your thoughts and feelings and being aware of how they affect your behaviour.
2. **Acknowledging your strengths and development needs**:
   (a) Having a realistic perception of your strengths and development needs—knowing your strengths and limitations and showing a commitment to continuous learning and self-development.
   (b) Self-belief—believing in your self-worth and capabilities.
3. **Self-mastery: managing your thoughts, feelings and behaviours in ways that promote behaviour contributing to career and organization success**:
   (a) Self-regulation: managing your reactions and emotions constructively.
   (b) Integrity: choosing ethical courses of action and being steadfast in your principles and beliefs.
   (c) Self-responsibility: assuming personal responsibility and accountability for your performance.
   (d) Adaptability: flexibility in handling change.
   (e) Emphasizing excellence: setting for yourself and confidently pursuing, challenging goals and high standards.
   (f) Initiative: taking independent action to change the direction of events.
   (g) Creativity and innovation: being receptive to new ideas and being able to generate alternative ways to view and define problems.

B. Core coaching skill-base

1. **Creating the foundations for business coaching**:
    (a) Working within established ethical guidelines and professional standards.
    (b) Agreeing on a clear and effective contract for the coaching relationship.
2. **Developing the business coaching relationship**:
    (a) Establishing trust and respect.
    (b) Establishing rapport.
3. **Promoting client understanding**:
    (a) Listening to understand.
    (b) Questioning effectively.
    (c) Communicating clearly.
    (d) Facilitating depth of understanding.
4. **Facilitating personal transformation**:
    (a) Promoting action.
    (b) Focusing on goals.
    (c) Building resiliency.
    (d) Managing termination of coaching.
5. **Professional development**:
    (a) Maintaining and improving professional skills.

C. Business and leadership coaching capabilities

1. **Alignment**:
    (a) Understanding the business and displaying a strong grounding in business knowledge and competences.
    (b) Demonstrating proficiency in systems thinking.
    (c) Aligning coaching initiatives with the business.
2. **Leadership knowledge and credibility**:
    (a) Acting as a strong and influential role model.
    (b) Possessing a thorough working knowledge of the world of the executive leader and leadership development.
    (c) Displaying highly developed communication and interpersonal competences.
3. **Coach as leader and developer of own business**:
    (a) Creating and managing business relationship networks.
    (b) Collaborating with other coaches.
    (c) Developing yourself in a business capacity.
4. **Creating and maintaining partnerships with all stakeholders in the business coaching process**.

5. **Understanding organizational behaviour and organizational development principles.**
6. **Assessment:**
   (a) Assessing the client.
   (b) Assessing the individual and organizational benefits of business coaching.
7. **Having respect for and knowledge about multicultural issues and diversity.**

The complete WABC competence framework can be found on the Association's website at www.wabccoaches.com.

European Mentoring and Coaching Council (EMCC)

The *EMCC Competence Standards* define core competences in four categories as a basis for the training of coaches and mentors, as follows (EMCC, 2008a:1–3):

1. **Who we are**—the incremental hierarchy of personal attributes for coaching and mentoring:
   (a) Beliefs and attitudes.
   (b) Self.
2. **Our skills and knowledge**—we will use during the coaching / mentoring process:
   (a) Communication skills.
   (b) Technical skills.
   (c) People development.
   (d) Business development.
3. **How we coach and mentor**—how we will demonstrate that we are able to apply what we have learned.
4. **How we manage the process**—what we will do as part of our coaching/mentoring practice to maintain and develop an effective and professional approach:
   (a) Managing the relationship.
   (b) Managing the contract.

The *EMCC Competence Standards* includes examples of how the competences should be demonstrated within each of the following six levels of practice (EMCC, 2008a:1–3):

- Foundation 3 (equivalent to the UK's National Vocational Qualification (NVQ) level 3);
- Foundation 4 (equivalent to NVQ 4);

- Intermediate (equivalent to an undergraduate degree or NVQ 5);
- Practitioner (equivalent to a postgraduate certificate);
- Advanced Practitioner (equivalent to a postgraduate diploma); and
- Master Practitioner (equivalent to a Master's degree).

The complete *EMCC Competence Standards* can be found on the Council's website at www.emccouncil.org.

Coaches and Mentors of South Africa (COMENSA)

During 2005–2006, Coaches and Mentors of South Africa (COMENSA) developed a simple framework of standards of professional competence for coaches, which defined competences in five functional areas at four levels of expertise. The five functional areas were (COMENSA, 2006a:1):

- questioning;
- listening;
- building rapport;
- delivering measurable results; and
- upholding ethical guidelines and professional standards.

The four levels of competence within each functional area ranged from Level 1 (i.e., unacceptable) to Level 4 (i.e., master/expert) (COMENSA, 2006a:1–3).

During 2007, COMENSA developed a revised competence framework, the draft *Membership Criteria and Standards of Competence (MCSC) Framework*, based on the EMCC's Competence Standards, defined in terms of the following "measurable outcomes" (COMENSA, 2007b: 21–26):

1. **Self-awareness/Who we are**—personal attributes for coaching:
   1.1 Beliefs and attitudes.
   1.2 Self-awareness.
2. **Managing the process**—what we will do as part of our coaching practice to maintain and develop an effective and professional approach:
   2.1 Managing the relationship.
   2.2 Managing the contract.
3. **Ability to coach**—skills we will use during the coaching process:
   3.1 Communication skills.
   3.2 Technical skills.
   3.3 People development skills.

4. **Facilitate learning and development**—how we will demonstrate that we are able to apply what we have learned.

The draft *MCSC Framework* includes examples of how the competences should be demonstrated within each of the following levels of practice (COMENSA, 2007b:22–26):

- Minimum competence standards for all coach practitioners.
- Registered Practitioner (in addition to minimum competence standards).
- Certified Practitioner (in addition to minimum competence standards).
- Master Practitioner (in addition to minimum competence standards).

The complete COMENSA draft *Membership Criteria and Standards of Competence Framework* can be found on the Association's website at www.comensa.org.za.

Specific competences required

This section includes excerpts from the competence frameworks developed by the ICF, WABC and the EMCC, outlining the specific competences stipulated by them for the following aspects of the coaching process:

1. **building the coaching relationship;**
2. **listening;**
3. **questioning;** and
4. **self-awareness.**

1. Building the coaching relationship

International Coach Federation (ICF)

The ICF (2008a:1–2) defines competences in **building the relationship** as follows:

Co-creating the relationship:
Establishing trust and intimacy with the client—ability to create a safe, supportive environment that produces ongoing mutual respect and trust:

a. Show genuine concern for the client's welfare and future.
b. Continuously demonstrate personal integrity, honesty and sincerity.

c. Establish clear agreements and keep promises.
d. Demonstrate respect for client's perceptions, learning style, personal being.
e. Provide ongoing support for and champion new behaviours and actions, including those involving risk-taking and fear of failure.
f. Ask permission to coach client in sensitive, new areas.

Worldwide Association of Business Coaches (WABC)

The WABC (2008b:5) defines business coaching competences in **building the relationship** as follows:

Core coaching skill-base:
Developing the business coaching relationship:
Establishing trust and respect:

- Demonstrate a genuine concern for the client's welfare and success.
- Demonstrate a strong belief in the boundless potential of others.
- Consistently work to establish trust and honest communication with the client.
- Establish clear agreements and keep promises.
- Clearly and candidly share your values, attitudes, beliefs and emotions when appropriate.
- Encourage the client to take on new and challenging tasks, while providing appropriate support.
- Create an environment of safety and security when dealing with sensitive issues.
- Create an environment of safety and security in which the client is able to share all sides of themselves (e.g., their ambitions, needs and fears).
- Be honest and truthful in difficult situations (e.g., be prepared to tell the client what they need to hear but others won't say).
- Establishing rapport:
- Have an open and responsive presence.
- Be comfortable sharing your intuitions with the client.
- Demonstrate a willingness to take risks and to enter the unknown.
- Have a very flexible approach to coaching and be able to adapt your style to what works best for the client.

- Make appropriate use of humour to make the work more fun.
- Be able to tolerate open expression of strong emotions directed at you without becoming defensive.
- Be able to manage the client's expression of strong emotions about their situation without getting caught up in their emotions.
- Be able to work with a variety of learning styles in individuals.
- Give objective feedback in a non-judgmental manner.

European Mentoring and Coaching Council (EMCC)

The *EMCC Competence Standards* define the following competences in **building the relationship** required by the respective EMCC member categories (EMCC, 2008a:3):

How we manage the process—what we will do as part of our coaching practice to maintain and develop an effective and professional approach:

Managing the relationship:
Foundation 3:

- establishes rapport;
- assists learner to clarify their goals;
- explores a range of options for achieving the goals aligned to organizational needs;
- enables learner to develop an action plan;
- supports learner in implementing the plan;
- reviews progress and achievement of the plan;
- keeps appropriate notes to ensure actions are followed;
- monitors the whole process; and
- manages the conclusion of the process.

Foundation 4:
Foundation 3 standards plus:

- demonstrates how they build and maintain the relationship;
- demonstrates a flexible approach;
- demonstrate effective session management;
- maintains commitment to goals; and
- develops trust effectively.

Intermediate:
Foundation 4 standards plus:

- works effectively with relevant policies and procedures of the organization;
- acts as an external source of motivation to support the learner in achieving their goals; and
- maintains trust and honest communication.

Practitioner:
Intermediate standards plus:

- draws on a range of techniques and methods to facilitate achievement of goals;
- adapts to organizational changes that impact on the contract agreement

Advanced Practitioner:
Practitioner standards plus:

- demonstrates an extensive understanding of adapting methodology and approaches.

Master Practitioner:
Advanced Practitioner standards plus:

- researches new understandings of interventions on coaching/mentoring relationships.

2. Listening

International Coach Federation (ICF)

The ICF (2008a) defines competences in **listening** as follows:

Communicating effectively:
Active listening—ability to focus completely on what the client is saying and is not saying, to understand the meaning of what is said in the context of the client's desires, and to support client self-expression:

- Attends to the client and the client's agenda and not to the coach's agenda for the client.

- Hears the client's concerns, goals, values and beliefs about what is and is not possible.
- Distinguishes between the words, the tone of voice, and the body language.
- Summarizes, paraphrases, reiterates, mirrors back what client has said to ensure clarity and understanding.
- Encourages, accepts, explores and reinforces the client's expression of feelings, perceptions, concerns, beliefs, suggestions, etc.,
- Integrates and builds on client's ideas and suggestions.
- "Bottom-lines" or understands the essence of the client's communication and helps the client get there rather than engaging in long descriptive stories.
- Allows the client to vent or "clear" the situation without judgment or attachment in order to move on to next steps.

Worldwide Association of Business Coaches (WABC)

The WABC (2008b) defines business coaching competences in **listening** as:

Core coaching skill-base:
Promoting client understanding:
   Listening to understand:

- Adjust easily to the client's agenda.
- Hear the client's expectations about what is and is not possible.
- Confirm understanding by observing and interpreting non-verbal signals (e.g., body language, facial expressions, tone of voice, etc.,).
- Use positive body language and non-verbal signals to demonstrate openness and undivided attention.
- Demonstrate active listening by seeking clarification, rephrasing the client's statements and summarizing to check understanding.
- Encourage the client to "say more"—create a positive climate for the client to express their feelings, perceptions, concerns, suggestions, etc.,
- Acknowledge the client's ideas and suggestions and build on them in discussions.
- Offer non-judgmental responses that encourage the client to explore and validate their feelings, concerns and aspirations.

- Use silence as an appropriate intervention to elicit more information.
- Listen to the client's emotional undercurrents.
- Pay attention to what the client isn't saying about issues discussed.

European Mentoring and Coaching Council (EMCC)

The *EMCC Competence Standards* define the following competences in **listening** required by the respective EMCC member categories (EMCC, 2008a:1–3):

Our skills and knowledge—we will use during the coaching process:

Communication skills:
Foundation 3:

- explain the value of whole-body listening.

Foundation 4:
Foundation 3 standards plus:

- explain potential blocks to effective listening.

Intermediate:
Foundation 4 standards plus:

- explain the principles of emotional intelligence and its use to improve communication.

Practitioner:
Intermediate standards plus:

- elicit deeper levels of communication through listening and questioning.

Advanced Practitioner:
Practitioner standards plus:

- formulate own tools and systems to improve effectiveness.

Master Practitioner:
Advanced Practitioner standards plus:

- show an extensive breadth of knowledge and/or experience in communicating and researching effectively within the coaching and mentoring community.

How we coach and mentor—how we will demonstrate that we are able to apply what we have learned:

Foundation 3:

• uses an active listening style.

Foundation 4:
Foundation 3 standards plus:
[N/A]
Intermediate:
Foundation 4 standards plus:

• recognizes and works with the emotional signals from the learner;
• combines listening and questioning to identify patterns of thinking and actions.

Practitioner:
Intermediate standards plus:
[N/A]
Advanced Practitioner:
Practitioner standards plus:
[N/A]
Master Practitioner:
Advanced Practitioner standards plus:

• researches development of professional standards in the coaching/ mentoring industry.

3. Questioning

International Coach Federation (ICF)

The ICF (2008a:2) defines competences in **questioning** as follows:

Communicating effectively:
Powerful questioning—Ability to ask questions that reveal the information needed for maximum benefit to the coaching relationship and the client:

• Asks questions that reflect active listening and an understanding of the client's perspective.
• Asks questions that evoke discovery, insight, commitment or action (e.g., those that challenge the client's assumptions).

- Asks open-ended questions that create greater clarity, possibility or new learning.
- Asks questions that move the client towards what they desire, not questions that ask for the client to justify or look backwards.

Worldwide Association of Business Coaches (WABC)

The WABC (2008b:5–6) defines business coaching competences in **questioning** as follows:

Core coaching skill-base:
Promoting client understanding:
Questioning effectively:

- Ask questions that reflect an understanding of the client's point of view.
- Ask challenging questions that help the client to self-discover.
- Pose open-ended questions that help the client to clarify issues.
- Ask questions that help the client to develop new perspectives and new possibilities for action and learning.
- Ask questions that evoke commitment to action.
- Ask questions that steer the client towards their desired outcomes.

European Mentoring and Coaching Council (EMCC)

The *EMCC Competence Standards* define the following competences in **questioning** required by the respective EMCC member categories (EMCC, 2008a:1–3):
Our skills and knowledge—we will use during the coaching process:
Communication skills:
Foundation 3:

- explain the principles of questioning and at least one framework;
- explain the why, what, how, when and where of feedback;
- use language appropriate to the needs of the learner.

Foundation 4:
Foundation 3 standards plus:

- explain the benefits/disadvantages of at least two questioning structures;
- demonstrate how different communication styles may affect understanding and relationships.

Intermediate:
Foundation 4 standards plus:

- explain the principles of emotional intelligence and its use to improve communication;
- explain the advantages/disadvantages of a range of questioning techniques and frameworks;
- explain particular styles of coaching and mentoring.

Practitioner:
Intermediate standards plus:

- explain how to match, pace, mirror and lead to help the learner;
- elicit deeper levels of communication through listening and questioning;
- use feedback to improve interaction with the learner.

Advanced Practitioner:
Practitioner standards plus:

- formulate owns tools and systems to improve effectiveness.

Master Practitioner:
Advanced Practitioner standards plus:

- show an extensive breadth of knowledge and/or experience in communicating and researching effectively within the coaching and mentoring community.

How we coach and mentor—how we will demonstrate that we are able to apply what we have learned:
Foundation 3:

- uses an appropriate questioning style;
- offers feedback in an appropriate style.

Foundation 4:
Foundation 3 standards plus:

- demonstrates use of 2 questioning approaches.

Intermediate:
Foundation 4 standards plus:

- recognises and works with the emotional signals from the learner;
- combines listening and questioning to identify patterns of thinking and actions.

Practitioner:
Intermediate standards plus:

- challenges in a way which demonstrably improves the learner's performance.

Advanced Practitioner:
Practitioner standards plus:
[N/A]
Master Practitioner:
Advanced Practitioner standards plus:

- researches development of professional standards in the coaching/ mentoring industry.

4. Self-awareness

International Coach Federation (ICF)

The ICF does not define specific competences for self-awareness.

Worldwide Association of Business Coaches (WABC)

The WABC (2008b:2–3) defines the following business competences for **self-awareness**:

Self-management—knowing oneself and self-mastery:
Knowing yourself: self-insight and understanding:
    Having ready access to your thoughts and feelings and being aware of how they affect your behaviour:

- Be aware of your own emotions and able to recognize what you're feeling at any given time.
- Know the reasons why you feel the way you do.
- Recognize how your feelings affect you and your work performance.

- Have a high degree of awareness of what is important to you and the contribution you want to make—your values, purpose and vision.
- Know what you want and go after it.
- Know when your self-talk is helpful.
- Know when your self-talk is unhelpful.

Self-mastery: managing your thoughts, feelings and behaviours in ways that promote behaviour contributing to career and organization success:

Self-regulation: managing your reactions and emotions constructively:

- Monitor and contain distressing emotions and regulate them so they don't keep you from doing the things you need to do.
- Maintain self-control under adverse or stressful conditions (e.g., maintain demeanour, composure and temperament).
- Manage your own behaviour to prevent or reduce feelings of stress.
- Be able to think clearly and to stay focused when under pressure.
- Accept negative feedback without becoming defensive.
- Talk yourself out of a bad mood.
- Distinguish between a client's contribution and your own contribution to your emotional reactions.

European Mentoring and Coaching Council (EMCC)

The *EMCC Competence Standards* define the following competences in **self-awareness** required by the respective EMCC member categories (EMCC, 2008a:1):

Who we are—the incremental hierarchy of personal attributes for coaching and mentoring:

Self:

Foundation 3:

- explains clearly their role in relation to the learner;
- explains clearly the implications of the coaching and mentoring relationship;
- demonstrates self-management and self-awareness.

Foundation 4:
Foundation 3 standards plus:

- receives and accepts feedback appropriately;

- uses a formal feedback process to assist their coaching and mentoring practice;
- behaves and acts in alignment with their values and beliefs and consistently does as they say.

Intermediate:
Foundation 4 standards plus:

- gains self-awareness from at least one personality type indicator or formal face to face feedback process (e.g., 360);
- operates to a clear code of ethics;
- demonstrates empathy in a broad range of settings and with a diverse range of people in both practice and reflection;
- demonstrates self-belief in their competence to coach and mentor within the limits of their own experience.

Practitioner:
Intermediate standards plus:

- demonstrates application of self-management and self-awareness consistently through practice and reflection;
- demonstrates self-belief in their ability to coach/mentor in a wide range of applications;
- develops self-awareness using at least three feedback processes, including personality indicators and self-reflection;
- demonstrates an ongoing process of review, reflection and revision of personal values, beliefs and attitudes to improve their coaching and mentoring.

Advanced Practitioner:
Practitioner standards plus:

- develops depth and breadth of expertise in self-awareness and self-management from study of and practice with a range of (at least three) psychometric tools;
- demonstrates application of psychometrics both in practice and reflection.

Master Practitioner:
Advanced Practitioner standards plus:

- demonstrates through practice and reflection the basics of brain function and human development and how this knowledge can help others to build coaching and mentoring capability.

BIBLIOGRAPHY

Abizadeh, A. (2001). Ethnicity, race, and a possible humanity. *World Order*, 33(1):22–34.

Achebe, C. (1977). An image of Africa. *The Massachusetts Review*, 18(4):782–794.

Achebe, C. (1988). *Hopes and Impediments: Selected essays 1965–1981*. New York, NY:Anchor Books.

Ahern, G. (2003). Designing and implementing coaching/mentoring competences: A case study. *Counselling Psychology Quarterly*, 16(4):373–383.

Aiken Hodge, D. (2006). *Towards Coaching Across Divides to Create Alliances—an Integral Approach*. Unpublished DProf dissertation. London: Middlesex University.

Allik, J., and McCrae, R. (2004). Toward a geography of personality traits: Patterns of profiles across 36 cultures. *Journal of Cross-Cultural Psychology*, 35:13–28.

American Manufacturing Association (AMA) (2008). *Coaching: A Global Strategy of Successful Practices*. New York, NY: AMA.

Ancona, D., and Bresman, H. (2007). *X-teams: How to Build Teams That Lead, Innovate and Succeed*. Cambridge, MA: Harvard Business School.

355

Argyris, C., and Schön, D. (1974). *Theory in Practice: Increasing Professional Effectiveness*. San Francisco, CA: Jossey-Bass.

Babcock, L., and Laschever, S. (2003). *Women Don't Ask: Negotiation and the Gender Divide*. Princeton, NJ: Princeton University Press.

Baek-Kyoo, B. (2005). Executive coaching: A conceptual framework from an integrative review of practice and research. *Human Resource Development Review*, 4:462–488.

Baez, F. (2006). Coaching across cultures. WABC *Business Coaching Worldwide eZine*, 2(4):20–23. Webpage: www.wabccoaches.com/bcw/2006_v2_i4/edge.html

Bandler, R. (1985). *Using Your Brain—For a Change: Neuro-Linguistic Programming*. Edited by C. Andreas and S. Andreas. Boulder, CO: Real People Press.

Bandler, R., and Grinder, J. (1992). *Reframing and the Transformation of Meaning*. Moab, UT: Real People Press.

Banks, M. (1996). *Ethnicity: Anthropological Constructions*. London: Routledge.

Barinaga, M. (1994). Surprises across the cultural divide. *Science*, 263(5152):1468–1469.

Bar-On, R. (1997). *The Emotional Quotient Inventory (EQ-i): A Test of Emotional Intelligence*. Toronto: Multi-Health Systems.

Beck, D.E., and Cowan, C.C. (1996). *Spiral Dynamics, Mastering Values, Leadership, and Change*. London: Blackwell.

Bell, E.L.J., and Nkomo, S.M. (2001). *Our Separate Ways: Black and White Women and the Struggle for Identity*. Cambridge, MA: Harvard Business School Press.

Bennett, J.L. (2006). An agenda for coaching-related research: A challenge for researchers. *Coaching Psychology Journal: Practice and Research*, 8(4):240–249.

Benz, K., and Maurya, S. (2007). Five keys to successful business coaching in India. WABC *Business Coaching Worldwide eZine*, 3(2):22–24. Webpage: www.wabccoaches.com/bcw/2007_v3_i2/hottopics.html

Bernthal, P.R., Bondra, J., and Wang, W. (2005). *Leadership in China: Keeping Pace With a Growing Economy*. Pittsburgh, PA: Development Dimensions International.

Bluckert, P. (2008). *Coaching Supervision: An Article by Peter Bluckert*. Leeds: PB Coaching. Webpage: www.pbcoaching.com/article-coaching-supervision.php

Boon, M. (1996). *The African Way*. Sandton: Zebra Press.

Bossuyt, M. (2002). *Prevention of Discrimination: The Concept and Practice of Affirmative Action*. Geneva: United Nations Economic and Social Council. Webpage: www.unhchr.ch/Huridocda/Huridoca.nsf/0/0aaa7775daf0bcebc1256c0c0031c5bd/$FILE/G0214014.pdf

Boud, D., Cohen, R., and Walker, D. (Eds.). (1996). *Using Experience for Learning*. Buckingham: SRHE and Open University Press.

Boud, D., and Walker, D. (1990). Making the most of experience. *Studies in Continuing Education, 12*(2):61–80.

Braaten, J. (1991). *Habermas's Critical Theory of Society*. New York, NY: State University of New York.

Bradberry, T., and Greaves, J. (2005a). *The Emotional Intelligence Quick Book*. New York, NY: Simon and Schuster.

Bradberry, T., and Greaves, J. (2005b). Heartless bosses. *Harvard Business Review, 83*(12):24.

Brennan, D. (2008). Coaching in the US: trends and challenges. *Coaching: An international journal of theory, research and practice, 1*(2):185–190.

Briggs Myers, I., and Myers, P.B. (1995). *Gifts Differing: Understanding Personality Type*. Palo Alto, CA: Davies-Black.

Buckingham, M., and Clifton, D.O. (2002). *Now, Discover Your Strengths*. London: Simon and Schuster.

Burger, A.P (Ed.). (1996). *Ubuntu: Cradles of Peace and Development*. Pretoria: Kagiso.

Caplan, S. (1970). *The Theory and Practise of Mental Health Consultation*. New York, NY: Basic Books.

Carter, E.A.K., and McGoldrick, M. (Eds.). (1990). *The Changing Family Life Cycle: A Framework for Family Therapy*. Boston, MA: Allyn and Bacon.

Carter, A., Wolfe, H., and Kerrin, M. (2005). Employers and coaching evaluation. *International Journal of Coaching in Organizations, 3*(4).

Cavanagh, M.J., and Grant, A.M. (2002). *Coaching Psychology: A Solution-focused, Cognitive-behavioural Approach*. University of Sydney: Coaching Psychology Unit. Webpage: www.psych.usyd.edu.au/coach

Caver, K.A., and Livers, A.B. (2002). Dear White Boss. *Harvard Business Review, 80*(11):76–81.

Chalkbored.com (2008). Webpage: www.chalkbored.com/lessons/ chemistry

Chen, A. (2007). The next Cultural Revolution. *Fast Company*, 116. Webpage: www.fastcompany.com/magazine/116/features-the-next-cultural-revolution.html

Clutterbuck, D. (2007). *Coaching the Team at Work*. London: Nicholas Brealey.

Coaches and Mentors of South Africa (COMENSA). (2006a). *Standards of Professional Competence*. Cape Town: COMENSA. Webpage: www.comensa.org.za/dotnetnuke/ProfessionalPractice/Competence Standards/tabid/80/language/en-ZA/Default.aspx

Coaches and Mentors of South Africa (COMENSA). (2006b). *Interim Policy on Supervision*. Cape Town: COMENSA. Webpage: www.comensa.org.za/dotnetnuke/   ProfessionalPractice/Supervision/tabid/79/language/en-ZA/Default.aspx

Coaches and Mentors of South Africa (COMENSA). (2006c). *Code of Ethics*. Cape Town: COMENSA.

Coaches and Mentors of South Africa (COMENSA). (2007a). *Revised Code of Ethics*. Cape Town: COMENSA. Webpage: www.comensa.org.za/dotnetnuke/ProfessionalPractice/CodeofEthics/tabid/78/language/en-ZA/Default.aspx

Coaches and Mentors of South Africa (COMENSA). (2007b). *Membership Criteria and Standards of Competence Framework*. Cape Town: COMENSA. Webpage: www.comensa.org.za/dotnetnuke/ProfessionalPractice/CompetenceStandards/tabid/80/language/en-ZA/Default.aspx

Connerley, M.L., and Pedersen, P.B. (2005). *Leadership in a Diverse and Multicultural Environment*. London: Sage.

Cormier, L., and Bernard, J. (1982). Ethical and legal responsibilities of clinical supervisors. *Personnel and Guidance Journal*, 60:486–491.

Coutu, D. (2004). Putting leaders on the couch: A conversation with Manfred F.R. Kets de Vries. *Harvard Business Review*, 82(1):64–71.

Covey, S.R. (1989). *Seven Habits of Highly Effective People*. London: Simon and Schuster.

Covey, S.R. (1990). *Principle-Centred Leadership*. London: Simon and Schuster.

Cox, E. (2007). *Collaborative Dialogue on the Research Agenda for Coaching*. Proceedings of a meeting of the Oxford Brookes Coaching and Mentoring Society on 14 December 2007. Mimeo.

Criticos, C. (1996). Experiential learning and social transformation for a post-apartheid learning future. In: Boud, D., Cohen, R., and Walker, D. (Eds.), *Using Experience for Learning* (pp. 157–168). Buckingham: SRHE and Open University Press.

Crocket, K. (1999). Supervision: a site of authority production. *New Zealand Journal of Counselling*, 20(1):75–83.

Cummings, T.G., and Worley, C.G. (2004). *Organization Development and Change*. Mason, OH: South-Western College Publishing.

Dagley, G. (2006). Human resources professionals' perceptions of executive coaching: Efficacy benefits and return on investment. *International Coaching Psychology Review*, 1(2):34–45.

DeLozier, J., and Grinder, J. (1987). *Turtles All the Way Down: Prerequisites to Personal Genius*. Santa Cruz, CA: Grinder, DeLozier and Associates.

Devenish, G. (2005). Understanding true meaning of Ubuntu is essential in politics. *Cape Times*, 17 May.

Dilts, R. (2003). *From Coach to Awakener*. Capitola, CA: Meta.

Ditzler, J. (1994). *Your Best Year Yet: The 10 Questions That Will Change Your Life Forever*. New York, NY: Warner.

Dolny, H. (2008). Personal communication. From Director: Coaching and Mentoring Unit, Global Leadership Centre. Johannesburg: Standard Bank of South Africa Ltd.

Downey, M. (2003). *Effective Coaching: Lessons From the Coach's Coach*. New York, NY: Texere.

Drefus, S., and Drefus, H. (1980). *A Five-Stage Model of the Mental Activities Involved in Directed Skill Acquisition*. Berkley, CA: University of California.

Dustin, M. (2007). *Gender Equality, Cultural Diversity: European Comparisons and Lessons*. London: LSE/The Nuffield Foundation. Webpage: www. lse.ac.uk/collections/genderInstitute/NuffieldReport_final.pdf

Dye, H., and Borders, L. (1990). Counselling supervisors: Standards of preparation and practice. *Journal of Counselling and Development*, 69(1):27–29.

Economist Intelligence Unit (EIU) and Korn/Ferry International (2007). *The Dream Team: Delivering Leadership in Asia*. Los Angeles: Korn/Ferry.

Eggers, J.H., and Clark, D. (2000). Executive coaching that wins. *Ivey Business Journal*, September, 65(1):66–70.

Elion, B., and Strieman M. (2001). *Clued-Up on Culture: A Practical Guide for all South Africans*. Cape Town: Juta Gariep.

Eriksen, T.H. (2001). *Small Places, Large Issues: An Introduction to Social and Cultural Anthropology*. London: Pluto Press.

European Mentoring and Coaching Council (EMCC). (2008a). *EQA—The European Quality Award*. Webpage: http://www.emccouncil.org/index.php?id = 80

European Mentoring and Coaching Council (EMCC). (2008b). *Code of Ethics*. Webpage: www.emccouncil.org/fileadmin/documents/EMCC_Code_of_Ethics.pdf

Faull, J. (2008). We can harness outrage over violence to rejuvenate democracy, bring change. *Cape Times*, 5 June.

Feldman, D.C., and Lankau, M.J. (2005). Executive coaching: A review and agenda for future research. *Journal of Management*, 31(6):829–848.

Fillery-Travis, A. (2007). *Where's the Evidence? First Steps into the Literature*. Mimeo.

Fillery-Travis, A. (2008a). Where's the evidence? First steps into the literature. Based on the evidence, WABC *Business Coaching Worldwide eZine*, 4(1):26–28. Webpage: www.wabccoaches.com/bcw/2008_v4_i1/based-on-the-evidence.html

Fillery-Travis, A. (2008b). *Current State of Knowledge Production in the UK*. Mimeo.

Fillery-Travis, A. (2009). Collaboration and research—all for one and one for all. WABC *Worldwide Business Coaching eZine*, 5(1). Webpage: www.wabccoaches.com/bcw/2009_v5_i1/based-on-the-evidence.html

Fillery-Travis, A., and Lane, D. (2006). Does coaching work, or are we asking the wrong question? *International Coaching Psychology Review*, 1(1):23–36.

Fillery-Travis, A., and Lane, D. (2008). How to develop your research interests. In: Palmer, S., and Bor, R. (Eds.), *The Practitioner's Handbook: A Guide for Counsellors, Psychotherapists and Counselling Psychologists* (pp. 176–192). London: Sage.

Flaherty, J. (1999). *Coaching: Evoking Excellence in Others*. Boston, MA: Butterworth-Heinemann.

Flaherty, J. (2005). *Coaching: Evoking Excellence in Others*. Oxford: Elsevier Butterworth-Heinemann.

Flaherty, J. (2008). *Detail of: Habermas' Domains of Competency*. Webpage: coaching.gc.ca/documents/coaching_essential_competences_for_leaders_e.asp

Foo, S.L. (2004). Asian perspectives in coaching. *Tomorrow's Life Coach*, 3(5):7–8.

Foy, N. (1994). *Empowering People at Work*. Aldershot, Hampshire: Gower.

Frankl, V. E. (1946). *Man's Search for Meaning*. London: Hodder and Stoughton.

Freire, P. (1973). *Education for Critical Consciousness*. New York, NY: Continuum.

Freud, S. (1960/1980). *The Psychopathology of Everyday Life*. Harmondsworth: Penguin.

Freud, S. (1974). *Introductory Lectures on Psychoanalysis*. Harmondsworth: Penguin.

Gallwey, W.T. (1974). *The Inner Game of Tennis: The Classic Guide to the Mental Side of Peak Performance*. New York, NY: Random House.

Gallwey, W.T. (2000). *The Inner Game of Work: Focus, Learning, Pleasure and Mobility in the Workplace*. New York. NY: Random House.

Gardiner, D. (1989). *The Autonomy of Supervision*. Milton Keynes: SRHE/Open University Press.

Gardner, H. (1983). *Frames of Mind*. New York, NY: Basic Books.

Gardner, H. (2006). *Multiple Intelligences*. Cambridge, MA: Perseus.

Garratt, B. (2001). *The Learning Organization: Developing Democracy at Work*. New York, NY: HarperCollins.

Garvey, R., Megginson, D., and Stokes, P. (2008). *Coaching and Mentoring: Theory and Practice*. London: Sage.

GCC Steering Committee. (2007). *Global Convention on Coaching: Visioning the Future Together*. Media release. Global Convention on Coaching.

Gladwell, M. (2000). *The Tipping Point: How Little Things Can Make a Big Difference*. Boston, MA: Little Brown.

Gladwell, M. (2008). *Outliers: The Story of Success*. London: Allen Lane.

Global Convention on Coaching (GCC). (2008a). *Current Reality*. Unpublished draft paper of the Working Group on Mapping the Field. Mimeo.

Global Convention on Coaching (GCC). (2008b). *Final Paper of the Working Group on Ethics*. Global Convention on Coaching. Dublin, July. Webpage: www.coachingconvention.org

Global Convention on Coaching (GCC). (2008c). *White Paper of the Working Group on a Research Agenda for Development of the Field*. Global Convention on Coaching. Dublin, July. Webpage: www.coachingconvention.org

Global Convention on Coaching (GCC). (2008d). *Final Paper of the Working Group on a Research Agenda for Development of the Field*. Global Convention on Coaching. Dublin, July. Webpage: www.coachingconvention.org

Global Convention on Coaching (GCC). (2008e). *Final Paper of the Working Group on a Knowledge Base for Coaching*. Global Convention on Coaching. Dublin, July. Webpage: www.coachingconvention.org

Global Convention on Coaching (GCC). (2008f). *White Paper of the Working Group on Core Competencies*. Global Convention on Coaching. Dublin, July. Webpage: www.coachingconvention.org

Global Convention on Coaching (GCC). (2008 g). *Dublin Declaration on Coaching Including Appendices.* Global Convention on Coaching. Dublin, August. Webpage: www.coachingconvention.org

Goldfried, M.R., and Wolfe, B.E. (1966). Psychotherapy practice and research: Repairing a strained alliance. *American Psychologist,* 51:1007–16.

Goldsmith, M., Lyons, L., and Freas, A. (Eds.). (2000). *Coaching for Leadership: How the World's Greatest Coaches Help Leaders Learn.* San Francisco, CA: Jossey-Bass/Pfeiffer.

Goleman, D. (1996). *Emotional Intelligence.* London: Bloomsbury.

Goleman, D. (1998). *Working with Emotional Intelligence.* New York, NY: Bantam Books.

Goleman, D. (2002). *The New Leaders: Transforming the Art of Leadership into the Science of Results.* London: Little, Brown.

Goleman, D., Boyatzis, R., and McKee, A. (2002). *The New Leaders.* London: Little, Brown.

Gorle, H.R. (2002). *Grief Theories: Elizabeth Kubler-Ross.* Webpage: www.bereavement.org/e_kubler-ross.htm

Grant, A.M. (2000). Coaching psychology comes of age. *PsychNews,* 4(4):12–14.

Grant, A.M. (2003a). The impact of life coaching on goal attainment, metacognition and mental health. *Social Behavior and Personality,* 31(3):253–264.

Grant, A.M. (2003b). *Keeping up with the Cheese! Research as a Foundation for Professional Coaching of the Future.* Keynote presentation to the International Coach Federation Conference Symposium on Research and Coaching, Denver, CO, November.

Grant, A.M. (2008). Coaching in Australia: A view from the ivory tower. *Coaching: An International Journal of Theory, Research and Practice,* 1(1):93–98.

Grant, A.M., and Cavanagh, M.J. (2006). *Toward a Profession of Coaching: Sixty-Five Years of Progress and Challenges for the Future.* Sydney: Coaching Psychology Unit, School of Psychology, University of Sydney.

Grant, A.M., and Cavanagh, M.J. (2007a). Evidence-based coaching: flourishing or languishing? *Australian Psychologist,* 42(4):239–254.

Grant, A.M., and Cavanagh, M.J. (2007b). The goal-focused coaching skills questionnaire: preliminary findings. *Social Behavior and Personality,* 35(6):751–760.

Grayson, D., and Larson, K. (2000). How to make the most of the coaching relationship. In: Goldsmith, M., Lyons, L., and Freas, A. (Eds.), *Coaching for Leadership: How the World's Greatest Coaches Help Leaders Learn* (pp. 121–130). San Francisco, CA: Jossey-Bass/Pfeiffer.

Griffiths, K.E and Campbell, M.A. (2008). Regulating the regulators: paving the way for international, evidence-based coaching standards. *International Journal of Evidence-Based Coaching and Mentoring,* 6(1):19–31.

Grouzet, F.M.E., Kasser, T., Ahuvia, A., Fernandez-Dols, J.M., Kim, Y., Lau, S., Ryan, R.M., Saunders, S., Schmuck, P., and Sheldon, K. (2005). The structure of goal contents across 15 cultures. *Journal of Personality and Social Psychology,* 89:800–816.

Hakim, C. (2000). *Work-Lifestyle Choices in the 21st Century.* New York, NY: Oxford University Press.

Hall, L.M., and Duval, M. (2003). *Coaching Conversations for Translational Change.* Clifton, CO: Neuro-Semantics Publications.

Hamlyn, J. (2005). *Theoretical Overview of Coaching.* Sandton: The People Business.

Hampden-Turner, C., and Trompenaars, F. (2000). *Building Cross-Cultural Competence: How to Create Wealth from Conflicting Values.* New Haven, CT: Yale University Press.

Hargrove, R. (2003). *Masterful Coaching: Inspire an "Impossible Future" While Producing Extraordinary Leaders and Extraordinary Results.* San Francisco, CA: Jossey-Bass/Pfeiffer.

HarperCollins. (2005). *Collins Dictionary and Thesaurus.* New York, NY: HarperCollins.

Harri-Augstein, S., and Thomas, L.F. (1991). *Learning Conversations, Self-Organised Learning: The Way to Personal and Organizational Growth.* London: Routledge.

Harvey, V., and Struzziero, J. (2000). *Effective Supervision in School Psychology.* Bethesda, MD: National Association of School Psychologists.

Hawkins, P., and Shohet, R. (1991). Approaches to the supervision of counsellors. In: Dryden, W., and Thorne, B. (Eds.), *Training and Supervision for Counselling in Action* (pp. 99–115). London: Sage.

Hawkins, P., and Shohet, R. (2000). *Supervision in the Helping Professions.* Buckingham: Open University Press.

Hay, J. (2007). *Reflective Practice and Supervision for Coaches.* New York, NY: Open University Press.

Haynes, R., Cory, C., and Moulton, P. (2003). *Professional Supervision in the Helping Professions: A Practical Guide*. Pacific Grove, CA: Brookes-Cole.

Heath, A., and Tharp, L. (1991). *What Therapists Say About Supervision*. Paper presented at the American Association of Marriage and Family Therapy Annual Conference, Dallas, Texas, November.

Hedricks, C.A., and Weinstein, H.P. (2001). *The Personality Profile of a Corporate Leader*. Republished conference paper of the American Psychological Association, Princeton, NJ: CALIPER.

Herrmann, N. (1996). *The Whole Brain Business Book*. New York, NY: McGraw-Hill.

Herskovits, M.J. (1955). *Cultural Anthropology*. New York, NY: Knopf.

Hofstede, G. (1997). *Cultures and Organizations: Software of the Mind*. New York, NY: McGraw-Hill.

Hofstede, G. (1999). Problems remain, but theories will change: the universal and the specific in 21st-century global management. *Organizational Dynamics*, 28(1):34–44.

Hofstede, G. (2001). *Culture's Consequences: Comparing Values, Behaviors, Institutions, and Organizations Across Nations*. Thousand Oaks, CA: Sage.

Hofstede, G. (2005). Foreword. In: M.L. Connerley and P.B. Pedersen, *Leadership in a Diverse and Multicultural Environment* (pp. ix–x). Thousand Oaks, CA: Sage.

Honey, P., and Mumford, A. (1986). *Using Your Learning Styles*. Maidenhead: Peter Honey.

Honey, P., and Mumford, A. (1992). *The Manual of Learning Styles*. Maidenhead: Peter Honey.

Houston, J. (1982). *The Possible Human*. Los Angeles, CA: Jeremy Tarcher.

Hu-Chan, M. (2007). Hybrid world: Coaching and the complexities of age, values and Asian business. WABC *Business Coaching Worldwide eZine*, 3(3):6–9. Webpage: www.wabccoaches.com/bcw/2007_v3_i3/feature.html

Hudson, F.M. (1998). *The Handbook of Coaching: A Resource Guide to Effective Coaching with Individuals and Organizations*. Santa Barbara, CA: Hudson Institute.

Hudson, F.M. (1999). *The Handbook of Coaching: A Comprehensive Resource Guide for Managers, Executives, Consultants, and Human Resource Professionals*. San Francisco, CA: Jossey-Bass.

Hudson, L. (1991). *Frames of Mind*. London: Penguin.

Husserl, E. (1962/1913). *Ideas: a General Introduction to Pure Phenomenology*. Volume 1. New York, NY: Collier Books.

Ibarra, H. (2003). *Working Identity: Unconventional Strategies for Reinventing Your Career*. Cambridge, MA: Harvard Business School Press.

Indian School of Business (ISB) (2007). Pioneering executive coaching in India. *ISB insight*, September. Webpage: www.isb.edu/isbinsight/ Insight_Sep07/Pioneering%20Executive.html

Insights (2008). *Insights Model*. Webpage: www.insights.co.uk

International Coach Federation (ICF). (2008a). *Core Competencies*. Lexington, KY: ICF. Webpage: www.coachfederation.org/research% 2Deducation/icf%2Dcredentials/core%2Dcompetencies/

International Coach Federation (ICF). (2008b). *ICF Code of Ethics*. Lexington, KY: ICF. Webpage: www.coachfederation.org/about%2Dicf/ ethics%2D%26%2Dregulation/icf%2Dcode%2Dof%2Dethics/

Jackson, B.G. (1999). The goose that laid the golden egg? A rhetorical critique of Stephen Covey and the effectiveness movement. *Journal of Management Studies, 36*(3):353–377.

Jackson, P., and Delehanty, H. (1995). *Sacred Hoops*. New York, NY: Hyperion.

Jacobi, J. (1942/1973). *The Psychology of C.G. Jung*. New Haven, CT: Yale University Press.

Jacobs, M. (Ed.). (1996). *In Search of Supervision*. Buckingham: Open University Press.

Janse van Rensburg, M. (2001a). *Executive Coaching and the Principles of African Humanism and Ubuntu*. Gordon Institute of Business Science, Pretoria: University of Pretoria.

Janse van Rensburg, M. (2001b). *Executive Coaching: A Natural Extension of the Principles of Ubuntu and African Humanism*. Research report for Master of Business Administration, Gordon Institute of Business Science. Johannesburg: University of Pretoria.

Jaques, E., and Clement, S.D. (1991). *Effective Leadership: A Practical Guide to Managing Complexity*. Oxford: Blackwell.

Jarvis, J. (2004). *Coaching and Buying Coaching Services: A Guide*. London: CIPD.

Javidan, M., and House, R.J. (2001). Cultural acumen for the global manager: lessons from Project GLOBE. *Organizational Dynamics, 29*(4):289–305.

Johnson, W.B., and Ridley, C.R. (2004). *The Elements of Mentoring*. New York, NY: Palgrave Macmillan.

Johwa, W. (2008). Stiff penalty for resisting job equity proposed. *Business Day*, 20 October.

Jones, R., and Jenkins, F. (Eds.). (2006). *Developing the Allied Health Professions*. Oxford: Radcliffe.

Jones, T. (2005). Chapter 7—Making local culture national: cultural management, state publications and local cultures. In: *Indonesian Cultural Policy, 1950–2003: Culture, Institutions, Government* (pp. 272–304). Unpublished PhD thesis. Perth, Western Australia: Curtin University of Technology. Webpage: adt.curtin.edu.au/theses/available/adt-WCU20061128.113236/unrestricted/09Chapter7.pdf, February 2009.

Jung, C. (1977). Psychological types. In: *Collected Works of C.G. Jung*. Volume 6. Bollingen Series XX. Princeton, NJ: Princeton University Press.

Kadushin, A. (1976). *Supervision in Social Work*. New York, NY, Columbia University Press.

Kaessmann, H., and Pääbo, S. (2002). The genetical history of humans and the great apes. *Journal of Internal Medicine, 251*(1)1–18.

Kanter, R.M., Stein, B.A., and Jick, T.D. (1992). *The Challenge of Organizational Change*. New York, NY: Free Press/Macmillan.

Kauffman, C.M., Russell, S.G., and Bush, M.W. (Eds.) (2008). *100 Coaching Research Proposal Abstracts*. International Coaching Research Forum. Cambridge, MA: The Coaching and Positive Psychology Initiative, McLean Hospital, Harvard Medical School and The Foundation of Coaching. Webpage: www.coachingresearchforum.org

Kets de Vries, M.F.R. (2006). *The Leader on the Couch*. London: Wiley.

Kilburg. R. (2002). *Executive Coaching: Developing Managerial Wisdom in a World of Chaos*. Washington, DC: American Psychological Association.

Kline, N. (1999/2004). *Time to Think: Listening with the Human Mind*. London: Ward Lock.

Kline, N. (2004). Keynote address. In: *Coaching in a Thinking Environment*. Wallingford: Time to Think.

Kline, N. (2005). *The Thinking Partnership programme: Consultant's guide*. Wallingford: Time to Think.

Kline, P., and Saunders, B. (1993). *Ten Steps to a Learning Organization*. Arlington, VA: Great Ocean.

Kluckholm, F., and Stroedbeck, F. (1961). *Variations in Value Orientations*. New York, NY: Harper and Row.

Knight, S. (1995). *NLP at Work*. London: Nicholas Brealey.

Kolb, D.A. (1984). *Experiential Learning: Experience as the Source of Learning and Development.* Upper Saddle River, NJ: Prentice Hall.

Kolb, D.A, Rubin, I.M., and McIntyre, J.M. (2001). *Organizational Psychology: An Experiential Approach to Organizational Behavior.* Upper Saddle River, NJ: Prentice-Hall.

Kottner, T. (2008). *A Short Brief on Coaching Evolution and Situation in Argentina.* Mimeo.

Kroeger, O., and Thuesen, J.M. (1988). *Type Talk: The 16 Personality Types That Determine How We Live, Love and work.* New York, NY: Dell.

Kroeger, O., Thuesen, J.M., and Rutledge, H. (2002). *Type Talk at Work: How the 16 Personality Types Determine Your Success on the Job.* New York, NY: Dell.

Krstić, I. (2003). Affirmative action in the United States and the European Union: Comparison and analysis. *Facta Universitatis, Series: Law and Politics,* 1(7):825–843. Webpage: facta.junis.ni.ac.rs/lap/lap2003/lap2003–06.pdf

Kuhn, T. (1962). *The Structure of Scientific Revolutions.* Chicago, IL: University of Chicago Press.

Landsberg, M. (1997). *The Tao of Coaching.* London: HarperCollins.

Landy, F.J. (2005). Some historical and scientific issues related to research on emotional intelligence. *Journal of Organizational Behavior,* 26:411–424.

Lane, D.A., and Corrie, S. (2006). *The Modern Scientist-Practitioner: A Guide to Practice in Psychology.* Hove: Routledge.

Langer, E. (1989). *Mindfulness.* Reading, MA: Addison-Wesley.

Langer, E. (1997). *The Power of Mindful Learning.* Reading, MA: Addison-Wesley.

Laske, O.E. (2004). Can evidence-based coaching increase ROI? *International Journal of Evidence-Based Coaching and Mentoring,* 2(2):41–53.

Lawton-Smith, C., and Cox, E. (2007). Coaching: is it just a new name for training? *International Journal of Evidence-Based Coaching and Mentoring,* Special Issue.

Legrain, E., and Fox, (2008). *Leadership Coaching: Inspiration from Asia.* Singapore: Banksia Coaching International. Webpage: www.banksia-coaching.com

Leong, F.T.L. (1994). Emergence of the cultural dimension: the roles and impact of culture on counseling supervision. *Counselor Education and Supervision,* 34(2):114–116.

Lévi-Strauss, C. (1958). *Race and History.* Paris: UNESCO.

Lidbetter, K. (2003). For good measure. *People Management,* 9(1):46.

Linley, P.A. (2006). Coaching research: Who? What? Where? When? Why? *International Journal of Evidence-Based Coaching and Mentoring*, 4(2).

Linnecar, R. (2008). The coaching frontier for business coaching. WABC *Business Coaching Worldwide eZine*, 4(2). Webpage: www. wabccoaches.com/bcw/2008_v4_i2/get-the-edge.html

Locke, E.A. (2005). Why emotional intelligence is an invalid concept. *Journal of Organizational Behavior*, 26:425–431.

Mackie, D. (2007). Evaluating the effectiveness of executive coaching: where are we now and where do we need to be? *Australian Psychologist*, 42(4):310–318.

Mahoney, M. (1991). *Human Change Processes*. New York, NY: Basic Books.

Mamdani, M. (2004). *Good Muslim, Bad Muslim*. Johannesburg: Jacana Media.

Manhire, B. (2000). Ode on a Grecian urn. Interview on *Kim Hill Show*. Wellington: Radio New Zealand, 5 May.

Manthei, R. (1997). *Counselling: The Skills of Finding Solutions to Problems*. Auckland: Longman.

Marx, K., and Engels, F. (1848). *Manifesto of the Communist Party*. Marx/Engels Internet Archive (marxists.org). Webpage: www.marxists.org/archive/marx/works/1848/communist-manifesto/index.htm, January 2009.

Maslow, A. (1968). *Toward a Psychology of Being*. New York, NY: Van Nostrand.

May, R. (1983). *The Discovery of Being*. New York, NY: Norton.

Mayer, J.D., and Salovey, P. (1997). What is emotional intelligence? In: Salovey, P., and Sluyter, D. (Eds.), *Emotional Development and Emotional Intelligence: Educational Applications*. New York, NY: Basic Books.

McDaniels, C. (1976). *Leisure and Career Development at Mid-Life*. Blacksburg, VA: Virginia Polytechnic Institute and State University.

McDermott, I., and Jago, W. (2001). *The NLP Coach: A Comprehensive Guide to Personal Well-Being and Professional Success*. London: Piatkus.

McLoughlin, M. (Ed.). (2006). *Sharing the Passion: Conversations with Coaches*. Cape Town: Advanced Human Technologies.

McLoughlin, M., and Stout Rostron, S. (2002). *NLP Coach Training Skills*. Unpublished programme.

McNab, P. (2005). *Towards an Integral Vision: Using NLP and Ken Wilber's AQAL Model to Enhance Communication*. Crewe: Trafford.

McWhinney, W., Webber, J.B., Smith, D.M., and Novokowsky, B.J. (1993). *Creating Paths of Change: Managing Issues and Resolving Problems in Organizations*. Venice, CA: Enthusion.

Mead, D. (1990). *Effective Supervision: A Task-Oriented Model for the Developing Professions*. New York, NY: Bruner/Mazel.

Megginson, D., and Clutterbuck, D. (2005). *Techniques for Coaching and Mentoring*. Oxford: Elsevier Butterworth-Heinemann.

Mike the Mentor. (2008a). *Classic Models: The 7-Eyed Supervision Model*. Webpage: www.mikethementor.co.uk

Mike the Mentor. (2008b). *Classic Models: The CLEAR Model*. Webpage: www.mikethementor.co.uk

MNet. (2008). Where do we come from? *Carte Blanche* Science and Technology feature broadcast September 2004. Webpage: www.mnet.co.za/Mnet/Shows/carteblanche

Morris, B., and Tarpley, N.A. (2000). So you're a player. Do you need a coach? *Fortune, 141*(4):144.

Mullen, J.D. (2006). Nature, nurture and individual change. *Behavior and Philosophy, 34*:1–17.

Ngũgĩ wa Thiong'o (1986). *Decolonizing the Mind*. Oxford: James Currey/Nairobi: EAEP.

Noer, D. (2000). The big three derailment factors in a coaching relationship. In: Goldsmith, M., Lyons, L., and Freas, A. (Eds.), *Coaching for Leadership: How the World's Greatest Coaches Help Leaders Learn* (pp. 317–324). San Francisco, CA: Jossey-Bass/Pfeiffer.

Nowack, K.M., and Wimer, S. (1997). Coaching for human performance. *Training and Development, 51*(10)28–32.

O'Connor, J., and Lages, A. (2004). *Coaching with NLP*. London: HarperCollins.

O'Connor, J., and Seymour, J. (1990). *Introducing NLP*. London: Aquarian/Thorsons.

O'Neill, M.B. (2000). *Coaching with Backbone and Heart: A Systems Approach to Engaging Leaders with Their Challenges*. San Francisco, CA: Jossey-Bass.

Olesen, M. (1996). Coaching today's executives. *Training and Development*, March, *50*(3):22.

Olson, K.R. (2007). Why do geographic differences exist in the worldwide distribution of extraversion and openness to experience? The history of human migration as an explanation. *Individual Differences Research, 5*(4):275–288.

Pampallis Paisley, P. (2006). *Towards a Theory of Supervision for Executive Coaching: An Integral Vision*. Unpublished DProf dissertation. London: Middlesex University.

Parsloe, E., and Wray, M. (2000). *Coaching and Mentoring: Practical Methods to Improve Learning*. London: Kogan Page.

Payne, W.L. (1983/1986). A study of emotion: developing emotional intelligence, self integration, relating to fear, pain and desire. *Dissertation Abstracts International*, 47:203A.

Pearson, K. (1996). Debate: this time 'supervision': who needs it? *NZAC Newsletter*, 16(4):14–15.

Peltier, B. (2001). *The Psychology of Executive Coaching: Theory and Application*. New York, NY: Brunner-Routledge.

Peters, T., and Austin, N. (1985). *A Passion for Excellence: The Leadership Difference*. New York, NY: Warner.

Peterson, D.B. (2007). Executive coaching in a cross-cultural context. *Consulting Psychology Journal: Practice and Research*, 59(4):261–271.

Peterson, D., and Little, B. (2008). Growth market. *Coaching at Work*, 3(1):44–47.

Pink, T. (2004). *Free Will: A Very Short Introduction*. Oxford: Oxford University Press.

Pinker, S. (2008). *The Sexual Paradox: Men, Women and the Real Gender Gap*. New York, NY: Scribner.

Pityana, B. (2001). Foreword. In: Elion, B., and Strieman, M., *Clued-Up on Culture: A Practical Guide for all South Africans*. Cape Town: Juta Gariep.

PricewaterhouseCoopers. (2007). *International Coach Federation Global Coaching Study*. Lexington, KY: International Coach Federation.

Proctor, B. (1994). Supervision: Competence, confidence, accountability. *British Journal of Guidance and Supervision*, 22(3):309–318.

Ramphele, M. (2008). *Laying Ghosts to Rest: Dilemmas of the Transformation in South Africa*. Cape Town: Tafelberg.

Revans, R.W. (1983). *The ABC of Action Learning*. Bromley: Chartwell Bratt.

Riso, D.R., and Hudson, R. (1999). *The Wisdom of the Enneagram*. New York, NY: Bantam.

Robbins, S.P. (2001). *Organizational Behavior*. Englewood Cliffs, NJ: Prentice-Hall.

Rogers, C.R. (1961/2004). *On Becoming a Person: A Therapist's View of Psychotherapy*. London: Constable and Robinson.

Rosinski, P. (2003). *Coaching Across Cultures: New Tools for Leveraging National, Corporate and Professional Differences*. London: Nicholas Brealey.

Russel, J. (1978). Sartre, therapy, and expanding the concept of responsibility. *American Journal of Psychoanalysis*, 38:259–69.

Saïd, E.W. (1991). *Orientalism. Western conceptions of the Orient.* London: Penguin.

Saïd, E.W. (1994). *Culture and Imperialism.* London: Vintage Books.

Salkovskis, P.M. (2002). Empirically grounded clinical interventions: cognitive-behavioural therapy progresses through a multi-dimensional approach to clinical science. *Behavioural and Cognitive Psychotherapy, 30*(11):3–9.

Salovey, P., and Mayer, J.D. (1990). Emotional intelligence. *Imagination, Cognition and Personality, 9*(3):185–211.

Scharmer, O. (2003). Mapping the Integral U: A conversation between Ken Wilber and Otto Scharmer, Denver, CO, 17 September. *Dialog on Leadership.* Webpage: www.dialogonleadership.org/interviews/Wilber.shtml

Scharmer, C.O. (2007). *Addressing the Blind Spot of Our Time: An Executive Summary of the New Book by Otto Scharmer: Theory U: Leading from the Future as it Emerges.* Theoryu.com. Webpage: www.theoryu.com/execsummary.html

Schneier, C.J. (1998). *Establishing Dimensions of South African Ethnicity.* Unpublished Masters dissertation. Johannesburg: University of the Witwatersrand.

Scott, A. (2007). In confidence. *People Management,* 22 February, 02:17. Webpage: www.peoplemanagement.co.uk/pm/articles/2007/02/inconfidence.htm

Scott, J.W. (1994). Deconstructing equality-versus-difference: Or, the uses of poststructuralist theory for feminism. In: Seidman, S. (Ed.), *The Postmodern Turn: New Perspectives on Social Theory* (pp. 282–298). Cambridge: Cambridge University Press.

Senge, P. (1990). *The Fifth Discipline: The Art and Practice of the Learning Organization.* New York, NY: Doubleday.

Senge, P., Scharmer, C.O., Jaworski, J., and Flowers, B.S. (2005). *Presence: Exploring Profound Change in People, Organizations and Society.* London: Nicholas Brealey.

Senghor, L. (1965). *On African Socialism.* New York, NY: Stanford.

Shaw, P., and Linnecar, R. (2007). *Business Coaching: Achieving Practical Results Through Effective Engagement.* London: Capstone.

Shrikanth, Gopal (2009). Coaching in the land of gurus and soothsayers. WABC *Business Coaching Worldwide eZine, 5*(1). Webpage: www.wabccoaches.com/bcw/2009_v5_i1/hot-topics.html

Spence, G.B. (2007a). GAS-powered coaching: Goal attainment scaling and its use in coaching research and practice. *International Coaching Psychology Review, 2*(2):155–167.

Spence, G.B. (2007b). Further development of evidence-based coaching: Lessons from the rise and fall of the human potential movement. *Australian Psychologist, 42*(4):255–265.

Spence, G.B., and Grant, A.M. (2007). Professional and peer life coaching and the enhancement of goal striving and well-being: An exploratory study. *The Journal of Positive Psychology, 2*(3):185–194.

Spinelli, E. (1989). *The Interpreted World: An Introduction to Phenomenological Psychology.* London: Sage.

Spinelli, E. (2005). *Existential Phenomenology.* Notes compiled by H. Dolny from lecture to i-Coach Academy, Cape Town, 8 February.

Steere, J. (1984). *Ethics in Clinical Psychology.* Cape Town: Oxford University Press.

Stern, L. (2008). *Executive Coaching: Building and Managing Your Professional Practice.* Hoboken, NJ: Wiley.

Sternberg, R.J. (1985). Implicit theories of intelligence, creativity, and wisdom. *Journal of Personality and Social Psychology, 49*(3):607–627.

Sternberg, R.J. (1997). *Thinking Styles.* Cambridge: Cambridge University Press.

Stevens, A. (1994). *Jung: A Very Short Introduction.* Oxford: Oxford University Press.

Storr, A. (1989). *Freud: A Very Short Introduction.* Oxford: Oxford University Press.

Stout Rostron, S. (2002). *Accelerating Performance: Powerful New Techniques to Develop People.* London: Kogan Page.

Stout Rostron, S. (2006a). The history of coaching. In: McLoughlin, M. (Ed.), *Sharing the Passion: Conversations with Coaches* (pp. 16–41). Cape Town: Advanced Human Technologies.

Stout Rostron, S. (2006b). Business coaching in South Africa. WABC *Business Coaching Worldwide eZine, 2*(2):7–10. Webpage: www.wabc-coaches.com/bcw/2006_v2_i2/ feature.html

Stout Rostron, S. (2006c). *Interventions in the Coaching Conversation: Thinking, Feeling and Behaviour.* Published DProf dissertation. London: Middlesex University.

Stout Rostron, S. (2008). Can coaching produce sustainable behavior change? WABC *Business Coaching Worldwide eZine, 4*(1):23–25.

Webpage: www.wabccoaches.com/bcw/2008_v4_i1/coaching-models-for-business-success.html

Sturrock, J. (2003). *Structuralism*. Oxford: Blackwell.

Sue-Chan, C., and Latham, G.P. (2004). The relative effectiveness of external, peer and self-coaches. *Applied Psychology: An International Review, 53*(2):260–278.

Swartz, L. (1998). *Culture and Mental Health: A Southern African View*. Oxford: Oxford University Press.

Tannen, D. (1995). The power of talk: Who gets heard and why. *Harvard Business Review*, September–October.

Thach, E.C. (2002). The impact of executive coaching and 360 feedback on leadership effectiveness. *Leadership and Organization Development Journal, 23*(4):205–214.

Thomas, A., and Bendixen, M. (2000). The management implication of ethnicity in South Africa. *Journal of International Business Studies. 31*(3):507–519.

Thorndike, R.K. (1920). Intelligence and its uses. *Harper's Magazine, 140*:227–335.

Ting, S., and Scisco, P. (2006). *The CCL Handbook of Coaching: A Guide for the Leader Coach*. San Francisco, CA: Jossey-Bass.

Todd, T.C., and Storm, C.L. (1997). *The Complete Systemic Supervisor*. Boston, MA: Allyn and Bacon.

Triandis, H.C. (1975). Cultural training, cognitive complexity and interpersonal attitudes. In: Brislin, R., Bochner, S., and Lonner, W. (Eds.), *Cross-Cultural Perspectives on Learning* (pp. 39–78). New York, NY: Wiley.

Underhill, B.O., McAnally, K., and Koriath, J. (2007). *Executive Coaching for Results*. San Francisco, CA: Berrett-Koehler.

UNESCO (1950). *The Race Question*. Paris: UNESCO. Webpage: unesdoc. unesco.org/images/0012/001282/128291eo.pdf

Useem, J. (2005). Jim Collins on tough calls. *Fortune, 151*(13):89–94.

Usher, C., and Borders, L. (1993). Practicing counselors' preferences for supervisory style and supervisory emphasis. *Counselor Education and Supervision, 33*(2):66–79.

Watson, O. (Ed.) (1968). *Longman Modern English Dictionary*. Harlow, Essex: Longman.

Watzlawick, P. (1978). *The Language of Change*. New York, NY: Basic Books.

Webster's (Eds.). (1983). *Webster's New Twentieth Century Dictionary*. New York, NY: Simon and Schuster.

Webster's (Eds.). (1989). *Webster's Encyclopedic Unabridged Dictionary of the English Language.* New York, NY: Random House.

Weiss, P. (2004). *The Three Levels of Coaching.* San Francisco, CA: An Appropriate Response. Webpage: www.newventureswest.com/three_levels.pdf

Weiten, W. (2000). *Psychology Themes and Variations: Brief Version.* Pacific Grove, CA: Wadsworth-Brooks/Cole.

West, L., and Milan, M. (2001). *The Reflecting Glass: Professional Coaching for Leadership Development.* New York, NY: Palgrave.

Wetzler, M. (2000). *Mountain Mist.* Audio CD produced for the Bristol Cancer Help Centre, UK. Durbanville: Creative Processes.

Whitmore, J. (2002). *Coaching for Performance: Growing People, Performance and Purpose.* London: Nicholas Brealey.

Whitmore, J. (2007a). *Corporate Coaching and Much More.* Mimeo.

Whitmore, J. (2007b). *Where Are We Coming From? Where Are We Going?* Mimeo.

Whitworth, L., Kimsey-House, H., and Sandahl, P. (1998). *Co-active Coaching: New Skills for Coaching People Toward Success in Work and Life.* Palo Alto, CA: Davies-Black.

Wilber, K. (1996). *A Brief History of Everything.* Dublin: Colourbooks.

Wilber, K. (1997). An integral theory of consciousness. *Journal of Consciousness Studies*, 4(1):71–92.

Wilber, K. (2000a). *A Theory of Everything: An Integral Vision for Business, Politics, Science and Spirituality.* Dublin: Gateway.

Wilber, K. (2000b). *Integral Psychology: Consciousness, Spirit, Psychology, Therapy.* Boston, MA: Shambhala.

Wilber, K. (2001). *A Brief History of Everything and a History of Everything.* Dublin: Gateway.

Wilber, K. (2006). *Integral Spirituality.* Boston, MA: Integral Books.

Williams, M.J. (1996). Are you ready for an executive coach? *Harvard Management Update*, October.

Wirth, L. (2001). *Breaking Through the Glass Ceiling: Women in Management.* Geneva: International Labour Office. Webpage: www.ilo.org/public/libdoc/ilo/2001/101B09_102_engl.pdf, January 2009

Wirth, L. (2004). *Breaking Through the Glass Ceiling: Women in Management: Update 2004.* Geneva: International Labour Office. Webpage: www.ilo.org/dyn/gender/docs/RES/292/F267981337/Breaking%20Glass%20PDF%20English.pdf, January 2009

Witherspoon, R. (2000). Starting smart: clarifying coaching goals and roles. In: Goldsmith, M., Lyons, L., and Freas, A. (Eds.), *Coaching for Leadership: How the World's Greatest Coaches Help Leaders Learn* (pp. 165–186). San Francisco, CA: Jossey-Bass/Pfeiffer.

Witherspoon, R., and White, R.P. (1996). Executive coaching: what's in it for you? *Training and Development*, March, *50*(3):14.

Worldwide Association of Business Coaches (WABC) (2008a). *Code of Business Coaching Ethics and Integrity*. Webpage: www.wabccoaches. com/includes/popups/code_of_ethics_2nd_edition_december_17_ 2007.html

Worldwide Association of Business Coaches (WABC) (2008b). *Business Coaching Definition and Competences*. Webpage: www.wabccoaches. com/includes/popups/definition_and_competencies.html

Yalom, I.D. (1980). *Existential Psychotherapy*. New York, NY: Basic Books.

Yalom, I.D. (1989). *Love's Executioner and Other Tales of Psychotherapy*. London: Penguin Books.

Yalom, I.D. (1995). *The Theory and Practice of Group Psychotherapy*. New York, NY: Basic Books.

Yalom, I.D. (2001). *The Gift of Therapy: Reflections on Being a Therapist*. London: Piatkus.

Zeus, P., and Skiffington, S. (2000). *The Complete Guide to Coaching at Work*. North Ryde, NSW: McGraw-Hill Australia.

Zohar, D., and Marshall, I. (2001). *Spiritual Intelligence: The Ultimate Intelligence*. London: Bloomsbury.

INDEX